Innovation and Sustainability Through Circular Economy in Businesses

Syed Abdul Rehman Khan
Xuzhou University of Technology, China

IGI Global
Scientific Publishing
Publishing Tomorrow's Research Today

Vice President of Editorial Melissa Wagner
Managing Editor of Acquisitions Mikaela Felty
Managing Editor of Book Development Jocelynn Hessler
Production Manager Mike Brehm
Cover Design Phillip Shickler

Published in the United States of America by
IGI Global Scientific Publishing
701 East Chocolate Avenue
Hershey, PA, 17033, USA
Tel: 717-533-8845
Fax: 717-533-8661
E-mail: cust@igi-global.com
Website: https://www.igi-global.com

Library of Congress Cataloging-in-Publication Data

Names: Khan, Syed Abdul Rehman, 1987- editor.
Title: Innovation and sustainability through circular economy in businesses / edited by Syed Abdul Rehman Khan.
Description: Hershey, PA : IGI Global Scientific Publishing, [2025] | Includes bibliographical references and index. | Summary: "This book will discuss innovative business methodologies and approaches supporting sustainability and circular economy (CE) ideology"-- Provided by publisher.
Identifiers: LCCN 2024052423 (print) | LCCN 2024052424 (ebook) | ISBN 9798369341230 (hardcover) | ISBN 9798369351512 (paperback) | ISBN 9798369341247 (ebook)
Subjects: LCSH: Circular economy. | Supply chain management. | Business logistics--Environmental aspects. | Industries--Environmental aspects.
Classification: LCC HC79.E5 I5148525 2025 (print) | LCC HC79.E5 (ebook) | DDC 658.4/083--dc23/eng/20241213
LC record available at https://lccn.loc.gov/2024052423
LC ebook record available at https://lccn.loc.gov/2024052424

British Cataloguing in Publication Data
A Cataloguing in Publication record for this book is available from the British Library.

Table of Contents

Detailed Table of Contents

This study investigates the rapid development of green knowledge management, digital transformation, green innovation adoption, and improved energy efficiencies that lead to enhanced corporate sustainability developments in light of knowledge management theory and green theory. The authors used a non-probability convenient sampling technique to gather data from 360 manufacturing firms and analyzed using PLS-SEM. The study's findings reveal that green knowledge management positively enhances digital transformation and innovation adoption for improved energy efficiency and a firm's sustainable development. This study provided valuable theoretical and practical enlightenment for managers and policymakers to promote digital transformation and green innovation adoption strategies to improve energy efficiency and sustainable development. The study has added a thoughtful contribution to the existing literature.

The textile and apparel (T&A) industry is one of the most crucial customer merchandise industries with a long supply chain regarded as one of the world's most polluting industries, especially when it accounts for the immense usage of natural resources, usage of hazardous raw materials, air and water pollution, and high carbon imprint. Circular economy principles are rooted in principles of environmental science and concepts of sustainable development which is why the textile and clothing manufacturing supply chain needs to start by not only controlling the pace of fashion but focusing on processes right from fiber manufacturing, production, textile wet processing, dyeing, finishing sizing, apparel manufacturing, retail, disposal, and recycling focusing on three specific areas to incorporate circular economy principles in the supply chain. These would be 1) the development of new business models increasing the timespan of clothing, 2) environmentally safe and renewable resources, and 4) recycling and upcycling solutions.

Technology will play an important role in the circular economy today and in the future as businesses strive to evolve capabilities to achieve sustainable goals. Innovations in supply chain operations are also picking up pace, and with the invention of cloud-based computing, supply chain integration is now digitally possible. However, the question remains whether the same digital supply chain capabilities would also be beneficial in improving or impacting the sustainable performance of business enterprises to create an ideal circular economy. Another important feature of cloud technology is software-as-a-service, providing supply chain software for users across the globe to provide organizations with capabilities like integration and resilience. Based on the cloud computing innovations in discussion and sustainability in the context of circular economy, the chapter brings forward an empirical study to understand the role of cloud technology, more importantly, SaaS, in building resilience and achieving sustainability in supply chains.

Blue wind energy is a brand-new concept that blends cutting-edge technology with offshore wind energy generation. This chapter initiates a comprehensive exploration of this novel approach, focusing on its potential applications to the intricate issues surrounding sustainable urbanization. It provides an overview of the key ideas of the chapter, which conducts an extensive investigation into the potential integration of blue wind energy, AI, and IoT to enable intelligent energy management in urban environments. It's critical to lessen conventional energy sources' negative environmental effects while still supplying the growing energy demands of urbanization. Urban areas use a great deal of energy, and traditional methods are neither sustainable nor good for the environment. When paired with AI and IoT integration, blue wind energy offers an enticing option for sustainable, efficient, and environmentally friendly energy management in cities. Appropriately integrating and maximizing these technologies is the issue.

The boards of directors serve as an important control unit in the effective management of sustainability reports. Various characteristics, such as the experience and skills of the board members, the presence of female members on the board, and the size of the board, can affect the company's approach to sustainability issues. Therefore, the boards of directors of companies have a critical role in understanding sustainability reports. The objective of this study is to investigate the correlation between the intricacy of sustainability reports and the attributes of the board. For this purpose, firms listed on the Borsa Istanbul (BIST) between 2014 and 2022 were selected as the sample. The complexity of the reports was evaluated on the basis of the length of pages, words, and characters within the reports. The findings indicate a positive relationship between board size, gender diversity within the board, and the length of sustainability reports. Furthermore, it was found that firms with effective audit committees tend to have shorter sustainability reports.

The pursuit of environmental sustainability has become imperative in today's world. This chapter aims to investigate the impact of the logistic performance index and ICT on the MENA region's environmental sustainability from 2012 to 2023. Using static as FE-DK and dynamic panel as System GMM model estimation, the results indicate that fossil fuel consumption with enhanced logistic performance negatively impacts environmental sustainability in MENA regions in the presence of foreign direct investment inflow, economic growth, and rapid urbanization. Results also suggest that ICT also causes degradation of the environment in the MENA region; therefore, the MENA region should prioritize attracting green and sustainable foreign investments while transitioning towards cleaner energy sources.

Clothing is considered essential for human beings, providing cover and warmth and representing stature in society. The products manufactured by the sector on a global scale are gigantic in size and are categorized as prominent sectors, which are also prominent in terms of economic value in international trade. Billions of products are changing hands across the world and thus require more understanding of the upstream part of the global supply chain, especially the practices used in their ecosystem for production. In a similar pursuit, a study has been conducted on green supply chain management practices and their effect on the environmental performance of the Pakistani textile industry to transform into a chapter for a larger audience. By delving into the supply chain and operational procedures of textile manufacturers in Pakistan, the chapter uncovers their GSCM practices and their effects on environmental performance through empirical testing.

This study aims to examine how numerous factors affect the sustainable business performance of major Pakistani enterprises using e-marketing as a mediating variable. Data was collected from 279 manufacturing companies in Pakistan using a cluster sampling technique. Notably, Amos revealed significant associations between e-marketing usage and sustainable business performance. The results showed partial mediation concerning e-marketing usage. The effective utilization of digital technologies assists in low-cost production and improves the flexibility and sustainability of manufacturing systems. Despite the lack of literature, digital marketing integrates to produce sustainability to overcome this problem. Therefore, this study has developed a unique framework to solve these difficulties and improve sustainable business performance.

The logistics services providers have come a long way. From the first-party logistics service provider, whereby all of the logistics-related activities are historically managed in-house, to the advanced technologically oriented fifth- (5PL) and even sixth-party logistics service providers (6PL). However, all these spectrums of logistics service providers fail to explicitly incorporate the circular nature of modern logistics activities. That is reverse logistics alongside forward logistics is an integral part of the logistics services. Therefore, this chapter proposes the need for a circular logistics service provider service (CPL) that incorporates the key aspects of reverse supply chains like recycling, reuse, and refurbishment (alongside more advanced technology, backed by more efficient overall logistics) and is logically linked with a greener overall supply chain.

Preface

This book is designed for both academic and professional audiences. It offers valuable insights for students studying business operations and sustainability. Additionally, it serves as a useful reference for practitioners in consulting and industry, providing both conceptual knowledge and a practical methodology.

The importance of sustainability and a circular economy in business operations has rapidly increased, as reflected in this book's content. This book provides a holistic view of green ideology and innovation within businesses.

ORGANIZATION OF THE BOOK

There are nine chapters in the book. A brief description of each of the chapters follows:

Chapter 1 explores the swift advancement of green knowledge management, digital transformation, the adoption of green innovations, and improved energy efficiencies, all of which contribute to enhanced corporate sustainability. It is framed within the perspectives of knowledge management theory and green theory. The authors employed a non-probability convenience sampling technique to collect data from 360 manufacturing firms, which was then analyzed using PLS-SEM. The findings indicate that green knowledge management positively influences digital transformation and the adoption of innovations, leading to improved energy efficiency and promoting sustainable development within firms.

Chapter 2 highlights the textile and apparel (T&A) industry as one of the most significant customer merchandise sectors. It has a long supply chain and is one of the most polluting industries globally. This is largely due to its extensive use of natural resources and hazardous raw materials, its contribution to air and water pollution, and its high carbon footprint.

Chapter 3 focuses on innovation and the circular economy in supply chain management. Technology is essential for the circular economy, both now and in the future, as businesses strive to improve their capabilities and reach their sustainability goals. Innovations in supply chain operations are growing rapidly, and with the rise of cloud-based computing, supply chain integration has become digitally feasible.

Chapter 4 discusses how Blue Wind Energy engages with the Internet of Things (IoT) and Artificial Intelligence (AI) within the framework of Industry 5.0. It highlights potential applications for sustainable urbanization. The chapter aims to offer valuable insights into the future development of energy systems that align with the principles of the fourth industrial revolution. By examining the benefits, challenges, and practical implications of this integrated approach, it outlines a pathway toward a more intelligent, sustainable, and environmentally friendly urban energy landscape in the era of Industry 5.0.

Chapter 5 examines the relationship between the complexity of sustainability reports and various characteristics of the board of directors. The study focused on firms listed on Borsa Istanbul (BIST) from 2014 to 2022. The complexity of the reports was assessed based on their length, including the number of pages, words, and characters. The findings reveal a positive correlation between board size and gender diversity and the length of sustainability reports. Additionally, it was observed that firms with strong audit committees tend to produce shorter sustainability reports.

Chapter 6 investigates the impact of the logistic performance index and information and communication technology (ICT) on environmental sustainability in the MENA region from 2012 to 2023. Using both static, fixed effects (FE-DK) and dynamic panel estimation methods (System GMM), the results indicate that fossil fuel consumption, combined with improved logistic performance, negatively affects environmental sustainability in the MENA region. Therefore, the MENA region needs to focus on attracting green and sustainable foreign investments while transitioning towards cleaner energy sources.

Chapter 7 describes the green supply chain practices in the textile industry. Clothing is essential for human beings, providing cover and warmth and representing societal stature. The products manufactured by the sector on a global scale are gigantic and are categorized as prominent sectors, which are also prominent in terms of economic value in international trade. This chapter analyzed the effect of green supply chain management practices on the environmental performance of the Pakistani textile industry.

Chapter 8 explores the various factors that influence enterprises' sustainable business performance, specifically examining e-marketing as a mediating variable. Data was collected from 279 manufacturing companies through a cluster sampling technique. Notably, the analysis using AMOS software revealed significant associations between the use of e-marketing and sustainable business performance. The results indicated partial mediation regarding the utilization of e-marketing. The effective use of digital technologies contributes to low-cost production and enhances the flexibility and sustainability of manufacturing systems.

Chapter 9 emphasizes the necessity of a circular logistics service provider (CPL) that integrates essential elements of reverse supply chains, such as recycling, reuse, and refurbishment. It also highlights the importance of advanced technology and improved overall logistics efficiency, contributing to a more sustainable supply chain.

Syed Abdul Rehman Khan
Xuzhou University of Technology, China

Acknowledgment

I want to express my deep appreciation to the many individuals who have played a crucial role in supporting me throughout this incredible journey. I am truly grateful to the insightful reviewers whose invaluable suggestions have significantly enhanced the quality of the book. I also want to extend my heartfelt thanks to my parents and teachers for their unwavering encouragement, especially to the esteemed Sufi Scholar Sahibzada Asim Maharvi, whose guidance and motivation have been instrumental in shaping my path.

Lastly, I want to thank you, the readers, for your time and engagement with this book. Your dedication to gaining a deeper understanding of the global circular economy and sustainability practices is truly commendable.

Acknowledgment

Chapter 1

The Influence of Green Knowledge Management on Digital Transformation, Green Innovation, Energy Efficiency, and Firm Sustainable Development: A Case of the Manufacturing Industry of Pakistan

Adnan Ahmed Sheikh
https://orcid.org/0000-0002-3546-5284
University of Buraimi, Oman

Muhammad Wisal
Air University, Islamabad, Pakistan

Bilal Hassan
https://orcid.org/0009-0002-8955-2516
Air University, Islamabad, Pakistan

Nadir Munir Hassan
Emerson University, Multan, Pakistan

DOI: 10.4018/979-8-3693-4123-0.ch001

Sajjad Khan
Emerson University, Multan, Pakistan

ABSTRACT

This study investigates the rapid development of green knowledge management, digital transformation, green innovation adoption, and improved energy efficiencies that lead to enhanced corporate sustainability developments in light of knowledge management theory and green theory. The authors used a non-probability convenient sampling technique to gather data from 360 manufacturing firms and analyzed using PLS-SEM. The study's findings reveal that green knowledge management positively enhances digital transformation and innovation adoption for improved energy efficiency and a firm's sustainable development. This study provided valuable theoretical and practical enlightenment for managers and policymakers to promote digital transformation and green innovation adoption strategies to improve energy efficiency and sustainable development. The study has added a thoughtful contribution to the existing literature.

1. INTRODUCTION

Currently, the sustainability field encompasses eco-friendly regulations, green technology use, environmental impact monitoring, and other innovative approaches (Geng et al., 2021; Jin et al., 2022). Society is seeking innovative methods to efficiently address social, economic, and environmental challenges to achieve sustainable development (Fernandes et al., 2022; Lu et al., 2020). The United Nations is worried about the sustainable development goals (SDGs). Considering this, SDG-17 recommendations have been proposed for global cooperation in 2015 by Chauhan et al. (2022) and Masuda et al. (2022). Resolute measures are required to address these crucial concerns (Masuda et al., 2021). Following the COVID-19 pandemic and its tumultuous effects, all nations must adopt a green recovery approach. This entails establishing collaborative mechanisms to attain reduced carbon emissions and providing economic, technological, and industrial assistance for comprehensive climate management.

Organisations diligently adhere to principles and procedures to produce and provide environmentally safe goods and services (Kumar & Barua, 2022). To effectively reduce greenhouse gas emissions in the real world and meet the goals of COP 26, governments were urged to embrace green innovation and implement digital transformation in the industry (UNCOP26, 2021). Consequently, firms have prioritised reconfiguring their operations and management systems, driven by the significance of promoting an environmentally sustainable approach (Ahmed et al., 2022). To ensure the long-term viability and enhance the functioning of businesses, it is crucial to prioritise innovation (Fan & Fan, 2020). Research has indicated that small and medium-sized enterprises (SMEs) have the capacity for ecological innovation, production, and consumption, as demonstrated by Klewitz and Hansen in 2014.

Academics believe that Knowledge management triggers economic development and the achievement of SDGs of the firms (Wang et al., 2021). Knowledge management is important and is considered a predictor of supporting sustainability (Chopra, Saini & Kumar, 2021). Vibrant firms contemplate different strategies to operate in completion and get an edge over others by incorporating knowledge and quality in processes and productions and eco-friendly procedures (Al-Qudah et al., 2022). Criteria of achievement and disaster of a firm depend upon the capability of managing knowledge (Zhang et al., 2022a). Most firms use knowledge to satisfy their customers and thus gain an edge over the other firms (Mohan et al., 2022). In the recent past, knowledge management has been very attractive in the corporate world. It is essential in framing strategies, in productions and in managing operative procedures (Pham et al., 2022). An active Knowledge management (KM) system can increase an organization's effectiveness and initiate the incorporation of climate in it (Ahmed et al., 2022).

Several firms have found green knowledge management as a dynamic tool for sustainable development (Yu et al., 2022). Green innovation helps businesses develop environmentally friendly products to complete SDGs (Ahmed et al., 2022). Firms need to emphasize clarifying green innovation into two forms: technical and managerial green innovation (Sianturi et al., 2022). Green technological innovation (GTI) carries maintainable skill and state-of-the-art technology together. GTI supports firms in developing environmental, economic, and production processes to produce new products with less material consumption (Song et al., 2022). The fundamental objectives of firms in green management innovation (GMI) are better management of operations and a decrease in ecological effects (Ullah et al., 2022). Knowledge management and its relationship with sustainable development have been examined in numerous research studies (Aamir et al., 2021). However, since the newness of the GKM conception, infrequent consideration is provided to GKM and corporate sustainable development. GKM has not been studied regarding digital transformation, green innovation, and improved energy efficiency in sustainable development. Incorporating these key constructs, this research wishes to fill the gap in the literature. This study has the following objectives: the research framework is shown in Figure 1.

Research Objectives

The study's main objective is to understand the influence of green knowledge management on corporate sustainable development.

1. To assess the relationships between green knowledge management and digital transformation.
2. To examine the relationship between green knowledge management and green innovation adoption.
3. To examine the relationship between digital transformation and green innovation adoption.
4. To examine the relationship between green innovation adoption and improved energy efficiency.
5. To examine the relationship between improved energy efficiency and corporate sustainable development.

Figure 1. Research Framework

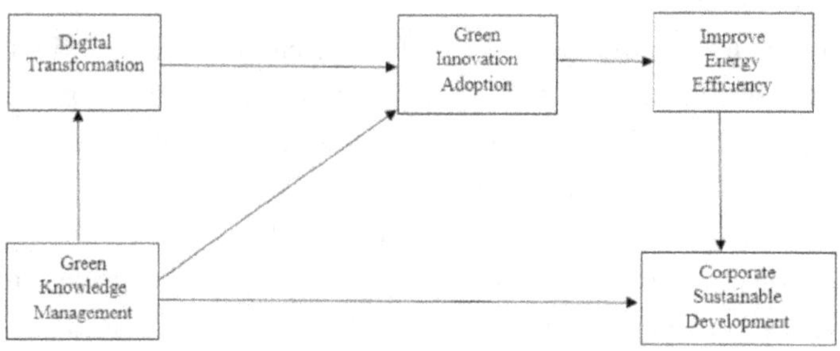

2. LITERATURE REVIEW AND HYPOTHESIS DEVELOPMENT

2.1 Corporate Sustainable Development

Every nation has to institute sustainable development goals to deal with ecological difficulties pertinent to human development. United Nations should address universal issues and disasters as a global institution (Montenegro et al., 2020). Therefore, universal issues like environmental change, societal disparity and environmental deprivation are taken seriously by the UN in its plan for 2030. It is all about sustainable development, focusing on reliable nationwide administrative clarifications (Coscieme, Mortensen & Anderson, 2020). Corporate sustainable development is composed of three points. The SDGs are further categorized into three: environmental sustainability, social well-being, and economic development and are projected to complete SDGs (Ripple et al., 2017). Governments will decide to defend the environment, encourage justice, and emphasise ecological development to attain human welfare (Coscieme et al., 2020). The first section of sustainability related to the environmental aspect concentrates on protecting the atmosphere, minimum usage of natural assets, fresh air and water preventing pollution, producing eco-friendly goods and fewer gas discharges (Song et al., 2022). The second section of sustainability related to the economic aspect concentrates on pulling down the operational costs, growing sales and efficient use of funds for better performance of the firms (Sianturi et al., 2022). The third section deals with societal sustainability, which focuses on firms' affiliation with people and society for human welfare (Abbas & Dogan 2022). In the same way, traditional life, communal justice and societal progress are the concerns of social sustainability. Corporate sustainable development has gained significance in sustainability literature.

2.2 Green Knowledge Management and Corporate Sustainable Development

Knowledge is a dynamic source of constant improvement for firms. Knowledge has two categories; tacit and explicit knowledge (Nonaka, 1994; Lee & Wong, 2015). Tacit knowledge can be transmitted and shared without difficulty. However, explicit knowledge cannot be simply transferred (Hubert, 1996; Cheng S. Lee, 2015). Green knowledge entails the ways to manage the sustainable performance of the firms. According to Zbuchea et al. (2019), green knowledge is quite different from other firms' assets, and firms need to consider the practical and social facets of GKM differently to benefit from it. For green creative performance at the individual level and firm levels, green knowledge is vital (Wang et al., 2020). Besides, people's green learning hints at organizations' new eco-knowledge, thus providing new philosophies, views, and way-outs towards new products and services. Firms which incorporate GKM in their systems can get more benefits by deciding which practices are useful for the firm. Corporate sustainable development is composed of three points. The SDGs are further categorized into three: environmental sustainability, social well-being, and economic development and are projected to complete SDGs (Ripple et al., 2017). Governments will decide to defend the environment, encourage justice, and emphasize ecological development to attain human welfare (Coscieme et al., 2020). The first section of sustainability related to the environmental aspect concentrates on protecting the atmosphere, minimum usage of natural assets, fresh air and water preventing pollution, producing eco-friendly goods and fewer gas discharges (Song et al., 2022). The second section of sustainability related to the economic aspect concentrates on pulling down the operational costs, growing sales and efficient use of funds for better performance of the firms (Sianturi et al., 2022). The third section deals with societal sustainability, which focuses on firms' affiliation with people and society for human welfare (Abbas & Dogan 2022). To achieve success in SDGs, firms must consider the sustainability of environmental, economic and social aspects entangled in GKM. For a substantial effect on their sustainable performance, firms put into practice green knowledge (Shahzad et al., 2020a). Many scholars have emphasised the importance of GKM, green innovation and firm performance, but little research has been done on the GKM's role in the CSD (Abbas & Sagsan, 2019). It is hypothesized that:

H1: Green knowledge management influences sustainable corporate development.

2.3 Green Knowledge Management and Digital Transformation

Green knowledge entails the ways to manage the sustainable performance of the firms. According to Zbuchea et al. (2019), green knowledge is quite different from other firms' assets, and firms need to consider the practical and social facets of GKM differently to benefit from it. For green creative performance at the individual level and firm levels, green knowledge is vital (Wang et al., 2020). Besides, people's green learning hints at organizations' new eco-knowledge, thus providing new philosophies, views, and way-outs towards new products and services. Firms which incorporate GKM in their systems can get more benefits by deciding which practices are useful for the firm. According to Clerck (2017), digital transformation is the usage of digital technologies and data to generate revenues, improve business processes and transform them into digital businesses. Academicians and practitioners have recently used digital transformation as a succeeding phase of digitalization. Sughra et al. (2017) have named various explanations of digital transformation with respect to diverse perspectives. Scholars are of the view that for sustainable performance and gaining a reasonable edge in the market, digital transformation can support firms as they use technology (Rehman et al., 2022). The use of technology to improve businesses completely puts digital transformation into the firms' performance (Westerman et al., 2011). Digital transformation has three components: operative procedures, customer experience and business models. Digital transformation can assist organizations in improving their commercial power and social impression and lessen their undesirable ecological impact (Hilali et al., 2020). Therefore, we assume that:

H2: Green knowledge management has a positive influence on digital transformation.

2.4 Green Knowledge Management and Green Innovation Adoption

Green knowledge entails the ways to manage the sustainable performance of the firms. According to Zbuchea et al. (2019), green knowledge is quite different from other firms' assets, and firms need to consider the practical and social facets of GKM differently to benefit from it. For green creative performance at the individual level and firm levels, green knowledge is vital (Wang et al., 2020). Besides, people's green learning hints at organization's new eco-knowledge, thus providing new philosophies, views, and way-outs towards new products and services. Firms which incorporate GKM in their systems can get more benefits by deciding which practices are useful for the firm. Implementing new practices, which include materials, products, procedures, services and guidelines for improving the organization's productivity and proficiency, constitutes innovation adoption of the firm. Green innovation adoption is defined as environmentally friendly innovation (Jun et al., 2019). According to Kemp (2010), green innovation is a new and modern method in the manufacturing and managerial process that decreases environmental threats and wastes, saves natural resources, and reduces energy consumption. Green innovation adoption can increase production with enhanced technological procedures (Wang, J. Abbas, & M.S. Sial et al., 2022). Adopting green innovation can minimize the ecological effect of firms' operational procedures. Thus, firms started to experience a rise in customers' confidence, trustworthiness, and accomplishment (Rehman et al., 2021). Knowledge management is significant for green innovation practice with respect to analysis (Chaithanapat et al., 2022). Green knowledge enhances the environmentally friendly performance of the firms (Gauthier & Zhang, 2020). It allows organizations to reduce the negative effects of production on the environment and helps to improve existing processes, ultimately decreasing energy consumption, avoiding pollution, and protecting natural resources. Thus, we posit that:

H3: Green knowledge management has a positive influence on green innovation adoption.

2.5 Digital Transformation and Green Innovation Adoption

According to Clerck (2017), digital transformation is the usage of digital technologies and data to generate revenues, improve business processes and transform them into digital businesses. In recent days, academicians and practitioners have used digital transformation as a succeeding phase of digitalization. Innovation makes the digital transformation into more creative administrative and functioning levels in business operations (Nambisan et al., 2017). Firms can assume operational characteristics providing improved services just like the firms those already experiencing digital operations by adopting green innovations (Bossert, 2016). Digital transformation with innovative technological improvements makes a firm compete in the marketplace with other relevant industries. Generally, the conversion of a firm into digital transformation puts it on the path of innovative and digital technologies in its procedures, thus cutting costs, minimizing waste and less environmental issues (Vial, 2019; Weill & Woerner, 2018). It is thus assumed that:

H4: Digital transformation has a positive influence on green innovation adoption.

2.6 Green Innovation Adoption and Improved Energy Efficiency

According to Kemp (2010), green innovation is a new and modern method in the manufacturing and managerial process that decreases environmental threats and wastes, saves natural resources, and reduces energy consumption. Green innovation adoption can increase production with enhanced technological procedures (Wang, J. Abbas, & M.S. Sial et al., 2022). Adopting green innovation can minimize the ecological effect of firms' operational procedures. Thus, firms started to experience a rise in customers' confidence, trustworthiness, and accomplishment (Rehman et al., 2021). Efficient energy use, or energy efficiency, uses less energy to achieve the same amount of service. Firms use energy in their day-to-day operations for production. Those firms are energy efficient in consuming energy, producing the same but using less energy. International Energy Agency states that one-third of 2050 world energy demand can be cut with the efficient use of energy by consuming less energy and reducing universal gas emissions. Energy efficacy and renewable energy are two bases of sustainable energy policy. Ecological development and renewable energy technology have a connection that is inspected by scholars (Matuszewska- Pierzynka, 2021; Noorollahi et al., 2020). Firms consider energy as a precarious element of economic progress and affluence. According to Tetteh and Asuah (2020), energy efficiency and economic growth are interconnected, and this connection is examined in 46 African nations. Every economic activity needs energy, and its availability is crucial for smooth business operations. This study investigates renewable energy mistreatment, recycling, efficient use of energy, and sources of renewable energy availability. Based on this we posit that:

H5: Green innovation adoption has a positive influence on improved energy efficiency.

2.7 Improved Energy Efficiency and Corporate Sustainable Development

International Energy Agency states that one-third of 2050 world energy demand can be cut with the efficient use of energy by consuming less energy and reducing universal gas emissions. Energy efficacy and renewable energy are two bases of sustainable energy policy. Ecological development and renewable energy technology have a connection that is inspected by scholars (Matuszewska- Pierzynka, 2021; Noorollahi et al., 2020). Firms use energy in their day-to-day operations for production. Those firms are energy efficient in consuming energy, producing the same but using less energy. Governments will decide to defend the environment, encourage justice, and emphasize ecological development to attain human welfare (Coscieme et al., 2020). The first section of sustainability related to the environmental aspect concentrates on protecting the atmosphere, minimum usage of natural assets, fresh air and water preventing pollution, producing eco-friendly goods and fewer gas discharges (Song et al., 2022). The second section of sustainability related to the economic aspect concentrates on pulling down the operational costs, growing sales and efficient use of funds for better performance of the firms (Sianturi et al., 2022). The third section deals with societal sustainability, which focuses on firms' affiliation with people and society for human welfare (Abbas & Dogan 2022). To achieve success in SDGs, firms must consider the sustainability of environmental, economic, and social aspects entangled with energy efficiency. Shereni (2019), also suggests that efficient energy use helps achieve organizational SDGs. Thus, we propose another hypothesis:

H6: Improved energy efficiency has a positive influence on corporate sustainable development.

2.8 Theoretical Development

The theory of knowledge management and green theory are applied in this study. Knowledge is a dynamic source of constant improvement for firms. Knowledge has two categories; tacit and explicit knowledge (Nonaka, 1994; Lee & Wong, 2015). Tacit knowledge can be transmitted and shared without difficulty. However, explicit knowledge cannot be simply transferred (Hubert, 1996; Cheng S. Lee, 2015). Green knowledge entails the ways to manage the sustainable performance of the firms. According to Zbuchea et al. (2019), green knowledge is quite different from other firms' assets, and firms need to consider the practical and social facets of GKM differently to benefit from it. For green creative performance at the individual level and firm levels, green knowledge is vital (Wang et al., 2020). Besides, people's green learning hints at organizations' new eco-knowledge, thus providing new philosophies, views, and way-outs towards new products and services. Green knowledge management has not yet been explored in future. It can be further investigated. GKM may be considered a subset of the broader, well-developed KM research stream. GKM is the domain of KM. Thus, KM is studied in different perspectives of object, process, and competency (Alavi and Leidner, 2001; Gauthier & Zhang, 2020). Knowledge management incorporates information technology for determining firms' policies (Alavi et al., 2005; Gauthier & Zhang, 2020). KM suggests that knowledge has three segments: creation, transfer, and application of knowledge for firm performance. Given this relationship to competitive advantage, KM should be considered an important variable that can provide significant insights into firm strategy.KM is pivotal for firms to gain a competitive edge. GKM progresses in the environmental aspect of corporate sustainability.

United Nations address universal issues and disasters as a global institution (Montenegro et al., 2020). Therefore, universal issues like environmental change, societal disparity and environmental deprivation are taken seriously by the UN in its plan for 2030. It is all about sustainable development, focusing on reliable nationwide administrative clarifications (Coscieme, Mortensen & Anderson, 2020). Corporate sustainable development is composed of three points. The SDGs are further categorized into three: environmental sustainability, social well-being, and economic development and are projected to complete SDGs (Ripple et al., 2017). Governments will plan to defend the environment, encourage justice, and emphasize ecological development to attain human welfare (Coscieme et al., 2020). According to Clerck (2017), digital transformation is the usage of digital technologies and data to generate revenues, improve business processes and transform them into digital businesses. Academicians and practitioners have recently used digital transformation as a succeeding phase of digitalization. Sughra et al. (2017) have given various explanations of digital transformation from diverse perspectives. Scholars are of the view that for sustainable performance and gaining a reasonable edge in the market, digital transformation can support firms as they use technology (Rehman et al., 2022). Knowledge management is significant for green innovation practice with respect to analysis (Chaithanapat et al., 2022). Green knowledge enhances the environmentally friendly performance of the firms (Gauthier & Zhang, 2020). It allows organizations to reduce the negative effects of production on the environment and helps to improve existing processes, ultimately decreasing energy consumption, avoiding pollution, and protecting natural resources. Firms consider energy as a precarious element of economic progress and affluence.

3. RESEARCH METHODOLOGY

3.1 Population and Sampling Procedure

This research considers green knowledge management and its relationship with corporate sustainable development. For this, manufacturing companies operating in Pakistan were incorporated. We conducted a non-probability convenient sampling technique to gather data. Managers were the respondents of this study, and data was collected through electronic means like email and WhatsApp. Likert scale of 5 points was used. Managers were considered for responses because they have the latest and adequate knowledge of company policies. Additionally, these managers enforce company policies within departments, so we have obtained data from these managers. Only companies registered on SECP and SMEDA were included in this study. First, according to Kline (2015), the minimum threshold level for structural equation modelling is 200. Second, the minimum threshold level can be measured by multiplying the total items by 5-10 responses to estimate the minimum sample size (Hair et al., 2017).

There were 31 items, multiplied by 5, resulting in 155, the smallest sample size necessary for this study. Big cities were chosen for data collection, like Karachi, Hyderabad, Lahore, Islamabad, Faisalabad, Peshawar, Gujranwala, Gujrat, Wazirabad and Multan. These cities have more industries and businesses. We collected data from October 2023 to December 2023. A total of 972 survey forms were disseminated. Received responses were 498; out of those, only 360 were acceptable. Out of 360, responses from small industries were 85, medium industries 124 and 151 from large industries. Of the respondents, there were 223 males and 137 females, whereas 6 respondents asked to hide their gender. Table 1 shows details of respondents.

Table 1. Demographics

Demographics of Respondents			
Particular	**Description**	**Values**	**%**
Firm Size	Large firms	151	41.94%
	Medium Firms	124	34.44%
	Small Firms	85	23.61%
Gender	Male	223	61.94%
	Female	137	38.05%
Job Position	Lower Management	127	35.27%
	Middle Management	155	43.65%
	Upper Management	78	21.67%

3.2 Measurement Instrument

The study used 31 items adopted from past research for the respondents' convenience. Green knowledge management was measured using 10 items adapted from Hung et al. (2014). Corporate sustainable development was measured using 6 items taken from Wang (2019). Green innovation adoption 6 items were adapted from Soewarno et al. (2019). Digital transformation was measured by the adapted 5 items from Nasiri et al. (2020). Improved energy efficiency was measured on 4 items adapted from Tan et al. (2017). All items were measured on a five-point Likert scale where (1=strongly disagree and 5 = strongly agree). The study used structural equation modelling (SEM) to analyze the relationships among variables. Statistical Package for Social Sciences (SPSS) 24 and (AMOS) were incorporated to analyze the data.

4. PRELIMINARY ANALYSIS AND RESULTS

We did data screening before data analysis; some of the missing, aberrant, and outliers were spotted and treated with means of identical values (Cousineau & Chartier, 2010). Results show skewness and kurtosis values are in the suggested threshold of ± 1 and ± 3, so data is normally distributed (Tabachnick & Fidell, 2007). Variance inflation factor (VIF) and tolerance value are inspected to inspect multicollinearity. VIF values <10 and tolerance values >0.10 indicated no multicollinearity issue (Hair et al., 2017). We used procedural and analytical remedies to check the common method bias (CBM) and resolved that the data do not have a CMB issue (Podsakoff et al., 2012).

4.1 Analysis of Measurement and Structural Model

The CFA is performed by 5 latent variables and 31 observed variables. In the first run of CFA, the model fit indicated poor fit. After modification and removing items, fit indices for measurement model values were in acceptable fit like; CMIN/DF =1.794, GFI = .856, AGFI = .831, CFI =.956, RMSEA = .049, NFI = .906, TLI = .950, IFI = .956, PCLOSE = .630. Furthermore, we examined the strength of measures of constructs by using reliability, convergent reliability, and discriminant validity (Fornell & Larcker, 1981). Cronbach's Alpha (α) of all constructs is within the suggested threshold, that is ($\alpha \geq 0.7$), and composite reliability surpasses the minimum threshold (CR $\geq$ 0.6) consequently, it indicates that all the constructs are reliable (Fornell and Lucker, 1981; Nunnally & Bernstein, 1994). Additional significant factor loadings (FL $\geq$ 0.6) (Steenkamp and Van Trijp, 1991), and average variance extracted (AVE $\geq$ 0.5) (Fornell and Larcker, 1981) were applied to institute convergent validity.

Table 2. Reliability and validity

Variables		CR	AVE	1	2	3	4	5
1.	CSD	0.87	0.65	0.81				
2.	DT	0.90	0.65	0.81	0.83			
3.	GII	0.89	0.70	0.81	0.73	0.72		
4.	GKM	0.88	0.67	0.71	0.80	0.69	0.74	
5.	IEE	0.87	0.57	0.82	0.77	0.72	0.72	0.785

Note: CR= composite reliability, AVE= average variance extracted

The table shows that the construct has convergent validity, as the AVEs of all latent constructs are above 0.5, and factor loadings of all items are more than 0.6 and significant at $p< 0.001$, which is desirable. Three methods were applied to inspect the divergent validity. First, the square root of the average variance extracted (AVE) must be greater than the inter-construct correlations (Fornell and Larcker, 1981). Next, we inspected the correlation confidence interval between the two constructs. The confidence interval around the correlation estimate did not include 1.00 (Hair et al., 2017). All the constructs are changed; Table 2 shows that no such case survives. Therefore, it confirms divergent validity. Third, strong and significant factor loadings (FL $\geq$ 0.6) of measurement items on their respective latent constructs rather than other constructs were witnessed, which shows an additional indication of divergent validity.

4.2 Testing of Hypotheses

Our results show that green knowledge management positively influences corporate sustainable development (H1: γ=0.37, $p<0.05$). It shows that green knowledge management and corporate sustainable development have a connection. This connection is supported by Abbas & Sagsan (2019), who discovered that corporate sustainable development and green knowledge management are interconnected. The results of this study confirm the findings of Lutchen (2018), which state that based on knowledge, firms can obtain better financial performance. Firms apply green knowledge in their operations and ultimately achieve corporate sustainability. Our results show that green knowledge management positively influences digital transformation (H2: γ=0.80, $p<0.05$). The results of our study support the idea that knowledge gained by employees is useful for accomplishing the firm's sustainable development goals. Green knowledge management significantly influences digital transformation. The findings suggest that acquiring new technology changes firms' fortune in establishing a solid platform for achieving sustainability goals. Our results show that green knowledge management positively influences (H3: $\gamma=0.29, p<0.05$), green innovation adoption. The results of our study support the idea that knowledge gained by employees is useful for accomplishing the firm's sustainable development goals. Green knowledge management and the adoption of green innovation are very significantly influenced. The findings suggest that acquiring new technology changes firms' performance in achieving sustainability goals. The results of our study support the findings of Song et al. (2020); green knowledge supports the efficient use of resources and technology adoption to achieve the overall goal of a firm's sustainable development goal. Firms can reduce waste and costs of production by adding green innovations in firms' operations. Our results show that digital transformation has a positive influence (H4: $\gamma=0.48, p<0.05$), on green innovation adoption. The results of our study support the idea that the conversion of the firm from traditional to digital enhances its efficiency in completing sustainable development goals. According to results, digital transformation very significantly influences digital transformation. The findings suggest that acquiring new technology changes firms' affluence in establishing a solid platform for achieving sustainability goals.

Table 3. Hypothesis Results

Hypothesis		Structural Paths			(γ)	t values	P-Values	Decision
H1	GKM		CSD		0.25	5.191	***	Supported
H2	GKM		DT		0.80	8.903	***	Supported
H3	GKM		GIA		0.29	6.592	***	Supported
H4	DT		GIA		0.48	6.736	***	Supported
H5	GIA		IEE		0.72	2.013	0.04	Supported
H6	IEE		CSD		0.63	2.083	0.03	Supported
H7	GKM		DT	GIA	0.39	6.796	0.01	Supported
H8	DT		GIA	IEE	0.35	6.270	0.00	Supported
H9	GIA		IEE	CSD	0.45	9.379	0.00	Supported

Note: (γ) = path coefficients; t-values $\geq \pm1.96$ $p<0.05$; $p<0.10$.

The results show that green innovation adoption positively influences (H5: $\gamma=0.72, p<0.05$) improved energy efficiency. The results of our study support that Abbas & Sagsan's (2019) green innovation adoption increases organizational growth in improved energy efficiency. According to the results, green innovation adoption significantly influences improved energy efficiency. The findings suggest that acquiring new technology changes firms' affluence in establishing a solid platform for achieving sustainability goals. Our results show that Improved energy efficiency has a positive influence on (H6: $\gamma=0.63$, $p<0.05$), sustainable corporate development, which confirms that our hypothesis H6 is accepted. Our results show that digital transformation mediates the relationship between GKM and green innovation adoption (H7: $\gamma=0.39$, $p<0.05$), supporting our hypothesis. Our results show that green innovation adaption mediates between digital transformation and improved energy efficiency (H8: $\gamma=0.35$, $p<0.05$). These findings show that firms must consider digital transformation to improve energy efficiency by considering green innovation practices. Finally, our results show that improved energy efficiency mediates the relationship (H9: $\gamma=0.45$, $p<0.05$), between green innovation adoption and sustainable corporate development.

Based on these results, it is proven that green knowledge management is vital for firms to attain sustainable goals. Firms that are more vibrant and proactive in adopting new technology with green knowledge management result in digital transformation and adoption of green innovation. Once firms become digitalized and innovative, they can reduce overhead costs, minimize raw material usage, recycle waste, and improve energy efficiency, ultimately achieving corporate sustainability. Adopting energy efficiencies in business processes will enhance their working capacity and improve production to meet market challenges.

5. DISCUSSION

This study has been conducted to inspect green knowledge management's relationship with corporate sustainable development with mediating effect of digital transformation, green innovation and improved energy efficiency in the small, medium, and large firms which are in Karachi, Hyderabad, Lahore, Islamabad, Faisalabad, Peshawar, Gujranwala, Gujrat, Wazirabad and Multan in Pakistan. Results of this study show that green knowledge management has a positive and significant influence on corporate sustainable development. If firms apply green knowledge management in operations, it will ultimately improve their sustainability. For long-term developmental plans, companies must consider knowledge sharing among employees to make them well-versed with the latest practices of digital transformation and innovation adoptions. By integrating Innovative and improved efficiencies in the firms, economies can be gained through reducing material waste, recycling, and producing environment-friendly products. Green innovations improve processes and make business operations smooth using new technologies. With modern innovations, firms can get benefits like a reduction in gas emissions and efficient use of natural resources, thus fulfilling firms' sustainability goals. Improved energy efficiency mediates green innovation adoption and corporate sustainable development. Improved energy efficiency helps in cleaning the environment. Improved energy efficiency in firms brings sustainable development, which is the firm's goal.

6. RESEARCH IMPLICATIONS

This research provides significant awareness for firms and practitioners regarding digital transformation, green innovation, and energy efficiency through green knowledge management. Organization managers must acknowledge the importance of implementing green knowledge management procedures to achieve sustainable corporate goals. The findings of this study suggest that companies and their management should apply green knowledge management practices in organizations. These managers must devise plans to provide training and workshops for staff development. Ultimately, firms will reduce their wastage and will be more environmentally friendly. The present study focuses on green practices and the firms' digital transformation. Once firms ensure that they adopt digital and innovative technology, they will attain sustainability. Managers must promote and implement green practices in their operations to reduce cost reduction, recycle, make minimum waste, control air pollution and water pollution, and, in the end, be environmentally friendly organizations.

This study considers the efficient use of resources in the firm's business operations, which will affect corporate sustainable development. The effects of performing green practices will provide results to the managers of small and medium firms and developing countries. Green knowledge management, digital transformation, innovation adoption, and improved energy efficiency create relationships among these constructs and impact firms' sustainable goals. This study has some theoretical implications as well. In this study, green theory and knowledge management theory are incorporated simultaneously. This study enhances the understating of green knowledge management and corporate sustainable development directly and indirectly through digital transformation, green innovation, and improved energy efficiency. With the better implementation of green practices, firms can increase performance.

7. LIMITATIONS AND FUTURE RESEARCH

This research has focused on small, medium, and upper management managers to get their responses for analysis and interpretation. In future research, supervisors can also be included in the responses because they directly oversee the firm's operations. There can be some other factors that can affect the sustainability of corporate development. This study has measured just green knowledge management, digital transformation, green innovation, and improved energy efficiency. This study is conducted in major cities of Pakistan, it can be tested in other cities of Pakistan and other countries as well. Future studies should consider those other factors. This study has applied green knowledge management as a predictor of a firm's sustainability; there are many other factors like recycling, etc. In future research, improved energy efficiency can be tested as a moderator of green knowledge management and corporate sustainable development.

7.1 Conclusion

This study explored the relationship between green knowledge management and sustainable corporate development. This relationship was tested regarding green knowledge management, digital transformation, green innovation adoption, improved energy efficiency, and firm sustainability. Green knowledge management positively impacts the digital transformation of firms. Once the firms become digitalized, the adoption of green innovation will be impacted. Green innovation adoption mediates between digital transformation and improved energy efficiency of the firm. Similarly, another aim was to investigate the mediating role of improved energy efficiency in the relationship between green innovation adoption and the firm's corporate sustainability.

REFERENCES

Aamir, A., Jan, S. U., Qadus, A., Nassani, A. A., & Haffar, M. (2021). Impact of knowledge sharing on sustainable performance: Mediating role of employee's ambidexterity. *Sustainability (Basel)*, 13(22), 12788. DOI: 10.3390/su132212788

Abbas, J., & Dogan, E. (2022). The impacts of organizational green culture and corporate social responsibility on employees' responsible behaviour towards the society.

Abbas, J., & Sağsan, M. (2019). Impact of knowledge management practices on green innovation and corporate sustainable development: A structural analysis. *Journal of Cleaner Production*, 229, 611–620. DOI: 10.1016/j.jclepro.2019.05.024

Ahmed, S., Naz, F., Abbas, Z., & Batool, K. H. (2022). Impact of green innovation on sustainable development with mediating effect of knowledge management. *Journal of Business Management Studies-JBMS*, 1(01), 1–16.

Al-Qudah, A. A., Hamdan, A., Al-Okaily, M., & Alhaddad, L. (2022). The impact of green lending on credit risk: Evidence from UAE's banks. *Environmental Science and Pollution Research International*, 30(22), 1–13. DOI: 10.1007/s11356-021-18224-5 PMID: 35067871

Alavi, M., Kayworth, T. R., & Leidner, D. E. (2005). An empirical examination of the influence of organizational culture on knowledge management practices. *Journal of Management Information Systems*, 22(3), 191–224. DOI: 10.2753/MIS0742-1222220307

Alavi, M., & Leidner, D. (2001). Knowledge management and knowledge management systems: Conceptual foundations and research issues. *Management Information Systems Quarterly*, 25(1), 107–136. DOI: 10.2307/3250961

Bossert, O. (2016). A two-speed architecture for the digital enterprise. *Emerging trends in the evolution of service-oriented and enterprise architectures*, 139-150.

Chaithanapat, P., Punnakitikashem, P., Oo, N. C. K. K., & Rakthin, S. (2022). Relationships among knowledge-oriented leadership, customer knowledge management, innovation quality and firm performance in SMEs. *Journal of Innovation & Knowledge*, 7(1), 100162. DOI: 10.1016/j.jik.2022.100162

Chauhan, C., Kaur, P., Arrawatia, R., Ractham, P., & Dhir, A. (2022). Supply chain collaboration and sustainable development goals (SDGs). Teamwork makes achieving SDGs dream work. *Journal of Business Research*, 147, 290–307. DOI: 10.1016/j.jbusres.2022.03.044

Chopra, M., Saini, N., Kumar, S., Varma, A., Mangla, S. K., & Lim, W. M. (2021). Past, present, and future of knowledge management for business sustainability. *Journal of Cleaner Production*, 328, 129592. DOI: 10.1016/j.jclepro.2021.129592

Clerck, J. (2017). Digitization, digitalization and digital transformation: the differences. I SCOOP. Available at: www. i-scoop. eu/digitization-digitalization-digital-transformation-disruption/

Coscieme, L., Mortensen, L. F., Anderson, S., Ward, J., Donohue, I., & Sutton, P. C. (2020). Going beyond gross domestic product as an indicator to bring coherence to the sustainable development goals. *Journal of Cleaner Production*, 248, 119232. DOI: 10.1016/j.jclepro.2019.119232

Cousineau, D., & Chartier, S. (2010). Outliers detection and treatment: A review. *International Journal of Psychological Research*, 3(1), 58–67. DOI: 10.21500/20112084.844

Daidj, N., Sugahara, S., & Ushio, S. (2017). *Value creation in management accounting and strategic management: An integrated approach*. John Wiley & Sons.

El Hilali, W., El Manouar, A., & Idrissi, M. A. J. (2020). Reaching sustainability during a digital transformation: A PLS approach. *International Journal of Innovation Science*, 12(1), 52–79. DOI: 10.1108/IJIS-08-2019-0083

Fan, C. L., & Fan, T. (2020). The emergence and development of the concept of national innovation system-ideological evolution and policy application. *Science of Science and Management of Science and Technology*, 5, 27.

Fernandes, A. J. C., Rodrigues, R. G., & Ferreira, J. J. (2022). National innovation systems and sustainability: What is the role of the environmental dimension? *Journal of Cleaner Production*, 347, 131164. DOI: 10.1016/j.jclepro.2022.131164

Fornell, C., & Larcker, D. F. (1981). Evaluating structural equation models with unobservable variables and measurement error. *JMR, Journal of Marketing Research*, 18(1), 39–50. DOI: 10.1177/002224378101800104

Geng, D., Hung, L. K., & Zhu, Q. (2021). Eco-innovation and its role for performance improvement among Chinese small and medium-sized manufacturing enterprises. *International Journal of Production Economics, 231*, 107869. .DOI: 10.1016/j.ijpe.2020.107869

Hair, J. F., Hult, G. T. M., Ringle, C. M., Sarstedt, M., & Thiele, K. O. (2017). Mirror, mirror on the wall: A comparative evaluation of composite-based structural equation modeling methods. *Journal of the Academy of Marketing Science*, 45(5), 616–632. DOI: 10.1007/s11747-017-0517-x

Hubert, S. O. (1996). Tacit knowledge: The key to the strategic alignment of intellectual capital. *Strategy and Leadership*, 24(2), 10–16.

Hung, S. W., Chen, P. C., & Chung, C. F. (2014). Gaining or losing? The social capital perspective on supply chain members' knowledge sharing of green practices. *Technology Analysis and Strategic Management*, 26(2), 189–206. DOI: 10.1080/09537325.2013.850475

Jin, C., Shahzad, M., Zafar, A. U., & Suki, N. M. (2022). Socio-economic and environmental drivers of green innovation: Evidence from nonlinear ARDL. *Ekonomska Istrazivanja*, 1–21. DOI: 10.1080/1331677X.2022.2026241

Jun, W., Ali, W., Bhutto, M. Y., Hussain, H., & Khan, N. A. (2019). Examining the determinants of green innovation adoption in SMEs: A PLS-SEM approach. *European Journal of Innovation Management*, 24(1), 67–87. DOI: 10.1108/EJIM-05-2019-0113

Kemp, R. (2010). Eco-innovation: Definition, measurement and open research issues. *Economics and Politics*, 27(3), 397–420.

Klewitz, J., & Hansen, E. (2014). Sustainability-oriented innovation of SMEs: A systematic review. *Journal of Cleaner Production*, 65, 57–75. DOI: 10.1016/j.jclepro.2013.07.017

Kline, R. B. (2015). *Principles and practice of structural equation modeling*. Guilford publications.

Kumar, S., & Barua, M. K. (2022). A modeling framework of green practices to explore their interrelations as a conduit to policy. *Journal of Cleaner Production*, 335, 130301. DOI: 10.1016/j.jclepro.2021.130301

Lee, C. S., & Wong, K. Y. (2015). Development and validation of knowledge management performance measurement constructs for small and medium enterprises. *Journal of Knowledge Management*, 19(4), 711–734. DOI: 10.1108/JKM-10-2014-0398

Lu, M. T., Tsai, J. F., Shen, S. P., Lin, M.-H., & Hu, Y.-C. (2020). Estimating sustainable development performance in the electrical wire and cable industry: Applying the integrated fuzzy MADM approach. *Journal of Cleaner Production*, 277, 122440. DOI: 10.1016/j.jclepro.2020.122440

Masuda, H., Kawakubo, S., Okitasari, M., & Morita, K. (2022). Exploring the role of local governments as intermediaries to facilitate partnerships for the Sustainable Development Goals. *Sustainable Cities and Society*, 82, 103883. DOI: 10.1016/j.scs.2022.103883

Masuda, H., Okitasari, M., Morita, K., Katramiz, T., Shimizu, H., Kawakubo, S., & Kataoka, Y. (2021). SDGs mainstreaming at the local level: Case studies from Japan. *Sustainability Science*, 16(5), 1539–1562. DOI: 10.1007/s11625-021-00977-0

Matuszewska-Pierzynka, A. (2021). Relationship between corporate sustainability performance and corporate financial performance: Evidence from US companies. *Equilibrium. Quarterly Journal of Economics and Economic Policy*, 16(4), 885–906. DOI: 10.24136/eq.2021.033

Mohan, J., Rathi, R., Kaswan, M. S., & Nain, S. S. (2022). Green lean six sigma journey: Conceptualization and realization. *Materials Today: Proceedings*, 50, 1991–1998. DOI: 10.1016/j.matpr.2021.09.338

Montenegro, R., Ribeiro, L. C., & Britto, G. (2020). The effects of environmental technologies: Evidences of different national innovation systems. *Journal of Cleaner Production*, 284, 124742. DOI: 10.1016/j.jclepro.2020.124742

Nambisan, S., Lyytinen, K., Majchrzak, A., & Song, M. (2017). Digital innovation management. *Management Information Systems Quarterly*, 41(1), 223–238. DOI: 10.25300/MISQ/2017/41:1.03

Nasiri, M., Ukko, J., Saunila, M., & Rantala, T. (2020). Managing the digital supply chain: The role of smart technologies. *Technovation*, 96, 102121. DOI: 10.1016/j.technovation.2020.102121

Nonaka, I. (1994). The dynamic theory of organizational knowledge creation. *Organization Science*, 5(1), 14–37. DOI: 10.1287/orsc.5.1.14

Ohene-Asare, K., Tetteh, E. N., & Asuah, E. L. (2020). Total factor energy efficiency and economic development in Africa. *Energy Efficiency*, 13(6), 1177–1194. DOI: 10.1007/s12053-020-09877-1

Østergaard, P. A., Duic, N., Noorollahi, Y., Mikulcic, H., & Kalogirou, S. (2020). Sustainable development using renewable energy technology. *Renewable Energy*, 146, 2430–2437. DOI: 10.1016/j.renene.2019.08.094

Pham, H. T., Pham, T., Truong Quang, H., & Dang, C. N. (2022). Impact of transformational leadership on green learning and green innovation in construction supply chains. *Engineering, Construction, and Architectural Management.*

Podsakoff, P. M., MacKenzie, S. B., & Podsakoff, N. P. (2012). Sources of method bias in social science research and recommendations on how to control it. *Annual Review of Psychology*, 63(1), 539–569. DOI: 10.1146/annurev-psych-120710-100452 PMID: 21838546

Rehman, S. U., Kraus, S., Shah, S. A., Khanin, D., & Mahto, R. V. (2021). Analyzing the relationship between green innovation and environmental performance in large manufacturing firms. *Technological Forecasting and Social Change*, 163, 120481. DOI: 10.1016/j.techfore.2020.120481

Rehman Khan, S. A., Ahmad, Z., Sheikh, A. A., & Yu, Z. (2022). Digital transformation, smart technologies, and eco-innovation are paving the way toward sustainable supply chain performance. *Science Progress*, 105(4), 00368504221145648. DOI: 10.1177/00368504221145648 PMID: 36573795

Ripple, W. J., Wolf, C., Newsome, T. M., Galetti, M., Alamgir, M., Crist, E., & Laurance, W. F. (2017). World scientists' warning to humanity: A second notice. *Bioscience*, 67(12), 1026–1028. DOI: 10.1093/biosci/bix125

Shahzad, M., Qu, Y., Zafar, A. U., Rehman, S. U., & Islam, T. (2020). Exploring the influence of knowledge management process on corporate sustainable performance through green innovation. *Journal of Knowledge Management*, 24(9), 2079–2106. DOI: 10.1108/JKM-11-2019-0624

Sianturi, N. M., Nofirman, N., Yulianti, E. B., Fatmawati, E., & Hendriarto, P. (2022). Relevancy technological innovation and community economic development in Indonesia. *Linguistics and Culture Review*, 6, 117–130. DOI: 10.21744/lingcure.v6nS3.2091

Soewarno, N., Tjahjadi, B., & Fithrianti, F. (2019). Green innovation strategy and green innovation: The roles of green organizational identity and environmental organizational legitimacy. *Management Decision*, 57(11), 3061–3078. DOI: 10.1108/MD-05-2018-0563

Song, M., Peng, L., Shang, Y., & Zhao, X. (2022). Green technology progress and total factor productivity of resource-based enterprises: A perspective of technical compensation of environmental regulation. *Technological Forecasting and Social Change*, 174, 121276. DOI: 10.1016/j.techfore.2021.121276

Song, M., Yang, M. X., Zeng, K. J., & Feng, W. (2020). Green knowledge sharing, stakeholder pressure, absorptive capacity, and green innovation: Evidence from Chinese manufacturing firms. *Business Strategy and the Environment*, 29(3), 1517–1531. DOI: 10.1002/bse.2450

Tabachnick, B. G., & Fidell, L. S. (2007). Using multivariate statistics.

Tan, K. H., Ji, G., Lim, C. P., & Tseng, M. L. (2017). Using big data to make better decisions in the digital economy. *International Journal of Production Research*, 55(17), 4998–5000. DOI: 10.1080/00207543.2017.1331051

Ullah, S., Khan, F. U., & Ahmad, N. (2022). Promoting sustainability through green innovation adoption: A case of manufacturing industry. *Environmental Science and Pollution Research International*, 29(14), 1–21. DOI: 10.1007/s11356-021-17322-8 PMID: 34746984

UNCOP26. (2021). COP26: Together for our planet. United Nations Climate Action. https://www.un.org/en/climatechange/cop26

Vial, G. (2019). Understanding digital transformation: A review and a research agenda. *The Journal of Strategic Information Systems*, 28(2), 118–144. DOI: 10.1016/j.jsis.2019.01.003

Wang, C., Fan, A. Y., & Qian, M. H. (2021). Research on evaluation index system of sustainable development of logistics enterprises. *Business and Economic Review*, 09, 87–90.

Wang, C. H. (2019). How organizational green culture influences green performance and competitive advantage: The mediating role of green innovation. *Journal of Manufacturing Technology Management*, 30(4), 666–683. DOI: 10.1108/JMTM-09-2018-0314

Wang, J., Xue, Y., Sun, X., & Yang, J. (2020). Green learning orientation, green knowledge acquisition and ambidextrous green innovation. *Journal of Cleaner Production*, 250, 119475. DOI: 10.1016/j.jclepro.2019.119475

Wang, S., Abbas, J., Sial, M. S., Álvarez-Otero, S., & Cioca, L. I. (2022). Achieving green innovation and sustainable development goals through green knowledge management: Moderating role of organizational green culture. *Journal of Innovation & Knowledge*, 7(4), 100272. DOI: 10.1016/j.jik.2022.100272

Weill, P., & Woerner, S. L. (2018). Is your company ready for a digital future? *MIT Sloan Management Review*, 59(2), 21–25.

Westerman, G., Calméjane, C., Bonnet, D., Ferraris, P., & McAfee, A. (2011). Digital transformation: A roadmap for billion-dollar organizations. *MIT Center for Digital Business and Capgemini Consulting*, 1, 1–68.

Yu, S., Abbas, J., Alvarez-Otero, S., & Cherian, J. (2022). Green knowledge management: Scale development and validation. *Journal of Innovation & Knowledge*, 7(4), 100244. DOI: 10.1016/j.jik.2022.100244

Zbuchea, A., Pînzaru, F., Busu, M., Stan, S.-O., & Bârgăoanu, A. (2019). Sustainable knowledge management and its impact on the performances of biotechnology organizations. *Sustainability (Basel)*, 11(2), 359. DOI: 10.3390/su11020359

Zhang, J., Cherian, J., Abbas Sandhu, Y., Abbas, J., Cismas, L. M., Negrut, C. V., & Negrut, L. (2022). Presumption of green electronic appliances purchase intention: The mediating role of personal moral norms. *Sustainability (Basel)*, 14(8), 4572. DOI: 10.3390/su14084572

Zheng, K., Zhang, Z., & Gauthier, J. (2020). Blockchain-based intelligent contract for factoring business in supply chains. *Annals of Operations Research*, 1–21.

Chapter 2
Circular Economy in Textile and Apparel Supply Chains

Neetu Singh
https://orcid.org/0000-0002-0338-9846
Symbiosis International University, India

ABSTRACT

The textile and apparel (T&A) industry is one of the most crucial customer merchandise industries with a long supply chain regarded as one of the world's most polluting industries, especially when it accounts for the immense usage of natural resources, usage of hazardous raw materials, air and water pollution, and high carbon imprint. Circular economy principles are rooted in principles of environmental science and concepts of sustainable development which is why the textile and clothing manufacturing supply chain needs to start by not only controlling the pace of fashion but focusing on processes right from fiber manufacturing, production, textile wet processing, dyeing, finishing sizing, apparel manufacturing, retail, disposal, and recycling focusing on three specific areas to incorporate circular economy principles in the supply chain. These would be 1) the development of new business models increasing the timespan of clothing, 2) environmentally safe and renewable resources, and 4) recycling and upcycling solutions.

INTRODUCTION

The textile and apparel (T&A after that) industry is one of the most crucial customer merchandise industries with a long supply chain (Cai & Choi, 2020). T&A accounts for 9% of the world's labor force,2% of G.D.P., and 4% of world exports,

DOI: 10.4018/979-8-3693-4123-0.ch002

centralized majorly around the world's emerging economies. (Khairul Akter et al., 2022). It is also regarded as one of the world's most polluting industries, especially when it accounts for the immense usage of natural resources (Niinimäki et al., 2020; Shirvanimoghaddam et al., 2020), usage of hazardous raw materials, air and water pollution, and high carbon imprint. Fashion is the fourth largest contributor of greenhouse gas, totaling 2.7 billion tons of carbon dioxide by 2030, falling short of housing, transport, and food (Dominick, 2023). The T&A supply chains are highly complex, with forward supply chain starting from yarn production, processing, fabric manufacturing, finishing, garment manufacturing, and retailing (Celep et al., 2022; Jana, 2022; Özen et al., 2020)and reverse supply chains consisting of reuse of old products and upcycling from consumers (Denizel & Schumm, 2024; Sandberg, 2023). For instance, apparel manufacturing requires enormous volumes of energy and water in fabric production. Pollution is another initial problem in the T&A industry. Without proper treatment before discharge, wet processing wastewater contains harmful chemical substances, which can lead to severe ecological damage by polluting waste gas, wastewater, and the fabric itself. (Nayak, 2020). The problems outlined above are common across domains in the T&A supply chain, including design, sourcing, fiber and clothing production, packing and delivery, usage and restoration, and waste management (Lorek & Spangenberg, 2014). Thus, the input and output of the fashion industry's textile product life cycle influenced the environment. Still, the scale of the effect was astonishing, partly because of the massive scale of the T&A industry, which is a $1.3 trillion industry.

While linear economies align with principles of mass manufacturing and disposal of waste, the circular economy follows natural laws of preservation (Gullingsrud & Perkins, 2015). The Circular Economy (C.E.) targets sustainability through restoring objects and design (Ghisellini et al., 2016). One way to mitigate the harmful effects of the T&A supply chain on the environment is to engage in a circular Economy (C.E.) which replaces the "end of life" concept (Alves et al., 2022, str. 4) and focuses more on a restorative and regenerative system minimizing waste and maximizing usage of resources (Kirchherr et al., 2017; Korhonen et al., 2018) Circular economy functions on four principals of nature focusing on waste as nutrients, resilience through diversity, collaborative renewable energy resources, and systematic connection between constituents (Muthu, 2019). Hence, the core of the Circular economy lies in recovering, restoring, and reusing tangible commodities, aiming at both economic and environmental recovery of resources and energy(Ashby et al., 2019). Closed-loop supply chains are "the design, control, and operation of a system to maximize value creation over the entire life cycle of a product with the dynamic recovery of value from different types and volumes of returns over time"(Guide & Van Wassenhove, 2009, str. 10).

Over the past few decades, sustainable supply chain management practices have incorporated ecological issues into business by decreasing unintentional destructive effects on the environment in manufacturing and purchasing. At the same time, C.E.s push the boundaries of environmental sustainability by highlighting the notion of innovative goods, creating a viable relationship between ecosystems and economic growth. This research, therefore, identifies four underlying themes—drivers, barriers, practices, and indicators of sustainable performance when applying a circular economy in the textile and apparel industry(Abbate et al., 2024; Jia et al., 2020a). Therefore, This research illustrates the relationship between these four themes and highlights challenges in circular economy implementation, providing suggestions and future research directions for managers in the textile and apparel industry.

LITERATURE REVIEW

Circular Economy in the Textile and Apparel Sector

Today's world is inundated with excessive economic growth and limited planetary resources, where assumedly improved efficiency at micro levels would reduce the global environmental impact of businesses (Habib et al., 2021). Hence, moving towards an economy using sustainable design, manufacturing, waste reduction, reuse, and recycling methods (circular economy) is gaining ground compared to the "take-make-dispose" models of linear economy focusing on the mass production of goods and waste generation.(Abbate et al., 2024). C.E. presents itself as a solution for unlimited planetary growth and limited resources. Still, some research refers to C.E. as the "myth of decoupling" (Desing et al., 2020, str. 2) between economic growth and resource consumption as when economic growth requires resource usage above 1%, the positive effects of recycling on resource depletion can be considered negligible(Lazarevic & Valve, 2017). The laws of thermodynamics state that materials and energy are irretrievably lost when used excessively and in a limitless manner due to entropy and cannot be cycled indefinitely due to physical and technological limitations (Nancy M. P. Bocken et al., 2017). Thus sustainable raw material extraction (Nancy M. P. Bocken et al., 2017) and safe disposal (Patnaik & Tshifularo, 2021) are essential to C.E.

C.E. principals focus on waste reduction, resource optimization, and regeneration of systems in nature (Jia et al., 2020b; Konstantin Malley, Ravneet Singh, 2020). The shift of products from an Industrial to a performance economy shows a perceptible change in the cost of liability from the consumer to the producer or a movement from "externalization of risks" towards "internalization of risks." Performance economy, therefore, works towards extending the lifecycle of products and services, material and resource conservation, better utilization of resources, waste prevention, substituting nonrenewable resources with renewable ones, and job creation (Radhakrishnan, 2021). The concept of Cradle to Cradle design philosophy works towards the philosophy of disassembly and returning to the soil as a biological or technical nutrient, thereby focusing on design innovation, creativity, and a continuous cycle (Adenle et al., 2024; Ellen, 2024; Henninger et al., 2020). Biomimicry uses nature as a model and a tool to create designs emulating nature to create products, processes, or ecosystems that are energy efficient and use renewable resources (Abate & Mavris, 2017; Coppola et al., 2023). Therefore, for C.E. to indicate absolute economic growth, resource usage should be decoupled from GDP growth and linked to improvement in resource efficiency (Jackson, 2020; Kjaer et al., 2019). The industrial ecology approach deals with the flow of material and energy for industrial and consumer activities segregated as type 1, II, and III and the impact of these flows. Type 1 Ecosystems are linear, focusing on mass production and waste generation; type II system is partially recyclable, focusing on limited energy and resources, generating limited waste, while type III is circular and focuses on 100% recycling and reuse with zero waste creation (U. N. Haq & Alam, 2023; Radhakrishnan, 2021). (Table 1)

Table 1. Industrial Ecology Approach Towards Circular Economy

Type 1 Ecology	Type 2 Ecology	Type 3 Ecology
Linear Economy	Reuse Economy	Circular Economy
Plan-Take-Make-Waste	Plan-Manufacturing,Recycling/Disposing	Plan -4 R approach of Reduce,Reuse,Recycle and Recover
Focus :Mass Production	Focus :Efficient usage of resources	Focus-Effective usage of resources and complete removal of waste
Methods -Production process using raw materials leading to non recyclable waste	Methods -Production using raw materials leading to non recyclable /recyclable waste	Methods-Production using Raw materials leading to recyclable waste
Material Flow-Linear -One way flow of resources from extraction to disposal	Material Flow-Quasi Cyclic -Conversion of waste into reusable materials	Material Flow-Cyclic-Resources are kept in use for as long as possible

Source: (Montag et al., 2021; Wiegand & Wynn, 2023)

Textile and Apparel Sector waste

The current state of the fashion, clothing, and textile industry concerns aspects of sustainability, with global fashion consumption going up by 400%more than two decades earlier with fast fashion accelerating the rate at which textile and clothing products are over-available, consumed, and stay valid for a minimal time duration(Audrey, 2024; Jia et al., 2020a).The availability of cheap trendy clothing at affordable prices in developing economies bolstered by an aspirational lifestyle of high-end cultures and propagated by social media influencers and celebrities satisfies the demands of low-income groups of consumers (Saha et al., 2021; Shirvanimoghaddam et al., 2020). The majority of fibers used to make apparel are synthetic (62%), followed by cotton (24%), and the remaining are fibers such as rayon and wool (14%) (Kabir et al., 2019; Khan & Islam, 2015; Nayak et al., 2019). The textile and apparel manufacturing industry generates substantial waste through all its processes (Table 1), with clothing, footwear, and housing textiles being the fifth most significant contributors to greenhouse gas emissions.(European Environment Agency, 2019).

Table 2. Waste generation during Textile and Apparel manufacturing Process Source: (Moazzem et al., 2022; Shah, 2011)

Process Raw Material	Raw Material (Input)	End Product(Output)	Material Waste	Environmental Impacts
Yarn manufacturing/Spinning	Natural and Synthetic fibres	Yarn	Lint, Damaged Yarn, Unfinished cones	Resource Consumption,Green House Gas Emissions.Air/Water pollution,Soil Degradation
Fabric manufacturing/Knitting and weaving	Natural and Synthetic yarn.	Greige Fabric	Fly fiber, Scrap yarn, greige or unfinished fabric.	Resource Consumption,Green House Gas Emissions.Air/Water pollution,Soil Degradation,Hazardous Waste
Wet processing/Dyeing, finishing,printing	Greige Fabric	Finished Fabric	Rejected Colored Fabric, Over finished fabrics.	Resource Consumption,Green House Gas Emissions.Air/Water pollution,Soil Degradation.Solid Waste
Apparel Manufacturing	Finished Fabric	Apparel	Cutting waste, Excess Development Samples,Sewing waste, Apparel rejects.	Solid and Hazardous Waste,Green house emissions
Retailing	Finished Apparel available to end use consumer	Retailed Apparel	Unbought Items,Packaging Waste	Green house emissions
Consumer Use	Finished Apparel used by the Consumer	Apparel	Consumer Discarded Apparel, Landfills	Energy Consumption,Resource Consumption(Washing+Drying)
EOL(End of life) Management	Discarded Apparel/Landfills	Reusable Textiles, Yarn & Apparel, Recyclable Textiles,	Blended Textiles and Yarn, Unsalvageable Apparel	Green house emissions(Landfills,Textile+Apparel Waste)

Of the 100 billion garments produced yearly, 92 million end up in landfills, with numbers projected at 134 million tons a year by the decade(Martina, 2023). The T&A industry is the world's second most polluting after oil, exuding 1.2 billion tons of greenhouse gas emissions (Jia et al., 2020a) using 25% of the world's carbon budget (Ellenmacarthurfoundation.org, 2021; U. N. Haq & Alam, 2023; Wojnowska-Baryła et al., 2024).With 20,000 liters of water required to produce one kilogram of cotton and dyeing and finishing processes of textile manufacturing responsible for 3% of global carbon emissions and 20% of water pollution (Khairul Akter et al., 2022; Martina, 2023), Impacts from the fashion industry tantamount towards 92 million tons of waste created per year along with 79 trillion liters of water consumed requiring urgent sustainability initiatives to curb the environmental impacts of the T&A industry by making changes to the fashion model using principals of circular economy (Peter John & Mishra, 2023).Circular economy principles are rooted in principles of environmental science and concepts of sustainable development (Piller, 2023), which is why the textile and clothing manufacturing supply chain needs to start by not only controlling the pace of fashion but focusing on processes right from fiber manufacturing, production, textile wet processing, dyeing, finishing sizing, apparel manufacturing, retail, disposal and recycling which are significant contributors towards energy, water consumption, pollution and carbon footprint(Table 2) (Peter John & Mishra, 2023; Yousaf MA & Aqsa R, 2023).

Table 3. World's most polluting fibers Source: (Georgette, Kilgore, 2024)

Material	Environmental Impact
Cotton	Negative impact on soil fertility and biodiversity.Hazardous to human helath and needs to be produced sustainably
Polyester	Contributor towrads plastic waste, causing microfiber pollution which is hazardous to human ,wildlife,aquatic and entre ecosystems health.
Nylon24	Contributor of plastic waste in landfills, oceans,air infiltrating and polluting the entire food chain.
Acrylic	Acrylic is a leding cause of cancer due to prevalense of inherent polyacrylonitrile-a synthetic resin prepared by the polymerization of acrylonitrile.
Viscose	Viscose production is highly dependant on chemical processes casuing water pollution and hazardous to both environment and human health.
Bamboo Viscose	Sustainable fibre, eco friendly and fast replinishment due to fast growth.
Acetate	Dependant on hazardous chemicals for processing.Production process emits toxic cehmicals often polluting water sources.
Wool	Most environmentally unfiendly fabric due to extensive chemical processing required,resulting in emiting toxic chemicals into water sources.
Leather	Leather tanning is destructive to human as well a senivironment health with chromium waste being the leading casue of pollution.
Fur	Unethical and reliant on harsh chemicals causing high level of pollution.

Global T&A models must focus on three specific areas to incorporate circular economy principles in the supply chain. These would be i) the Development of new business models increasing the timespan of clothing, ii) Environmentally safe and renewable resources, and iii) Recycling and Upcycling solutions(Ellenmacarthurfoundation.org, 2024).

Development of New Business Models in Textless and Fashion

New business models focusing on circular economy principles in the fashion industry refer to a regenerative approach aiming to reduce the usage of natural resources, use sustainable materials, minimize waste through recycling, and use renewable energy during production. With the advent of fast fashion and the massive availability of clothing to consumers at affordable prices, the life span of apparel has been reduced to a few weeks, increasing usage and disposal. This results in massive usage of virgin textile fibers, both natural and artificial, having a huge environmental impact and usage of nonrenewable sources. Therefore, new innovative business models in Textile and Apparel need to focus on eight key aspects (N.M.P. Bocken et al., 2014; Nancy M. P. Bocken et al., 2017). These are i)Maximization of material and energy efficiencies ii)Value creation from waste iii)Sustainable and renewable substitution of resources iv)Deliver functionality instead of ownership iv)Adoption of a stewardship role vii) Repurposing of business focusing on the betterment of society and environment and viii) Development of scale-up solutions. Therefore, new business models in fashion and textiles need to focus on increasing the life span of garments and recovering and recycling raw materials throughout the T&A supply chain process(Bas, 2023; Marques et al., 2020). Clothing rental services such as Rent the Runaway focus on reducing the cheap fast fashion alternatives to the consumer by preferring designer clothing on rent, thereby aiming to reduce overconsumption and repairing and reselling platforms like Renewal Workshop partner with brands towards repairing and upcycling returned garments, ensuring their longevity. Community initiatives towards clothing swap and community wardrobe sharing enable consumers to exchange clothing they no longer wear as an alternative to new purchases. Zero waste and upcycling design techniques are also some models aiming at utilizing leftover materials and eliminating waste from the production process, wherein brands like Zero Waste Daniel, Tom Adam, and Herd e are pioneers (Romaily, 2022). Moreover, utilizing textile fibers from recycling is far more sustainable than producing new virgin fib(ETP Fibres Textile Clothing - European Technology Platform, b. d.).

Design

Circular economy fashion design practices focus on making durability exciting, ensuring clothes stay in circulation for (Ellenmacarthurfoundation.org, 2024). Enabling Cradle to Cradle design fashion products demands redesigning and reshaping product design and manufacturing systems to enable a closed-loop system or a continuous cycle of reuse (A. Mishra et al., 2023). Design for longevity addresses two aspects: Design for durability and design for long-lasting (Dan & Østergaard,

2021; Dissanayake & Weerasinghe, 2020). Durable products extend the product life cycle, reducing consumption and slowing resource loops (Mölsä et al., 2022; Muthu, 2020).Thus suitable quality materials, seams, dyes and manufacturing system along with repair, return and replacement and warrantees by retailers ensure that clothing meets changing consumer needs, enable customer loyalty and instrumental in consumer reuse, upcycling and recycling all ensure durable products (Corvellec & Stål, 2017; Ellenmacarthurfoundation.org, 2024).Designing quintessential timeless apparel, trans-seasonal extending beyond a fashion season, and increasing styling options enabling wearing a garment in different ways are all design interventions leading towards the longevity of apparel (Niinimäki, 2024). Design for customization using 3D body scan, virtual prototyping, and personalization of correct fit ensures consumer purchase of well-fitted clothing, allowing customer satisfaction at the purchase stage (Dissanayake, 2020). Customization also ensures additional features to the customers, transcending beyond traditional resource-intensive technologies such as dyeing, printing embellishments, etc., which are resource-centric and cause pollution. Design for disassembly ensures easy disassembly of products for repair and recycling and involves the appropriate selection of materials, component design, product architecture, and selection of sewing and fastening methods to make it feasible (Abuzied et al., 2020; Favi et al., 2019).Wear2™sewing thread is an invention that uses microwaveable dissolvable threads to facilitate disassembly when required. Current systems allow for only 1% of recyclable clothing, so it is essential to align clothing design that is easily recyclable and recoverable (Niinimäki, 2017). Composting textiles is another method of ensuring recycling, but it is difficult to do so due to the need to blend fibers. Thus, increasing the use of mono materials and minimizing surface coating in textiles can maximize recycling (Manshoven Saskia, Maarten Christis et al., 2019; Sandvik & Stubbs, 2019). Candiani Denim company from Italy focuses on innovative sustainable fabric, custom fits, and transparent sourcing and manufacturing processes, making it "the greenest textile company in the Blue World" (Colucci & Vecchi, 2021, str. 6).

Fibre Production, Spinning, and Fabric Production

Global fiber production doubled in the last 20 years to reach 113 million metric tons in 2019 and expected to reach a potential growth of 149 million metric tons by 2030.(Exchange, 2022; Shirvanimoghaddam et al., 2020) The value-adding process of textile and clothing consists of six levels: (i) Fibre production: Production of fibers by growing, harvesting, and cleaning fibers, which is called ginning. (ii) Spinning: Conversion of fibers into yarn by spinning, e.g., cotton fiber. The synthetic fibers are made from polymers extruding through spinneret for yarn production, which can involve either wet or dry spinning techniques. (iii) Fabric Production: Convert yarn into fabric through weaving and knitting.(iv) Wet Processing: Using chemicals and dyes to make fabric whiter, colorful, or attractive(v)Clothing: Using fabric to cut, sew, iron, pack, and distribute as completed apparel to the end consumer.(vii) Garment maintenance during its life cycle: Washing, drying, conditioning, ironing, and maintaining the apparel quality and (viii)Disposal or reuse/recycling of waste/ discarded apparel. The entire fiber-to-yarn conversion stage requires intensive use of pesticides, synthetic pesticides, synthetic fertilizers, and various chemicals, leading to high energy consumption, soil exhaustion, and destruction, including disturbance of soil water table balance(Table 3, Table 4) (Kabir et al., 2019; Khan & Islam, 2015; Pensupa et al., 2017; Wojciechowska, 2021).

Table 4. Energy consumption during production of different polymers (Source: (Chen et al., b. d.)

Polymer/Fiber	Energy Consumption(MJ/kg of fiber)
Natural polymers	
Flax	10
Cotton	55
Wool	63
Synthetic Polymers	
Viscose	100
Polypropylene	115
Polyester	125
Acrylic	175
Nylon	250

Table 5. Energy consumption during various textile processes and machine-wise breakdown Source: (Roy Choudhury, 2014)

Sector	Electrical Energy Consumption
Process	
Spinning	41
Weaving Preparatory	5
Weaving Preparatory	13
Humidification	19
Wet Processing	10
Lighting	4
Others	8
Machine-Wise Breakdown	
Blow Room	11
Carding	12
Drawing Machine	5
Combing Machine	1
Simplex	7
Ring spinning machines	37
Open end Machines	20
Winding Machine	7

Natural artificial or regenerated textiles formulate the basis of all textiles. Natural fibers are categorized as animal hair or crop fibers, while synthetic fibers are created by polymerizing small molecules into larger ones(Sinclair, 2015). Artificial fibers account for 75% of all fibers produced in the world, totaling 113 million tons in 2021(Textile, 2023; Wojnowska-Baryła et al., 2024). Polyethylene terephthalate (P.E.T.), account for the largest share (54%) of total fiber production. The production volume of polyester increased from 57 million tons in 2020 to 61 million tons in 2021. Fibers make up 98% of finished clothing, with 73% of fibers ending in landfills and only 12% recycled(Andrew et al., 2017).

During the yarn production stage the yarn processing of cotton in spinning operation " cotton lint" or short fibers accumulate around the machine and floor as waste (Khairul Akter et al., 2022). Additionally, damaged, failed quality and left-over yarns are also causing of waste. Material waste during knitting and weaving consists of fly fibers and greige/unfinished fabrics. During wet processing dyeing, finishing, printing, and washing stages, the fabrics are colored using dyes and treated with chemicals for the desired finish where fabric rejection happens due to excess processing or material waste (U. N. Haq & Alam, 2023; Kumar et al., 2023; Shamsuzzaman et al., 2023). Finally cutting an apparel production generates cut fabrics, leftovers an apparel rejects as waste. A significant consideration to allowing fiber recycling is sorting, which becomes difficult due to blending yards, which are chemically challenging to segregate and are commercially non-viable. Secondly fiber sorting is economically expensive and costs more than virgin fibers, thereby requiring more innovation and investment. as the share of recycled fibers increased from 8.4% to 8.9% in 2021 due to maximum usage of bottle-based polyester fiber but less than 1% global fiber market came from recycled textiles in 2021(Exchange, 2022). Some strategies to sort fiber for recycling include RFID- Radio Frequency Identification (RFID) yarns are added to apparel, and infrared sensors are employed to track the garment at all stages from manufacturing, shipping, retail, use, and recycling. Solvent technologies enable dissolvable dissolving materials for recycling or using high temperatures to dissolve a blend of fibers, dissolving one and leaving the other a solid. A mix of cotton polyester fabrics can be segregated by first dissolving cotton cellulose to leave polyester behind, combining the retrieved cellulose with other recycled sources, like Lyocell, Rayon, Cupro, and Acetate fibers.

Poor-quality fibers are later used to make pulp and paper(Chen et al., b. d.; Furferi et al., 2022). Bio-sorting is another effective way of using living organisms and enzymes to consume part of the fabric and leave others behind. Bio recycling using enzymes also enables the depolymerizing of textile waste into its original fibers (Burik Alexander, 2018). Asia Pacific Rayon (A.P.R.) is pilot-testing the creation of viscose from pre and post-consumer textiles. Asahi Kasei's Bemberg is a cupro fiber made in Japan from 100% cotton linter, a pre-consumer-consumer residue of cotton processing. Birla's Liva Reviva is also a new development of viscose fiber made from 20% pre-consumer cotton plus a small amount of post-consumer cotton waste up to 5%(Exchange, 2022). Creating new fibers using pineapple, orange, and algae waste creates new sustainable, eco-friendly fibers (Ananas-anam, 2024; Hmfoundation, 2017; Orangefiber, 2024).

Dyeing/Finishing

Textile finishing is an important process in textiles contributing significantly towards the CO_2 emissions and carbon footprint through usage of energy and usage of chemicals and lubricants. In a continuous textile process, 40% of CO_2 emissions disseminate during washing and steaming, 50% by drying, and 10% by chemical usage. In Knitwear production, 60% of emissions happen during the heating of water (Alam et al., 2023; Shamsuzzaman et al., 2023). According to a Lenzing group report, 63% of fibers are petrochemical derived while synthetic and polymers are made from petroleum extracts like nylon, acrylic, polyester, and polypropylene, which emit significant carbon dioxide (Lenzing, 2024; S. Mishra & Das, 2023). Some easy-to-use and environment-friendly materials are Bamboo and Hemp, which are easy to cultivate, hypo-allergic and fast-growing, and silk, which does not use harsh dyeing (Seidu et al., 2024).

Some of the changes required are substituting input material, such as replacing chemical dyes with natural dyes. Modification of technology used in dyeing using floating treatment macrocosms augmented with dye-degrading bacterial or biocatalyst immobilization on fibers and textiles for wastewater treatment (Kumar et al., 2023; Morshed et al., 2021; Mustafa et al., 2023; Yousaf MA & Aqsa R, 2023) and optimizing chemical usage by utilizing automated dosing machines. A membrane photocatalytic reactor (M.P.R.) would enable more sustainable operation in removing dyes to decolorize, detoxify, and treat industrial dye wastewater (Desa et al., 2019). Using biopolymers instead of synthetic petroleum-based fibers is a shift from synthetic to bio-based fibers, which is more sustainable for the environment . Similarly, the usage of layers of biopolymers on the surface of textiles electrophoretic deposition brings interesting environmentally friendly possibilities for surface modification (Jahandideh et al., 2021; Pabjańczyk-Wlazło et al., 2022). The use of alternative processes, like pulsating rinse technology, reduces water wastage and lowers the water temperature during dyeing to reduce energy wastage. Finally, introducing smart textiles and functional clothing offers more functionalities in T&A. These technologies enable layering of enzymes on textiles, nano-coating of textile surfaces, plasma for nanoscale modifications and incorporating functional biomaterials, and micro and nano capsulation onto materials by increasing functionality and not limiting breathability, pliability, and strength of textiles and apparel (Klinkhammer et al., 2024; Kumar Singh, 2021).

Digitalization in clothing manufacturing through tracing and documenting the chemicals and materials used in products and addressing the current concerns about what goes into textiles and apparel and will align a better flow of information between all entities of the supply chain (Alicke Knut, Rexhausen Daniel, 2017; Zhu et al., 2016).C&A, the European fashion retailer uses a certification process to assess products and materials for safety on both humans and environment, using design for future and manufacturing methods which are first Cradle to Cradle Certified™ Gold products using 100% organic cotton, pesticide, and fertilizer free, recyclable and produced in a socially sustainable manner (C&A, 2024). For their dyeing process, C&A has aligned itself with Dystar to develop an eco-friendly color palette of about 100 shades using C2C gold-certified primary colors from the range of DyStar Levafix® and Remazol® reactive dyes, which received C2C Gold level certification for material Health from C2CPII in 2016 (Engin, 2017).

Apparel Production

The primary energy usage and GHG (greenhouse gas emissions) during T&A manufacturing are generally during the raw material production and end usage stages (Allwood et al., 2006; Paul & Mercedes, 2009). L.C.A. (Life cycle assessment) of finished apparel indicates post-industrial, pre-consumer, and post-consumer waste at textile processing, spinning and weaving as droppings, kitty dust, noil, pneumafil, sweeping waste, selvage waste, sizing waste, knot, gaiting or tying-in-waste, chindi, residual waste, etc.(Goyal Ashvani, 2021).Cutting section waste accounts for a huge portion of garment costing due to unwanted waste produced, such as fabric leftovers, cutting waste, spreading loss, cutting rejects, etc. (Cao et al., 2022; Vadicherla et al., 2017). Apparel waste happens as swatch waste, cutting, and trim waste, cut and sew operations, sampling yardage, rejected apparel, and unsold clothing(Doctor & Khatwani, 2022). An analysis of garment factory production states that an estimated 26.5% of waste is generated during knit T-shirt production, while 13.57% is unavoidable cutting section waste(Md. & Md., 2016). Stream mapping of the textile-apparel production chain estimates a loss of 0.70 USD in every piece of apparel export due to textile-apparel material waste, with 87% of global textile waste managed through landfills with 90% of this waste having the potential to be converted into valued added items through recycling (Moazzem et al., 2021). The environmental cost of this material waste is substantial, with landfills contributing towards greenhouse gas (GHG) emissions and materials waste producing ash and carbon dioxide gases when generating heat energy, materials producing toxic chemical waste when processing, and clogging rivers, drains, filling landfills resulting in environment pollution (Awasthi et al., 2019; Sivaram et al., 2019). Taking the environmental hazards into consideration, the concept of the circular economy provides the best fit to the waste management solution in the T&A industry right from reducing waste during processing, cutting, and manufacturing, reducing negative impacts of carbon emissions, recycling and reusing a product becomes a more viable alternative than discarding it in trash or landfills. (Fortuna & Diyamandoglu, 2017; Saha et al., 2021). Waste valorization and repurposing of pre-consumer waste through recycling can create secondhand products, which facilitate the recovery of T&A products (Cao et al., 2022). High-quality products can be made through the reclamation of pre-consumer waste, such as home products, different-sized apparel, and novel merchandise for the circular fashion industry (Aus et al., 2021; Khairul Akter et al., 2022).

Filipaa K, founded in 1993, is a Scandinavian brand situated in Stockholm, Sweden,, producing garments as sustainably as possible. The garments go through a life cycle assessment where every phase of the life cycle is examined, from raw material to the afterlife, and adjusted to cause a minimum carbon footprint on the ecosystem through a traceability system. The brand offers an extended 10-year warranty and care for its products, provides rental services for its clothing, and has an old clothes collection initiative for a 15% discount to positively influence the four R's: reduce, repair, reuse, and recycle of apparel (KFilippa, 2020; Larsson, 2018; Muthu, 2019). In line with other industries the current production of T&A have huge potential for automation and upgradation.3D printed garments a new age technology creating customized fitted garments for consumers have been explored by designers such as Iris van Herpen (n.d.) and Belgian fashion designer Bruno Pieters while brands like Adidas have tested in store production technology using 3D knitting which knits clothes within hours and lead to high quality, durable customized garments with minimal wastage(Narayanan, 2021; Tony, 2017).

Apparel Retailing

The primary carbon footprint during apparel retail and apparel consumption by consumers is in the form of GHG (Green House Gas) emissions, which are a result of transportation and domestic energy consumption during washing, drying, and maintenance of apparel (Demirdelen et al., 2023; Muthu, 2020). The highest energy consumption for finished apparel comes from transportation between multiple suppliers, distribution centers, and stores. The largest contribution at the user's end comes from machine washing, high-temperature machine washing, electric drying, tumble drying, and ironing, which contribute majorly to energy consumption (Jain et al., 2024; Rath et al., 2023).To meet the United Nations sustainable goals program, most retailers need to strive to meet the Sustainable Development Goals(S.D.G.)by 2030, marking particular goal number 12, focusing on sustainable consumption and production (Cai & Choi, 2020).Shopping malls, online retail, and app retailing have been persuading consumers to adapt to the fast fashion trend and indulge heavily in fashion, making the fashion cycles smaller and the rate of apparel disposal higher. To solve hyper-consumption, retailers are now trying to involve themselves in eco-fashion by making season less, customized, and slow-fashion garments, encouraging repairs and recycling through their C.S.R. (Corporate Social Responsibility) initiatives (H&M, 2024; Overdiek, 2018).

Hence, retailers need to focus on sustainable product design, sourcing, packaging, and business model strategies incorporating a circular economy in the supply chain. Circular economy in retail is heavily dependent on software's to track products from origin to recycling determining when an item should be picked up, restocked, reordered, replenished, returned to vendor as reverse supply chain (R.F.S.C.)enabling suppliers, manufactures and third party collaborators across industries to achieve sustainability (M. Haq et al., 2023; Wu et al., 2023).This avoids transport, return costs reducing Co_2 emissions reducing landfills (Frei et al., 2020).Brands like John

Lewis are collaborating with social enterprises like Stuffstr to offer an app for re-selling unwanted fashion products purchased from John Lewis (R.Smithers, 2018). Brands consider refurbished secondary markets as a threat, assuming it would eat into their new product market. However secondary markets provide a profitable venture to capitalize on rejects, and surplus as they cost lesser than making fresh products from start and are actually profitable (U. N. Haq & Alam, 2023; Persson & Hinton, 2023).

The change in business model to C.E. requires customer understanding towards a new mode from selling products to selling services (product service systems) and making them interested in products which are refurbished, recycled and upcycled indicating an equivalent prestige as new ones (Akbar & Hoffmann, 2018).Ensuring customer feedback towards product quality resulting in defects, controlling excessive choices, hence resulting in returns, making return barriers higher (Albinsson et al., 2023; Zhang et al., 2023).The annual environmental impact of household clothing can be considered equivalent to filling 1000 bathtubs with the carbon emissions equaling driving a car 6000 miles (Millward-Hopkins et al., 2023; Rick, 2020). Also garments requiring extreme maintenance lead towards more energy usage (Trust, 2018), with climatic and cultural elements also playing a crucial role in environmentally friendly clothing habits where American washing habits have been proven to be more unsustainable than Chinese consumers (Guo & Kim, 2023).hence educating consumers about washing and cold water and line drying would prove to be 90% more sustainable than user washing in machines.

Textile and Apparel Recycling

As the current literature states currently there are several barriers towards textile and apparel recycling, these include separation of blends, separation of additives & trims, restoration of quality and ensuring all processes are sustainable (Leonas, 2017). Globally an estimated 92 million tons of textiles go to landfill and pose a serious threat to recycling with the problem exacerbated by the mixtures of various natural and synthetic fibres making recycling difficult (Khairul Akter et al., 2022; QUT, 2024).Separating blended fabrics, additives and trims complicates the recycling process which is not only difficult and requires special processes especially towards removal of chemicals and hazardous substances from materials (Maria & Hanna, 2016).Restoration of fiber quality is also difficult during disassembly and recyclable material quality is severely degraded. Besides technical challenges, recycling can only be considered viable when it matches current production prices and not exceed it, Also emission and resource usage during recycling should not exceed those during garment production stage. The cost of using different technologies to meet the recycling requirements of separating fabric waste is also a detrimental factor and not financially viable which is why incorporating social aspects into principals of circular economy are necessary towards building reciprocity and responsibility during recycling(Moreau et al., 2017). Despite several challenges it's important to focus on all aspects of the T&A supply chain to focus on principals of circularity. Starting from design enabling creation of garments using lesser blended materials, easier disassembly, customization and focusing on quality, durability and longevity of apparel will align apparel design towards recycling (Shafqat & Saccavini, 2023). Mono materials make disassembly easier Gaining access to clothes otherwise ending up in landfills is also important towards creating a recovery system. Enabling recycling possible at low cost focusses on digitization for easy traceability, recovery using RFID technology which acts as a digital passport and enabling surface sorting of waste through a chip. E.U. projects "Trash-2-Cash" and Content Thread are such RFID technologies enabling digital sorting informing sorters an recyclers about the type of materials and chemicals used in each garment enabling easier sorting and preventing degradation of fabric and of materials (Hmfoundation, 2017).Circular System Texloop™ and Takihyo a Japanese company converts pre consumer and post-consumer materials to high value materials by preserving the original fiber quality through mechanical/hydrothermal process(Exchange, 2022).Over the last five years BlockTexx® has developed, tested, patented and commercialized our chemical separation technology called S.O.F.T. (separation of fibre technology) enabling difficult to recycle clothing made from blends of polyester and cotton fibres to be processed and recycled at commercial scale (BlockTexx, 2024; QUT, 2024).Aalto University's loncell is a technology in-development which turns textiles into new textiles using a solvent called ionic liquid Hence by focusing on ways to repair, reuse, refurbish, remanufacture and recycle companies can implement circular economy principals in textile and apparel supply chains (Stahel, 2016). Gucci usage of recycled cotton increased to 74% from 61% in 2021 while recycled, responsibly sourced wool and cashmere increased to 60% up from 47% the same year. In 2022 the brand also maintained their 100% target for responsibly sourced precious metals and 100% paper from responsibly managed forest sources(Gucci, 2021).Candiani Denim uses ReGen as part of their denim project initiative. It's made with 100% regenerated fibres – 50% recycled cotton recovered from their own production and 50% recycled lyocell, made using Lenzing's patented Refibra technology, in both the warp and the weft (Colucci & Vecchi, 2021).Goonj, an N.G.O. in India working on social and economic development of poor rural communities, has pioneered a business model to Recover, Reuse and Recycle clothing and other goods discarded in the cities of India. It is a remarkably sophisticated operation involving, repair, re-manufacturing, upcycling and re-distribution; it has also achieved considerable scale and now employs 600 people in its processing centers handling more than 5,500 tons per year(Alan, 2020)

Textile and Apparel Upcycling

Focusing on technological processes in textile and apparel recycling enables traceability, transparency, standardization, atomization and enable connection of different stake holders and processes across supply chain (Sandvik & Stubbs, 2019). Digital platforms also enhance resource availability by connecting supply and demand of "textile waste" enabling people with waste to find places and material suppliers to get it upcycled or recycled enabling creation of a circular model(Schwab, 2016). Textile & Apparel waste can be divided into two categories unsold goods, which are at retailers end and pre consumer waste generated mainly by fibre, fabric and garment producers (Domina & Koch, 1997).End of life strategies for textile and apparel include usage of biodegradable fabric, creation of new life through redesign and recycling, recycling textiles, organize collection and take back systems of apparel to life through reuse(C. T. Loop, 2024). Reuse or Upcycling implies repurposing the same fabric, materials such as clothing, textiles or fabrics and transforming them by enhancing value (Aus et al., 2021).Various creative techniques such as embroidery, screen printing, tie and dye, embellishments, repair are employed din upcycling garments to give them a unique upcycled look. This process not only prevents landfills and disposal of clothing & textiles but also enhances longevity leading towards reduction in carbon foot print by using existing material and reducing associated greenhouse emissions from their extraction, transportation and processing. Top atelier a 2019-21 research project funded by Vlaanderen Circulair, provides consultancy to designers over various forms of upcycling (C. T. Loop, 2024).Gucci as part of its sustainability efforts works with several nonprofit organizations and was able to reuse around 3500 tons of leather leftovers, 298 tons of textile leftovers and 67 tons of metal scraps in the year 2021 (Gucci, 2021). The British designer Christopher Raeburn has been collaborating with the branding company Avery Dennison R.B.I.S. (Retail Branding and Information Solutions) for many years in order to create designs using old parachutes and life boats. With a significant cultural shift in the last few years items which were earlier considered as second hand are now being considered vintage by consumers, which is why supporting an industry wide move towards circular economy would add €160 billion in value by 2030.Brands like Zara, H&M and Marks & Spencer's are therefore starting to become more circular by introducing collection pointes for old clothes at their stores (Trust, 2018).This is also leading towards emergence of new models such as Rent-the Runway where used clothing can be rented and brands like M.U.D. Jeans leasing their products for a year with free repairs after which they can be exchanged for a new pair and returned for recycling or upcycling (Braithwaite, 2018).

CONCLUSION

The final ingredient towards achieving circular economy and driving the shift towards a sustainable fashion industry is the will to change. For example brands like H&M are committed since 2017 to become 100% circular by 2030 implying they will only be using sustainable circular economy principals of production, usage, reuse and recycling (Trust, 2018). Sustainable brands specially in sports and luxury by incorporating circular economy in their production process are utilizing and minimizing waste. Nike reduces waste during production awhile brands like DavyJ, Patagonia and Levis use garbage to convert into feasible apparel (Leonas, 2017; Moorhouse & Moorhouse, 2017; Nayak et al., 2019). Designers like Dame Vivienne Westwood's are also pushing the sustainability agenda by advising consumers to buy less, choose well and make their clothing last. The consumer is slowly waking up to the concept of slow fashion which is sustainable by adhering to ethical and sustainable sourcing, manufacturing, distribution, retail and recycling standards. The Textile and Apparel supply chains are consciously becoming more environmentally conscious by adopting circular economy principals gaining superiority over the traditional linear economy systems all the while making themselves attractive to the consumers by safeguarding their revenues and making the consumers pay more for sustainable green apparel (Mölsä et al., 2022).

Recommendation

The recommendations for a future sustainability using circular economy principals in the fashion industry are therefore to produce less, through better forecasting, better fit quality models, and usage of software technology to monitor returns and adapt business models across the supply chain focusing on profitability which is less product centric(Figure 1).The next step would be towards elimination of waste from the manufacturing systems by "cut-make-trim innovation" which focus on elimination of waste during right from pattern creation, sewing, embellishment itself .the cutting wastage itself ranges from 6-25% of fabric which can be reduced through zero waste designs, effective pattern cutting, minimal seam creation and reduction of garment complexity (Gabe, 2023; Good, 2020; McQuillan, 2019).Elimination of waste from the supply chain using Artificial Intelligence (A.I.) which would enable performance assessment, continuous quality improvement, implementation of improvement plans and reassessing results. The Hong Kong Polytechnic University has developed a fabric defect detection system known as "Wise eye: which used advanced technology such as Artificial Intelligence(A.I.) and Deep Learning for quality improvement in textile industry (Ren et al., 2022; Systems, 2024).Reduction of carbon footprint by getting off coal and other fossil fuels and moving on to renewable energy sources is an urgent an necessary step which needs to be taken to attain circular Economy in T&A supply chain. Brands therefore need to elect suppliers and incentivize those willing to invest in clean renewable energy sources, usage of sustainable materials, waste reducing manufacturing, distribution, retail and recycling systems. California label Christy Dawn helps fund framers transition from conventional agriculture systems to wards regenerative agriculture (Rachel, 2021).Using waste from pineapple, algae and to create new fibres and usage of straw based packaging from waste materials all lead towards reutilization of waste from the system towards circular economy systems (Ananas-anam, 2024; Resources, 2024). ReBlend a Dutch circular fashion startup converts textile waste into fibres and yarns for interior design pieces by using no hazardous chemicals or solvents during recycling (C. the Loop, 2024). Finally, following the principals of the 3 R's: reuse, recycle, and reuse, brands need to increase visibility for consumers to actively engage in upcycling, recycling.

Figure 1. Future direction for circular economy implementation in T&A supply chains

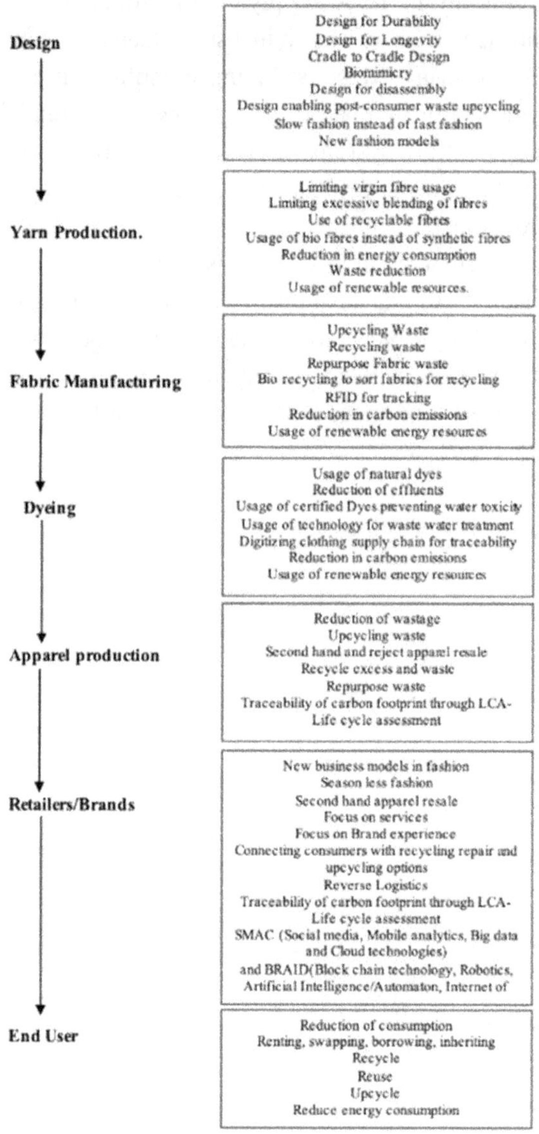

Future Direction

The adoption barriers towards implementation of circular supply chain in the T&A industry are high costs of research and development, lack of control due to multiple stakeholders and lack of relevant technology enabling data tracking, sorting of materials, logistics and agile response system. Enabling circular supply chain would therefore entail effective data aggregation and sharing, product development and implementing new technologies enabling collaboration, garment collection, waste sorting, and recycling accelerated with digital transformation to create new sustainable business models (Sandvik & Stubbs, 2019).

The first area of focus would be to influence consumers towards reduction in consumption patterns, reuse and recycle and movement towards better environmentally friendly design and product development (Rath et al., 2023). The second research are focuses LCA (lifecycle assessment) methodology along the supply chain and usage of technology to interpret and control the environmental impacts along the supply chain (Abbate et al., 2024; Chowdhury et al., 2023).Hence electric tools, automated systems and technology driven devices give way to large amount of data to be collected, processed, transmitted and stored. These technologies are known as SMAC (Social media, Mobile analytics, Big data and Cloud technologies) and BRAID(Block chain technology, Robotics, Artificial Intelligence/Automaton, Internet of things and Digital Fabrication) enabling traceability, Life cycle assessment, resource usage and, carbon footprint throughout the supply chain enabling implementation of circularity practices in Textile and Apparel supply chain (Jain et al., 2024; Wiegand & Wynn, 2023).The third area of focus would be on Corporate social responsibility of corporates and brands towards incorporating and implementing sustainable practices aiming towards a circular supply chain. focusing on waste reduction, recycling and reverse supply chain requiring a change in both the consumer and brand mindset (Long & Gui, 2023). Finally the fourth area of research and future direction would be towards creation of new fashion models, such as slow fashion focusing on longevity of the product cycle and reducing consumption, in order to safeguard the environment, resources, an economy. As compared to fast fashion models, slow fashion models are still not financially profitable, requiring more research on the causes, implications and solutions towards addressing the same in future.

REFERENCES

Abate, G., & Mavris, D. N. (2017). CFD Analysis of Leading Edge Tubercle Effects on Wind Turbine Performance. *15th International Energy Conversion Engineering Conference*, 1–2. DOI: 10.2514/6.2017-4626

Abbate, S., Centobelli, P., Cerchione, R., Nadeem, S. P., & Riccio, E. (2024). Sustainability trends and gaps in the textile, apparel and fashion industries. V. *Environment, Development and Sustainability*. Advance online publication. DOI: 10.1007/s10668-022-02887-2 PMID: 36788931

Abuzied, H., Senbel, H., Awad, M. & Abbas, A. (2020). A review of advances in design for disassembly with active disassembly applications. *Engineering Science and Technology, an International Journal*. DOI: 10.1016/j.jestch.2019.07.003

Adenle, Y. A., Haideri, S., & Sandouka, I. (2024). Understanding the best practices of cradle to cradle in furnishings, carpet, and textile industries–A case studies analysis and conceptual model. *Cleaner and Circular Bioeconomy*, 8, 100088. DOI: 10.1016/j.clcb.2024.100088

Akbar, P., & Hoffmann, S. (2018). Under which circumstances do consumers choose a product service system (PSS)? Consumer benefits and costs of sharing in PSS. *Journal of Cleaner Production*, 201, 416–427. DOI: 10.1016/j.jclepro.2018.08.010

Al Alam, M. A., Biswas, M. K., Mahiat, T., Chowdhury, R. B., Biswas, K. F., Hossain, M. M., & Sujauddin, M. (2023). Taking stock of the share of global environmental burden of knitwear production in Bangladesh: Constructing the life cycle inventory. *Journal of Cleaner Production*, 412, 137376. DOI: 10.1016/j.jclepro.2023.137376

Alan, B. (2020). *A quantified case study of the value in the circular economy for clothing and textiles*. Goong.org. https://www.linkedin.com/pulse/quantified-case-study-value-circular-economy-clothing-braithwaite

Albinsson, P. A., Chaudhuri, H. R., Das, A., Ray, S. & Nayak, L. (2023). Marketing Sustainable Fashion: Trends and Future Directions. *Sustainability, 15*(7), 6202. DOI: 10.3390/su15076202

Alexander, B. (2018). *Carbios Breaks Down Plastic Textile Waste With Enzymes*. Labiotech. https://www.labiotech.eu/trends-news/carbios-plastic-textile-waste-enzymes/

Allwood, J. M., Soren, L. E., Cecilia, R. de M. & Nancy, B. (2006). *Well dressed? The present and future sustainability of clothing and textiles in the United Kingdom.* University of Cambridge. https://www.researchgate.net/publication/282249347_Well_Dressed_The_Present_and_Future_Sustainability_of_Clothing_and_Textiles_in_the_United_Kingdom

Alves, L., Ferreira Cruz, E., Lopes, S. I., Faria, P. M., & Rosado da Cruz, A. M. (2022). Towards circular economy in the textiles and clothing value chain through blockchain technology and IoT: A review. V. *Waste Management & Research*, 40(1), 3–23. Advance online publication. DOI: 10.1177/0734242X211052858 PMID: 34708680

Ananas-anam. (2024). *Home - Ananas Anam.* https://www.ananas-anam.com/

Andrew, M., Rob, O., Dr, H. S., Laura, B., Camille, G. & Lukas, F. (2017). *A New Textiles Economy: Redesigning Fashion's Future.*

Ashby, A., Callegaro, A. M., Adeyeye, K. & Granados, M. (2019). The Spiral Economy: A Socially Progressive Circular Economy Model? *Sustainable Development Goals and Sustainable Supply Chains in the Post-global Economy* (pp. 67–94). Springer Nature. https://doi.org/DOI: 10.1007/978-3-030-15066-2_5/COVER

Ashvani, G. (2021). *Management of spinning and weaving wastes. Waste Management in the Fashion and Textile Industries.* Woodhead Publishing. DOI: 10.1016/C2018-0-04057-8

Audrey, S. (2024). *What Is Fast Fashion, Anyway? The Good Trade.* https://www.thegoodtrade.com/features/what-is-fast-fashion/

Aus, R., Moora, H., Vihma, M., Unt, R., Kiisa, M., & Kapur, S. (2021). Designing for circular fashion: Integrating upcycling into conventional garment manufacturing processes. *Fashion and Textiles*, 8(1), 34. DOI: 10.1186/s40691-021-00262-9

Awasthi, M. K., Sarsaiya, S., Chen, H., Wang, Q., Wang, M., Awasthi, S. K., Li, J., Liu, T., Pandey, A., & Zhang, Z. (2019). *Global Status of Waste-to-Energy Technology. Current Developments in Biotechnology and Bioengineering.* Elsevier. DOI: 10.1016/B978-0-444-64083-3.00003-8

Bas, F. (2023). *The Circular Fashion Economy: A Sustainable Shift Towards a Greener Future - EcoMatcher.* EcoMatcher. https://www.ecomatcher.com/the-circular-fashion-economy-a-sustainable-shift-towards-a-greener-future/

BlockTexx. (2024). *Technology — BlockTexx®.* blocktexx.com. https://www.blocktexx.com/technology

Bocken, N. M. P., Olivetti, E. A., Cullen, J. M., Potting, J., & Lifset, R. (2017). Taking the Circularity to the Next Level: A Special Issue on the Circular Economy. *Journal of Industrial Ecology*, 21(3), 476–482. DOI: 10.1111/jiec.12606

Bocken, N. M. P., Short, S. W., Rana, P., & Evans, S. (2014). A literature and practice review to develop sustainable business model archetypes. *Journal of Cleaner Production*, 65, 42–56. DOI: 10.1016/j.jclepro.2013.11.039

Braithwaite, N. (2018). *Clothing rental could be the key to a stylishly sustainable fashion industry*. theconversation.com. https://theconversation.com/clothing-rental-could-be-the-key-to-a-stylishly-sustainable-fashion-industry-100106

C&A. (2024). *Cradle-to-Cradle describes a circular economy in which products are recycled without waste. Find out how C2C works here.*https://www.c-and-a.com/eu/cz/shop/circular-economy-for-products

Cai, Y.-J., & Choi, T.-M. (2020). A United Nations' Sustainable Development Goals perspective for sustainable textile and apparel supply chain management. *Transportation Research Part E, Logistics and Transportation Review*, 141, 102010. DOI: 10.1016/j.tre.2020.102010 PMID: 32834741

Cao, H., Cobb, K., Yatvitskiy, M., Wolfe, M., & Shen, H. (2022). Textile and Product Development from End-of-Use Cotton Apparel: A Study to Reclaim Value from Waste. *Sustainability (Basel)*, 14(14), 8553. DOI: 10.3390/su14148553

Celep, G., Tetik, G. D., Yilmaz, F., Celep, G., Tetik, G. D., & Yilmaz, F. (2022). *Limitations of Textile Recycling: The Reason behind the Development of Alternative Sustainable Fibers*. Next-Generation Textiles. DOI: 10.5772/intechopen.105118

Chen, X., Memon, H. A., Wang, Y., Marriam, I. & Tebyetekerwa, M. (n.d.). Circular Economy and Sustainability of the Clothing and Textile Industry. *Materials Circular Economy, 1*, 3. DOI: 10.1007/s42824-021-00026-2

Chowdhury, M. M. H., Rahman, S., Quaddus, M. A., & Shi, Y. (2023). Strategies to mitigate barriers to supply chain sustainability: An apparel manufacturing case study. *Journal of Business and Industrial Marketing*, 38(4), 869–885. DOI: 10.1108/JBIM-04-2021-0233

Colucci, M., & Vecchi, A. (2021). Close the loop: Evidence on the implementation of the circular economy from the Italian fashion industry. *Business Strategy and the Environment*, 30(2), 856–873. DOI: 10.1002/bse.2658

Coppola, C., Vollero, A., & Siano, A. (2023). Developing dynamic capabilities for the circular economy in the textile and clothing industry in Italy: A natural-resource-based view. *Business Strategy and the Environment*, 32(7), 4798–4820. DOI: 10.1002/bse.3394

Corvellec, H., & Stål, H. I. (2017). Evidencing the waste effect of Product-Service Systems (PSSs). *Journal of Cleaner Production*, 145, 14–24. Advance online publication. DOI: 10.1016/j.jclepro.2017.01.033

Dan, M. C., & Østergaard, T. (2021). Circular Fashion: The New Roles of Designers in Organizations Transitioning to a Circular Economy. *The Design Journal*, 24(6), 1001–1021. Advance online publication. DOI: 10.1080/14606925.2021.1936748

Demirdelen, T., Aksu, İ. Ö., Yilmaz, K., Koç, D. D., Arikan, M., & Şener, A. (2023). Investigation of the Carbon Footprint of the Textile Industry: PES- and PP-Based Products with Monte Carlo Uncertainty Analysis. *Sustainability (Basel)*, 15(19), 14237. DOI: 10.3390/su151914237

Denizel, M., & Schumm, C. Z. (2024). Closed loop supply chains in apparel: Current state and future directions. *Journal of Operations Management*, 70(2), 190–223. DOI: 10.1002/joom.1274

Desa, A. L., Hairom, N. H. H., Ng, L. Y., Ng, C. Y., Ahmad, M. K., & Mohammad, A. W. (2019). Industrial textile wastewater treatment via membrane photocatalytic reactor (MPR) in the presence of ZnO-PEG nanoparticles and tight ultrafiltration. *Journal of Water Process Engineering*, 31, 100872. Advance online publication. DOI: 10.1016/j.jwpe.2019.100872

Desing, H., Brunner, D., Takacs, F., Nahrath, S., Frankenberger, K., & Hischier, R. (2020). A circular economy within the planetary boundaries: Towards a resource-based, systemic approach. *Resources, Conservation and Recycling*, 155, 104673. Advance online publication. DOI: 10.1016/j.resconrec.2019.104673

Dissanayake, D. G. K. (2020). *Does Mass Customization Enable Sustainability in the Fashion Industry? V*. Fashion Industry - An Itinerary Between Feelings and Technology., DOI: 10.5772/intechopen.88281

Dissanayake, D. G. K., & Weerasinghe, D. (2020). *Does Mass Customization Enable Sustainability in the Fashion Industry? Fashion Industry - An Itinerary Between Feelings and Technology*. IntechOpen. DOI: 10.1007/s43615-021-00090-5

Doctor, S. J., & Khatwani, P. A. (2022). Solid Textile Wastes : Different Types and their Causes of Generation. *Journal of the Textile Association, 83*(1), 422–426. https://doi.org/https://doi.org/10.17605/OSF.IO/QC6DT

Domina, T., & Koch, K. (1997). The Textile Waste Lifecycle. *Clothing & Textiles Research Journal*, 15(2), 96–102. DOI: 10.1177/0887302X9701500204

Dominick, A.-F. (2023). *The Fashion Industry Needs to Reduce Its Carbon Footprint | Industry Insights*. https://www.ana.net/miccontent/show/id/ii-2023-01-sustainable-fashion

Ellen, F. M. (2024). *Schools of thought that inspired the circular economy*. https://www.ellenmacarthurfoundation.org/schools-of-thought-that-inspired-the-circular-economy

Ellenmacarthurfoundation.org. (2021). *Recycling and the circular economy: what's the difference?* Ellen Macarthur Foundation. https://www.ellenmacarthurfoundation.org/articles/recycling-and-the-circular-economy-whats-the-difference

Ellenmacarthurfoundation.org. (2024). *Fashion and the circular economy*. https://www.ellenmacarthurfoundation.org/fashion-and-the-circular-economy-deep-dive

Engin, B. (2017). *DyStar and Circular Fashion Time with C&A - Textilegence*. https://www.textilegence.com/en/circular-fashion-time-with-ca-and-dystar/

ETP Fibres Textile Clothing -European Technology Platform. (n.d.). *Towards a 4th Industrial Revolution of Textiles and Clothing A Strategic Innovation and Research Agenda for the European Textile and Clothing Industry*.

European Environment Agency. (2019). *Textile waste — European Environment Agency*. https://www.eea.europa.eu/media/infographics/textile-waste/view

Exchange, T. (2022). *Preferred Fiber and Materials Market Report 2022 - Textile Exchange*. https://textileexchange.org/knowledge-center/reports/materials-market-report-2022/

Favi, C., Marconi, M., Germani, M., & Mandolini, M. (2019). A design for disassembly tool oriented to mechatronic product de-manufacturing and recycling. *Advanced Engineering Informatics*, 39, 62–79. Advance online publication. DOI: 10.1016/j.aei.2018.11.008

Fortuna, L. M., & Diyamandoglu, V. (2017). Disposal and acquisition trends in second-hand products. *Journal of Cleaner Production*, 142, 2454–2462. DOI: 10.1016/j.jclepro.2016.11.030

Frei, R., Jack, L., & Krzyzaniak, S. (2020). Sustainable reverse supply chains and circular economy in multichannel retail returns. *Business Strategy and the Environment*, 29(5), 1925–1940. DOI: 10.1002/bse.2479

Furferi, R., Volpe, Y., & Mantellassi, F. (2022). Circular Economy Guidelines for the Textile Industry. *Sustainability (Basel)*, 14(17), 11111. DOI: 10.3390/su141711111

Gabe. (2023). *Cut, Make, Trim Clothing Manufacturing Explained – Gabe Clothing*. gabeclothing.ca. https://gabeclothing.ca/blogs/building-a-clothing-brand/cmt-clothing-manufacturing-explained

Georgette, K. C. O. C. (2024). *Carbon Footprint of Polyester vs Cotton vs Wool vs Leather vs Nylon (Calculator)*. https://8billiontrees.com/carbon-offsets-credits/carbon-footprint-of-polyester/

Ghisellini, P., Cialani, C., & Ulgiati, S. (2016). A review on circular economy: The expected transition to a balanced interplay of environmental and economic systems. *Journal of Cleaner Production*, 114, 11–32. Advance online publication. DOI: 10.1016/j.jclepro.2015.09.007

Good, F. F. (2020). Fashion for Good Resource Library. https://reports.fashionforgood.com/report/state-of-the-circular-innovations-in-the-indian-fashion-and-textile-industry/

Gucci. (2021). *Presenting the First Gucci Equilibrium Impact Report – Gucci Equilibrium*. https://equilibrium.gucci.com/presenting-the-first-gucci-equilibrium-impact-report/

Guide, V. D. R.Jr, & Van Wassenhove, L. N. (2009). The evolution of closed-loop supply chain research. *Operations Research*, 57(1), 10–18. Advance online publication. DOI: 10.1287/opre.1080.0628

Gullingsrud, A., & Perkins, L. (2015). *Designing for the Circular Economy: Cradle to Cradle® Design. V Sustainable Fashion What's Next?* Bloomsbury Publishing Inc. DOI: 10.5040/9781501312250.ch-012

Guo, W. & Kim, E. (2023). Categorizing Chinese Consumers' Behavior to Identify Factors Related to Sustainable Clothing Consumption. *Sustainability, 15*(7), 6126. DOI: 10.3390/su15076126

Habib, M. A., Bao, Y., Nabi, N., Dulal, M., Asha, A. A. & Islam, M. (2021). Impact of Strategic Orientations on the Implementation of Green Supply Chain Management Practices and Sustainable Firm Performance. *Sustainability, 13*(1), 340. DOI: 10.3390/su13010340

Haq, M., Moazzam, M., Khan, A. S., & Ahmed, W. (2023). The impact of reverse logistics process coordination on third party relationship quality: A moderated mediation model for multichannel retailers in the fashion industry. *Journal of Retailing and Consumer Services*, 73, 103362. DOI: 10.1016/j.jretconser.2023.103362

Haq, U. N., & Alam, S. M. R. (2023). Implementing circular economy principles in the apparel production process: Reusing pre-consumer waste for sustainability of environment and economy. *Cleaner Waste Systems*, 6, 100108. DOI: 10.1016/j.clwas.2023.100108

Henninger, C. E., Cano, M. B., Boardman, R., Jones, C., McCormick, H., & Sahab, S. (2020). *Cradle-to-Cradle Versus Consumer Preferences in the Fashion Industry. Encyclopedia of Renewable and Sustainable Materials*. Elsevier. DOI: 10.1016/B978-0-12-803581-8.10893-8

H&M. (2024). *Sustainability - H&M Group*. https://hmgroup.com/sustainability/

Hmfoundation. (2017). *GCA winners – H&M Foundation*. https://hmfoundation.com/gca/winners/

Jackson, T. (2020). *The Myth of Decoupling. Prosperity without Growth*. Routledge. DOI: 10.4324/9781849774338-10/MYTH-DECOUPLING-TIM-JACKSON

Jahandideh, A., Ashkani, M., & Moini, N. (2021). *Biopolymers in textile industries. Biopolymers and their Industrial Applications*. Elsevier. DOI: 10.1016/B978-0-12-819240-5.00008-0

Jain, A., Sharma, A., Jately, V., & Azzopardi, B. (2024). *Sustainable energy solutions with artificial intelligence, blockchain technology, and internet of things*. CRC Press. https://www.routledge.com/Sustainable-Energy-Solutions-with-Artificial-Intelligence-Blockchain-Technology-and-Internet-of-Things/Jain-Sharma-Jately-Azzopardi/p/book/9781032392752

Jana, P. (2022). *Challenges in the Traditional Fashion and Textile Supply Chain. Lean Supply Chain Management in Fashion and Textile Industry*. Springer. DOI: 10.1007/978-981-19-2108-7_2

Jia, F., Yin, S., Chen, L., & Chen, X. (2020a). The circular economy in the textile and apparel industry: A systematic literature review. *Journal of Cleaner Production*, 259, 120728. Advance online publication. DOI: 10.1016/j.jclepro.2020.120728

Jia, F., Yin, S., Chen, L., & Chen, X. (2020b). The circular economy in the textile and apparel industry: A systematic literature review. *Journal of Cleaner Production*, 259, 120728. DOI: 10.1016/j.jclepro.2020.120728

Kabir, S. M. F., Chakraborty, S., Hoque, S. M. A., & Mathur, K. (2019). Sustainability Assessment of Cotton-Based Textile Wet Processing. *Cleanroom Technology*, 1(1), 232–246. DOI: 10.3390/cleantechnol1010016

KFilippa. (2020). *Filippa-K-sustainability-report 2020*.

Khairul Akter, M. M., Haq, U. N., Islam, M. M., & Uddin, M. A. (2022). Textile-apparel manufacturing and material waste management in the circular economy: A conceptual model to achieve sustainable development goal (SDG) 12 for Bangladesh. *Cleaner Environmental Systems*, 4, 100070. DOI: 10.1016/j.cesys.2022.100070

Khan, M. M. R., & Islam, M. M. (2015). *Materials and manufacturing environmental sustainability evaluation of apparel product: knitted T-shirt case study*. Textiles and Clothing Sustainability. DOI: 10.1186/s40689-015-0008-8

Kirchherr, J., Reike, D., & Hekkert, M. (2017). Conceptualizing the circular economy: An analysis of 114 definitions. V. *Resources, Conservation and Recycling*, 127, 221–232. Advance online publication. DOI: 10.1016/j.resconrec.2017.09.005

Kjaer, L. L., Pigosso, D. C. A., Niero, M., Bech, N. M., & McAloone, T. C. (2019). Product/Service-Systems for a Circular Economy: The Route to Decoupling Economic Growth from Resource Consumption? *Journal of Industrial Ecology*, 23(1), 22–35. Advance online publication. DOI: 10.1111/jiec.12747

Klinkhammer, K., Hohenbild, H., Hoque, M. T., Elze, L., Teshay, H., & Mahltig, B. (2024). Functionalization of Technical Textiles with Chitosan. *Textiles*, 4(1), 70–90. DOI: 10.3390/textiles4010006

Knut, A., & Daniel, R. S. A. (2017). *Supply Chain 4.0 in consumer goods | McKinsey*. McKinsey & Company. https://www.mckinsey.com/industries/consumer-packaged-goods/our-insights/supply-chain-4-0-in-consumer-goods

Korhonen, J., Honkasalo, A., & Seppälä, J. (2018). Circular Economy: The Concept and its Limitations. *Ecological Economics*, 143, 37–46. Advance online publication. DOI: 10.1016/j.ecolecon.2017.06.041

Kumar, R., Chakraborty, P., Chakraborty, S., Basak, B., & Jeon, B.-H. (2023). *Synergy of textile dyeing wastewater treatment along with water reclamation using membrane-enabled approach. Current Developments in Bioengineering and Biotechnology*. Elsevier. DOI: 10.1016/B978-0-323-91235-8.00015-2

Kumar Singh, M. (2021). *Textiles Functionalization - A Review of Materials, Processes, and Assessment. Textiles for Functional Applications*. IntechOpen. DOI: 10.5772/intechopen.96936

Larsson, E. (2018). *Filippa K's Fashion Manifest: Long Lasting Simplicity. Sustainable Fashion: Let. Part F625*. Springer Nature. DOI: 10.1007/978-3-319-74367-7_8

Lazarevic, D., & Valve, H. (2017). Narrating expectations for the circular economy: Towards a common and contested European transition. *Energy Research & Social Science*, 31, 60–69. DOI: 10.1016/j.erss.2017.05.006

Lenzing. (2024). *Circular economy.* https://www.lenzing.com/sustainability/sustainability-management/circular-economy

Leonas, K. K. (2017). The Use of Recycled Fibers in Fashion and Home Products. *Textile Science and Clothing Technology* (pp. 55–77). DOI: 10.1007/978-981-10-2146-6_2

Long, X. & Gui, L. (2023). Waste Not Want Not? The Environmental Implications of Quick Response and Upcycling. https://doi.org/DOI: 10.1287/msom.2022.0040

Loop, C. (2024). *ReBlend - Case - Close The Loop.* https://www.close-the-loop.be/en/case/299/reblend

Loop, C. T. (2024). *End of life - Phase - Close The Loop.* https://www.close-the-loop.be/en/phase/3/end-of-life

Lorek, S., & Spangenberg, J. H. (2014). Sustainable consumption within a sustainable economy - Beyond green growth and green economies. *Journal of Cleaner Production*, 63, 33–44. Advance online publication. DOI: 10.1016/j.jclepro.2013.08.045

Malley, K., & Singh, R. T. D. (2020). *2nd Law of Thermodynamics - Chemistry LibreTexts.* https://chem.libretexts.org/Bookshelves/Physical_and_Theoretical_Chemistry_Textbook_Maps/Supplemental_Modules_(Physical_and_Theoretical_Chemistry)/Thermodynamics/The_Four_Laws_of_Thermodynamics/Second_Law_of_Thermodynamics

Maria, E., & Hanna, L. (2016). *Critical aspects in design - Mistra Future Fashion.* http://mistrafuturefashion.com/2016-1-critical-aspects/

Marques, A. D., Marques, A., & Ferreira, F. (2020). Homo Sustentabilis: Circular economy and new business models in fashion industry. *SN Applied Sciences*, 2(2), 306. Advance online publication. DOI: 10.1007/s42452-020-2094-8

Martina, I. (2023). *10 Concerning Fast Fashion Waste Statistics.* https://earth.org/statistics-about-fast-fashion-waste/

McQuillan, H. (2019). Waste, so What? A reflection on waste and the role of designers in a circular economy. *Nordes 2019: Who Cares?*, 1–9. DOI: 10.21606/nordes.2019.017

Md, R. M., & Md, H. M. (2016). Investigation of fabric wastages in Knit T-Shirt manufacturing industry in Bangladesh. *International Journal of Research in Engineering and Technology*, 05(10), 212–215. DOI: 10.15623/ijret.2016.0510035

Millward-Hopkins, J., Purnell, P., & Baurley, S. (2023). Scenarios for reducing the environmental impacts of the UK clothing economy. *Journal of Cleaner Production*, 420, 138352. DOI: 10.1016/j.jclepro.2023.138352

Mishra, A., Dutta, P., Jayasankar, S., Jain, P., & Mathiyazhagan, K. (2023). A review of reverse logistics and closed-loop supply chains in the perspective of circular economy. *Benchmarking*, 30(3), 975–1020. DOI: 10.1108/BIJ-11-2021-0669

Mishra, S., & Das, A. P. (2023). *Microbial Remediation of Synthetic Microfiber Contaminated Wastewater. Microbial Technologies in Industrial Wastewater Treatment*. Springer Nature Singapore. DOI: 10.1007/978-981-99-2435-6_17

Moazzem, S., Crossin, E., Daver, F., & Wang, L. (2022). Environmental impact of apparel supply chain and textile products. *Environment, Development and Sustainability*, 24(8), 9757–9775. DOI: 10.1007/s10668-021-01873-4

Moazzem, S., Wang, L., Daver, F., & Crossin, E. (2021). Environmental impact of discarded apparel landfilling and recycling. *Resources, Conservation and Recycling*, 166, 105338. DOI: 10.1016/j.resconrec.2020.105338

Mölsä, K. M., Horn, S., Dahlbo, H., & Rissanen, M. (2022). Linear, reuse or recycling? An environmental comparison of different life cycle options for cotton roller towels. *Journal of Cleaner Production*, 374, 133976. DOI: 10.1016/j.jclepro.2022.133976

Montag, L., Klünder, T., & Steven, M. (2021). Paving the Way for Circular Supply Chains: Conceptualization of a Circular Supply Chain Maturity Framework. *Frontiers in Sustainability*, 2(11), 9111. DOI: 10.3389/frsus.2021.781978

Moorhouse, D. & Moorhouse, D. (2017). Sustainable Design: Circular Economy in Fashion and Textiles. *The Design Journal, 20*(sup1), S1948–S1959. DOI: 10.1080/14606925.2017.1352713

Moreau, V., Sahakian, M., van Griethuysen, P., & Vuille, F. (2017). Coming Full Circle: Why Social and Institutional Dimensions Matter for the Circular Economy. *Journal of Industrial Ecology*, 21(3), 497–506. DOI: 10.1111/jiec.12598

Morshed, M. N., Behary, N., Bouazizi, N., Guan, J., & Nierstrasz, V. A. (2021). An overview on biocatalysts immobilization on textiles: Preparation, progress and application in wastewater treatment. V. *Chemosphere*, 279, 130481. Advance online publication. DOI: 10.1016/j.chemosphere.2021.130481 PMID: 33894516

Mustafa, G., Zahid, M. T., Ullah, F., Zia, I., Younas, A., Batool, T., & Zahid, I. (2023). *Bacterial tools for the removal and degradation of synthetic dyes from the wastewater. Current Developments in Bioengineering and Biotechnology*. Elsevier. DOI: 10.1016/B978-0-323-91235-8.00022-X

Muthu, S. S. (2019). *Circular Economy in Textiles and Apparel. Circular Economy in Textiles and Apparel: Processing, Manufacturing, and Design*. Elsevier. DOI: 10.1016/C2017-0-03221-4

Muthu, S. S. (2020). Life cycle assessment and product carbon footprint modelling of textile products. *Assessing the Environmental Impact of Textiles and the Clothing Supply Chain* (pp. 131–141). Elsevier. DOI: 10.1016/B978-0-12-819783-7.00007-7

Narayanan, V. (2021). *Foundations for 3D Machine Knitting*. Carnegie Mellon University.

Nayak, R. (2020). *Sustainable technologies in yarn and fabric manufacturing. Sustainable Technologies for Fashion and Textiles*. Elsevier. DOI: 10.1016/C2018-0-00610-6

Nayak, R., Akbari, M., & Maleki Far, S. (2019). Recent sustainable trends in Vietnam's fashion supply chain. *Journal of Cleaner Production*, 225, 291–303. Advance online publication. DOI: 10.1016/j.jclepro.2019.03.239

Niinimäki, K. (2017). *Sustainable consumer satisfaction in the context of clothing. Product-Service System Design for Sustainability*. Routledge. DOI: 10.4324/9781351278003-7

Niinimäki, K. (2024). *Designing for (Extended) Product and Material Lifetimes. Recycling and Lifetime Management in the Textile and Fashion Sector*. CRC Press. DOI: 10.1201/9781003044413-3/DESIGNING-EXTENDED-PRODUCT-MATERIAL-LIFETIMES-KIRSI-NIINIM

Niinimäki, K., Peters, G., Dahlbo, H., Perry, P., Rissanen, T., & Gwilt, A. (2020). The environmental price of fast fashion. *Nature Reviews. Earth & Environment*, 1(4), 189–200. DOI: 10.1038/s43017-020-0039-9

Orangefiber. (2024). *Orange Fiber • Sustainable fabrics from citrus juice by-products*. https://orangefiber.it/

Overdiek, A. (2018). Opportunities for slow fashion retail in temporary stores. *Journal of Fashion Marketing and Management*, 22(1), 67–81. Advance online publication. DOI: 10.1108/JFMM-05-2017-0042

Özen, M., Demircan, G., Kisa, M., & Ilik, Z. (2020). *Investigation of usability of waste textile fabrics in composites. Emerging Materials Research*. Thomas Telford Ltd. DOI: 10.1680/jemmr.18.00106

Pabjańczyk-Wlazło, E. K., Puszkarz, A. K., Bednarowicz, A., Tarzyńska, N., & Sztajnowski, S. (2022). The Influence of Surface Modification with Biopolymers on the Structure of Melt-Blown and Spun-Bonded Poly(lactic acid) Nonwovens. *Materials (Basel)*, 15(20), 7097. Advance online publication. DOI: 10.3390/ma15207097 PMID: 36295163

Patnaik, S., & Tshifularo, C. A. (2021). *Management of wastes in garment manufacturing. Waste Management in the Fashion and Textile Industries*. Elsevier. DOI: 10.1016/B978-0-12-818758-6.00004-1

Paul, U., & Mercedes, B. (2009). *Carbon Labelling: Public Perceptions of the Debate*. https://www.researchgate.net/publication/236146858_Carbon_Labelling_Public_Perceptions_of_the_Debate

Pensupa, N., Leu, S. Y., Hu, Y., Du, C., Liu, H., Jing, H., Wang, H., & Lin, C. S. K. (2017). Recent Trends in Sustainable Textile Waste Recycling Methods: Current Situation and Future Prospects. V. *Topics in Current Chemistry*, 375(5), 76. Advance online publication. DOI: 10.1007/s41061-017-0165-0 PMID: 28815435

Persson, O., & Hinton, J. B. (2023). Second-hand clothing markets and a just circular economy? Exploring the role of business forms and profit. *Journal of Cleaner Production*, 390, 136139. DOI: 10.1016/j.jclepro.2023.136139

Peter John, E., & Mishra, U. (2023). A sustainable three-layer circular economic model with controllable waste, emission, and wastewater from the textile and fashion industry. *Journal of Cleaner Production*, 388, 135642. DOI: 10.1016/j.jclepro.2022.135642

Piller, L. W. (2023). Designing for circularity: Sustainable pathways for Australian fashion small to medium enterprises. *Journal of Fashion Marketing and Management*, 27(2), 287–310. DOI: 10.1108/JFMM-09-2021-0220

QUT. (2024). *Separation and recycling of fast fashion fibres - TextileR: Future Textile Industries*. QUT TextileR. https://research.qut.edu.au/textiler/research/demonstrating-effective-recycling-of-fast-fashion-fibres/

Rachel, C. (2021). *Fashion's sustainability agenda: Where to start | Vogue Business*. Vogue Business. https://www.voguebusiness.com/sustainability/fashions-sustainability-agenda-where-to-start

Radhakrishnan, S. (2021). *Circular Economy in Textiles and Fashion. Environmental Footprints and Eco-Design of Products and Processes*. Springer. DOI: 10.1007/978-981-16-3698-1_6

Rath, S. R., Chu, W., Terzioğlu, N., & Wever, R. (2023). *Designing Interventions for Sustainability: A Conceptual Framework for Information Scoping in the Design Research Phase. EcoDesign for Sustainable Products, Services and Social Systems I.* Springer Nature Singapore. DOI: 10.1007/978-981-99-3818-6_29

Ren, Z., Fang, F., Yan, N., & Wu, Y. (2022). State of the Art in Defect Detection Based on Machine Vision. *International Journal of Precision Engineering and Manufacturing-Green Technology*, 9(2), 661–691. DOI: 10.1007/s40684-021-00343-6

Resources, N. S. (2024). *How straw-based packaging can help optimize your supply chains and fight climate change?*https://www.nefab.com/news-insights/2022/how-straw-based-packaging-can-help-optimize-your-supply-chains-and-fight-climate-change/

Rick, L. (2020). *Textile and Clothes Recycling Facts and Figures.* https://www.liveabout.com/textile-recycling-facts-and-figures-2878122

Romaily, C. (2022). *10 Zero Waste Fashion Brands For A Sustainable Wardrobe.* https://pebblemag.com/zero-waste-fashion/

Roy Choudhury, A. K. (2014). Environmental Impacts of the Textile Industry and Its Assessment Through Life Cycle Assessment. *Roadmap to Sustainable Textiles and Clothing* (str. 1–39). DOI: 10.1007/978-981-287-110-7_1

Saha, K., Dey, P. K., & Papagiannaki, E. (2021). Implementing circular economy in the textile and clothing industry. *Business Strategy and the Environment*, 30(4), 1497–1530. Advance online publication. DOI: 10.1002/bse.2670

Sandberg, E. (2023). Orchestration capabilities in circular supply chains of post-consumer used clothes – A case study of a Swedish fashion retailer. *Journal of Cleaner Production*, 387, 135935. DOI: 10.1016/j.jclepro.2023.135935

Sandvik, I. M., & Stubbs, W. (2019). Circular fashion supply chain through textile-to-textile recycling. *Journal of Fashion Marketing and Management*, 23(3), 366–381. DOI: 10.1108/JFMM-04-2018-0058

Saskia, M., Christis, M., & An, V. (2019). Textiles and the environment in a circular economy. *European Topic Centre on Waste and Materials in a Green Economy.*

Schwab, K. (2016). *The Fourth Industrial Revolution.* World Economic Forum. www.weforum.org

Seidu, R. K., Eghan, B., & Acquaye, R. (2024). A Review of Circular Fashion and Bio-based Materials in the Fashion Industry. *Circular Economy and Sustainability*, 4(1), 693–715. DOI: 10.1007/s43615-023-00303-z

Shafqat, A. R., & Saccavini, A. (2023). *Eco-design of Textiles. Textile Science and Clothing Technology*. Springer. DOI: 10.1007/978-3-031-49479-6_3

Shah, R. (2011). Examine the Role of Different Actors Across The Textile -Fashion Supply Chain To Understand the issues Regarding Growth Of Eco-Labeled Sustainable Textile Products [Thesis]. The University of Manchester, Manchester, UK.

Shamsuzzaman, M., Islam, M. M., Hasan, H. M. R. U., Khan, A. M., & Sayem, A. S. M. (2023). Mapping environmental sustainability of knitted textile production facilities. *Journal of Cleaner Production*, 405, 136900. DOI: 10.1016/j.jclepro.2023.136900

Shirvanimoghaddam, K., Motamed, B., Ramakrishna, S., & Naebe, M. (2020). Death by waste: Fashion and textile circular economy case. *The Science of the Total Environment*, 718, 137317. DOI: 10.1016/j.scitotenv.2020.137317 PMID: 32088483

Sinclair, R. (2015). *Understanding Textile Fibres and Their Properties. Textiles and Fashion*. Elsevier., DOI: 10.1016/B978-1-84569-931-4.00001-5

Sivaram, N. M., Gopal, P. M. & Barik, D. (2019). Toxic Waste From Textile Industries. *Energy from Toxic Organic Waste for Heat and Power Generation*, 43–54. DOI: 10.1016/B978-0-08-102528-4.00004-3

Smithers, R. (2018). *Money for old socks: John Lewis to buy back clothes to cut waste | John Lewis | The Guardian*. https://www.theguardian.com/business/2018/jun/18/money-for-old-socks-john-lewis-to-buy-back-clothes-to-cut-waste

Stahel, W. R. (2016). The circular economy. *Nature*, 531(7595), 435–438. DOI: 10.1038/531435a PMID: 27008952

Systems, Z. (2024). *Defect Detection Using Artificial Intelligence In Software Testing – Learning From Other Industries*. https://www.zucisystems.com/blog/defect-detection-using-artificial-intelligence-in-software-testing-learning-from-other-industries/

Textile, E. (2023). *Standards - Textile Exchange*. https://textileexchange.org/standards/

Tony, C. (2017). *Adidas pursues rival Nike with in-store personalisation and manufacturing*. The Drum. https://www.thedrum.com/news/2017/03/21/adidas-pursues-rival-nike-with-store-personalisation-and-manufacturing

Trust, C. T. (2018). *Three sustainability trends shaping the future of the fashion industry*. https://www.carbontrust.com/news-and-insights/insights/three-sustainability-trends-shaping-the-future-of-the-fashion-industry

Vadicherla, T., Saravanan, D., Muthu Ram, M., & Suganya, K. (2017). *Fashion Renovation via Upcycling. Textiles and Clothing Sustainability*. Springer. DOI: 10.1007/978-981-10-2146-6_1

Wiegand, T., & Wynn, M. (2023). Sustainability, the Circular Economy and Digitalisation in the German Textile and Clothing Industry. *Sustainability (Basel)*, 15(11), 9111. DOI: 10.3390/su15119111

Wojciechowska, P. (2021). *Fibres and textiles in the circular economy. Fundamentals of Natural Fibres and Textiles*. Elsevier. DOI: 10.1016/B978-0-12-821483-1.00019-X

Wojnowska-Baryła, I., Bernat, K., Zaborowska, M., & Kulikowska, D. (2024). The Growing Problem of Textile Waste Generation—The Current State of Textile Waste Management. *Energies*, 17(7), 1528. DOI: 10.3390/en17071528

Wu, K. J., Tseng, M. L., Yang, W. H., Ali, M. H., & Chen, X. (2023). Re-shaping sustainable value chain model under post pandemic disruptions: A fast fashion supply chain analysis. *International Journal of Production Economics*, 255, 108704. DOI: 10.1016/j.ijpe.2022.108704

Yousaf, M. A., & Aqsa, R. (2023). Integrating Circular Economy, SBTI, Digital LCA, and ESG Benchmarks for Sustainable Textile Dyeing: A Critical Review of Industrial Textile Practices. *Global NEST Journal*, 25(7), 39–51. DOI: 10.30955/gnj.005145

Zhang, D., Frei, R., Wills, G., Gerding, E., Bayer, S., & Senyo, P. K. (2023). Strategies and practices to reduce the ecological impact of product returns: An environmental sustainability framework for multichannel retail. *Business Strategy and the Environment*, 32(7), 4636–4661. DOI: 10.1002/bse.3385

Zhu, X., Song, B., Ni, Y., Ren, Y., & Li, R. (2016). *Business Trends in the Digital Era. Business Trends in the Digital Era: Evolution of Theories and Applications*. Springer Singapore. DOI: 10.1007/978-981-10-1079-8

ADDITIONAL READING

Ashvani, G. (2021). Management of spinning and weaving wastes. In *Waste Management in the Fashion and Textile Industries* (1st ed., pp. 61–82). Woodhead Publishing. DOI: 10.1016/C2018-0-04057-8

Awasthi, M. K., Sarsaiya, S., Chen, H., Wang, Q., Wang, M., Awasthi, S. K., Li, J., Liu, T., Pandey, A., & Zhang, Z. (2019). Global Status of Waste-to-Energy Technology. In *Current Developments in Biotechnology and Bioengineering* (pp. 31–52). Elsevier. DOI: 10.1016/B978-0-444-64083-3.00003-8

Dissanayake, D. G. K. (2020). Does Mass Customization Enable Sustainability in the Fashion Industry? In *Fashion Industry - An Itinerary Between Feelings and Technology*. DOI: 10.5772/intechopen.88281

Jackson, T. (2020). The Myth of Decoupling. In *Prosperity without Growth* (1st ed., pp. 86–105). Routledge. DOI: 10.4324/9781849774338-10/MYTH-DECOUPLING-TIM-JACKSON

Muthu, S. S. (2019). Circular Economy in Textiles and Apparel. In *Circular Economy in Textiles and Apparel: Processing, Manufacturing, and Design*. Elsevier. DOI: 10.1016/C2017-0-03221-4

Radhakrishnan, S. (2021). Circular Economy in Textiles and Fashion. In *Environmental Footprints and Eco-Design of Products and Processes* (pp. 163–202). Springer. DOI: 10.1007/978-981-16-3698-1_6

Rath, S. R., Chu, W., Terzioğlu, N., & Wever, R. (2023). Designing Interventions for Sustainability: A Conceptual Framework for Information Scoping in the Design Research Phase. *EcoDesign for Sustainable Products, Services and Social Systems I* (pp. 429–446). DOI: 10.1007/978-981-99-3818-6_29

Wojciechowska, P. (2021). Fibers and textiles in the circular economy. In *Fundamentals of Natural Fibres and Textiles* (pp. 691–717). Elsevier. DOI: 10.1016/B978-0-12-821483-1.00019-X

KEY TERMS AND DEFINITIONS

AI: Artificial intelligence is technology enabling computers and machines to simulate human intelligence and problem-solving capabilities.

Automation: Use of machines and technology eliminating human intervention resulting in high efficiencies, streamlining of processes and reduction in human errors.

Big Data: Large quantity of structured, semi-structured and unstructured data collected, for predictive modeling, machine learning applications and other analytical capabilities.

Blockchain: Data base or ledger shared amongst compute network nodes. Used for maintaining secure and decentralized transactions and used in cryptocurrency.

CE: Circular economy is an economy focusing on using sustainable design, manufacturing, waste reduction, reuse, and recycling methods.

Cloud Technologies: Cloud technology enables users access to storage, files, data and servers through their computers, mobile devices, smartphones and wearables enabling saving of data in a remote location different from the end user.

Digital Fabrication: Data fabrication is a design and production system amalgamating 3D modeling systems with computer aided design to drive manufacturing systems.

E.U.: European Union is a union of 27-member states of Europe. It's a political entity combining characteristics of both a confederation and a federation.

GDP: Gross Domestic Product is the monetary value of goods and services bought by the end user at a given time in an economy.

GHG: Green House Gas emissions which are harmful gases released in the environment during textile and apparel manufacturing, transportation, consumption and waste process. These gases are a result of energy consumption during each stage released into the environment.

Internet of Things (IOT): IOT is a network of physical objects which connect with each other through sensors, technologies and software.

LCA: Life Cycle Assessment measures the environmental impact of a product or service.

Mobile Analytics: Analyzing mobile user behavior and track app data for user behavior and experience.

PET: Polyethylene terephthalate is a thermoplastic polymer resin of the polyester family used in fibres for clothing, containers, glass fibres or engineering equipment.

RFID: Radio-frequency Identification is a wireless system using tags and sensors. Antennas in the reader emit radio waves to interpret the signals received from the RFID tags.

RFSC: Reverse fashion supply chain is opposite to the normal supply chain with fashion apparel/textiles moving back to the vendor/supplier or retailer, picked up through reverse logistics system and then cleaned, sorted, restored, repacked and reused.

Robotics: Usage of mechanical, electrical engineering and computer science technologies to create machines, which can assist, replicate, and substitute human effort in completing complex tasks. These machines which act like humans are known as robots.

SDG: Sustainable development goals by United Nations aimed as a blue print to create a sustainable future for all.

Social Media: Interactive technologies facilitating creation, sharing and aggregation of content, ideas, and expressions.

SOFT: Separation of fibre technology separates cotton/polyester and wool/ polyester blends using a patented technology by Block Texx to recycle blended waste textiles and fibres from waste and landfills.

T&A: Textile and Apparel Sector has a supply chain starting from yarn production, processing, fabric manufacturing, finishing, garment manufacturing, and retailing.

Chapter 3
Cloud-Enabled Supply Chain Integration for Sustainable Firms:
An Empirical Study on Technology and the Circular Economy Relationship

Noor-Ul-Ain Hanif
Jinnah University for Women, Karachi, Pakistan

Musawir Ali Soomro
Institute of Business Management, Karachi, Pakistan

Sherbaz Khan
Jinnah University for Women, Karachi, Pakistan

Adeel Shah
https://orcid.org/0000-0001-8477-5310
Institute of Business Management, Karachi, Pakistan

ABSTRACT

Technology will play an important role in the circular economy today and in the future as businesses strive to evolve capabilities to achieve sustainable goals. Innovations in supply chain operations are also picking up pace, and with the invention of cloud-based computing, supply chain integration is now digitally possible. However, the question remains whether the same digital supply chain capabilities would also be beneficial in improving or impacting the sustainable performance of business enterprises to create an ideal circular economy. Another important feature

DOI: 10.4018/979-8-3693-4123-0.ch003

of cloud technology is software-as-a-service, providing supply chain software for users across the globe to provide organizations with capabilities like integration and resilience. Based on the cloud computing innovations in discussion and sustainability in the context of circular economy, the chapter brings forward an empirical study to understand the role of cloud technology, more importantly, SaaS, in building resilience and achieving sustainability in supply chains.

1. INTRODUCTION

The field of supply chain management has benefited from many useful studies in management science for a very long time for developing strategies. From extracting natural resources to processing them into manufactured goods and finally delivering them to the consumer, activities offer a very diverse array of research material that goes on to give impetus to scholars and practitioners alike. Similarly, supply chains have evolved to mitigate risks of disruptions, which are of many types that a Supply Chain (SC) will encounter, with most of them coming from within the SC in the form of manufacturing line breakdowns, demand fluctuations, information technology problems, sustainability problems, and quality problems (Abbas et al., 2022). Thus, the SCM literature has evolved into a well-documented discipline that has spawned a range of new streams in research, helping to resolve these challenges. The true magnitude of research output associated with sustainable supply chain management (SSCM) is gradually becoming substantial (Khan et al., 2021). Initial attributes of SSCM were oriented to environmental issues, besides the more conventional economic themes, due to the fact that the sustainability perspective was embedded into SCM (Lazar et al., 2021). Later, it has been expanded to include social issues, mainly since Elkington introduced in 1994 the term "triple bottom line" encompassing (Elkington, 1997).

Interestingly, the ideas of green and SSCM have grown at the same time as the circular economy (CE) discourse, which has been around for a long time in industrial ecology literature and practice (Ehrenfeld, 1995). However, there are some important differences in how they work. Sustainable supply chain management tries to make businesses more eco-friendly by reducing the flow of materials or the unwanted bad effects of production and usage (Dong et al., 2016). Recently, there has been a rise in global apprehension regarding the depletion of natural resources, environmental degradation, and the escalating volume of refuse produced by our linear economic model. In response to these obstacles, the Circular Economy (CE) has acquired momentum as a more sustainable alternative to the conventional linear economic model (Fig. 1.1) (Vela, 2023).

Figure 1. Circular Economy vs. Linear Economy (World, 2023)

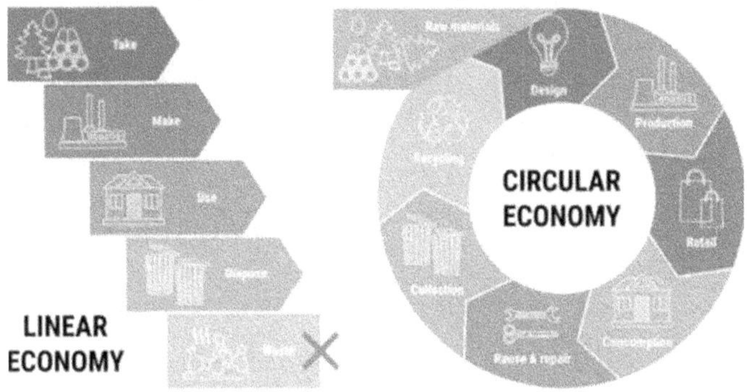

The Circular Economy promotes the transition from a product-based to a service-based model. As opposed to purchasing products outright, consumers have the option of accessing them as services, such as leasing or subscription models. This change encourages manufacturers to develop products that are both durable and reusable, as they are still accountable for the maintenance and end-of-life treatment of the products. Consequently, circular SCM has been significantly helped by technological and digital advancements. Blockchain, data analytics, and IoT devices can facilitate the sharing of information across the SC, optimize resource utilization, and enable traceability (Vela, 2023). Today's contemporary innovation technology has placed our world on the edge of the fourth industrial revolution. Industry 4.0 encapsulates the evolution of technology, specifically emphasizing the digitization of production plants and warehouse automation. This concept delimits four principal domains within the realm of Internet 4.0, which are smart factories, Cyber-Physical Systems (CPS), the Internet of Things (IoT), and the Internet of Services (IoS) (Ryalat et al., 2023). It is all about adopting IoT, information, and services for the next production paradigm.

Figure 2. Software as a Service (Lee, 2024)

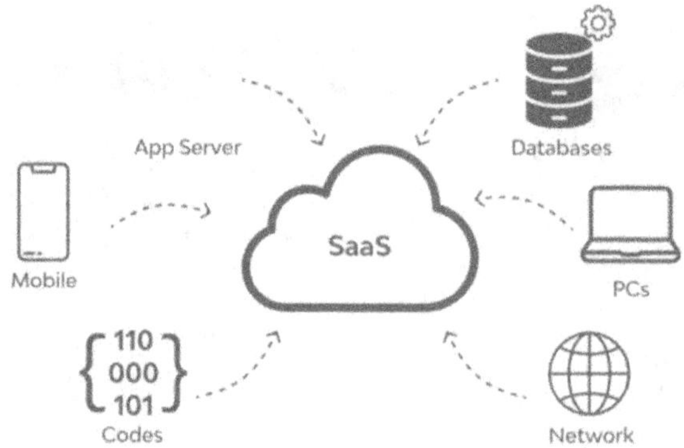

SaaS (Software as a service) solutions often offer scalability, allowing companies to easily adapt to changes in demand or business growth (Bentaher & Rajaa, 2022). SaaS typically eliminates the necessity for companies to make substantial investments in their IT infrastructure. It also provides regular updates and upgrades to its software, ensuring that users have access to the latest features and security patches (Chauhan et al., 2022). SaaS solutions often come with managed services, reducing the burden on internal IT teams. SaaS solutions often provide cloud-based access, enabling collaboration and accessibility from various locations and devices (Fig. 1.2). Without SaaS, collaboration may be limited to on-premises systems, potentially hindering the ability of remote teams or partners to participate in the supply chain management process. By using cloud-based, firms can easily customize as per their requirement, and data security and breach probability also decrease. The chapter studies the mediation effect of intention to adopt SAAS and its continued use and SAAS integration in the supply chain on its sustainability (Martins et al., 2019).

The interplay of the real and virtual worlds is another important new turning point in the development of industries, as independent processes will be optimized through decentralized intelligence and intelligent networks. Thus, technological developments have made possible a view of Industry 4.0 that entails not only the paradigmatic shift from "centralized" to "decentralized" production but also one turning conventional logic in the production process upside down. Wang et al. (2016) have observed that industrial production machinery is no longer merely a "process" for the product; rather, it is a system that is interconnected with the product to provide exact instructions. By integrating cloud-based software, companies can save huge costs and work on sustainability in their supply chain (Alcácer & Cruz-Machado, 2019). Likewise, Circular Economy principles promote local solutions and decentralized approaches. Local manufacturing, repair, and recycling facilities can be encouraged by the Circular Economy to mitigate the environmental consequences of transportation and stimulate regional economic growth. Localized systems may more effectively adapt to the unique requirements and opportunities of their respective regions (Vela, 2023).

In consultation with the supply chain head of a company, valuable insights were gained regarding the challenges encountered by the business in the context of SV operations. The company's SC head highlighted the need for increased automation and enhanced efficiency in the SC processes. The company is already using the latest technology in its operations. However, it is still not automated and requires human resources, which may cause business loss due to human error, unavailability, or biases. The Head of Supply Chain emphasized the growing significance of adopting modern technologies, specifically drawing attention to the potential benefits of SaaS in the pursuit of sustainability to overcome their hassles. The company discovered a significant connection between cloud-based supply chain integration and sustainability; there has been a concentrated effort to comprehend the complexities of this link. This revelation serves as the motivation for the present research, aiming to delve into the role of SaaS and its continued use alongside the integration of cloud-based solutions in SCM, with a primary focus on sustainability. Through investigating these aspects, this research hopes to provide significant understandings that not only address the challenges faced by the company but also advance the broader understanding of technology-driven solutions in fostering SSC practices for the development of the circular economy.

1.1 Problem Statement

Advancements in technology during the past decades have undoubtedly improved the performance of an organization; however, at the same time, it has raised further expectations toward making business operations sustainable (Chauhan et al., 2022). This study aims to find out the impact of cloud-based SC integration on a firm's sustainability and support of SC resilience. To explore this, this study is going to consider the other factors that can impact this relationship. One of the factors is an intention to adopt SaaS, and another factor is perceived complexity. The gap that is being observed is a non-optimization of resources in supply chain operations. By some means, supply chain operations that could be done by technology are currently utilizing human resources, which is not in favor of the sustainability of the industry. These supply chain operations include temperature controlling during smart warehousing, tracking of machine operations during outsourcing, and others. Therefore, in this chapter, we investigate the role of SAAS, how it fits into the picture, and whether using it in conjunction with cloud-based SC Integration makes businesses more sustainable. Additionally, this study explores the role of SC resilience in attaining a firm's sustainability and the development of the circular economy.

1.2 Objective of the Study

The research's central thesis is to study the role of Cloud-based SC Integration in attaining the firm's sustainability along with the mediating impact of SAAS adoption and supply chain resilience when Perceived complexity is negatively affecting the relationship of SAAS adoption and firm sustainability in the development of Pakistan's CE. This study will contribute to the literature by determining how to use the cloud if SAAS has an impact on supply chains and helps businesses become sustainable. Further, this study will help practitioners understand how these technologies impact SC performance and, consequently, the sustainability of businesses. In this way, the present study will assist businesses in realizing how to leverage technology for maximum effectiveness and minimal environmental impact.

First of all, a literature review sets the scene for the remainder of the study, developing the conceptual model and testing the hypotheses. The results and analysis follow this. The last sections are dedicated to discussing the findings with an examination of the practical and managerial implications. Broad strokes for further study are provided toward the very end of this work.

2. LITERATURE REVIEW

2.1. Resource-Based View (RBV)

A theory called the Resource-Based View (RBV) is widely accepted and thought to be a good base for this study. Additionally, cloud-based technology can help a business build a supply chain, which can give it an edge over its competitors. Researchers at RBV say that physical resources, like ICT and technical staff, can only give a company a competitive edge if they perform better than rivals' similar assets (Barney, 1991). In general, it is contended that investment in ICT is a method of capacity building that can be used to improve a company's competitive advantage (Bharadwaj, 2000). ICT capability is a resource that generates rent, as the procurement and distribution of goods generate a set of complementary resources that are exclusive to the firm and unmatched by its competitors.

2.2. Relationship Between Cloud Enabled Supply Chain Integration and Firm's Sustainability

Cloud technology is a service model that is "enabled by Information & Communication Technologies (ICT)" and allows for the on-demand delivery of hardware and software services in a self-service manner over the Internet to end-user customers who are not dependent on devices or locations. Cloud technology is relatively still in its infancy, at least within a supply chain context. Accordingly, an empirical examination will be warranted to help managers understand the potential for cross-firm logistics process integration that it offers. This research will focus on the adoption intention decision since cloud computing technology is gaining growing interest from many firms. In contrast, a diffusion level within industrialized practices has yet to be reached. Even though numerous studies have been carried out on SCI issues by utilizing ICT as the foundation for the flow of information between functions which are dispersed across players, the state of affairs remains below par (Prajogo & Olhager, 2012), the majority of these studies have concentrated on SCI as a single concept, it can have both positive and negative effects on performance. Further, cloud computing has several technical issues, such as security, platform reliability, privacy, additional bandwidth cost, and vendor lock-in. However, cloud computing has many advantages, such as cost savings, high availability, and easy scalability, especially in SaaS, and it will continue to grow in popularity compared to on-premises IT investment.

Cloud computing comes in many forms, such as software as a service (SaaS), platform as a service (PaaS), and infrastructure as a service (IaaS). These types of computing offer many advantages over traditional ICT systems (Fig. 1.3). Additionally, using virtual clouds is a good way to improve resources since ICT is getting better and cloud-based computing (also called hybrid cloud) is becoming more popular. Cloud computing will be a cheap choice if ICT tools like electronic data exchange (EDI) and warehouse management systems can be used across different parts of an organization (technological breadth) to link important customers and suppliers. This is due to the fact that on-premises investment is negligible. Cloud technologies, which are distinguished by their "on-demand and scalable computing power, rapid deployment capability, minimal infrastructure needs, and low cost," can serve as an invaluable edge in the SC operations of large, medium, and small businesses. Thus, A resource that encourages the integration of the supply chains of partners is cloud-based technology, thereby granting a competitive edge over other organizations.

Based on this logic, develop hypotheses as below:

H1: Cloud-enabled SC Integration affects the intention to adopt SaaS positively.

H2: Intension to adopt SaaS effects on firms' sustainability positively in the development of the circular economy.

Figure 3. SaaS – PaaS – IaaS (Lee, 2024)

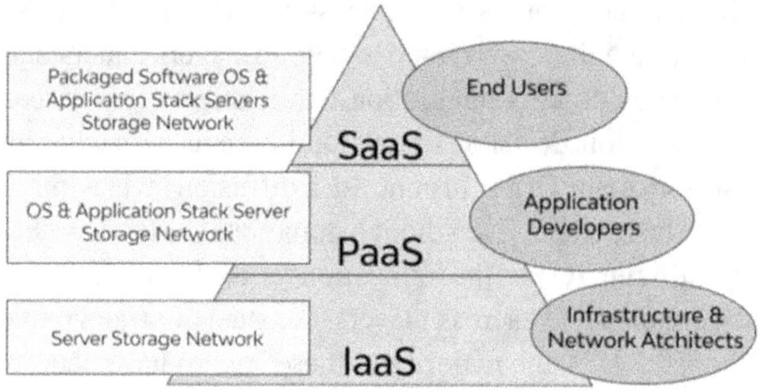

2.3. Moderation Effect Perceived Complexity

Uncertainty theory and empirical research show that companies are more likely to copy other companies that are good at using technologies that they still need to familiarize themselves with (i.e., a high degree of perceived complexity).

Perceived complexity is derived from the diffusion of innovation (DoI). This refers to the degree to which an innovation is perceived as difficult to understand and implement (Rogers, 1995). Innovations that necessitate the acquisition of new skills and comprehension are adopted more rapidly than those that are more straightforward to comprehend. The DoI theory investigates the manner, rationale, and velocity at which new technologies and concepts are implemented within organizations. In the realm of information systems, DoI has been implemented in numerous investigations. Relative advantage, complexity, compatibility, observability and trialability are among the variables that the theory suggests determine the rate of innovation adoption (Rogers, 1995). Through the application of DoI, research has consistently demonstrated that the adoption of innovations is significantly influenced by technical complexity, technical compatibility, and relative advantage (Bradford & Florin, 2003). Internal factors, such as compatibility and relative advantages, are more likely to facilitate the adoption and implementation of innovations within the firms. Perceived complexity influences both internal and external factors. The review of the predictors, linkages, and biases in the adoption of IT innovation by individuals and organizations by Jeyaraj et al. (2006) summarizes independent factors and variables in the literature. The authors mentioned above suggest that complexity is a mere prognostic and has a detrimental impact on a business's decision about adopting a new technology. Based on this rationale:

H3: Perceived complexity moderates the relationship between the intention to adopt SaaS and Firms' sustainability in the development of the circular economy.

2.4. Relationship Between Cloud Enabled Supply Chain Integration, SC Resilience, and Firm's Sustainability

A platform that is well-integrated and powered by cloud services facilitates the real-time transfer of data among partners in an extended chain (Bentaher & Rajaa, 2022). This is possible as the cloud operates on an internet protocol that makes it possible to communicate promptly with suppliers and customers. This way, if the logistics processes of key suppliers and customers are integrated, seamless information flow in relation to production planning, sales forecasts, delivery status, order tracking and tracing, and stock level can be assured. This is achieved through the use of cloud technology. Cloud services are expected to provide adequate support for logistics activities within a company, particularly those related to safety stock, inventory turnover, order processing, labor cost, and accurate pricing. Like any other traditional form of ICT, cloud technology will also make the flow of information, material, funds, and demand information between partners easier. Cloud technology can thus reduce one of the periodic problems of an SC, which is the bullwhip effect (Shee & Kaswi, 2015), and improve the inventory status at each partner down the chain. The cloud services can thus enable a set of processes across-chain partners to provide an effective consumer response through much better inventory reordering when the supply is perfectly aligned. Just-in-time is a replenishment program that is implemented between a manufacturer and its suppliers. It is believed that the cloud utilizes the internet to facilitate improved collaboration between buyers and suppliers. Currently, ICT can accomplish this through a diverse array of technologies, including WMS, ERP, and EDI (Autry et al., 2010). Nevertheless, it is believed that cloud-based services perform this function more efficiently, as evidenced by their flexibility, reduced cost, mobility, scalability, and shared resources (Zhang et al., 2010).

In addition, cloud computing facilitates the real-time storage and analysis of data on the SC, which can be accessed as needed. Consequently, IoT and cloud computing can allow for the free flow, on-demand processing, and effective deployment of the information that is required throughout the SC, thus enhancing organizational resilience. Moreover, even though big data analytics may result in large amounts of data arising, being collected, and integrated throughout the SC, businesses are able to identify and extract relevant information for making scientific decisions about SC disruptions (Gunasekaran et al., 2017). In summary, the efficiency of production is significantly enhanced by the development of more advanced information processing capabilities. A firm's market information is also essential. Instability in the SC can result from a lack of understanding of consumer behavior and market dynamics. For instance, Kodak should have paid more attention to market information and manufactured numerous films that were ultimately discontinued, resulting in bankruptcy. Mastering consumer demand is also essential for the preservation of normalcy downstream in the SC. The appropriate digital technologies facilitate the rapid monitoring and transfer of preferential customer demand to the firm in order to ensure uptime. Consequently, digital technologies have the potential to enhance the firm's resilience.

The study proposes the following hypotheses:

H4) Cloud-based SC integration positively affects SC resilience.

H5) SC Resilience positively affects the firm's sustainability in the development of the circular economy.

The proposed hypotheses of the study are summarized in Table 1.

Table 1. Hypotheses Summary

S. No	Hypotheses
H1	Cloud-enabled SC integration positively affects the intention to adopt SaaS.
H2	Intention to adopt SaaS positively affects firms' sustainability in the development of the circular economy.
H3	Perceived complexity is moderating the relationship between the Intention to adopt SaaS and Firms' sustainability in the development of the circular economy.
H4	Cloud-based SC integration positively affects SC resilience.
H5	SC Resilience positively affects the firm's sustainability in the development of the circular economy.

2.5. Theoretical Framework

Figure 4. Theoretical Framework Based on Hypothesis Development

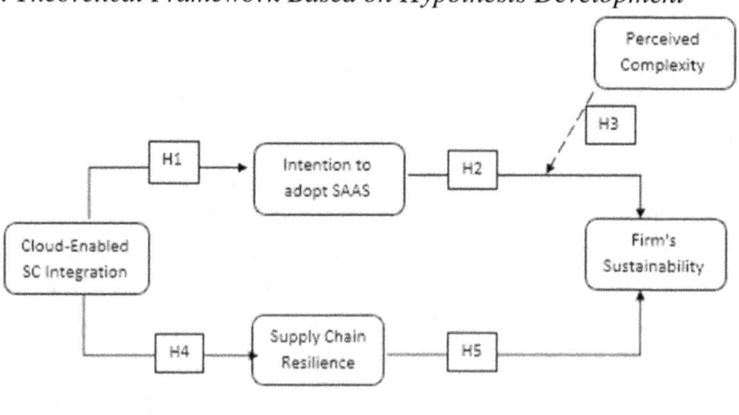

3. METHODOLOGY

3.1. Research Design

Research philosophy is a set of ideas about how to do a study that is based on assumptions about what is true and how knowledge works. Philosophy addresses fundamental questions that arise in all areas of human thought and behavior and cannot be resolved by a single strategy. There are multiple philosophies present to classify the papers or methods accordingly. For this study, positivism research philosophy is used as it will help obtain objective results for the investigation. This implies that the objective of positivism is to scientifically evaluate these hypotheses while simultaneously obtaining mathematical or logical evidence through statistical analysis. In order to provide precise, objective, and quantitative data, positivists consistently employ large samples (Pathak & Thapaliya, 2022).

This present study is a causal explanatory study because it examines the relationship between the independent variable (IV), Cloud-Enabled SC Integration, and the dependent variable (DV), the firm's sustainability and perceived complexity to adopt as moderators. Further, the paper is classified as Quantitative as a survey-based research tool is used for this study. The questionnaire that is given to participants in the study includes a Likert scale. There are multiple sections to the questionnaire.

3.2 Population and Sampling Design

The population is the whole group of people, events, or interesting things that the researcher wants to learn more about. The Web-based survey method was used to gather information for this study. This method's data collection from the managers is cost-effective. According to Ansari and Kant (2017), a web-based survey is conducted to collect data. Fawcett et al. (2007) assert that this type of survey is effective in the collection of data among managers. For this study, the target population was selected from the list of small and medium to large firms working along with the company and registered under. The target audience for this study is working people who have experience with supply chains or who are taking steps to start using it to create a more SSC by adopting cloud-based solutions. The data was collected by by the authors from the targeted companies. The autors distributed 345 questionnaires and received 310 questionnaires, indicating an acceptable response rate.

The sample population in this research is selected using non-probability sampling. Non-probability sampling is a simple, quick, and affordable technique to collect data, but it depends on research competence because it only requires a partial survey frame (Vehovar et al., 2016).

3.3. Data Collection Tools

In this research, devices or techniques used to get data from subjects or sources in order to answer research questions or objectives are referred to as data-collecting tools. There are several tools at one's disposal. The questionnaires and surveys are used as the data-collecting tools for this study. In data collecting tools, the term "measures" refers to the precise tools or methods used to qualify or quantify a certain idea or variable of interest. These measurements are essential for getting consistent and similar data, which enables researchers to make insightful study findings (Rovshenov & Sarsar, 2023).

A Likert scale was chosen because it is one of the very common psychometric tools in the areas of survey and research methods used to understand what people feel, think, or believe about any subject. The response options under a Likert scale are usually scaled, normally from "Strongly Disagree" to "Strongly Agree." Moreover, one of the most important stages in the data collection for publications involves questionnaire design. It involved the act of formulating a number of questions and response options that represented reliable data to be obtained from subjects. Therefore, the authors take great care in filtering only relevant participants by incorporating screening questions in the survey and are also collecting demographics of participants in order to further divide the population, if necessary, for this research.

Further, to avoid common method variance, the study included its list of aids to respondents' psychological breaks by breaking up the survey into several sections. This adds a marker variable as well. The mark variable refers to the technique used in questionnaire survey architecture for data gathering (Jordan et al., 2019). The authors have also pre-tested the questionnaire by getting it checked by the research supervisor, and based on that, a pilot test of the same was conducted. A full-scale pilot testing phase engages a cohort of 10-12 professional postgraduate working-class students of a prestigious university in Karachi (Pakistan) to test the practical applicability and clarity of the refined questionnaire. These students or professionals, equipped with advanced knowledge in relevant fields, provided valuable insights into the questionnaire's functionality and comprehensibility.

As the study targets professionals in the supply chain industry, the authors have considered ethical considerations in the questionnaire, which includes respondents' voluntary participation, honoring their anonymity, and allowing them to leave the survey at any point if they do not feel comfortable without justifying their reasons.

3.4. Data Analysis

In this study, PLS-SEM with SMART PLS software is the method employed to evaluate the hypothesis. Because PLS-SEM offers enormous promise for SEM-based research, it is being used (Hair et al., 2011). Its ability to display elements and composites has been valued by research over the orders, making it an effective strategy for research. It can also be used for forecasting (Henseler et al., 2014). PLS-SEM is indeed a nonparametric statistical method that does not anticipate that information will typically be disseminated (Hair Jr et al., 2014). A questionnaire was developed to validate the conceptual framework. The indicator determining Industry 4.0 was adapted from the work of Gao et al. (2022). Sustainable Supply Chain indicators were taken from Gupta et al. (2020). For Big Data practices Gunasekaran et al. (2017). For Block Chain Technology, Hoxha and Sadiku (2019) and finally, for Top Management Support (Lai et al., 2018). Some questions were taken from these papers due to their divergence from the main concept. The respondents' profile is depicted in Table 2.

Table 2. Respondent Profile

Demographics	Category
Gender	Male
	Female
Age	Below 20
	20 - 30
	31 - 40
	41 - 50
	Above 50
Education	Under Graduate
	Graduate
	Post Graduate
	PHD
Professional Experience	Below 3 Experience
	3 to 6 years
	7 to 10 years
	More than 10 years

continued on following page

Table 2. Continued

Demographics	Category
Supply Chain Department	Logistics
	Production
	Procurement
	Merchandising
	None

4. ANALYSIS AND RESULTS

4.1. Descriptive Analysis

This section of the investigation has assessed the internal consistency and convergent validity, which are summarized in Table 3. The findings indicate that the highest Cronbach's alpha values are for Firm's Sustainability (α 0.898), while the lowest is for Perceived complexity (α 0.722). The results also indicate that the composite values are all greater than 0.70, and the AVE values are all greater than 0.50, confirming that the constructs do not deviate from the requirements of convergent validity (Hair & Alamer, 2022).

Table 3. Constructs Reliability and Validity

Constructs	Cronbach's alpha	Composite reliability	Average variance extracted (AVE)
Cloud enabled SC integration	0.827	0.832	0.743
Firm Sustainability	0.898	0.901	0.526
Intention to Adopt SaaS	0.816	0.817	0.731
Perceived Complexities	0.722	0.784	0.691
SC Resilience	0.777	0.735	0.640

4.2. Discriminant Validity

This investigation has implemented Fornell and Larcker's (1981) criteria to evaluate discriminant validity. Table 1.4 summarizes the findings. The AVE square root values are higher than the Pearson Correlation values, which indicates that the constructs employed in the study are distinctive (Fornell & Larcker, 1981). The study tested the hypotheses by bootstrapping. The results related to hypotheses are illustrated in Table 5.

The results support all five hypotheses: (1) cloud-based SC integration affects intention to adopt technology ($p < 0.05$), (2) cloud-based SC integration effect SC resilience ($p < 0.05$), (3) Intention to adopt technology affect firms technology ($p < 0.05$) (4) SC resilience affect firms sustainability ($p < 0.05$) (5) Perceived complexity moderates the relationship between intention to adopt technology and firms sustainability ($p < 0.05$).

Table 4. Discriminant Validity

Constructs	Cloud enabled SC integration	Firm Sustainability	Intention to Adopt SaaS	Perceived Complexities	SC Resilience	Perceived Complexities x Intention to Adopt SaaS
Cloud enabled SC integration						
Firm Sustainability	0.881					
Intention to Adopt SaaS	0.861	0.933				
Perceived Complexities	0.723	0.413	0.733			
SC Resilience	0.760	0.576	0.785	0.880		
Perceived Complexities x Intention to Adopt Saas	0.179	0.110	0.128	0.170	0.188	

Table 5. Hypothesis Results

Constructs	β	T statistics	P values	Results
Cloud enabled SC integration -> Intention to Adopt SaaS	0.712	20.327	0.000	Accepted
Cloud enabled SC integration -> SC Resilience	0.614	15.300	0.000	Accepted
Intention to Adopt SaaS -> Firm Sustainability	0.421	10.093	0.000	Accepted
SC Resilience -> Firm Sustainability	0.237	4.847	0.000	Accepted
Perceived Complexities x Intention to Adopt SaaS -> Firm Sustainability	- 0.050	2.508	0.012	Accepted

4.3. R-Square

The minimum number of R squares is between 0 and 1, with 0.75 being very strong, 0.50 being moderate, and 0.25 being very weak (Achar, 2016). In Table 6, the result for R-squares, all the values of R-square presented, showed that the variables have strong explanatory power since they are all above 0.33.

Table 6. R-Square

	R-Square	R-Square Adjusted
Firm Sustainability	0.801	0.799
Intention to Adopt technology	0.506	0.505
SC Resilience	0.377	0.376

4.5. VIF Analysis

Variance Inflation Factor or VIF is the measure of multicollinearity in regression (Adeboye et al., 2014). The high VIF value indicates the problem of multicollinearity because of a high level of correlation between independent variables (Gwelo, 2019). In other words, one can consider a VIF of more than 3.3 as problematic (Diamantopoulos & Siguaw, 2006).

Table 7 shows that constructs are not correlated with each other as none of their values are greater than 3.3.

Table 7. Variance Inflation Factor

	f-Square
Cloud enabled SC integration -> Intention to Adopt SaaS	1.026
Cloud enabled SC integration -> SC Resilience	0.606
Intention to Adopt technology -> Firm Sustainability	0.352
SC Resilience -> Firm Sustainability	0.099
Perceived Complexities x Intention to Adopt SaaS -> Firm Sustainability	0.016

5. DISCUSSIONS

This study aimed to explore the impact of Cloud-Enabled SC Integration on Firm's Sustainability within the context of Pakistan's circular economy. The findings from the hypothesis testing provide significant insights into the dynamics between cloud technologies, supply chain resilience, and sustainable business practices.

The integration of cloud technologies into supply chains increases the willingness of firms to adopt SaaS solutions, as manifested in the positive relationship between cloud-enabled SC and the intention to adopt SaaS ($\beta = 0.712$, $p < 0.001$). The finding is therefore supported by extant literature that shows that cloud technologies increase operational efficiencies and flexibility, hence making SaaS adoption more attractive for any business (Wang et al., 2021). Similarly, Shee et al. (2018) assessed the effect of cloud-enabled process integration on supply chain performance and firm sustainability. The outcome of the research showed that cloud-based technologies enhance operational efficiencies and are, therefore, additional reasons toward the adoption of SaaS by businesses. Further, the role that SaaS can play in diffusing sustainable practices is underlined by the large positive influence of the intention to use SaaS on firm sustainability ($\beta = 0.421$, $p < 0.001$). Herein, SaaS will help in developing a circular economy through efficient management of resources and reduction of environmental impact by bringing optimum process management with minimum wastage, validating findings from Novais et al. (2019). This finding is also supported by prior research conducted by Chauhan et al. (2023), which placed importance on the role of digital technologies, including SaaS, in achieving sustainability within supply chains through efficient processes and responsiveness.

On the other hand, the intention to employ a SaaS-firm sustainability relationship is negatively moderated by perceived complexity with a β of -0.050 at $p = 0.012$. The result showcases that perceived complexities in the implementation of SaaS can act as a restraint on its positive impacts on sustainability. It could be that some firms are affected in terms of employee training, data security issues, and integration of technology, which may lower the benefit attained from SaaS adoption (Raut et al., 2018). This lines up with the results of Rogers (1995) and Greenhalgh et al. (2018), who found that technological complexity can impede the adoption of new technologies. Moreover, the integration of cloud-based SCs substantially improves the resilience of the SC ($\beta = 0.614$, $p < 0.001$). Real-time visibility, agility, and responsiveness in supply chains are critical for establishing resilience against disruptions, and firms can achieve these by utilizing cloud technologies (Ivanov & Dolgui, 2021). Furthermore, finally, the sustainability of a firm is positively influenced by supply chain resilience ($\beta = 0.237$, $p < 0.001$). The continuity and efficacy of operations are guaranteed by a resilient supply chain, which is beneficial for sustainable practices and contributes to the overarching objectives of a circular economy (Tang

& Tomlin, 2008). This is consistent with the findings of Shee et al. (2018), who emphasized the importance of cloud-enabled process integration in improving the resilience of the supply chain, which in turn affects the sustainability of the firm.

5.1 Theoretical Implications

Theoretically, the chapter contributes to technology adoption and supply chain management literature in several ways. This work extends extant models of technology acceptance by including the moderating role of perceived complexity in such a way that it gives a nuanced view of how complexities can dampen such positive effects that the new technologies bring forth (Greenhalgh et al., 2018). By doing so, the following refines extant theoretical frameworks that have given very little attention to barriers for the integration of technologies and, consequently, how those barriers could be overcome. The chapter also integrates the literature on cloud computing with sustainability studies through the empirical demonstration of the link between cloud-enabled SCI and sustainability outcomes. This provides a comprehensive framework explaining how digital integration can drive sustainable practices in supply chains (Kang et al., 2018). This has contributed to the theory of supply chain resilience through some empirical evidence on the role that could be played by cloud technologies in enhancing agility and responsiveness, but generally the resilience of the supply chain. Finally, based on resource-based theory, research illustrates how cloud-enabled SCI can become a strategic resource in enhancing firm performance and sustainability in the dynamic market environment with competitive advantages (Shee et al., 2018).

5.2 Practical Implications

This chapter therefore provides major practical contributions to the supply chain management and business operations sectors. First, it provides details on how cloud-enabled SCI can enhance operational efficiency. Supply chain managers are able to develop or leverage cloud computing technologies in processes that reduce their operational costs, enhance their agility, and increase their overall performance regarding their supply chains (Shee et al., 2018). The chapter further calls upon firms to adopt cloud technologies as part of their sustainability strategies by associating SaaS adoption with better sustainability outcomes. Efficient management and reduction of waste associated with the approach can bring tremendous environmental benefits, conforming to the global goals of sustainability. Also, the sharing of data in real time, combined with greater coordination, can allow firms to deal better with risks and maintain continuous operations, thereby mitigating supply chain risks (Ivanov & Dolgui, 2021). The chapter also covers the challenges of adopting

SaaS solutions through the elaboration that perceived complexity has a negative effect on adoption. Businesses can develop certain strategies, like comprehensive training programs and robust support systems, to mitigate these complexities and therefore make a shift to SaaS easier (Kaine & Wright, 2022). Finally, the insights developed can be presented to policymakers and investors to illustrate the economic and environmental value that cloud technologies generate when deployed within supply chains; subsidizing incentivizing digital transformation initiatives may enhance their wider sector adoption and sustainability.

5.3 Conclusion

The chapter aims to find out the factors that can support making an organization more sustainable for the development of Pakistan's circular economy. This study considered a cloud-enabled supply chain (IV) as a main factor in checking the impact on firms' sustainability (DV). To strengthen this relationship, the intention to adopt SaaS and Supply Chain Resilience was also added; after the collection of data from respondents and running tests on Smart PLS, it was found that the proposed hypotheses were correct. However, in addition to this, the present study also checks one moderation relation in this research, and the moderator is Perceived Complexity, which is moderating the relation of intention to adopt SaaS and Firms' sustainability in the development of Pakistan's circular economy. This chapter provides theoretical insights into the interplay between technology adoption, supply chain resilience, and sustainable business practices, contributing to both academic and practical knowledge. Businesses can leverage these findings to navigate modern challenges, fostering sustainable practices that support the development of a circular economy.

5.4 Limitations and Future Recommendations

This study underscores the importance of cloud-enabled SC integration in enhancing firm sustainability and developing a circular economy. While cloud technologies and SaaS adoption offer significant benefits, addressing perceived complexities is crucial to fully realizing their potential. Strengthening supply chain resilience through cloud integration is a key strategy for achieving sustainable business practices. Besides its strengths, this present study has some limitations. The study depended on respondents' knowledge regarding cloud-based SC integration and its impact on SC performance in the development of Pakistan's circular economy. This also restricted the current study to a small population that understood the concepts. Also, this study is restricted to Karachi, Pakistan. The strength of respondents and experts from whom data is collected is restricted to 310 only. This study is restricted to 5 variables. Respondents who know cloud technology and have an awareness of the concept of SC resilience are restricted from filling in data. In order to enhance the generalizability of the study, future researchers may increase the sample size and select a different sample. Further, using Smart PLS-SEM as the statistical approach, the study was validated to ensure the results were reliable and real. However, this study can be examined through other statistical approaches, such as DEMATEL or Fuzzy. Future researches might be conducted to investigate management support as a moderator between cloud-based SC integration and a firm's performance, and best practices that can enhance a firm's sustainability can be explored in future.

REFERENCES

Abbas, U., Hassan, S., & Miko, N. (2022). Sustainability practices and supply chain resilience in the development of a circular economy: A study of Nigeria. *Journal of Economics and Technology Research*, 3(4), 30–46. DOI: 10.22158/jetr.v3n4p30

Achar, A. P. (2016). Assessment of PLS-SEM path model for coefficient of determination and predictive relevance of consumer trust on organic cosmetics. *Ushus Journal of Business Management*, 15(4), 1–19.

Adeboye, N., Fagoyinbo, I., & Olatayo, T. (2014). Estimation of the effect of multicollinearity on the standard error for regression coefficients. *Journal of Mathematics*, 10(4), 16–20.

Alcácer, V., & Cruz-Machado, V. (2019). Scanning the industry 4.0: A literature review on technologies for manufacturing systems. *Engineering Science and Technology, an International Journal, 22*(3), 899-919.

Ansari, Z. N., & Kant, R. (2017). A state-of-art literature review reflecting 15 years of focus on sustainable supply chain management. *Journal of Cleaner Production*, 142, 2524–2543. DOI: 10.1016/j.jclepro.2016.11.023

Autry, C. W., Grawe, S. J., Daugherty, P. J., & Richey, R. G. (2010). The effects of technological turbulence and breadth on supply chain technology acceptance and adoption. *Journal of Operations Management*, 28(6), 522–536. DOI: 10.1016/j.jom.2010.03.001

Barney, J. (1991). Firm resources and sustained competitive advantage. *Journal of Management*, 17(1), 99–120. DOI: 10.1177/014920639101700108

Bentaher, C., & Rajaa, M. (2022). Supply chain management 4.0: A literature review and research framework. *European Journal of Business and Management Research*, 7(1), 117–127. DOI: 10.24018/ejbmr.2022.7.1.1246

Bharadwaj, A. S. (2000). A resource-based perspective on information technology capability and firm performance: An empirical investigation. *Management Information Systems Quarterly*, 24(1), 169–196. DOI: 10.2307/3250983

Bradford, M., & Florin, J. (2003). Examining the role of innovation diffusion factors on the implementation success of enterprise resource planning systems. *International Journal of Accounting Information Systems*, 4(3), 205–225. DOI: 10.1016/S1467-0895(03)00026-5

Chauhan, N., Kumar, V., & Dixit, S. (2023). To achieve sustainability in a supply chain with Digital integration: A TISM approach. *International Journal of Experimental Research and Review*, 30, 442–451. DOI: 10.52756/ijerr.2023.v30.041

Chauhan, S., Singh, R., Gehlot, A., Akram, S. V., Twala, B., & Priyadarshi, N. (2022). Digitalization of supply chain management with industry 4.0 enabling technologies: A sustainable perspective. *Processes (Basel, Switzerland)*, 11(1), 96. DOI: 10.3390/pr11010096

Diamantopoulos, A., & Siguaw, J. A. (2006). Formative versus reflective indicators in organizational measure development: A comparison and empirical illustration. *British Journal of Management*, 17(4), 263–282. DOI: 10.1111/j.1467-8551.2006.00500.x

Dong, C., Shen, B., Chow, P.-S., Yang, L., & Ng, C. T. (2016). Sustainability investment under cap-and-trade regulation. *Annals of Operations Research*, 240(2), 509–531. DOI: 10.1007/s10479-013-1514-1

Ehrenfeld, J. R. (1995). Design for environment: A new framework for strategic decisions. *Environmental Quality Management*, 4(4), 37–51. DOI: 10.1002/tqem.3310040406

Elkington, J. (1997). Cannibals with forks: The triple bottom line of 21st century business, Capstone. Oxford Capestone.

Fawcett, S. E., Osterhaus, P., Magnan, G. M., Brau, J. C., & McCarter, M. W. (2007). Information sharing and supply chain performance: The role of connectivity and willingness. *Supply Chain Management*, 12(5), 358–368. DOI: 10.1108/13598540710776935

Fornell, C., & Larcker, D. F. (1981). Evaluating structural equation models with unobservable variables and measurement error. *JMR, Journal of Marketing Research*, 18(1), 39–50. DOI: 10.1177/002224378101800104

Gao, J., Zhang, B., Guo, X., Baker, T., Li, M., & Liu, Z. (2022). Secure partial aggregation: Making federated learning more robust for industry 4.0 applications. *IEEE Transactions on Industrial Informatics*, 18(9), 6340–6348. DOI: 10.1109/TII.2022.3145837

Greenhalgh, T., Wherton, J., Papoutsi, C., Lynch, J., Hughes, G., A'Court, C., Hinder, S., Procter, R., & Shaw, S. (2018). Analysing the role of complexity in explaining the fortunes of technology programmes: Empirical application of the NASSS framework. *BMC Medicine*, 16(1), 1–15. DOI: 10.1186/s12916-018-1050-6 PMID: 29754584

Gunasekaran, A., Papadopoulos, T., Dubey, R., Wamba, S. F., Childe, S. J., Hazen, B., & Akter, S. (2017). Big data and predictive analytics for supply chain and organizational performance. *Journal of Business Research*, 70, 308–317. DOI: 10.1016/j.jbusres.2016.08.004

Gupta, H., Kusi-Sarpong, S., & Rezaei, J. (2020). Barriers and overcoming strategies to supply chain sustainability innovation. *Resources, Conservation and Recycling*, 161, 104819. DOI: 10.1016/j.resconrec.2020.104819

Gwelo, A. S. (2019). Principal components to overcome multicollinearity problem. *Oradea Journal of Business and Economics*, 4(1), 79–91. DOI: 10.47535/1991ojbe062

Hair, J., & Alamer, A. (2022). Partial Least Squares Structural Equation Modeling (PLS-SEM) in second language and education research: Guidelines using an applied example. *Research Methods in Applied Linguistics*, 1(3), 100027. DOI: 10.1016/j.rmal.2022.100027

Hair, J. F., Ringle, C. M., & Sarstedt, M. (2011). PLS-SEM: Indeed a silver bullet. *Journal of Marketing Theory and Practice*, 19(2), 139–152. DOI: 10.2753/MTP1069-6679190202

Hair, J. F.Jr, Sarstedt, M., Hopkins, L., & Kuppelwieser, V. G. (2014). Partial least squares structural equation modeling (PLS-SEM): An emerging tool in business research. *European Business Review*, 26(2), 106–121. DOI: 10.1108/EBR-10-2013-0128

Henseler, J., Dijkstra, T. K., Sarstedt, M., Ringle, C. M., Diamantopoulos, A., Straub, D. W., Ketchen, D. J.Jr, Hair, J. F., Hult, G. T. M., & Calantone, R. J. (2014). Common beliefs and reality about PLS: Comments on Rönkkö and Evermann (2013). *Organizational Research Methods*, 17(2), 182–209. DOI: 10.1177/1094428114526928

Hoxha, V., & Sadiku, S. (2019). Study of factors influencing the decision to adopt the blockchain technology in real estate transactions in Kosovo. *Property Management*, 37(5), 684–700. DOI: 10.1108/PM-01-2019-0002

Ivanov, D., & Dolgui, A. (2021). A digital supply chain twin for managing the disruption risks and resilience in the era of Industry 4.0. *Production Planning and Control*, 32(9), 775–788. DOI: 10.1080/09537287.2020.1768450

Jeyaraj, A., Rottman, J. W., & Lacity, M. C. (2006). A review of the predictors, linkages, and biases in IT innovation adoption research. *Journal of Information Technology*, 21(1), 1–23. DOI: 10.1057/palgrave.jit.2000056

Kaine, G., & Wright, V. (2022). Relative advantage and complexity: Predicting the rate of adoption of agricultural innovations. *Frontiers in Agronomy*, 4, 967605. DOI: 10.3389/fagro.2022.967605

Kang, M., Yang, M. G., Park, Y., & Huo, B. (2018). Supply chain integration and its impact on sustainability. *Industrial Management & Data Systems*, 118(9), 1749–1765. DOI: 10.1108/IMDS-01-2018-0004

Khan, S. A. R., Yu, Z., Golpira, H., Sharif, A., & Mardani, A. (2021). A state-of-the-art review and meta-analysis on sustainable supply chain management: Future research directions. *Journal of Cleaner Production*, 278, 123357. DOI: 10.1016/j.jclepro.2020.123357

Lai, Y., Sun, H., & Ren, J. (2018). Understanding the determinants of big data analytics (BDA) adoption in logistics and supply chain management: An empirical investigation. *International Journal of Logistics Management*, 29(2), 676–703. DOI: 10.1108/IJLM-06-2017-0153

Lazar, S., Klimecka-Tatar, D., & Obrecht, M. (2021). Sustainability orientation and focus in logistics and supply chains. *Sustainability (Basel)*, 13(6), 3280. DOI: 10.3390/su13063280

Lee, I. (2024). SaaS –Software – As – A – Service https://www.wallarm.com/what/what-is-saas

Martins, R., Oliveira, T., Thomas, M., & Tomás, S. (2019). Firms' continuance intention on SaaS use–an empirical study. *Information Technology & People*, 32(1), 189–216. DOI: 10.1108/ITP-01-2018-0027

Novais, L., Maqueira, J. M., & Ortiz-Bas, Á. (2019). A systematic literature review of cloud computing use in supply chain integration. *Computers & Industrial Engineering*, 129, 296–314. DOI: 10.1016/j.cie.2019.01.056

Pathak, K., & Thapaliya, S. (2022). Some philosophical paradigms and their implications in health.

Prajogo, D., & Olhager, J. (2012). The effect of supply chain information integration on logistics integration and firm performance. *International Journal of Production Economics*, 135(1), 514–522. DOI: 10.1016/j.ijpe.2011.09.001

Raut, R., Priyadarshinee, P., Gardas, B. B., Narkhede, B. E., & Nehete, R. (2018). The incident effects of supply chain and cloud computing integration on the business performance: An integrated SEM-ANN approach. *Benchmarking*, 25(8), 2688–2722. DOI: 10.1108/BIJ-07-2017-0170

Rogers, E. M. (1995). Diffusion of Innovations: modifications of a model for telecommunications. *Die diffusion von innovationen in der telekommunikation*, 25-38.

Rovshenov, A., & Sarsar, F. (2023). Research trends in programming education: A systematic review of the articles published between 2012-2020. *Journal of Educational Technology and Online Learning*, 6(1), 48–81. DOI: 10.31681/jetol.1201010

Ryalat, M., ElMoaqet, H., & AlFaouri, M. (2023). Design of a smart factory based on cyber-physical systems and Internet of Things towards Industry 4.0. *Applied Sciences (Basel, Switzerland)*, 13(4), 2156. DOI: 10.3390/app13042156

Shee, H., & Kaswi, S. (2015). Behavioral causes of the bullwhip effect: Multinational vs. local supermarket retailers. *Operations and Supply Chain Management: An International Journal*, 9(1), 1–14. DOI: 10.31387/oscm0230156

Shee, H., Miah, S. J., Fairfield, L., & Pujawan, N. (2018). The impact of cloud-enabled process integration on supply chain performance and firm sustainability: The moderating role of top management. *Supply Chain Management*, 23(6), 500–517. DOI: 10.1108/SCM-09-2017-0309

Tang, C., & Tomlin, B. (2008). The power of flexibility for mitigating supply chain risks. *International Journal of Production Economics*, 116(1), 12–27. DOI: 10.1016/j.ijpe.2008.07.008

Vehovar, V., Toepoel, V., & Steinmetz, S. (2016). *Non-probability sampling* (Vol. 1). The Sage Handbook of Survey Methods.

Vela, R. A. (2023). Circular Economy and Supply Chain Management: Circular SCM, a Sustainable Pathway for the Future. https://www.linkedin.com/pulse/circular-economy-supply-chain-management-scm-sustainable-vela/

Wang, G., Zhang, G., Guo, X., & Zhang, Y. (2021). Digital twin-driven service model and optimal allocation of manufacturing resources in shared manufacturing. *Journal of Manufacturing Systems*, 59, 165–179. DOI: 10.1016/j.jmsy.2021.02.008

Wang, S., Wan, J., Zhang, D., Li, D., & Zhang, C. (2016). Towards smart factory for industry 4.0: A self-organized multi-agent system with big data based feedback and coordination. *Computer Networks*, 101, 158–168. DOI: 10.1016/j.comnet.2015.12.017

World, B. N. (2023). The Circular Supply Chain Is Driving Corporate Decarbonization.

Zhang, Q., Cheng, L., & Boutaba, R. (2010). Cloud computing: State-of-the-art and research challenges. *Journal of Internet Services and Applications*, 1(1), 7–18. DOI: 10.1007/s13174-010-0007-6

Chapter 4
The Fifth Industrial Revolution:
Blue Wind Energy for Environmentally Responsible Urbanization and Intelligent Energy Management

K. Madhura
Presidency University, Bangalore, India

Shalini Ninoria
Teerthanker Mahaveer University, India

Arvind Tripathy
KIIT University, India

Tanushree Sharma
Manipal University Jaipur, India

Vivek Deshpande
Vishwakarma Institute of Information Technology, India

Ankur Gupta
https://orcid.org/0000-0002-4651-5830
Vaish College of Engineering, India

Sabyasachi Pramanik
https://orcid.org/0000-0002-9431-8751
Haldia Institute of Technology, India

ABSTRACT

Blue wind energy is a brand-new concept that blends cutting-edge technology with offshore wind energy generation. This chapter initiates a comprehensive exploration of this novel approach, focusing on its potential applications to the intricate issues surrounding sustainable urbanization. It provides an overview of the key ideas of the chapter, which conducts an extensive investigation into the potential integration of blue wind energy, AI, and IoT to enable intelligent energy management in urban environments. It's critical to lessen conventional energy sources' negative environmental effects while still supplying the growing energy demands of urbanization.

DOI: 10.4018/979-8-3693-4123-0.ch004

Urban areas use a great deal of energy, and traditional methods are neither sustainable nor good for the environment. When paired with AI and IoT integration, blue wind energy offers an enticing option for sustainable, efficient, and environmentally friendly energy management in cities. Appropriately integrating and maximizing these technologies is the issue.

INTRODUCTION

The world has to address the triple trifecta of rising energy use, climate change, and fast urbanization if it is to reach sustainable development. One sensible solution to these difficult issues is blue wind energy, which highlights the very vital need of investigating other energy sources. With its towering wind turbines linked to ground stations, Blue Wind Energy is leading the way in wind power invention. This section delves into the possibilities of blue wind energy as a crucial component of industry 5.0. It has been considered as a revolutionary industrial process that integrates green energy, IoT, and AI. The need for innovative and environmentally friendly solutions is rising in anticipation of Industry 5.0, which is characterized by the complete integration of digital along with physical technologies. Urbanization is a hallmark of modern society; it increases energy use as well as necessitates a shift in thinking toward greener practices. Within the context of Industry 5.0, this study investigates the game-changing possibilities of Energy as green power for cities, when coupled with AI and IoT. The goal is to bring about new age of smart management. There has to be innovative and long-term solutions to the energy crisis since conventional energy is becoming more problematic due to issues. Blue Wind Energy is an environmentally friendly and practical method of generating wind power. Because of the necessity for affordable and environmentally friendly energy sources in highly populated areas, renewable energy is relevant when thinking about urbanization. Ideas from Industry 5.0, are compatible of the possible effects of Energy systems. Incorporating AI into the Energy system may boost its efficiency, the technology's speed and accuracy in analyzing massive information. Smart and networked energy are now within reach, thanks to IoT, which paves the way for effective energy management via seamless communication and device control. The growing energy demands of urbanized landscapes may be creatively and comprehensively met via the combination of Energy, IoT, and AI within the Industry 5.0.

Literature Review

Rapid urbanization in the 21st century has brought several problems, the most pressing of which is the ever-increasing need for energy in highly populated regions. As metropolitan areas develop, traditional energies become more and more unsustainable from an ecological and financial standpoint. Given these challenges, academics, policymakers, and corporate executives now need to concentrate on the need of moving toward sustainable (Ullah, S. et al. 2024) and renewable energy (Dadashi, Z. et al. 2024) sources. A kind of wind energy known as "blue wind energy" seems to be a workable solution for supplying cities with the increasing amounts of electricity they need. By using wind currents across vast bodies of water, it taps into the enormous energy potential of offshore wind, unlike conventional wind power. Onshore wind farms have certain land use issues; this new method improves energy generation efficiency while reducing some of those issues. In light of the worldwide threats caused by climate change, the intrinsic sustainability of this holds the potential for a future of energy that is both more robust and less harmful to the environment. Combining AI with the IoT expands the capabilities of these systems, in keeping with the tenets of Industry 5.0. With its powerful data analysis and ML features, AI has power to transform energy production and consumption optimization. These systems can predict when repairs might be required, adapt to changing weather conditions, and overall boost output with AI helping them. Connected devices enabled by the IoT may work as one, enabling sensors, turbines, and energy grids to interact in a simplified way. In the era of Industry 5.0, sustainable urbanization depends on smart energy management, which this link helps to make possible. Since the entrance of Industry 5.0, combining of digital technologies, integration of AI, IoT has been a great leap forward in the development of smart and sustainable urban energy systems. This paper will investigate the advantages, drawbacks, and viability of implementing such a comprehensive approach in the always shifting environment of Industry 5.0 to have understanding of complicated features of this integration. With an eye toward fulfilling the demands of a world fast urbanizing, we want to provide perceptive data that will guide the development of intelligent energy infrastructures both robust and ecologically sensitive.

Significance

As advised by (Harrison-Atlas et al. 2024), merging Blue Wind Energy offers fresh method to satisfy the energy demands of ever urbanized areas. For many important reasons, one must understand and seize the possibilities afforded by this integration. First of all, it is well known that as urban populations grow conventional energy sources are becoming increasingly insufficient. The ecosystem suffers from this as well. Like Blue Wind Energy, offshore wind power offers a cleaner, greener energy source than onshore choices and helps to minimize land use problems. The technologies under investigation have the power to change people's opinions on sustainable urbanization and provide a workable answer for the problem of satisfying the energy consumption of growing cities. Energy systems using IoT and AI also fit Industry 5.0, the concept guiding us into a new age of smart, networked technologies. By allowing performance optimization, predictive maintenance, and real-time decision-making, IoT and AI have transformed intelligent energy management. Along with increasing efficiency of energy consumption, this creates the foundation for adaptable and strong metropolitan energy systems. The chapter is significant as it contributes to a greater conversation on sustainable in framework. (Ha, 2024) claims that the study clarifies our knowledge of how AI and IoT are linked in Blue Wind Energy (Khanh, P. T. et al. 2023), thereby enabling us to create more ecologically friendly cities. Scholars, legislators, and business leaders seeking sustainable urban energy planning might find this paper helpful. Figure 1 helps one understand the relevance of this chapter.

Figure 1. Capabilities of 5th Industrial Revolution

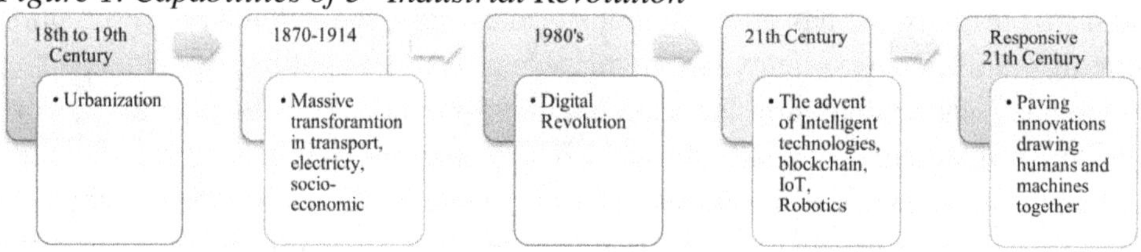

This chapter offers a thorough plan for the use of renewable energy in metropolitan environments, therefore supporting ongoing global attempts to address climate change. We can construct a future where cities are more sustainable and resilient by combining Energy with AI (Ng c, T. H. et al. 2023) and IoT, hence transcending mere technological integration. At the junction of historical technical development and pressing environmental issues, this study may provide the path for smart technology, green energy, and urbanization to live peacefully in the age of Industry 5.0.

Objectives

Figure 2 displays the objective of the chapter. By demonstrating blue wind energy as practical green energy along with outlining potential avenues for innovations in area of urban management, study aspires to provide informative analysis that enhances conversation around sustainable energy.

Figure 2. Chapter's Goal

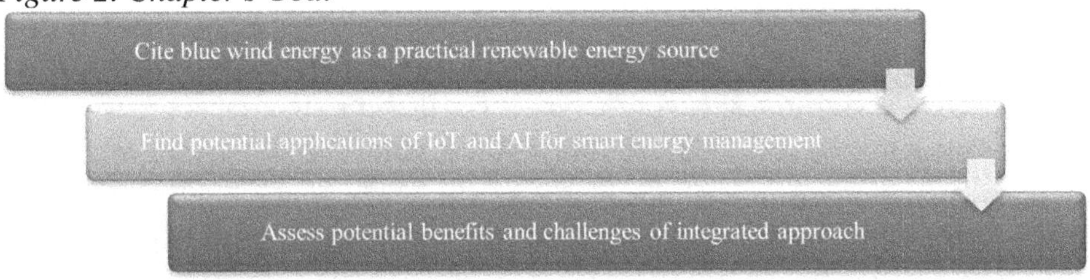

Synopsis, Description, and Tenets of Blue Wind Energy

A fresh approach to wind power is provided by Blue Wind Energy, which makes advantage of wind resources that are located offshore. Blue Wind Energy (Choudhary, S. et al., 2022) is a company that deploys wind turbines offshore in order to alleviate various problems that are associated with typical onshore wind farms. This company builds on previous research in the field of wind energy. It is a viable option for the generation of sustainable energy in coastal locations since this planned migration has various characteristics that make it a promising choice. The kinetic energy of the wind is harnessed over wide regions of water using blue wind power, which results in the generation of electricity. There is a connection between the term "blue" in the name "Blue Wind Energy" and the ocean vistas that are often used as the backdrop for these wind farms. Blue Wind Energy, by using offshore areas, is able to maximize the amount of space that is accessible while also minimizing the visual effect on terrestrial ecosystems. The aesthetic issues and land use restrictions that are connected with onshore wind projects are effectively addressed in order to accomplish this goal. A scientific investigation of the dynamics of wind is the foundation of Blue Wind Energy. When compared to onshore settings, offshore locations provide a more reliable and efficient source of electricity since the wind speeds are greater and more consistent. Both capacity factors and energy output may be improved by permitting the wind to blow from behind big bodies of water that are exposed to the air. One further benefit of offshore wind farms is that they provide a reduction in the transmission losses that are involved with the delivery of power across long distances. Because of this, the distribution of the energy that is generated to areas with a population is made easier. Towers that are linked to the ocean bottom are often used by blue wind energy projects in order to provide support for their gigantic turbines. Wind turbines are devices that spin blades that are attached to a generator in order to transform the mechanical energy of the wind into electricity that can be used. Through the use of underwater cables, the energy that is created is transported to the shore, where it has the potential to be incorporated into the electric infrastructure that is already in place. The use of blue wind energy is very beneficial to the environment since it lessens the production of greenhouse gases, lessens the reliance on fossil fuels, and lessens the harm that is produced by conventional energy sources. The use of turbines that are larger and more robust might be considered for the purpose of enhancing the effectiveness of offshore energy production (Pramanik, S. et al., 2022). In the field of renewable energy, Blue Wind Energy represents a significant step forward that will change the game. Offshore wind resources are essential in this regard since they provide power that is dependable, sustainable over the long term, and better for the environment. During a time when the world is under intense pressure to transition to renewable energy sources, Blue Wind Energy's ambitions demonstrate what offshore wind technology is capable of achieving to construct a more favorable energy future.

Benefits and issues of Wind Energy

Clean, renewable Blue Wind Energy's many benefits have to be overcome if it is to realize their full potential and guarantee their position in the future of sustainable energy. More industrial, legislative, and scientific advancement would be needed to solve these issues and make Energy more effective component of global energy.

Blue Wind Energy's Advantages

The advantages of blue wind power—a green alternative—are by using the large and consistent offshore wind resources, blue wind energy has shown to be plentiful and consistent renewable energy source. By placing your wind turbine offshore—where the wind is stronger and more consistent—you may generate more power. Arguments About Land Use Avoidance: An alternative to onshore wind farms not vying for limited land resources are blue wind energy systems. Resolving concerns with habitat loss and aesthetics, offshore turbine locations reduce land use conflicts and decrease impacts on terrestrial ecosystems. This allows these systems to operate closer to their maximum capacity, which in turn increases their total energy output. The offshore farms of Blue Wind Energy are strategically located near major population areas, which is advantageous for producing renewable energy since many cities are located near coasts. This proximity lowers the energy transmission losses and the long-distance power transfer expenses. Blue Wind Energy lowers greenhouse gas emissions and fossil fuel use, therefore supporting the global battle against climate change. Offshore wind farms less damage local ecosystems and animals than their onshore counterparts.

Challenges of Blue Wind Energy

A very high initial outlay Initial outlay for establishing and maintaining offshore wind farms is significant. The whole cost of erecting and installing turbines at sea, complete with the required infrastructure, might be relatively costly compared to land-based wind projects.

- Problems brought on by technological advancement: Working in demanding offshore environments creates technological difficulties. Modern technologies are required if turbines are to be dependable and long-lasting in high winds, strong wave pressure, and corrosive waters.
- Challenge with planning and execution: Offshore wind turbine transportation and installation are difficult tasks needing specific boats and tools. Building and maintaining turbines in deep sea presents significant difficulty.
- Connection to the Grid: A connecting offshore wind farm to onshore power grid necessitates construction of cables underwater, which may be a costly and technically demanding process. Stable and effective grid connection is critical for Blue Wind Energy to reach its full potential.

Wind farms nevertheless provide a greener alternative to conventional energy sources, despite the fact that they may have certain limited environmental impacts during building and operation. The visual landscape, marine habitats, and shipping waterways are among areas that might undergo changes.

Need for Energy and Sustainable Urban Development

The inevitable trend of global urbanization has ushered in an unprecedented period of city development and population concentration in metropolitan regions. This revolutionary process has increased the need for energy at the same time as it is a symbol of human development. According to (Li, Y. et al. 2024), this makes sustainable urbanization crucial and necessitates a paradigm shift in city design, building, and energy systems. The primary challenge presented by the growth of urbanization is the increasing need for energy to meet needs of rising populations. In addition to being massive energy users, cities are also actual hubs for technological advancement, business activity and cultural vibrancy.

How Smart Cities Affect Global Energy Consumption

Their concentrations of people, companies, and new technology make "smart cities" essential for the picture of global energy use. Thanks to industrialization, transportation systems, and the varied energy needs of city dwellers, cities worldwide are major consumers of energy resources. Urban energy consumption is large and complicated, hence cities must solve sustainability problems if they want to lower the environmental effect of this use. Strategies to support renewable energy sources, smart technology integration into cities, and energy efficiency are becoming importance given the fast rate of urbanization. Cities therefore not only use a lot of energy but also play a vital part in worldwide campaign for more reliable and ecologically responsible energy.

Importance of Using Renewable Energy Sources

The struggle against environmental damage, energy insecurity, and climate change has to give renewable energy sources top priority. Green energy is here to stay as sustainable substitute. It is created by solar, wind, water, geothermal heat among other sustainable sources. Rather than depending on limited fossil fuels or exhausting valuable resources, green energy uses Earth's natural processes to satisfy our energy needs. According to (Osman, et al. 2024), this transition is necessary to lower air pollution, promote environmental sustainability, and thus lessen negative consequences. Green energy improves energy security as it diversifies energy mix and lessens dependence on sensitive to global volatility fossil fuel supply, which depends on. A nation's economic and geopolitical stability are less affected by the geopolitics of oil-producing areas and the caprices of changing oil prices. A possible way toward energy independence may be green energy technology, which enables countries to produce electricity locally and lessens reliance on ups and downs of the global energy market. Scientific and economic advancement are both aided by shifting to renewable energy sources. Developing business job creation and R&D are both bolstered by investments in renewable energy. The green energy industry may stimulate economic growth, according to (Mahmud, H. et al. 2024), by creating skilled jobs and catapulting nations to global clean energy. Green energy is way to go if we want to slow global warming, make our planet more sustainable, and provide a steady and varied supply of power in the future. A more equitable and sustainable global energy landscape is possible because of this change, which helps countries become economically prosperous and energy independent. It occurs while reducing effect of environment in case of conventional energy sources.

Impact of Urbanization on Energy Consumption

Urbanization has far-reaching and varied impacts on energy use. The energy demand in cities is always rising due to factors such as population density, infrastructural development, and economic activity concentration. This is caused by the fact that more and more people are moving to cities. Greater energy consumption to power homes, companies, and industries, as well as an increase in fuel consumption to power automobiles, are all results of urbanization. The proliferation of technological equipment and the development of energy-intensive structures are two factors that exacerbate the problem of urban energy consumption. As a direct outcome of rising living standards, more people are choosing to live in urban areas, leading to an increase in the demand for energy-intensive services.

Offshore Wind Energy

To take advantage of stronger and more regular winds, offshore wind farms are located at or close to the water's edge, as opposed to the more conventional onshore wind farms. Because it can capture the immense wind power across large areas of water, offshore wind energy represents a giant leap forward for renewable energy. As a sustainable energy source, it's little wonder this innovative project is getting a lot of attention; it solves several issues with traditional onshore wind farms while offering obvious benefits. Offshore wind power mostly benefits from the much high speed wind often seen over open water. Power is proportional to cube of wind speed, meaning that wind turbines generate more power in conditions of greater wind speeds. As a result, offshore wind farms may have higher capacity factors and run at or near their full production levels more consistently. The exceptional efficiency of offshore wind generation enables a substantial expansion of renewable energy consumption. In addition, land use limitations are less of a concern for offshore wind projects than for onshore wind farms. The vast rivers may allow large wind farms without affecting or harming the surrounding land. In densely populated places, where there may not be as many ideal onshore spots, this comes in handy. Offshore wind generation has undeniable environmental impacts. If we want to produce electricity without adding to climate change or other dangerous pollutants, offshore wind power is a sustainable and clean substitute for traditional power stations that use fossil fuels. When compared to onshore wind turbines, offshore wind farms are less visually and aurally disruptive due to their submerged nature. Offshore wind energy development is fraught with challenges. Because of great expense of marine-resistant infrastructure, foundations, and turbines, outright capital expenditures for offshore wind projects might be more than those for onshore ones. Connecting to building, and maintaining the grid at offshore locations creates particular logistical problems that need for specific boats and innovative technology solutions. Offshore wind farms have rapidly grown in the last several years thanks in part to government subsidies combined with private investment. Because of their lengthy coasts, the United Kingdom, Denmark, and China are driving offshore wind development. Offshore wind energy is becoming practical and efficient because to developments in grid connection, floating platforms, and turbine technology. Consequently, shift to carbon-neutral energy system depends on offshore wind generation ever more in relevance.

Advantages of Offshore Wind Farms

Offshore wind farms are becoming well-known in the renewable energy sector because to their many benefits. Stronger and more constant winds might be experienced in offshore locations than in onshore ones. This feature helps offshore wind farms to increase their capacity factors and increase their energy output via more efficient conversion of wind energy into electricity. If the wind speeds were to increase over open water, enabling each turbine to produce more power, the total energy generated by offshore wind farms may be greater. Larger turbines, only feasible offshore, allow one to collect more wind energy and produce more electricity. This feature of offshore wind farms makes them more trustworthy and helps to balance the grid. Considering the prevalence of cities along coastlines, one may purposefully find offshore wind turbines near highly populous areas. Reducing the transmission losses and power prices helps to distribute energy more effectively across great distances. Offshore wind energy improves the environment more than conventional energy sources running on fossil fuels. A trained and long-lasting workforce may be achieved via this, since it encompasses engineering, manufacturing, installation, and continuous operations jobs. Improvements in Design, Materials, and Construction Methods: Offshore wind technology is undergoing continuous research and development, which is leading to advancements in several areas. Offshore wind farms are becoming more cost-effective, environmentally friendly, and efficient thanks to these innovations. The benefits of offshore wind farms are shown in Figure 3.

Figure 3. Advantages of Offshore Wind Farms

- Increases wind velocity
- Enhanced production of energy
- Mitigation of Sight and Noise impacts
- Nearby Population Centers
- Potentiality of Greater Turbine Sizes
- Technological progress
- Growth in the economy and employment
- Advantages for the environment

Challenges and the Advancement of Technology

Compared to onshore facilities, the initial investment needed to create offshore wind farms is far larger. Problems with Logistics with Installation: Offshore wind turbine transportation along with installation, especially in deeper seas, could be challenging. Foundation installation and grid connection are technologically difficult processes that need specialist boats, adding another layer of complication to the project. Upkeep and Fixtures: Offshore turbines may be difficult to reach and repair because of the salt water's corrosive effects and the severe marine environment. The establishment of cost-effective and efficient maintenance plans is crucial to sustainability of offshore wind farms in long run. Link to the Grid: The technically demanding and expensive procedure of undersea cable construction must be completed in order to connect offshore wind turbines to the onshore power system. Harnessing offshore wind energy to its greatest potential depends on dependable and effective grid connections. Offshore wind farms produce environmental problems because of the hazards they provide to humans, marine life, and migratory paths. One of the toughest challenges is figuring out how to both safeguard marine life and benefit the surroundings from renewable energy sources.

Advancements in Technology Managing

Clearer image of the possible ecological consequences of offshore wind farms is result of developments in environmental impact assessment techniques. Projects might be designed to have less of an effect on marine ecosystems and species with this information at hand. If offshore wind energy is to fully realize, overcoming these limitations will demand constant study and innovation as technology develops. Because offshore wind is profitable, environmentally friendly, and widely used, these developments have helped it to become more and more popular as a renewable energy source.

Prominent Offshore Wind Energy Projects

Numerous well-known initiatives have shown offshore wind energy to have a promising future.

Industry 5.0 Uses AI and IoT for Management of Energy

Via constantly monitoring power distribution networks for problems and quickly addressing them, smart grid energy management combining AI and IoT sensors improves the dependability and resilience of smart grids via Industry 5.0 IoT sensors. By allowing more finely-grained control of equipment and processes to reach energy efficiency objectives, IoT-enabled industrial devices enhance demand-side management. Using AI along with IoT helps industry 5.0, management of energy go well beyond conventional control along with monitoring. AI-powered cognitive computing systems analyze and react to fresh energy data, therefore improving energy consumption patterns. ML algorithms fed real-time data from IoT sensors might enable quick judgments on load balancing, equipment failure avoidance, and energy consumption profile modification. With this degree of intelligent automation, cost savings and sustainability objectives are more readily reached while operational efficiency is improved.

IoT and predictive analytics help management of energy resources promote proactive maintenance. AI systems might look for trends in IoT device performance that would point to malfunctioning equipment. Predictive maintenance allows important energy infrastructure to remain operating for more years with fewer downtime and cost. Industry 5.0 emphasizes on integrating intelligent technologies to signify the change from reactive along with manual management of energy practices to dependable, self-optimizing systems. As part of Industry 5.0, integrating IoT and AI into energy management has numerous possible advantages; but, there are certain negative effects to take into account as well. An immediate issue of national security is fixing flaws in AI systems and guaranteeing that devices can interact with one another. Their effective implementation also depends on the acceptance of such modern technology as well as large expenditures in associated infrastructure and training. Moreover essential to provide flawless integration across many industrial ecosystems is consideration of standards and interoperability.

Industry 5.0's Use of AI to Optimize Energy Output

AI is essential for making energy systems smarter, more sustainable, and more efficient. Industry 5.0 describes this meeting point of digital and physical technologies. The ability of AI to analyze complex data sets in real time makes it an indispensable tool for energy production management, forecasting, and improvement. Machine learning algorithms use weather patterns, present energy usage measurements, and historical data to provide accurate demand estimates. Businesses may make better use of their resources and reduce waste with the aid of these predictive skills, which allow them to dynamically adjust their energy output. Optimizing energy production with the use of AI cuts down on overproduction by bringing supply and demand closer together. As part of Industry 5.0, energy system optimization is enhanced by combining AI and the IoT. Smart meters and sensors are two examples of IoT devices that continually provide data on equipment performance and consumption of energy. Systems powered by AI scour this data for patterns, inefficiencies, and growth opportunities. To decrease energy consumption and avoid expensive down-time, predictive maintenance might be enabled by AI that can identify equipment problems. Adebayo et al. (2024) states that cognitive computing systems augmented with AI continuously adapt to new energy scenarios via learning. These systems are capable of autonomously balancing loads, responding to demand, and using energy storage. The adaptability of AI paves the way for building energy systems. It optimizes themselves in response to fluctuations in supply, demand, along with environmental factors. In case of optimizing energy production, AI has a lot to offer Industry 5.0. Gains in efficiency boost industrial competitiveness, sustainability, and savings. Energy optimization guided by AI further enhances grid stability, especially in cases where renewable energy sources, such as solar and wind, with fluctuating outputs, are employed significantly. By intelligently regulating energy production and consumption, AI helps create a more robust and adaptable energy environment, in line with the aims of Industry 5.0. Still, there are a number of issues that need fixing, including privacy and data security concerns as well as a lack of qualified individuals to build and oversee AI systems. For AI technology to be easily integrated into many industrial settings, standardization and interoperability are also crucial.

Real-time Control and Monitoring Applications of IoT

IoT real-time monitoring is a key element of this revolutionary technology that has many uses. Numerous IoT uses use real-time control.

- Smart Cities: IoT is essential to the growth of smart cities since it allows for the management and monitoring of various municipal systems in real-time. Through the use of cameras and sensors, smart traffic management systems constantly assess traffic conditions, allowing for the improvement of signal timings and the redirection of automobiles to alleviate congestion. Through the use of IoT devices, authorities are able to quickly adapt to changing circumstances by monitoring air quality, public safety, and waste management.
- Industrial-IoT: IIoT is a subset of the IoT that enables real-time monitoring and management of production processes by manufacturers and other businesses. Various sensors installed on machines record vital statistics such as temperature and equipment performance. Reduced downtime and increased production efficiency are the results of predictive maintenance. Such maintenance has been made possible due to real-time data.
- Smart Buildings: By monitoring occupancy and other environmental factors, smart thermostats are able to fine-tune the indoor climate. Security systems provide real-time monitoring and access management, while lighting systems with IoT capabilities allow for remote brightness adjustment.
- Agriculture: As a result of IoT, precision agriculture is changing the face of the agricultural industry. With the use of field sensors, we can track the temperature, moisture level, and overall health of our crops. Irrigation systems may use data to make adjustments to water distribution, which might lead to more efficient use of resources. The ability of drones to monitor IoT devices is constantly evolving and improving.

Coastal Cities and Wind Power

Blue Wind Energy is offshore wind farm that considers both the aesthetic considerations and the scarcity of land for onshore wind farms. Such type of wind Energy makes better use of space and ensures more dependable and efficient energy production. A number of major cities are located near beaches, which increases the likelihood that Blue wind energy will be part of energy mix of these rapidly developing towns. Blue Wind Energy's principles are absolutely correct with regard to environmentally responsible city planning. The massive arrays of turbines used by offshore wind farms are fastened to the ocean floor, which helps to decrease emissions of greenhouse gases and other problems created by conventional power plants. This technology lessens the environmental impact of urban energy usage by rapidly transitioning to a low-carbon future via the production of vast amounts of clean electricity. Another important part of creating sustainable cities is the decentralization of power production, which Blue Wind Energy lays the groundwork for. Many cities are exploring the possibility of using offshore wind resources to diversify their energy sources, enhance energy security, and decrease their dependence on centralized power infrastructure. The purpose of smart cities is to make metropolitan zones more adaptable, efficient, and responsive to human needs. Distributed energy systems are required to achieve this goal, which is a rather popular notion. Consistent with this trend, Blue Wind Energy operates as a decentralized organization. Despite its many advantages, using blue wind energy into urbanization projects remains a challenging task. Significant initial capital expenditures, logistical hurdles at offshore locations, and environmental concerns are important considerations. Because these challenges are being actively addressed via ongoing technological improvements, government aid, and stakeholder involvement, Blue Wind Energy has the potential to become an important element of sustainable urbanization strategy. Blue Wind Energy is a progressive as well as inventive business that offers a renewable substitute in case of fossil fuels. Such fossil fuels power expanding cities throughout globe. Incorporating Blue Wind Energy into metropolitan energy portfolios is a crucial move toward cleaner, more environmentally friendly, and more efficient power generation. This is especially critical as urbanization continues to accelerate. Future city energy use of wind power will be impacted by blue wind energy, which is game-changer in fight for resilient and sustainable urban growth.

Significance of Smart Grids in Area of Urban Energy Distribution

Integrating smart grids with energy storage technology is crucial to improving urban energy distribution and efficiently managing the challenges brought about by growing urbanization. Because they improve grid stability and dependability by giving real-time visibility into the whole energy network, smart grids have various applications in urban energy distribution. Smart grids use cutting-edge communication technologies, smart meters, and sensors to track energy consumption, system health, and issues. According to (Jayasingh, R. et al. 2022), real-time monitoring enables the discovery of issues early on, quick reaction to blackouts, and optimization of grid performance, all of which contribute to a reliable power supply for urban enterprises and people. Consumers are given the ability to actively engage in energy management using smart grids' demand response systems. Connecting smart meters to devices that can access the internet allows consumers to get real-time information about their energy use, costs, and environmental effect. With this knowledge, consumers may make informed decisions, such moving power-hungry activity to off-peak hours when renewable energy production is at its greatest or electricity rates are at their lowest. Achieving grid balance, optimizing energy consumption patterns, and reducing peak demand are all made easier with demand-side flexibility. To mitigate power interruptions and the unpredictable nature of renewable energy, smart grids in conjunction with energy storage devices are a great asset. Batteries and other technology make efficient energy storage and release feasible. They are a stopgap measure to control market supply and demand. By increasing the use of renewable energy sources in urban networks, this function helps to stabilize the grid and reduces reliance on backup power from fossil fuels. All urban transportation would be powered by electricity in future, owing to smart networks and energy storage. When fully integrated into smart grids, electric cars (EVs) may serve as portable power storage, which bodes well for their future. During times of high demand, bidirectional charging might return excess power to the grid, or it could employ abundant and inexpensive energy sources. This two-way flow, according to (Soni, J. et al. 2024), makes the grid more flexible and helps make urban mobility more sustainable in general. The distribution of energy in urban areas cannot be accomplished without smart grids if we are to build an efficient, modern, and environmentally friendly energy scene. Smart grids enhance consumer engagement in energy recovery via dependable and efficient use of current technology, data analytics, real-time communication, and traditional power networks. By lowering the barriers to integration of renewable energy sources into metropolitan networks, smart grids and energy storage technology may make city energy infrastructure more resilient and eco-friendly. Smart networks and energy storage are crucial for building a sustainable and future-proof urban environment in light of the ever-increasing size of cities.

How IoT and AI Support Efficient Energy Storage and Distribution

Working together, AI and IoT will shortly usher in a new era of effective energy distribution and storage. Major nervous system nodes in an ecosystem are the widespread IoT sensors of energy networks and storage systems, constantly spewing a torrent of data on energy usage, grid efficiency, and storage capacity. AI driven algorithms search through this data, extract pertinent information, and provide reasonable conclusions. Real-time IoT data and artificial intelligence's predictive analytics, an intelligent energy ecosystem capable of adaptation and survival in any environment is within grasp. Through predictive maintenance—a major use of AI and IoT—embedded sensors may monitor the energy infrastructure to ascertain its current state and possible failure dates. Data from IoT devices, demand response, and load management taken together let utilities improve energy distribution, load balancing, and peak demand lowering via AI-driven decision-making. Some of the ways researchers are trying to make energy storage systems more efficient are monitoring system performance using IoT sensors along with AI algorithms optimizing charging along with discharging cycles in real-time depending on demand and grid condition. Consequently, usage of stored energy as well as general efficiency improves. One such field where IoT and AI cooperate is renewable energy. AI algorithms for pattern identification and analysis are fed real-time data gathered from IoT sensors housed on solar and wind energy. Although their natural volatility makes it more difficult, this feature facilitates integration of renewable energy sources into grid. Modern cyber security depends critically on AI systems' capacity to rapidly identify suspicious activity in network traffic and reduce digital age risks (Andrushia, A. D. et al., 2023). If done, the networked equipment in the energy infrastructure will be dependable and safe. IoT and AI are helping energy distribution and storage enter a new era more intelligent, adaptable, and environmentally benign. Real-time data, predictive analytics, and adaptive decision-making taken together provide the foundation for a sustainable and strong energy future. With its support, the complexity of current energy needs may be better controlled for customers as well as utilities.

CONCLUSION

An unparalleled alliance combining blue wind energy and game-changing powers of AI and IoT might help redefining sustainable urbanization and energy management in era of Industry 5.0. Blue Wind Energy is a paradigm of creative thinking that provides a reasonably priced, sustainable answer to growing energy needs of metropolitan areas. Using dominant winds of ocean, offshore wind farms generate energy, therefore reducing land shortage problem and consequent sharp drop in greenhouse gas emissions. Made possible by AI and IoT, smart grids define benchmark for clever and effective electricity distribution in cities. Including renewable energy sources, demand response systems, predictive maintenance, and real-time monitoring has fundamentally changed modern urban energy management and consumption. Apart from improving grid reliability, distributed architecture of smart grids allows users more agencies and creates path for urban energy systems that are both flexible and responsive. Drive for renewable energy is emphasizing batteries more as AI and IoT aid. By controlling their intermittent character, which in turn lowers dependency on traditional backup power sources, these developments facilitate integration of renewable energy sources into municipal networks. They improve approaches for real-time archiving as well. The transforming possibilities of AI and IoT in energy storage sector are shown by evolution of predictive analytics and use of bidirectional energy flow between storage devices and grid. These networked technologies have immense far-reaching potential. Efficiency, stability, and flexibility, constant developments in machine learning frameworks, AI algorithms, and IoT sensor technologies port forward for urban energy systems. These technologies will be widely used in fast growing notion of "smart cities," which are distinguished, hence supporting sustainability and resilience.

As Industry 5.0 grows, new, more complex energy management solutions arising from these networked systems will become more important. In different metropolitan environments, interoperability, cyber security protocols, and standards will define the degree of cooperation among these technologies. Research institutions, businesses, and governments all have to cooperate to address these challenges and fully use these revolutionary energy technologies. Blue wind, energy storage, smart grids, AI and IoT will all drive the clever, flexible energy systems of future cities. When fully embraced, these technologies will change urban energy consumption and distribution patterns, hasten the shift to a cleaner, safer energy future, and profoundly affect sustainable urbanization. Creative mix sets a benchmark for next strategies addressing important problems in urban energy management and sustainable development. These linked technologies provide promise for a more safe, efficient and ecologically responsible energy future in front of rising urban population, changing temperature, and energy transition.

REFERENCES

Adebayo, T. S., & Samour, A. (2024). Renewable energy, fiscal policy and load capacity factor in BRICS countries: Novel findings from panel nonlinear ARDL model. *Environment, Development and Sustainability*, 26(2), 4365–4389. DOI: 10.1007/s10668-022-02888-1

Andrushia, A. D., Neebha, T. M., Patricia, A. T., Sagayam, K. M., & Pramanik, S. (2023). Capsule Network based Disease Classification for VitisVinifera Leaves. *Neural Computing & Applications*. Advance online publication. DOI: 10.1007/s00521-023-09058-y

Choudhary, S., Narayan, V., Faiz, M., & Pramanik, S. (2022). Fuzzy Approach-Based Stable Energy-Efficient AODV Routing Protocol in Mobile Ad hoc Networks. In Ghonge, M. M., Pramanik, S., & Potgantwar, A. D. (Eds.), *Software Defined Networking for Ad Hoc Networks*. Springer. DOI: 10.1007/978-3-030-91149-2_6

Dadashi, Z., Mahmoudi, A., & Rashidi, S. (2022). Capacity and strategies of energy production from renewable sources in Arab countries until 2030: A review from renewable energy potentials to environmental issues. *Environmental Science and Pollution Research International*, 29(32), 47837–47866. DOI: 10.1007/s11356-022-20544-z PMID: 35522406

Ha, L. T. (2024). A wavelet analysis of dynamic connectedness between geopolitical risk and renewable energy volatility during the COVID-19 pandemic and Ukraine-Russia conflicts. *Environmental Science and Pollution Research International*, 31(12), 17994–18009. DOI: 10.1007/s11356-023-26033-1 PMID: 36914932

Harrison-Atlas, D., Glaws, A., King, R. N., & Lantz, E. (2024). Artificial intelligence-aided wind plant optimization for nationwide evaluation of land use and economic benefits of wake steering. *Nature Energy*, 9(6), 735–749. Advance online publication. DOI: 10.1038/s41560-024-01516-8

Jayasingh, R., Kumar, R. J. S., Telagathoti, D. B., Sagayam, K. M., & Pramanik, S. (2022). Speckle noise removal by SORAMA segmentation in Digital Image Processing to facilitate precise robotic surgery. *International Journal of Reliable and Quality E-Healthcare*, 11(1), 1–19. Advance online publication. DOI: 10.4018/IJRQEH.295083

Khanh, P. T., Ng c, T. H., & Pramanik, S. (2023). Future of Smart Agriculture Techniques and Applications. In Khang, A., & Global, I. G. I. (Eds.), *Advanced Technologies and AI-Equipped IoT Applications in High Tech Agriculture*. DOI: 10.4018/978-1-6684-9231-4.ch021

Li, Y., Janik, P., & Schwarz, H. (2024). Aggregated wind power characteristic curves and AI for the regional wind power infeed estimation. *Electrical Engineering*, 106, 655–671. DOI: 10.1007/s00202-023-02005-z

Mahmud, H., & Roy, J. (2024). Energy sector sustainability for a fast-growing economy like Bangladesh: An empirical assessment. *Sustainability Science*, 19(1), 51–73. DOI: 10.1007/s11625-023-01385-2

Ng c, T. H., Khanh, P. T., & Pramanik, S. (2023). Smart Agriculture using a Soil Monitoring System. In Khang, A., & Global, I. G. I. (Eds.), *Advanced Technologies and AI-Equipped IoT Applications in High Tech Agriculture*. DOI: 10.4018/978-1-6684-9231-4.ch011

Osman, A. I., Redpath, D., Lichtfouse, E., & Rooney, D. W. (2024). Synergy between vertical farming and the hydrogen economy. *Environmental Chemistry Letters*, 22(1), 1–6. DOI: 10.1007/s10311-023-01648-5

Pramanik, S. (2022). An Effective Secured Privacy-Protecting Data Aggregation Method in IoT. In Odhiambo, M. O., Mwashita, W., & Global, I. G. I. (Eds.), *Achieving Full Realization and Mitigating the Challenges of the Internet of Things*. DOI: 10.4018/978-1-7998-9312-7.ch008

Soni, J., & Bhattacharjee, K. (2024). Multi-objective dynamic economic emission dispatch integration with renewable energy sources and plug-in electrical vehicle using equilibrium optimizer. *Environment, Development and Sustainability*, 26(4), 8555–8586. DOI: 10.1007/s10668-023-03058-7

Ullah, S., Luo, R., Adebayo, T. S., & Kartal, M. T. (2024). Paving the ways toward sustainable development: The asymmetric effect of economic complexity, renewable electricity, and foreign direct investment on the environmental sustainability in BRICS-T. *Environment, Development and Sustainability*, 26(4), 9115–9139. DOI: 10.1007/s10668-023-03085-4

Chapter 5
The Impact of Board Qualifications on the Complexity of Sustainability Reports

Abdullah Kürşat Merter
https://orcid.org/0000-0001-6874-1890
Gebze Technical University, Turkey

Yavuz Selim Balcioğlu
https://orcid.org/0000-0001-7138-2972
Gebze Technical University, Turkey

Sedat Çerez
Gebze Technical University, Turkey

Gökhan Özer
Gebze Technical University, Turkey & Kyrgyz-Turkish Manas University, Turkey

ABSTRACT

The boards of directors serve as an important control unit in the effective management of sustainability reports. Various characteristics, such as the experience and skills of the board members, the presence of female members on the board, and the size of the board, can affect the company's approach to sustainability issues. Therefore, the boards of directors of companies have a critical role in understanding sustainability reports. The objective of this study is to investigate the correlation between the intricacy of sustainability reports and the attributes of the board. For this purpose, firms listed on the Borsa Istanbul (BIST) between 2014 and 2022 were selected as

DOI: 10.4018/979-8-3693-4123-0.ch005

the sample. The complexity of the reports was evaluated on the basis of the length of pages, words, and characters within the reports. The findings indicate a positive relationship between board size, gender diversity within the board, and the length of sustainability reports. Furthermore, it was found that firms with effective audit committees tend to have shorter sustainability reports.

1. INTRODUCTION

In today's world, the concept of sustainability has gained significant importance not only in everyday life, but also in the business world. Firms evaluate their outputs not only in terms of financial performance, but also considering social, environmental, and economic impacts. Therefore, firms determine their strategies regarding business models taking into account increasing environmental and social pressures and shaping them based on sustainability. In this context, sustainability reports are of critical importance to measuring firms' sustainability performance. Additionally, in today's world, financial indicators are not sufficient to comprehensively examine a company's activities and their environmental outcomes (Cho et al., 2022). Therefore, sustainability reports are seen as an important tool for companies to communicate with various stakeholders.

Although definitions of sustainability may vary between companies, many agree on the importance of conducting sustainability reports. The publication of sustainability reports by large corporations has become increasingly significant in today's business world. Most major companies worldwide publish sustainability reports (Landrum & Ohsowski, 2018). Sustainability reporting by large corporations provides an opportunity to enhance their corporate image (Robinson, 2004) and to provide transparency to stakeholders. Furthermore, through these reports, companies demonstrate that they operate in an environmentally friendly and socially responsible manner, thus gaining the trust of consumers, investors, and other stakeholders. Thus, reporting on sustainability issues constitutes an important part of the dialogue between firms and stakeholders (Gray et al., 1995).

Sustainability reporting is a document that evaluates a company's environmental, social, and economic performance and communicates these indicators to various stakeholder groups. Through sustainability reports, companies communicate the extent to which they have achieved sustainability goals and their future sustainability goals to stakeholders. These reports comprehensively demonstrate how a company performs in terms of environmental impacts, social responsibility practices, employee rights, supply chain management, and many other areas.

In many countries, sustainability reporting, which involves assessing and presenting firms' environmental, social, and economic performance to stakeholders, is based on a voluntary basis (Nilipour et al., 2020), and Türkiye is among these countries. However, in some countries, such as the United States and Canada, sustainability reporting is a mandatory practice governed by laws and regulations (Brockett & Rezaee, 2012). Whether reporting is mandatory or voluntary, there is a wide variety of sustainability data reported by businesses (Nazari et al., 2017), and the subjectivity inherent in sustainability reports provides firms with various options for explanations (Abu Bakar & Ameer, 2011).

The complexity of reports represents readability (Smeuninx et al., 2016). According to Rennekamp (2012), investors respond more strongly to easily readable information and weakly to difficult-to-read texts. For investors to use these reports effectively, they must be readable. If the readability of the report is low, some readers may have difficulty obtaining the information they trust for decision making (Dyer et al., 2017; Ebaid, 2024; Luo et al., 2017). There are numerous studies in the literature on the complexity of reports. However, no studies have been found in Türkiye, a developing country, that examine the relationship between the readability of reports and the board of directors.

Boards of directors are an important control unit in effectively managing sustainability reports. Therefore, they play an important role in the preparation stage of the report. Various characteristics, such as experience, skills, or the presence of female members within the board, as well as the size of the board, can influence a company's approach to sustainability issues. Thus, the boards of directors of companies play a critical role in understanding sustainability reports. The objective of this study is to investigate the correlation between the intricacy of sustainability reports and the attributes of the board of directors. Investigate how the complexity of reports is affected by the characteristics of the board of directors. Firms in developing countries often face more pressure on sustainability issues. Society, governments, various organisations, and investors increasingly have expectations and demands related to sustainability. Therefore, in this study, firms operating in Borsa Istanbul between 2014 and 2022 were selected as a sample. The study excluded financial institutions such as banks, insurance companies, real estate investment trusts, and holding companies because they are subject to distinct regulations and accounting practices.

The subsequent sections of the study are organized in the following manner: The second section presents the literature on the subject and the hypothesis formulated. The third section provides information on the dataset, variables, and methodology. The fourth section examines the findings of the analysis, while the final section presents the conclusions of the investigation.

2. LITERATURE REVIEW AND HYPOTHESIS DEVELOPMENT

2.1. Literature Review

Managers may use the choice of whether or not to disclose inside information or the complexity of disclosures as a manipulation tool (Satt & Iatridis, 2023). In the face of events that can affect financial performance, such as low profitability or various adverse events, managers may resort to various methods, such as reducing transparency (Chi & Wang, 2008; Farooq et al., 2021). Moreover, complex language is often used by corporate managers to raise information processing costs and delay market reactions (Chan & Li, 2008). Furthermore, the flagging hypothesis argues that more successful companies are motivated to disclose more information (Oyelere et al., 2003). According to the opportunistic perspective of positive accounting theory (PAT), managers choose the reporting method in their own self-interest (Watts & Zimmerman, 1978; 1986). Consequently, they may misrepresent or obfuscate the true financial indicators in order to mislead the various parties that use this information (Pajuste et al., 2021).

Li (2008) investigates the correlation between the readability of annual reports and both firm performance and earnings. The study analyzes 55,719 observations of firms operating from 1993 to 2003. The findings indicate that firms with lower earnings tend to have more intricate annual reports. Ertuğrul et al. (2017) discovered that banks enforce more stringent credit contract conditions and charge higher interest rates to companies whose reports are challenging to comprehend. Furthermore, bond market investors expect greater rates of return from companies that generate annual reports that are less comprehensible (Bonsall & Miller, 2017). Lim et al. (2018) examine the effects of firms' business strategies on annual report readability. As a result of the findings, they observed that firms that prefer an efficiency-orientated defensive strategy have more readable 10-K reports compared to those that follow an innovation-orientated investigative strategy. Luo et al. (2018) examined the relationship between annual report readability and agency costs for firms operating in China between 2001 and 2015. They applied OLS regression analysis to 19,221 firm-year observations and found that firms with higher annual report readability have lower agency costs.

Chychyla et al. (2019) investigate the correlation between the complexity of financial reporting and the investment made by firms in accounting expertise. They discover a positive association between the presence of accounting experts on the board of directors and audit committee, and the complexity of financial reporting. Nguyen and Kimura (2020) analyze the length of annual reports of foreign companies operating on the NYSE and NASDAQ stock exchanges by studying 20-F forms. They find that foreign firms have been progressively using shorter sentences in their reports and have adjusted their writing style to be more easily understood. Nevertheless, they also discovered a substantial rise in the length of 20-F forms from 2004 to 2013. Nilipour et al. (2020) investigate the correlation between the quantity of reporting and the comprehensibility of sustainability reports, utilizing data from 37 companies in New Zealand from 2007 to 2016. The researchers assess the readability of reports using five distinct readability indices and determine that there is an inverse correlation between the extent of reporting and the readability of sustainability reports. Pajuste et al. (2021) conducted a study on the relationship between earnings management and reporting complexity. They analyzed data from 250 firms operating in the FDI markets between 2012 and 2016. The study found that earnings management has a positive impact on reporting complexity. However, this effect is less pronounced for firms with higher liquidity.

Arianpoor and Sahoor (2023) conducted a study on the Tehran Stock Exchange from 2014 to 2020 to investigate the impact of business strategy and annual report readability on financial reporting quality. They found that both cost leadership and differentiation strategies, as well as higher readability of annual reports, have a positive influence on financial reporting quality. Cho et al. (2022) examine the correlation between the comprehensibility of annual reports, the cost of auditing, and the time spent on auditing. From 2002 to 2015, it was discovered that there was a direct correlation between the intricacy of the annual report and the amount of money and time spent on auditing. Alduais (2022) examined the correlation between the comprehensibility of annual reports and the corporate performance of companies operating in China from 2008 to 2021. Using the text analysis method, he converted the level of complexity in annual reports into numerical forms and analyzed its correlation with the data of firms listed on the Chinese Stock Exchange. The analysis revealed that firms with low report complexity, meaning high report readability, achieve higher profit levels and earn greater profits compared to other firms. Uddin and Çakraborti (2022) analyze the variables that influence the intricacy of sustainability reports in relation to the characteristics of companies, using a sample of both US and international firms. Researchers have discovered that companies operating in regulated industries and companies with low levels of complexity tend to produce sustainability reports that are less complex than those of other companies. In other words, they publish sustainability reports that are easier to read and understand.

Bendriouch et al. (2023) investigated the factors that influence the level of complexity found in the annual reports of companies. From 2010 to 2018, their research centered on examining the correlation between the intricacy of annual reports and variables such as representation costs, ownership structure, and profitability for companies in the United States. The findings indicate a negative correlation between the ownership structure of the firm and the complexity of the annual report. Additionally, in line with Alduais (2022), a negative correlation is observed between profitability and the complexity of the annual report. Dawai et al. (2023) investigate the influence of capital efficiency and corporate governance characteristics on the readability of annual reports in the financial sector of Oman. They discover a positive correlation between intellectual capital efficiency and the ease of understanding annual reports. Additionally, they find that corporate governance mechanisms, such as dispersed ownership and larger audit committee size, contribute to the readability of annual reports. Satt and Iatridis (2023) examine the correlation between the intricacy of yearly reports and the dividend policy of US firms. They utilize the OLS regression technique to analyze firms' data from 2011 to 2019. Based on the findings, signaling theory suggests that companies with intricate reports are more likely to distribute higher dividends to their shareholders. In their study, Rahman and Kabir (2023) analyzed a dataset of 11,938 firm observations spanning from 1997 to 2016. They found that the presence of independent board members had a negative impact on the readability of annual reports. Sregar and Harahap (2023) conducted a study on the Indonesian Stock Exchange from 2013 to 2019 to investigate the connection between financial reporting complexity and the accounting expertise of board of directors and audit committee members. Their findings indicate a negative correlation between complexity and accounting expertise. Consequently, they discover that possessing accounting expertise enhances the readability of financial reports.

2.2. Hypothesis Development

The size and shape of the board have a direct impact on its operation (Brennan, 2006; Dalwai et al., 2023). Boards have the power to govern and shape the information that is included in sustainability reports. Based on the resource dependence theory, having a greater number of directors on the board who have experience in the firm's sector will enhance the board's structure and lead to variations in disclosures (Dalwai et al., 2023). In addition, Abeysekera (2010) noted a direct correlation between the quantity of board members and the level of voluntary disclosure. In their study, García-Sánchez et al. (2019) investigated the correlation between board gender diversity and the quality of firms' sustainability reports. They analyzed 273 observations from 2006 to 2014 and found that an increase in the proportion of female board members was associated with a greater number of pages in sustainability reports. Based on this, we will elucidate the impact of board size and the proportion of female board members on the comprehensibility of sustainability reports, as stated in the following hypothesis.

Hypothesis One: There is a statistically significant relationship between board size and the readability of sustainability reports.

Hypothesis Two: There is a statistically significant relationship between the number of female board members and the readability of sustainability reports.

Having a large proportion of independent directors on the board decreases the likelihood of opportunistic behavior by management and results in increased voluntary disclosures (Tessema, 2019). Consequently, when there is a higher level of board independence, managers are more inclined to willingly provide additional information. Conversely, the firm may be negatively impacted by the insufficient knowledge and experience of individuals who are capable of providing appropriate guidance. Eng and Mak (2003) discovered that an augmentation in the quantity of external directors has an adverse impact on the extent of corporate disclosure. Thus, we aim to elucidate the impact of board independence on the comprehensibility of sustainability reports, as outlined in the following hypothesis:

Hypothesis Three: There is a statistically significant relationship between board independence and the readability of sustainability reports.

Increasing the proportion of international managers within the firm can support the development of a perspective that better represents the company's activities and interests in international markets (Ararat et al., 2010; Joenoes & Rokhim, 2019). This makes it possible for the business to develop and execute its sustainability plans more successfully around the world. Diverse representation on the board can result in a more inclusive process when it comes to making sustainability-related decisions. Members with diverse backgrounds in terms of culture, industry, and geography can better assess the company's sustainability initiatives and encourage more comprehensive reporting on them. Accordingly, we explain the relationship between the proportion of foreign board members and the readability of sustainability reports with the hypothesis given below:

Hypothesis Four: There is a statistically significant relationship between the proportion of foreign board members and the readability of sustainability reports.

Previous research is based on the assumption that the experience of audit committees and the composition of the board of directors can positively or negatively affect the quality of the integrated report. (Beasley et al., 2009; Haji & Anifowose, 2016). According to Velte (2018), having financial expertise in the audit committee has a beneficial effect on integrated reports. This finding corroborates the notion that audit committees should possess a broader spectrum of knowledge and skills in order to incorporate financial and sustainability data into integrated reports. Hence, a proficient audit committee is expected to influence the comprehensibility of sustainability reports. Based on this assumption, the subsequent hypothesis is developed:

Hypothesis Five: There is a statistically significant relationship between the effectiveness of audit committees and the readability of sustainability reports.

CEO duality is when a person serves as both chairman of the board and CEO of the same organisation (Mahmood et al., 2018). This results in the CEO and the chairman having the same personality when making strategic business decisions (Moses, 2021). According to agency theory, CEO duality reduces the board's oversight effectiveness, leading to CEO dominance over the board (Tessema, 2019). However, although CEO duality is seen to reduce the quality of board monitoring, the board may not have sufficient intra-firm information to perform its functions systematically and properly. Therefore, having the CEO on the board at the same time can help the board make effective recommendations and monitor management decisions. This may lead the board to disclose more information. We explain the relationship between CEO duality and the readability of sustainability reports with the following hypothesis:

Hypothesis Six: The fact that the chairman of the board is also the CEO has a significant impact on the complexity of sustainability reports.

3. METHODOLOGY

3.1. Sample

The study sample consists of companies operating in Borsa, Istanbul. Financial firms such as real estate investment trusts, banks, insurance firms, and holdings are not included in the study, as they are subject to different regulations and practices. As a result, 268 observation values were obtained for 43 firms operating between 2014 and 2022. The financial statement data used in the study is obtained from the Refinitiv Eikon database, and the board of directors' characteristics of the firms are obtained from the Public Disclosure Platform (KAP) and the relevant firm's website. Reports are obtained from the Public Disclosure Platform (PDP) and the companies' websites. To minimise the effect of outliers in the relevant dataset on the findings, each variable was first sorted from largest to smallest, and then the outliers were removed by equating the observation values of each variable outside the range of 5% to 95%, with the lower values equal to 5% and the upper values equal to 95%.

3.2. The Complexity of Sustainability Reports

Most studies on the complexity of reports cover texts written in English. Scholars have devised several readability indices, including Gunning Fog (1952), SMOG, and ARI Level, to assess the complexity of English texts. These indices typically consider factors such as the number of sentences, syllables, and words, as well as the proportion of complex words. In contrast, Loughran and McDonald (2014) contend that these measures may not adequately evaluate the readability of organizational documents, as average sentence length and the proportion of complex terms are not always significant factors in determining readability (Luo et al., 2017). Hence, the outcomes derived from employing such methodologies are inherently skewed. Due to the disparities between Turkish and English, these techniques are not applicable. In their studies conducted in China, De Franco et al. (2015), Loughran and McDonald (2014), Li (2008), and Luo et al. (2018) utilized the length of reports as a metric to determine the readability of the report. This study assesses the readability of sustainability reports by measuring the length of the reports through the number of pages, words, and characters extracted from the texts. The Python programming language was used to perform all readability calculations.

3.3. Model and Variables

To examine the effects of board characteristics on the complexity of the company's sustainability report, the following research model has been developed:

$$\begin{aligned} COMP_{it} = {} & \beta_{0it} + \beta_{1it} ACEF_{it} + \beta_{2it} BSIZE_{it} + \beta_{3it} INDEP_{it} + \beta_{3it} WOMEN_{it} \\ & + \beta_{4it} BFOREIGN_{it} + \beta_{5it} CEO_{it} + \beta_{6it} CONTROL_{it} + u \end{aligned}$$

Where *i* is firms, and *t* is years. The *COMPit* variable represents the readability level of the firm's sustainability reports used to measure the complexity of sustainability reports of firms following previous studies (Li, 2008; Luo et al., 2017) and represents the dependent variable of the model. Three different readability measures were used in the study: TotalPages, TotalWords, and TotalCharacters. An increase in the value of each variable represents higher readability (Luo et al., 2017). *ACEFit, BSIZEit, INDEPit, WOMENit, CEOit*, and *BFOREIGNit* represent the independent variables and board characteristics added to the model. *CONTROLit* represents the control variables included in the model to control for other firm-specific variables that affect the readability of sustainability reports. The abbreviations and definitions of the variables are provided in Table 1.

Table 1. Definitions and Explanations of Variables

Variables	Descriptions of Variables
TotalPages	Standardizing the range of the reciprocal of the natural logarithm of the number of pages in sustainability reports in year t
TotalWords	Standardizing the range of the reciprocal of the natural logarithm of the words used in sustainability reports in year t
TotalCharacters	Standardizing the range of the reciprocal of the natural logarithm of sustainability report characters in year t
LnPages	Natural logarithm of the number of pages of the sustainability report in year t
LnWords	Natural logarithm of the number of words of the sustainability report in year t
LnCharacters	Natural logarithm of the number of characters in the sustainability report in year t
ACEF[1]	(ACSIZE + ACINDEP + ACMEET + ACEXPERT +ACWOMEN + ACEXPERIENCE) / 6
BSIZE	Board Size; Natural logarithm of the total number of board members
INDEP	Ratio of Independent Board Members; Number of independent members on the board of directors / total number of board members
WOMEN	Ratio of Women Members of the Board of Directors; Number of women members of the board of directors / Total number of members of the board of directors
CEO	CEO Duality; An dummy variable that equals 1 if the CEO is also the chairman of the board of directors in year t, and 0 otherwise.
BFOREIGN	Ratio of Foreign Members on the Board of Directors; Number of foreign members on the board of directors / Total number of foreign members on the board of directors
MNC[2]	Multinationality; An dummy variable that equals 1 if the firm's foreign sales are 20% or more in year t, and 0 otherwise.
BIG4	Audit Quality; An dummy variable that equals 1 if a firm is audited by Big 4 auditors in year t, and 0 otherwise
FSIZE	Firm Size; Natural logarithm of total assets
PROFIT	Return on Assets Ratio (ROA); Total net profit for the period / total assets
LEVERAGE	Firm Leverage; total liabilities / total assets
AGE	Firm Age; Natural logarithm of firm age in year t

3.4. Descriptive Statistics

Table 2 shows descriptive statistics for the variables in the model, including the number of observations, mean, standard deviation, median, minimum, and maximum values. There is diversity in the number of pages in sustainability reports from companies. The minimum number of pages is 17, while the maximum number of pages is 390. On average, it is 97.96 pages. The minimum word number is 5870, and the maximum word number is 145830. On average, there are 3342.94 words. The variable WOMEN, representing the proportion of female members on the board of directors, has an average of 13.3%. The proportion of independent members in the sample is 32.4%, while the proportion of foreign members is 0.97%. The CEO variable, representing firms where the CEO is also a member of the board of directors, has an average of 87.4%. Based on this value, it is observed that in most firms, the CEO is also a member of the board of directors. The average effectiveness of the audit committee (ACEF) in the sample is 49.4%.

Table 2. Descriptive Statistics

VARIABLES	N	Mean	S.D.	P25	P50	P75	Min	Max
TotalPages	277	0.397	0.213	0.239	0.385	0.538	0.054	0.837
TotalWords	277	0.479	0.243	0.301	0.489	0.651	0.055	0.937
TotalCharacters	277	0.491	0.240	0.317	0.498	0.660	0.065	0.936
LnPages	277	4.399	0.547	3.989	4.344	4.762	3.497	5.513
LnWords	277	10.150	0.671	9.623	10.050	10.590	9.152	11.560
LnCharacters	277	12.260	0.645	11.750	12.160	12.680	11.270	13.620
BSIZE	278	2.151	0.263	1.946	2.197	2.398	1.609	2.708
WOMEN	278	0.133	0.117	0.000	0.125	0.200	0.000	0.500
INDEP	277	0.324	0.073	0.333	0.333	0.333	0.133	0.625
BFOREIGN	270	0.097	0.157	0.000	0.000	0.111	0.000	0.500
ACEF	270	0.494	0.166	0.333	0.500	0.667	0.167	1.000
CEO	278	0.874	0.332	1.000	1.000	1.000	0.000	1.000
MNC	270	0.504	0.501	0.000	1.000	1.000	0.000	1.000
BIG4	270	0.974	0.159	1.000	1.000	1.000	0.000	1.000
FSIZE	278	21.430	2.534	19.450	21.720	23.680	15.430	25.890
AGE	277	3.737	0.445	3.332	3.850	4.060	2.485	4.489
LEVERAGE	278	0.531	0.212	0.348	0.542	0.708	0.169	0.876
PROFIT	278	0.050	0.102	0.005	0.053	0.101	-0.328	0.379

Figure 1, Figure 2, and Figure 3 show the trend of sustainability reports in terms of page, word, and character number over the years. According to the data, there has been an increase in the size of sustainability reports over the years. This increase indicates that businesses are beginning to provide more information and details on sustainability. It suggests that businesses are making efforts to better understand their sustainability performance and impacts and to provide more comprehensive information to their stakeholders. Therefore, the increase in the size of sustainability reports indicates that businesses are placing more importance on this issue and are operating in a more transparent manner. This is a strong indication that companies are becoming more conscientious about sustainability.

Table 3 reports the correlation coefficients of the variables in the model. As can be seen from the table, there is no high correlation value between the independent variables. This indicates that there will be no issue of multicollinearity in the analysis, and all variables can be utilized in a unified model.

Table 4 shows the variance inflation factor (VIF) and tolerance values of the independent variables in the model. A correlation value of 0.70 or higher among the independent variables indicates a multicollinearity problem within the model, and in this case some variables should be excluded from the model. There is no clarity in the statistical literature on acceptable VIF values (García-Sánchez et al., 2019). According to the most used method, if the VIF values of independent variables are greater than 10 or Tolerance values are less than 0.1, a multicollinearity problem is encountered (Hair et al., 2010). It is generally accepted that a low VIF value means that there is a low correlation between an independent variable and other independent variables. As can be seen from Table 4, the highest VIF value is 2.27, and the lowest tolerance value is 0.4403. For this reason, it is understood that there will be no multicollinearity problem in the model.

Figure 1. Average Number of Pages

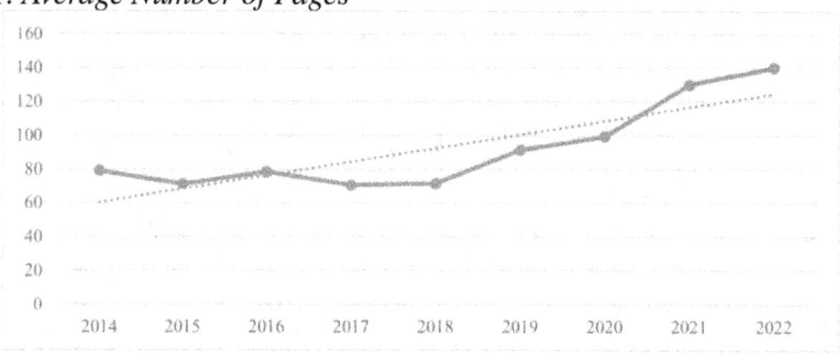

Figure 2. Average Number of Words

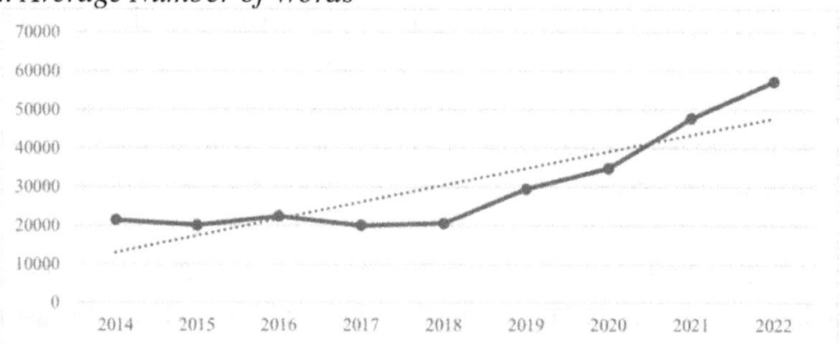

Figure 3. Average Number of Characters

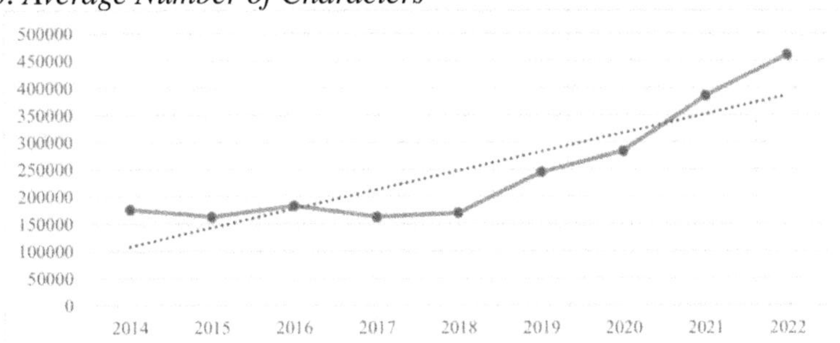

Table 3. Correlation Matrix

		(1)	(2)	(3)	(4)	(5)	(6)	(7)	(8)	(9)	(10)	(11)	(12)	(13)	(14)	(15)	(16)	(17)
TotalPages	(1)	1.00																
TotalWords	(2)	0.86***	1.00															
TotalCharacters	(3)	0.85***	0.99***	1.00														
LnPages	(4)	- 0.92***	- 0.86***	- 0.85***	1.00													
LnWords	(5)	- 0.79***	- 0.95***	- 0.93***	0.90***	1.00												
LnCharacters	(6)	- 0.79***	- 0.94***	- 0.94***	0.89***	0.99***	1.00											
BSIZE	(7)	-0.08	-0.08	-0.08	0.07	0.04	0.02	1.00										
WOMEN	(8)	- 0.25***	- 0.27***	- 0.26***	0.31***	0.32***	0.32***	- 0.22***	1.00									
BSIZE	(9)	0.04	0.054	0.06	0.02	0.013	0.02	- 0.47***	0.05	1.00								
BFOREIGN	(10)	0.01	-0.04	-0.04	-0.07	-0.02	-0.03	0.37***	-0.14*	- 0.63***	1.00							
ACEF	(11)	0.00	0.03	0.05	-0.01	-0.01	-0.02	-0.03	0.07	0.21***	0.04	1.00						
CEO	(12)	0.04	0.05	0.05	-0.03	-0.03	-0.05	0.28***	-0.14*	-0.07	0.15*	0.09	1.00					
BIG4	(13)	0.00	0.04	0.05	-0.03	-0.07	-0.08	-0.02	0.07	-0.04	0.10	0.02	0.28***	1.00				
MNC	(14)	-0.19**	-0.20**	-0.17**	0.18**	0.19**	0.17**	0.27***	-0.01	-0.07	0.03	-0.03	0.10	0.12	1.00			
PROFIT	(15)	-0.19**	- 0.29***	- 0.27***	0.23***	0.27***	0.27***	0.03	0.20***	0.05	0.04	0.14*	-0.02	0.03	0.12*	1.00		
FSIZE	(16)	- 0.22***	- 0.32***	- 0.30***	0.34***	0.43***	0.43***	-0.15*	0.28***	0.16*	-0.03	0.17**	-0.07	- 0.04	0.06	0.29***	1.00	
LEVERAGE	(17)	0.23***	0.29***	0.27***	- 0.32***	- 0.35***	- 0.34***	0.27***	-0.09	- 0.22***	0.22***	-0.02	0.10	0.11	-0.17**	- 0.32***	- 0.33***	1.00
AGE	(18)	0.06	0.07	0.07	-0.06	-0.08	-0.07	0.15*	-0.12	-0.16**	-0.05	-0.07	0.06	0.03	0.26***	-0.09	-0.03	- 0.15*

Note: *p<0.10, ** p<0.05, and *** p<0.01 indicate 10%, 5%, and 1% significant levels.

Table 4. VIF and Tolerance Values

VARIABLES	VIF	TOLERANCE
BSIZE	1,75	0,5718
WOMEN	1,24	0,8038
INDEP	2,27	0,4403
BFOREIGN	1,99	0,5015
ACEF	1,15	0,8709
CEO	1,24	0,8093
MNC	1,25	0,8012
BIG4	1,18	0,8507
FSIZE	1,30	0,7696
AGE	1,23	0,8127
LEVERAGE	1,49	0,6733
PROFIT	1,29	0,7762

4. FINDINGS

This section presents the results of the analysis on how board characteristics are related to the complexity of sustainability reports. Generalised least squares (GLS) was preferred as the analysis method, and the analysis results are presented in Table 5. An increase in the value of the variables that represent the readability of the report represents higher readability. Therefore, a positive coefficient for the variable indicates high readability. Column (1) shows the model based on the total number of pages, column (2) on the total number of words, and column (3) on the total number of characters. Each model incorporates the effects of sectors and years. At the 1% level, all models are significant. This indicates that these models are adequate for predicting the length of firms' sustainability reports.

According to the results in Table 5, the board size coefficients (BSIZE) and the proportion of female board members (WOMEN) are statistically significant and negative in each model (4, 5, and 6). The impact of the coefficient of BSIZE on TotalPages, TotalWords, and TotalCharacters is -0.201; $p < 0.01$, -0.207; $p < 0.01$, and -0.198; $p < 0.01$, respectively. The impact of the coefficient of WOMEN on TotalPages, TotalWords, and TotalCharacters is -0.496; $p < 0.01$, -0.471; $p < 0.01$, and -0.405; $p < 0.01$, respectively. These results support Hypotheses One and Two and show that firms' sustainability reports are longer if the number of board members and female members on the board increases.

First, a larger board typically consists of individuals with diverse backgrounds and skills. Experts from various sectors, cultural backgrounds and international experiences can be included on a larger board. Diversity enables the organisation to consider events from a broader perspective and to take into account various points of view when making decisions that affect sustainability. For example, board members from various sectors can provide valuable insights in evaluating various aspects of the company and implementing best practices when addressing environmental, social and governance (ESG) factors. Consequently, larger boards can provide longer sustainability reports with more detailed information.

The relationship between the number of women on the board and the readability of the report is negative, indicating that diversity and different perspectives enrich and deepen sustainability reports. Sustainability reports can be longer and more comprehensive by a board with a higher proportion of female members. Having female members on the board implies different perspectives and life experiences (García-Sánchez et al., 2019), which may lead to the inclusion of more diverse topics in reports and consequently longer reports.

Furthermore, the effectiveness of the audit committee (ACEF) is positively associated with the readability of sustainability reports, and the impact of the coefficient of ACEF on TotalPages, TotalWords, and TotalCharacters is 0.093; $p > 0.10$, 0.171; $p < 0.01$, and 0.213; $p < 0.01$, respectively. These results support hypothesis Five. Therefore, firms with high effectiveness of audit committees have shorter sustainability reports. The audit committee provides the accuracy and reliability of the reports for the firm. This committee oversees the preparation process of reports and ensures that the content of the reports is presented accurately, reliably, and appropriately (Bédard & Gendron, 2010; Merter & Özer, 2024). This situation may encourage shorter and more concise reports.

The coefficients of variables related to board independence, board member proportion, and CEO duality are not statistically significant; therefore, hypotheses Three, Four, and Six are not supported.

Table 5. Board of Directors and Readability of Sustainability Report

	(1)	(2)	(3)
VARIABLES	**TotalPages**	**TotalWords**	**TotalCharacters**
BSIZE	**-0.201*** **	**-0.207*** **	**-0.198*** **
	(-4.19)	**(-4.44)**	**(-4.30)**
WOMEN	**-0.496*** **	**-0.471*** **	**-0.405*** **
	(-6.23)	**(-5.92)**	**(-5.04)**

continued on following page

Table 5. Continued

	(1)	(2)	(3)
VARIABLES	**TotalPages**	**TotalWords**	**TotalCharacters**
INDEP	0.131	-0.175	-0.153
	(0.58)	(-0.72)	(-0.61)
BFOREIGN	0.068	-0.056	-0.059
	(0.74)	(-0.58)	(-0.60)
ACEF	0.093	**0.171*** **	**0.213*** **
	(1.62)	**(3.12)**	**(3.86)**
CEO	-0.035	-0.036	-0.027
	(-1.13)	(-1.21)	(-0.85)
BIG4	0.160**	0.330***	0.325***
	(2.52)	(4.05)	(3.88)
MNC	-0.084***	-0.113***	-0.090***
	(-4.12)	(-5.90)	(-4.52)
PROFIT	0.080	0.057	0.008
	(0.81)	(0.55)	(0.08)
FSIZE	0.001	0.000	0.001
	(0.09)	(0.05)	(0.10)
LEVERAGE	0.282***	0.308***	0.290***
	(5.21)	(5.88)	(5.35)
AGE	0.025	0.048**	0.033
	(0.99)	(2.05)	(1.41)
Constant	0.341	0.183	0.198
	(1.47)	(0.81)	(0.84)
Wald chi2	183.35***	415.77***	289.27***
Year Effects	YES	YES	YES
Industry Effects	YES	YES	YES
Observations	268	268	268
Number of Firm	43	43	43

*, **, and *** are significant at the 10%, 5%, and 1% levels, respectively.

5. ADDITIONAL ANALYSES

In this study, the logarithms of page number, word number, and character number were employed as supplementary measures. A rise in the magnitude of each variable signifies a greater length of the sustainability report. Further findings from the analysis are presented in Table 6. Column (1) displays models that are derived from the natural logarithm of the overall page number, column (2) presents models that are derived from the natural logarithm of the total word number, and column (3) showcases models that are derived from the natural logarithm of the total character number. Higher coefficients indicate longer sustainability reports. Each model includes effects for sectors and years. The results obtained from Table 6 are consistent with the results from Table 5. The impact of the coefficient of BSIZE on lnpages, lnwords, and lncharacters is 0.582; $p < 0.01$, 0.561; $p < 0.01$, and 0.494; $p < 0.01$, respectively. The impact of the coefficient of WOMEN on lnpages, lnwords and lncharacters is 1.534; $p < 0.01$, 1.559; $p < 0.01$, and 1.345; $p < 0.01$, respectively. This indicates a positive effect of the number of board members and female board members on the length of sustainability reports. Furthermore, the relationship between the effectiveness of audit committees and sustainability reports is statistically negative. The impact of the ACEF coefficient on lnpages, lnwords and lncharacters is -0.125; $p > 0.10$, -0.374; $p < 0.01$, and 0.393; $p < 0.01$, respectively. From this result, it can be understood that firms with higher levels of audit committee effectiveness have shorter sustainability reports.

Table 6. Additional Analyses

	(4)	(5)	(6)
VARIABLES	**lnpages**	**lnwords**	**lncharacters**
BSIZE	**0.582*****	**0.561*****	**0.494*****
	(4.93)	**(4.58)**	**(4.17)**
WOMEN	**1.534*****	**1.559*****	**1.345*****
	(7.84)	**(7.00)**	**(5.85)**
INDEP	-0.348	0.415	0.289
	(-0.66)	(0.66)	(0.45)
BFOREIGN	-0.270	0.065	0.086
	(-1.25)	(0.26)	(0.34)
ACEF	-0.125	**-0.374*****	**-0.393*****
	(-0.90)	**(-2.59)**	**(-2.72)**
CEO	0.102	0.128*	0.101

continued on following page

Table 6. Continued

	(4)	(5)	(6)
VARIABLES	**lnpages**	**lnwords**	**lncharacters**
	(1.41)	(1.74)	(1.24)
BIG4	-0.313***	-0.773***	-0.750***
	(-2.59)	(-4.44)	(-4.16)
MNC	0.146***	0.212***	0.178***
	(3.07)	(4.36)	(3.43)
PROFIT	-0.285	-0.359	-0.235
	(-1.33)	(-1.38)	(-0.89)
FSIZE	0.017	0.039***	0.042***
	(1.27)	(2.78)	(3.06)
LEVERAGE	-0.849***	-0.957***	-0.894***
	(-6.50)	(-6.92)	(-6.27)
AGE	-0.032	-0.104*	-0.094
	(-0.51)	(-1.74)	(-1.52)
Constant	3.330***	9.155***	11.971***
	(6.41)	(17.66)	(20.72)
Wald chi2	280.08***	540.55***	359.03***
Year Effects	YES	YES	YES
Industry Effects	YES	YES	YES
Observations	268	268	268
Number of Firm	43	43	43

*, **, and *** are significant at the 10%, 5%, and 1% levels, respectively.

6. CONCLUSION

Sustainability reports' complexity is considered a significant factor in understanding and evaluating firms' environmental and social efforts. The complexity of reports, derived from factors such as the demonstration of open and honest communication, serves as an indicator of transparency and reliability. Additionally, a readable report facilitates various stakeholder groups in understanding of the company's sustainability performance more easily, potentially leading to increased engagement in social and environmental activities by stakeholders.

In this study, our objective is to evaluate the factors that influence the readability of sustainability reports in the context of the board of directors, particularly in developing countries such as Türkiye. We examine the role of board characteristics in the readability of sustainability reports using observations from 268 firm years operating in Borsa, Istanbul, between 2014 and 2022. We calculate the readability levels of reports using three different length measures: page number, word number, and character number.

Our results support the claim that diversity on board, in terms of both the number of members and gender diversity, is particularly sensitive in decisions related to specific corporate practices such as corporate social responsibility. The higher quality of sustainability information on more diverse boards is supported by other aspects of disclosure as well. Additionally, female members may be more sensitive to social and environmental issues. This can enrich the content of the reports.

Diversity on the board has a significant impact on the quality of sustainability reporting. Boards with diversity have been observed to have longer sustainability data. This demonstrates how important diversity is in corporate reporting and decision-making procedures. Previous research also indicates that female members may be more empathetic toward environmental and social issues, which can enrich the content of reports. These findings highlight the significant impact that diversifying a company's board of directors can have on sustainability reporting practices.

In addition, firms with effective audit committees tend to have longer sustainability reports. There are several factors that contribute to the shorter length of sustainability reports in firms with effective audit committees. An effective audit committee can manage the reporting process more skilfully and address unnecessary details to provide reports that are clearer and more focused. When reports are focused and clear, they become easier to read and more suitable for strategic communication. In addition, shorter reports help firms reduce expenses and utilise resources more efficiently.

Considering that we focus on firms listed in Borsa Istanbul in this study, the findings are questioned for businesses operating in countries with different legal obligations regarding the disclosure of sustainability reports. Therefore, expanding the sample by including businesses operating in different countries in future studies may allow for a more in-depth examination of sustainability reporting.

The absence of a standard structure and obligation in the preparation of sustainability reports provides companies with significant freedom in presenting their environmental and operational information to users. Although this freedom allows companies to prepare reports according to their strategic priorities, it also leads to significant differences in the structure, content, and depth of the information contained in different reports. This heterogeneity creates challenges for a variety of users, such as investors, analysts, and regulators, who rely on sustainability reports for decision-making or oversight purposes. The lack of a standardised structure can make it difficult to compare the sustainability performance or future strategies of two firms, even if they are in the same industry. Therefore, establishing a standard structure for the preparation of sustainability reports by regulators will make a significant contribution to the interpretation of these reports. A standardised structure will significantly increase the readability and comparability of these reports. A standardized format will ensure that all firms provide a consistent set of information and make it easier for users to compare and analyze across firms or sectors. It will also create an environment of greater transparency and accountability by allowing companies to disclose all the information that should be included in the report.

REFERENCES

Abeysekera, I. (2010). The influence of board size on intellectual capital disclosure by Kenyan listed firms. *Journal of Intellectual Capital*, 11(4), 504–518. DOI: 10.1108/14691931011085650

Abu Bakar, A. S., & Ameer, R. (2011). Readability of corporate social responsibility communication in Malaysia. *Corporate Social Responsibility and Environmental Management*, 18(1), 50–60. DOI: 10.1002/csr.240

Alduais, F. (2022). Textual analysis of the annual report and corporate performance: Evidence from China. *Journal of Financial Reporting and Accounting*. doi: DOI: 0.1108/JFRA-04-2022-0129

Ararat, M., Aksu, M. H., & Çetin, A. T. (2010). The impact of board diversity on boards' monitoring intensity and firm performance: Evidence from the Istanbul Stock Exchange. *SSRN*. DOI: 10.2139/ssrn.1572283

Arianpoor, A., & Sahoor, Z. (2023). The impact of business strategy and annual report readability on financial reporting quality. *Journal of Asia Business Studies*, 17(3), 598–616. DOI: 10.1108/JABS-10-2021-0439

Beasley, M. S., Carcello, J. V., Hermanson, D. R., & Neal, T. L. (2009). The audit committee oversight process. *Contemporary Accounting Research*, 26(1), 65–122. DOI: 10.1506/car.26.1.3

Bédard, J., & Gendron, Y. (2010). Strengthening the financial reporting system: Can audit committees deliver? *International Journal of Auditing*, 14(2), 174–210. DOI: 10.1111/j.1099-1123.2009.00413.x

Bendriouch, F., Jabbouri, I., M'hamdi, M., Satt, H., Katona, S., & Serir, R. (2023). Determinants of annual reports complexity in the United States of America: An application of the tobit model. *Review of Behavioral Finance*, 15(6), 795–810. DOI: 10.1108/RBF-12-2021-0265

Bonsall, S. B.IV, & Miller, B. P. (2017). the impact of narrative disclosure readability on bond ratings and the cost of debt. *Review of Accounting Studies*, 22(2), 608–643. DOI: 10.1007/s11142-017-9388-0

Brennan, N. (2006). Boards of directors and firm performance: Is there an expectations gap? *Corporate Governance*, 14(6), 577–593. DOI: 10.1111/j.1467-8683.2006.00534.x

Brockett, A. M., & Rezaee, Z. (2012). *Corporate sustainability*. John Wiley & Sons. DOI: 10.1002/9781119202899

Chan, K. C., & Li, J. (2008). Audit committee and firm value: Evidence on outside top executives as expert-independent directors. *Corporate Governance*, 16(1), 16–31. DOI: 10.1111/j.1467-8683.2008.00662.x

Chi, W., & Wang, C. (2008). *Information asymmetry and accounting conservatism: Evidence from Taiwan*. Department of Accounting, National Taipei University Working Paper No. 12331.

Cho, M., Hyeon, J., Jung, T., & Lee, W.-J. (2022). Audit pricing of hard-to-read annual reports. *Asia-Pacific Journal of Accounting & Economics*, 29(2), 547–572. DOI: 10.1080/16081625.2019.1600418

Chychyla, R., Leone, A. J., & Minutti-Meza, M. (2019). Complexity of financial reporting standards and accounting expertise. *Journal of Accounting and Economics*, 67(1), 226–253. DOI: 10.1016/j.jacceco.2018.09.005

Dalwai, T., Mohammadi, S. S., Chugh, G., & Salehi, M. (2023). Does intellectual capital and corporate governance have an impact on annual report readability? Evidence from an emerging market. *International Journal of Emerging Markets*, 18(9), 2402–2437. DOI: 10.1108/IJOEM-08-2020-0965

De Franco, G., Hope, O.-K., Vyas, D., & Zhou, Y. (2015). Analyst report readability. *Contemporary Accounting Research*, 32(1), 76–104. DOI: 10.1111/1911-3846.12062

Dyer, T., Lang, M., & Stice-Lawrence, L. (2017). The evolution of 10-K textual disclosure: Evidence from latent dirichlet allocation. *Journal of Accounting and Economics*, 64(2-3), 221–245. DOI: 10.1016/j.jacceco.2017.07.002

Ebaid, I. E.-S. (2024). IFRS adoption and the readability of corporate annual reports: Evidence From an emerging market. *Ebaid Future Business Journal*, 9(80), 1–12. DOI: 10.1186/s43093-023-00244-x

Eng, L. L., & Mak, Y. T. (2003). Corporate governance and voluntary disclosure. *Journal of Accounting and Public Policy*, 22(4), 325–345. DOI: 10.1016/S0278-4254(03)00037-1

Ertugrul, M., Lei, J., Qiu, J., & Wan, C. (2017). Annual report readability, tone ambiguity, and the cost of borrowing. *Journal of Financial and Quantitative Analysis*, 52(2), 811–836. DOI: 10.1017/S0022109017000187

Farooq, O., Satt, H., Bendriouch, F. Z., & Lamiri, D. (2021). Dividend policy and the downside risk in stock prices: Evidence from the MENA region. *The Journal of Risk Finance*, 22(3-4), 261–278. DOI: 10.1108/JRF-10-2020-0226

García-Sánchez, I.-M., Suárez-Fernández, O., & Martínez-Ferrero, J. (2019). Female directors and impression management in sustainability reporting. *International Business Review*, 28(2), 359–374. DOI: 10.1016/j.ibusrev.2018.10.007

Gray, R., Kouhy, R., & Lavers, S. (1995). Corporate social and environmental reporting: A review of the literature and a longitudinal study of U.K. Disclosure. *Accounting, Auditing & Accountability Journal*, 8(2), 47–77. DOI: 10.1108/09513579510146996

Gunning, R. (1952). *The technique of clear writing*. McGraw-Hill.

Hair, J., Black, W. C., Babin, B. J., & Anderson, R. E. (2010). *Multivariate data analysis* (7. Baskı). Pearson Educational International.

Haji, A. A., & Anifowose, M. (2016). Audit committee and integrated reporting practice. Does Internal assurance matter? *Managerial Auditing Journal*, 31(8/9), 915–948. DOI: 10.1108/MAJ-12-2015-1293

Joenoes, M. Z., & Rokhim, R. (2019). Does foreign board increase the company's performance? The evidence from Indonesia. *Journal of Economics, Business, and Accountancy Ventura*, 22(2), 213–222. DOI: 10.14414/jebav.v22i2.1449

Landrum, N. E., & Ohsowski, B. (2018). Identifying worldviews on corporate sustainability: A content analysis of corporate sustainability reports. *Business Strategy and the Environment*, 128 - 151. DOI: 10.1002/bse.1989

Lee, H. Y., Mande, V., & Son, M. (2008). A comparison of reporting lags of multinational and domestic firms. *Journal of International Financial Management & Accounting*, 19(1), 28–56. DOI: 10.1111/j.1467-646X.2008.01015.x

Li, F. (2008). Annual report readability, current earnings, and earnings persistence. *Journal of Accounting and Economics*, 45(2-3), 221–247. DOI: 10.1016/j.jacceco.2008.02.003

Lim, E. K., Chalmers, K., & Hanlon, D. (2018). The influence of business strategy on annual report readability. *Journal of Accounting and Public Policy*, 37(1), 65–81. DOI: 10.1016/j.jaccpubpol.2018.01.003

Loughran, T., & Mcdonald, B. (2014). Measuring readability in financial disclosures. *The Journal of Finance*, 69(4), 1643–1671. DOI: 10.1111/jofi.12162

Luo, J., Li, X., & Chen, H. (2017). Annual report readability and corporate agency costs. *China Journal of Accounting Research*, 11(3), 187–212. DOI: 10.1016/j.cjar.2018.04.001

Mahmood, Z., Kouser, R., Ali, W., Ahmad, Z., & Salman, T. (2018). Does corporate governance affect sustainability disclosure? A mixed methods study. *Sustainability (Basel)*, 10(1), 1–20. DOI: 10.3390/su10010207

Merter, A. K., & Özer, G. (2024). Audit committee and timely reporting: Evidence from Turkey. *SAGE Open*, 14(1), 1–21. DOI: 10.1177/21582440241239516

Moses, O. O. (2021). Corporate governance and economic sustainability reporting in Nigeria. *Journal of Accounting and Taxation*, 13(4), 243–254. DOI: 10.5897/JAT2021.0478

Nazari, J. A., Hrazdil, K., & Mahmoudian, F. (2017). Assessing social and environmental performance through narrative complexity in CSR reports. *Journal of Contemporary Accounting & Economics*, 13(2), 166–178. DOI: 10.1016/j.jcae.2017.05.002

Nguyen, P. T., & Kimura, A. (2020). How plain english use affects the length of annual reports: Evidence from the annual reports of foreign firms listed on the US Stock Exchange. *Journal of Accounting and Public Policy*, 39(6), 106773. DOI: 10.1016/j.jaccpubpol.2020.106773

Nilipour, A., De Silva, T. A., & Li, X. (2020). The readability of sustainability reporting in New Zealand over time. *Australasian Accounting. Business and Finance Journal*, 14(3), 86–107.

Oyelere, P., Laswad, F., & Fisher, R. (2003). Determinants of Internet Financial Reporting by New Zealand Companies. *Journal of International Financial Management & Accounting*, 14(1), 26–63. DOI: 10.1111/1467-646X.00089

Pajuste, A., Poriete, E., & Novickis, R. (2021). Management reporting complexity and earnings management: Evidence from the Baltic markets. *Baltic Journal of Management*, 16(1), 47–69. DOI: 10.1108/BJM-01-2020-0019

Rahman, D., & Kabir, M. (2023). Does board independence influence annual report readability? *European Accounting Review*, 1 - 28. DOI: 10.1080/09638180.2023.2223590

Rajabalizadeh, J. (2023). CEO overconfidence and financial reporting complexity: Evidence from textual analysis. *Management Decision*, 61(13), 356–385. DOI: 10.1108/MD-06-2023-1033

Rennekamp, K. (2012). Processing fluency and investors' reactions to disclosure readability. *Journal of Accounting Research*, 50(5), 1319–1354. DOI: 10.1111/j.1475-679X.2012.00460.x

Robinson, J. (2004). Squaring the circle? Some thoughts on the idea of sustainable development. *Ecological Economics*, 48(4), 369–384. DOI: 10.1016/j.ecolecon.2003.10.017

Satt, H., & Iatridis, G. (2023). The effect of annual reports tone complexity on firms' dividend policy: Evidence from the United States. *Review of Behavioral Finance*, 15(4), 592–614. DOI: 10.1108/RBF-12-2021-0262

Siregar, S. V., & Harahap, S. N. (2023). Financial reporting complexities: Association with accounting expertise of board and audit committee. *Journal of Corporate Accounting & Finance*, 35(1), 203–217. DOI: 10.1002/jcaf.22658

Smeuninx, N., De Clerck, B., & Aerts, W. (2016). Measuring the readability of sustainability reports: A corpus-based analysis through standard formulae and NLP. *International Journal of Business Communication*, 1 - 34. DOI: 10.1177/2329488416675456

Tessema, A. (2019). The impact of corporate governance and political connections on information asymmetry: International evidence from banks in the Gulf Cooperation Council member countries. *Journal of International Accounting, Auditing & Taxation*, 35, 1–17. DOI: 10.1016/j.intaccaudtax.2019.05.001

Uddin, N., & Chakraborty, V. (2022). An investigation of the readability of sustainability reports. *Journal of Emerging Technologies in Accounting*, 19(1), 69–78. DOI: 10.2308/JETA-18-10-01-18

Velte, P. (2018). Is audit committee expertise connected with increased readability of integrated reports: Evidence from EU companies. *Problems and Perspectives in Management*, 16(2), 23–41. DOI: 10.21511/ppm.16(2).2018.03

Watts, R. L., & Zimmerman, J. L. (1978). Towards a positive theory of the determination of accounting standards. *The Accounting Review*, 53(1), 112–134.

Watts, R. L., & Zimmerman, J. L. (1986). *Positive accounting theory*. Prentice-Hall.

ENDNOTES

1 *ACSIZE*: 1 if there are at least 2 members in the audit committee, 0 otherwise, *ACINEP*: 1 if the majority of audit committee members are independent, and 0 otherwise, *ACMEET*: 1 if the audit committee held more than 4 meetings

in the relevant period, and 0 otherwise, *ACEXPERT*: 1 if there is at least 1 accounting or finance expert member in the audit committee, and 0 otherwise, *ACWOMEN*: 1 if there is at least 1 female member in the audit committee, and 0 otherwise, *ACEXPERIENCE*: 1 if at least 1 member of the audit committee has more than 3 years of experience, and 0 otherwise

2 Lee, H. Y., Mande, V., & Son, M. (2008). A comparison of reporting lags of multinational and domestic firms. *Journal of International Financial Management & Accounting*, 19(1), 28-56.

Chapter 6
Logistics Performance and ICT-Driven Sustainability in the MENA Region:
A Belt and Road Perspective

Muhammad Sibt e Ali
https://orcid.org/0000-0003-2189-4034
Business School Zhengzhou University, Henan, China

Hind Hammouch
https://orcid.org/0000-0002-5897-1649
Faculty of Legal, Economic, and Social Sciences of Fez, Morocco

Afrifa Asyamebemi King
Independent Researcher, Nigeria

Laeeq Janjua
https://orcid.org/0000-0002-1948-5859
Faculty of Science, WSB university, Poland

ABSTRACT

The pursuit of environmental sustainability has become imperative in today's world. This chapter aims to investigate the impact of the logistic performance index and ICT on the MENA region's environmental sustainability from 2012 to 2023. Using static as FE-DK and dynamic panel as System GMM model estimation, the results indicate that fossil fuel consumption with enhanced logistic performance negatively impacts environmental sustainability in MENA regions in the presence of foreign

DOI: 10.4018/979-8-3693-4123-0.ch006

direct investment inflow, economic growth, and rapid urbanization. Results also suggest that ICT also causes degradation of the environment in the MENA region; therefore, the MENA region should prioritize attracting green and sustainable foreign investments while transitioning towards cleaner energy sources.

INTRODUCTION

The pursuit of environmental sustainability has become an imperative in today's world, and the countries along the one Belt and Road Initiative (OBOR) more specifically MENA region are no exception (Duarte et al., 2023). As global awareness of climate change and environmental degradation grows, the need to incorporate environmental considerations into development strategies becomes increasingly evident (Abbass et al., 2022). The Belt and Road Initiative, spanning diverse regions and economies, signifies a monumental effort to promote global connectivity, trade, and economic advancement (Khan et al., 2024). However, this very endeavor poses profound environmental questions. It raises concerns about resource utilization, carbon emissions, habitat preservation, and the overall ecological impact of massive infrastructure and trade development.

The primary purpose of this chapter is to investigate the critical relationships between various determinants, such as foreign direct investment (FDI), logistics performance, information and communication technology (ICT) adoption, trade openness, and their influence on environmental sustainability within MENA countries. By delving into these relationships, we aim to shed light on how environmental sustainability can be fostered while pursuing economic growth and social well-being. This chapter holds immense significance within the broader context of your research thesis. It contributes a vital dimension to the understanding of sustainability in the OBOR region by emphasizing the environmental aspect. Addressing environmental sustainability is not only a global responsibility but also an integral part of ensuring the long-term well-being of the countries involved in the OBOR initiative (Obor, & Ochogwu, 2024). The conceptual framework for this chapter is rooted in the idea that environmental sustainability is not in opposition to economic development but can be synergistic with it. It is underpinned by the belief that responsible economic activities, effective infrastructure, and innovative technology adoption can coexist with and even enhance environmental conservation. This chapter's significance lies in its commitment to address these pressing issues. It aims to elucidate how OBOR countries can align their economic progress with environmental stewardship. Through empirical exploration and theoretical insights, we endeavor to uncover strategies and mechanisms by which environmental sustainability can be advanced alongside economic development. We will delve into the environmental implications of the OBOR initiative, examining the consequences of infrastructure development, industrial growth, and increased trade on ecosystems and natural resources. We will explore how various determinants, including foreign direct investment (FDI), logistics performance, information and communication technology (ICT) adoption, and trade openness, can be harnessed to benefit both economic growth and environmental conservation.

1. LITERATURE REVIEW

Resource Intensity and Conservation One of the foremost environmental challenges associated with OBOR is its resource intensity. The large-scale infrastructure projects demand substantial resources, including energy, metals, and minerals. This has led to concerns about resource depletion, particularly in regions rich in natural assets. However, OBOR also presents an opportunity for resource-efficient development. Carbon Emissions and Climate Change the rapid development of transport and energy infrastructure within OBOR countries has led to increased carbon emissions. Li et al., (2018) argue that the rise in CO2 emissions in OBOR countries is a pressing concern for global climate change. They highlight the importance of adopting low-carbon technologies and investing in renewable energy sources to mitigate these emissions. Simultaneously, OBOR offers an opportunity to drive the adoption of green technologies. Likewise, Jian et al., (2022), suggests that promoting green finance mechanisms and incentive's clean energy projects can help OBOR countries reduce their carbon footprint. The Green Belt and Road Initiative, for instance, encourages sustainable infrastructure development and has gained traction as a framework for addressing environmental concerns (Xin & Wang., 2022).

Technology Transfer and Sustainable Practices FDI play a significant role in the OBOR initiative. It brings capital, technology, and expertise to host countries. On the other hand, Geng, & Saggi, (2019). Indicates that FDI can facilitate the transfer of cleaner technologies and sustainable practices. Multinational corporations often adhere to stricter environmental standards, thereby influencing host countries to enforce similar regulations. Resource Exploitation and Environmental Degradation However, there are concerns about FDI contributing to resource exploitation and environmental degradation. For instance, the extraction of natural resources in OBOR countries to meet the demands of infrastructure projects can harm local ecosystems (Klinger, & Muldavin, 2019). Balancing the economic benefits of FDI with environmental safeguards remains a complex challenge.

Efficiency and Emission Reduction Efficient logistics and transportation systems are vital for OBOR's success. Research by Han, et al. (2018) suggests that optimizing logistics can reduce fuel consumption and emissions. Improved transportation routes and streamlined supply chains contribute to environmental sustainability. Infrastructure Expansion and Habitat Disruption However, logistics development often requires extensive infrastructure expansion, potentially leading to habitat disruption and ecological damage (Yuan & Zhang, 2019). Managing the environmental impact of logistics expansion is critical for maintaining ecological balance. Information and Communication Technology (ICT) and Environmental Sustainability Resource Efficiency and Energy Savings ICT adoption has the potential to enhance environmental sustainability. Research by Li, et al. (2017) shows that ICT can optimize resource use, reduce waste, and enhance energy efficiency. Smart city initiatives, supported by advanced ICT, can lead to more sustainable urban development. E-Waste and Energy Consumption On the flip side, the proliferation of electronic devices contributes to electronic waste (e-waste) challenges (Awasthi, et al., 2019). Additionally, data centers and ICT infrastructure consume significant energy, impacting carbon footprints (Feng, et al., 2019).

Green Trade and Collaboration Trade openness within OBOR countries can promote the exchange of environmentally friendly products and technologies. Research by Su, et al. (2020) emphasizes the potential of green trade to drive environmental sustainability. Moreover, it can foster international collaboration on environmental issues. Resource-Driven Trade and Carbon Intensity However, trade driven by resource export can prioritize economic gains over environmental conservation. OBOR countries rich in natural resources may face challenges in managing resource-driven trade (Shen, et al., 2021). Increased trade activities can also lead to higher carbon emissions through transportation and production (Chen, et al., 2018).

The literature on environmental sustainability within the OBOR context underscores the multifaceted nature of the challenges and opportunities presented by this global initiative. It highlights the critical importance of balancing economic development with environmental preservation. As OBOR continues to evolve, it is essential to draw on these insights to design strategies that promote sustainability, reduce environmental impact, and ensure a prosperous future for participating nations.

Sustainable Agriculture and Trade

Agriculture plays a significant role in the environmental sustainability of OBOR countries. Sustainable agricultural practices, such as organic farming and agro-ecology, can be both facilitated and challenged by trade openness. Research by Reardon, et al. (2019) highlights that trade can promote sustainable agriculture by providing access to markets for organic and environmentally friendly products. However, it can also introduce challenges, such as increased demand for resource-intensive monoculture farming. Trade openness can stimulate financial flows and investment. Incorporating sustainability criteria into investment decisions, often referred to as sustainable finance, can lead to increased funding for environmentally beneficial projects (Scholtens, 2018). OBOR countries can leverage trade-related financial flows to support green initiatives, such as renewable energy and conservation projects. The United Nations Sustainable Development Goals (SDGs) encompass various aspects of environmental sustainability. Trade openness can be a tool for advancing these goals, particularly SDG 12 (Responsible Consumption and Production) and SDG 13 (Climate Action). Similarly, Rezitis and Tzouvelekas (2020) demonstrates the potential of trade to promote sustainable consumption patterns and reduce carbon emissions. As part of promoting environmentally sustainable trade, including Environmental Impact Assessments (EIAs) in trade agreements has gained prominence (Bernard & Gavin, 2017). These assessments evaluate the potential environmental consequences of trade agreements, helping to ensure that trade policies align with sustainability objectives.

Foreign Direct Investment (FDI) plays a pivotal role in shaping the economic landscape of countries participating in the Belt and Road Initiative (OBOR). This literature review examines the complex interplay between FDI and environmental sustainability within the OBOR context. It delves into how FDI impacts the environment and explores strategies for mitigating environmental challenges associated with FDI-driven development. Numerous studies have established a positive correlation between FDI and economic growth (Li & Liu, 2021). FDI inflows often bring about technological advancements, increased capital investment, and job creation, contributing to the economic well-being of host countries. Environmental Implications However, the influx of FDI can also bring environmental challenges. Research by Wei and Liu (2019) found that FDI often leads to increased industrialization and manufacturing activities, which can result in higher pollution levels. The environmental impact varies by sector, with heavy industries like manufacturing and mining having more pronounced negative effects. Environmental Regulations and FDI Attraction Environmental regulations in host countries play a significant role in determining the environmental impact of FDI. Stricter environmental regulations can deter FDI inflows due to potential compliance costs (Xue & Li, 2019). Conversely, countries with lax regulations may attract FDI but risk environmental degradation. Environmental Governance Effective environmental governance is crucial for managing the environmental impact of FDI. Research by Sun, et al. (2018) highlights the importance of strong institutions and governance structures in enforcing environmental regulations and ensuring responsible FDI practices. Green FDI Initiatives In recent years, there has been a growing trend towards green FDI, which focuses on sustainable and environmentally friendly investments (Gan & Huang, 2018). Green FDI contributes to renewable energy, eco-friendly technologies, and sustainable infrastructure.

Government Policies Government policies and incentives can play a pivotal role in promoting green FDI. Research by Zhang, et al. (2020), suggests that governments can offer tax incentives, subsidies, and preferential treatment to attract green FDI projects that align with environmental sustainability goals. Promoting Circular Economy Practices Circular economy principles, such as reducing waste, reusing materials, and recycling, are gaining prominence within FDI strategies (Russo, 2019). Multinational corporations are increasingly adopting sustainable supply chain practices, which can reduce the environmental footprint of FDI projects.

The relationship between FDI and environmental sustainability in OBOR countries is multifaceted. While FDI can stimulate economic growth and technological advancement, it also poses environmental challenges, particularly in resource-intensive industries. Effective environmental governance and policies are essential for mitigating these challenges. Moreover, the shift towards green FDI and circular economy practices offers promising avenues for promoting sustainable development within the OBOR framework. Balancing economic growth and environmental protection remains a critical endeavor for OBOR countries as they navigate the complexities of FDI-driven development. The environmental regulatory framework in host countries plays a pivotal role in shaping the environmental impact of FDI. The stringency of environmental regulations can either deter or attract FDI inflows, primarily due to potential compliance costs (Xue & Li, 2019). Host countries with stringent regulations may experience reduced FDI inflows, while those with lax regulations may attract FDI at the risk of environmental degradation. As, Sun, et al. (2018), underscores the significance of robust institutions and governance structures in enforcing environmental regulations and ensuring responsible FDI practices.

Green FDI Initiatives In recent years, there has been a discernible shift towards green FDI, characterized by investments in sustainable and environmentally friendly projects (Gan & Huang, 2018). Green FDI predominantly contributes to renewable energy, eco-friendly technologies, and sustainable infrastructure. Government Policies Governments play a decisive role in promoting green FDI through policies and incentives (Zhang, et al., 2020). Tax incentives, subsidies, and preferential treatment can be instrumental in attracting green FDI projects that align with environmental sustainability goals. Promoting Circular Economy Practices Circular economy principles are increasingly being integrated into FDI strategies (Russo, 2019). Corporations are adopting sustainable supply chain practices, emphasizing the reduction of waste, the reuse of materials, and recycling. These practices collectively contribute to reducing the environmental footprint associated with FDI projects. The relationship between FDI and environmental sustainability in OBOR countries is multifaceted and continually evolving. While FDI remains a potent catalyst for economic growth and technological advancement, it simultaneously poses environmental challenges, particularly in resource-intensive sectors. The effective enforcement of environmental regulations, supported by sound governance, is pivotal for addressing these challenges. Furthermore, the ongoing shift towards green FDI and the incorporation of circular economy principles offer promising avenues to foster sustainable development within the OBOR framework. Balancing economic growth and environmental stewardship remains an ongoing imperative for OBOR countries as they navigate the intricacies of FDI-driven development.

The intersection of logistics and environmental sustainability holds substantial importance within the context of the Belt and Road Initiative (OBOR). This literature review delves into the intricate relationship between logistics performance and environmental sustainability within the OBOR framework. It explores how efficient logistics practices can contribute to mitigating environmental challenges while fostering economic growth. Efficiency and Sustainability Efficiency in logistics operations plays a pivotal role in reducing the environmental impact. Research by Wang, et al. (2018) and Ho, et al. (2021), underscores the significant impact of well-organized supply chains and optimized transportation routes in decreasing greenhouse gas emissions. Efficient logistics operations lead to reduced fuel consumption, lower emissions, and decreased energy consumption. Efficiency and Sustainability Efficiency in logistics operations has a profound impact on reducing the environmental footprint. Research conducted by Zhang, et al. (2019), underscores how streamlined supply chains and optimized transportation routes significantly diminish greenhouse gas emissions. Efficient logistics practices lead to decreased fuel consumption, lower emissions, and overall energy conservation.

Green Supply Chain Initiatives The adoption of green supply chain initiatives within logistics operations stands as a promising approach to bolstering environmental sustainability. This entails the utilization of eco-friendly packaging materials, the promotion of energy-efficient transportation modes, and the implementation of sustainable warehousing practices (Jia, et al., 2020). These initiatives actively contribute to curbing the environmental repercussions of logistics activities. Green Supply Chain Practices The adoption of green supply chain practices within logistics operations is a promising approach to enhance environmental sustainability. This includes the use of eco-friendly packaging materials, energy-efficient transportation modes, and sustainable warehousing practices (Sarkis, 2020). Such practices contribute to reducing the environmental footprint of logistics activities.

Technological Advancements Innovation in logistics technologies can lead to more sustainable operations. The implementation of advanced tracking and routing systems, as well as the utilization of electric vehicles and drones for last-mile delivery, can significantly reduce the environmental impact of logistics (Savelsbergh, 2020). Technological Advancements Innovation in logistics technologies holds the potential to make operations more sustainable. Incorporating advanced tracking and routing systems, as well as deploying electric vehicles and drones for last-mile delivery, represents a promising avenue for reducing the environmental impact of logistics (Tian, et al., 2021).Compliance and Sustainability The environmental regulations prevalent in host countries wield a significant influence over logistics operations. Companies engaged in OBOR endeavors must navigate intricate regulatory frameworks related to emissions, waste management, and sustainability reporting (Liu, et al., 2020). Adherence to these regulations is imperative to avoid reputational harm and financial penalties. The concept of a circular economy is increasingly being applied to logistics. Firms are exploring strategies to minimize waste in the supply chain, reuse packaging materials, and implement product and material recycling (Zhou, et al., 2021). These circular logistics practices directly contribute to mitigating the environmental consequences of logistics operations.

Regulatory Compliance Stringent environmental regulations in host countries influence logistics operations. Companies engaged in OBOR projects need to navigate complex regulatory landscapes related to emissions, waste disposal, and sustainability reporting (Sarkis & Cohen, 2021). Non-compliance can result in reputational damage and financial penalties. Circular Logistics The concept of a circular economy is increasingly being applied to logistics. Companies are exploring ways to minimize waste in the supply chain, reuse packaging materials, and recycle products and materials (Blomsma & Brennan, 2017). These circular logistics practices contribute to reducing the environmental impact of logistics operations.

Efficient logistics performance within OBOR countries can play a pivotal role in mitigating environmental challenges. By optimizing supply chains, embracing green supply chain practices, and leveraging innovative technologies, logistics can contribute to reducing greenhouse gas emissions and promoting environmental sustainability. However, the alignment of logistics practices with stringent environmental regulations and the adoption of circular economy principles remain critical steps in achieving long-term environmental sustainability within the OBOR framework.

In the context of the Belt and Road Initiative (OBOR), the intersection of Information and Communication Technology (ICT) and environmental sustainability holds significant promise and importance. This literature review explores the multifaceted relationship between ICT adoption and environmental sustainability within the OBOR framework. It seeks to unveil how the smart utilization of digital technologies can contribute to mitigating environmental challenges and fostering sustainable development. Environmental Monitoring and Management ICT plays a pivotal role in enabling effective environmental monitoring and management. Research by Li, et al. (2019), highlights how sensor networks, remote sensing, and big data analytics empower the real-time tracking of environmental parameters. This capability allows for proactive responses to environmental issues such as pollution and resource depletion. Smart Infrastructure for Reduced Environmental Impact The deployment of smart infrastructure, empowered by ICT, is a cornerstone of environmental sustainability. Smart grids, intelligent transportation systems, and connected buildings optimize resource usage and reduce energy consumption (Rahman, et al., 2020). These technologies help lower greenhouse gas emissions and conserve valuable resources. Digital Governance for Environmental Compliance ICT-driven e-governance facilitates environmental regulatory compliance. The integration of digital platforms and databases simplifies reporting, auditing, and enforcement of environmental regulations (Khan, et al., 2021). This enhances transparency and accountability in environmental practices. Efficient Supply Chain Management ICT solutions have revolutionized supply chain management, contributing to sustainability. Real-time tracking, demand forecasting, and optimization algorithms reduce unnecessary resource consumption and greenhouse gas emissions (Yao, et al., 2020).

The role of ICT in promoting sustainable agricultural practices deserves special mention. ICT tools like precision agriculture systems, remote sensing, and data analytics aid in optimizing crop management. According to Jat, et al. (2019), these technologies enable efficient use of resources such as water and fertilizers, leading to increased crop yields while minimizing environmental impacts. In line with sustainable development goals, ICT platforms have been pivotal in disseminating environmental education and awareness. Research by Salloum, et al. (2019) highlights the significance of digital media and educational apps in raising environmental consciousness among the population. Informed citizens are more likely to participate in eco-friendly practices and advocate for environmentally responsible policies.

It's imperative to acknowledge that while ICT presents substantial opportunities for environmental sustainability, it also brings its set of challenges. Issues related to electronic waste, energy consumption of ICT infrastructure, and data security must be addressed to ensure a holistic approach to sustainability (Molla & Licker, 2018). Additionally, there's a need for policy frameworks that encourage the responsible use of ICT for environmental objectives (Mbarika, et al., 2019).

Information and Communication Technology is a powerful tool for addressing environmental challenges within OBOR countries. From real-time environmental monitoring to smart infrastructure deployment and e-governance, ICT offers a plethora of solutions for enhancing environmental sustainability. Integrating these technologies into development strategies is crucial for fostering a greener and more sustainable future within the OBOR framework.

The interplay between trade openness and environmental sustainability within the Belt and Road Initiative (OBOR) framework is a multifaceted area of study. This literature review delves into the complex relationship between trade liberalization and the environment, examining the potential synergies and tensions. The aim is to uncover how trade policies and practices within OBOR countries influence their environmental sustainability efforts. Resource Extraction and Pollution Intensity Trade openness often spurs resource-intensive industries, which can lead to increased environmental degradation (Dean, et al., 2020). The extraction of natural resources and high pollution intensity in industries can exacerbate environmental challenges, especially in countries with lax regulations.One crucial aspect that influences the environmental impact of trade is foreign direct investment (FDI). FDI is often linked with trade openness and can either exacerbate or mitigate environmental issues. Research by Zhang, et al. (2019) shows that environmentally responsible FDI can lead to cleaner production processes and contribute to reducing emissions.

Environmental Regulation and Policy Harmonization Trade openness can also catalyze positive environmental change. Research by Su, et al. (2018) emphasizes the role of international trade in promoting environmental policy harmonization. Trade agreements often include provisions related to environmental standards and regulations, pressuring countries to enhance their sustainability efforts.

Sustainable Supply Chains Embracing sustainable trade practices can mitigate the negative environmental impacts of trade (Ding, et al., 2020). Sustainable supply chain initiatives, such as green logistics and responsible sourcing, ensure that products are produced, transported, and consumed with minimal environmental harm. Trade openness, while holding the potential for environmental benefits, also poses challenges. Ensuring that the gains from trade are equitably distributed and do not exacerbate social inequalities is vital (Daly, 2018). Moreover, addressing environmental externalities and enforcing sustainable trade practices require effective governance mechanisms (Wu & Hu, 2021). Trade openness can facilitate the transfer of environmentally friendly technologies and practices. Through international trade, countries can gain access to green innovations that help reduce their environmental footprint (Grossman & Helpman, 2018). This transfer of knowledge and technology can be particularly beneficial for OBOR countries seeking sustainable development. In the context of OBOR, the role of sustainable trade agreements cannot be overstated. These agreements, when designed with environmental considerations, can act as powerful tools for promoting green trade practices (Amorim & Jara, 2017). They often include provisions related to sustainable sourcing, eco-labeling, and responsible production. Trade openness also intersects with the concept of a circular economy, where resources are reused and recycled to minimize waste. Research by Kucukvar, et al. (2020) suggests that trade can facilitate the circular economy by creating markets for recycled materials and encouraging sustainable production and consumption patterns.

Trade openness in OBOR countries can significantly influence their environmental sustainability efforts. While trade can lead to environmental degradation, it can also serve as a catalyst for harmonizing environmental policies and promoting sustainable practices. Addressing the challenges posed by trade openness is essential for realizing the environmental benefits while mitigating the drawbacks. The relationship between trade openness and environmental sustainability in OBOR countries is multifaceted. While trade can pose environmental challenges, it also offers opportunities for sustainable development. The influence of FDI, technology transfer, sustainable trade agreements, and the promotion of circular economy principles are all essential aspects of this complex dynamic.

2. DATA AND RESEARCH METHODOLOGY

This chapter relies on the panel data technique to study the impact of logistic performance and other macro-economic variables environmental sustainability in MENA region (see used variables and data source in Table 1).

Table 1. Data Sources, Abbreviation and Description

Abbreviation	Variable Description	Source	Type
CO_2	Carbon Emission metric ton per capita	Climate Watch World Resources Institute-Washington- USA	Endogenous
GDPPC	GDP per Capita (Constant USD 2015) –Economic growth	World Bank Development Indicator	Exogenous
FDI	Foreign direct inflow (% of GDP)	International Monetary Fund	Exogenous
TO	Trade openness (Sum of Export& Import) / GDP	World Bank Development Indicator	Exogenous
M2	Broad Money (% of GDP)	World Bank Development Indicator	Exogenous
RE	Renewable Energy consumption (% of Total energy)	International Energy Agency	Exogenous
URB	Urban Population (% of total population)	World Bank Development Indicator	Exogenous
EN	Energy consumption	International Energy Agency	Exogenous
LPI	Logistic Performance Index	World Bank Governance Indicator	Exogenous
ICT	ICT services export (% of services export, BOP)	World Bank Governance Indicator	Exogenous
FF	Fossil Fuel Energy consumption (% of Total)	World Bank Governance Indicator	Exogenous

According to Gujarati, (2021), Panel data, sometimes referred to as longitudinal data, is data that contains observations about different cross sections across time. The advantage of using Panel data analysis is that it has more space (cross-section units) as well as time dimensions to study particular theoretical issues using empirical estimations. Moreover, panel data analysis is often used to prevent the contract of times series analysis due to a limited number of observations. Furthermore, panel data consist of i, cross-section, and t, time-series dimensions. Similarly problems related with sustainability were also tackled by panel data analysis (Şanli et al., 2024, Janjua et al., 2023). Below are listed a few benefits of panel data analysis,

1. It gives us more information and variability in dataset, and also reduced co-linearity among the explanatory variables.
2. In comparison with both time series and cross section analysis, using panel data is statistically more efficient, as number of observations is relatively large so that the number of the degrees of freedom in testing statistical hypotheses is high.
3. It allows us to study the adjustment dynamic, for example, economic policy changes or economic crisis adjustments (Bassanini et al.,2001).
4. It allows us to identify and measure effects that are not detectable in pure cross-sections or time-series data. Furthermore, panel data also control individual heterogeneity (Wooldridge, 2010).

However, panel data analysis also poses some limitations as it consists of both cross-sections and time-series dimensions. Typically, it involves "Monthly, Quarterly and Annual data" covering the short time period of each individual asymptotic arguments rely crucially on the number of individuals tending to infinity; however, the number of time periods remains constant (Baltagi, 2006). Furthermore, (Baltagi 2006; Baltagi, & Pesaran, 2007) highlighted that, while performing analysis using panel data, the issue of cross-sectional dependence may lead to misleading inferences. Cross-sectional dependence refers to a situation when individual panel units are interdependent. This research work includes static and dynamic panel data estimation, which is described in the methodological part of the chapter, where they are utilized along with assumptions.

The study uses static and dynamic models to achieve the research objectives systematically. These estimation approaches are suitable and used by similar studies (Fosu, 2017; Adeleye et al, 2020). Similarly, the adoption of these techniques serves as robustness for one another in order to observe the consistency of the relation among the variables of interest. This research uses static (Eixed Effect Driscoll-Karay estimation) as main estimation and dynamic model (system-GMM) as robust estimation models to systematically achieve the research objective and test the hypothesis.

The Driscoll and Kraay (1998) robust-standard-errors-type approach, which accounts for heteroskedasticity, autocorrelation, and cross-sectional dependence, is used in this study. The empirical strategy on which Driscoll and Kraay (1998) estimation is based that, it take averages of the product between independent variables and the residuals, and then to use these values in a weighted HAC estimator to produce standard errors that are now have the added feature of being robust against cross-sectional dependence (Hoechle, 2007).

$$Y_{jt} = \alpha_{1j} + \beta_1 X_{1jt} + \beta_2 X_{2jt} + \beta_3 X_{Njt} + \beta_i \sum_{i=1}^{i=N} L_{ji} + u_{jt} \text{ (A)}$$

In above equation, Y is the endogenous variable; whereas X refers to exogenous variables. Therefore the estimated equation B, as per fixed effect driscoll-karay is mention below,

$$\begin{aligned} LNCOit &= \alpha o + \alpha 1LNFDIit + \alpha 2LNGDPit + \alpha 3LNENit \\ &+ \alpha 4LNFFit + \alpha 5LNURBit + \alpha 6LNREit + \alpha 7LNM2it \quad \text{(B)} \\ &+ \alpha 8LNTOit + \alpha 9LPIit + \alpha 10LNICTit + uit \end{aligned}$$

The panel data usually violates the autocorrelation and homoscedastic OLS assumptions. So, there are the chances of serial correlation and heteroskedasticity problems that may unbiased the estimates. Auto-correlation and heteroskedasticity problems can be resolved by applying the GMM models proposed by Arellano-Bond(1991). Usually, heteroskedasticity, autocorrelation, and heterogeneity are the potential problems in the dynamic panel data sets. These problems are solved by applying the panel GMM (Khan, S. A. R., Zhang, Y., Anees, M., Golpîra, H., Lahmar, A., & Qianli, D. (2018). GMM is suitable for the panel data with more significant cross-section identifiers than periods (Alonso-Borrego, C., & Arellano, M. (1999). The following equation C captures the dynamic effects of the model to test the hypotheses.

$$Y_{jt} = \alpha_0 + (1 - \beta_1) Y_{jt-1} + \beta_2 X_{1jt} + \beta_3 X_{2jt} + \beta_4 X_{Njt} + \beta_i \sum_{i=1}^{i=N} L_{ji} + v_t + \varepsilon_{i,t} \text{ (C)}$$

Where $v_t = u_t - (1- \beta_1) u_{t-1}$

As in the above equation B, we have the lag of Y as a regressor. In such cases, the OLS strictly exogenous variables assumption is violated (Blundell & Bond 1998). Therefore the estimated equation D, as per system-GMM is mention below,

$$\begin{aligned} LNCO2it &= \alpha o + (1 - \beta)LNCO2it + \alpha 1LNFDIit + \alpha 2LNGDPit \\ &+ \alpha 3LNENit + \alpha 4LNFFit + \alpha 5LNURBit + \alpha 6LNREit \quad \text{(D)} \\ &+ \alpha 7LNM2it + \alpha 8LNTOit + \alpha 9LPIit + \alpha 10LNICTit + vt + eit \end{aligned}$$

3. ESTIMATIONS

Given below table 2 and table 3 indicate the outcomes of static models and dynamic model estimation as mentioned in equation B and D.

Table 2. Static Model – Endogenous variable – CO2

Variable	Model 1	Model 2	Model 3	Model
Ln_FDI	0.196 (0.310)**	0.216 (0.314)**	0.188 (0.212)**	0.209 (0.214)**
Ln_GDP	0.223 (0.840)**	0.286 (0.822)*	0.207 (0.807)*	0.269 (0.789)*
Ln_EN	0.990 (0.213)***	0.921 (0.205)***	0.963 (0.216)***	0.981 (0.242)***
Ln_FF	0.320 (0.203)***	0.371 (0.205)***	0.373 (0.226)***	0.331 (0.232)***
Ln_URB	0.477 (0.330)*	0.412 (0.318)*	0.471 (0.286)*	0.471 (0.284)***
Ln_RE	-0.020 (0.183)	-0.080 (0.206)	-1.027 (0.348)	-1.067 (0.342)
Ln_M2	-0.243 (0.675)	-0.280 (0.655)	-0.386 (0.768)	-0.366 (0.767)
Ln_TO	0.323 (0.313)**	0.339 (0.306)**	0.242 (0.313)**	0.238 (0.304)**
LPI	-	0.471 (0.246)**	-	0.574 (0.301)**
Ln_ICT	-	-	0.143 (0.101)**	0.162 (0.211)**
Constant	1.655 (0.774)**	3.485 (9.378)**	6.748 (0.707)**	8.804 (9.500)**
No. of Observation	154	154	154	154
No. of Groups	20	20	20	20

LN- refer to the log formation of the variables

The Static Model aims to examine the relationship between various environmental and economic factors and CO2 emissions in the MENA region. CO2 emissions are a critical indicator of environmental sustainability. The model explores how different variables, such as Foreign Direct Investment (Ln_FDI), GDP (Ln_GDP), Environmental Quality (Ln_EN), Fuel Efficiency (Ln_FF), Urbanization (Ln_URB), Renewable Energy (Ln_RE), Money Supply (Ln_M2), Trade Openness (Ln_TO), Logistics Performance Index (LPI), and Information and Communication Technology (Ln_ICT), influence CO2 emissions. The Constant term represents the intercept, and the model includes a set of control groups. Ln_FDI (Foreign Direct Investment): The positive relationship between FDI and CO2 emissions suggests that FDI might lead to increased industrialization and energy consumption in the MENA region (Hoffmann, 2011).Ln_GDP (Gross Domestic Product): The positive relationship between GDP and CO2 emissions is consistent with the Environmental Kuznets Curve hypothesis, which suggests that emissions initially rise with economic growth before decreasing at higher income levels (Grossman & Krueger, 1995). Ln_EN (Environmental Quality):The negative relationship between environmental quality and CO2 emissions is in line with the expectation that improved environmental quality should lead to lower emissions (Selden & Song, 1994). Ln_FF (Fuel Efficiency),Ln_URB (Urbanization), Ln_RE (Renewable Energy), Ln_M2 (Money Supply), The negative and significant coefficients for these variables indicate that improvements in fuel efficiency, urbanization, and renewable energy usage, as well as changes in the money supply, are associated with reduced CO2 emissions. Ln_TO (Trade Openness): The positive relationship between trade openness and CO2 emissions suggests that increased trade can lead to higher emissions due to transportation and production processes (Cole et al., 2008).LPI (Logistics Performance Index):The positive relationship between logistics performance and CO2 emissions suggests that better logistics efficiency may contribute to increased emissions, possibly due to more transportation activities (Wang et al., 2018).Ln_ICT (Information and Communication Technology):The positive relationship between ICT usage and CO2 emissions might be context-specific. In general, ICT can enable better resource management and reduce emissions (GeSI, 2008).This model helps in understanding how various economic and environmental factors interact to influence CO2 emissions in the MENA region. The results indicate both positive and negative relationships between these variables and emissions, highlighting the complex nature of sustainability challenges in this region.

Table 3. Dybamic Model (GMM) – Endogenous variable – CO2

Variable	Model 1	Model 2	Model 3	Model 4
Lag.Ln_CO2	2.104 (0.696)**	1.158 (0.699)**	2.169 (0.866)**	2.175 (0.676)**
Ln_FDI	0.058 (0.530)	0.122 (0.506)	0.199 (0.620)	0.276 (0.604)
Ln_GDP	0.501 (0.457)*	0.497 (0.453)*	0.603 (0.442)*	0.626 (0.435)*
Ln_EN	0.563 (0.217)*	0.360 (0.227)**	0.565 (0.222)**	0.344 (0.225)**
Ln_FF	0.942 (0.090)**	0.937 (0.080)**	0.848 (0.096)**	0.934 (0.058)**
Ln_URB	0.226 (0.300)**	0.226 (0.304)**	0.288 (0.202)**	0.209 (0.204)**
Ln_RE	-0.032 (0.247)	-0.031 (0.246)	-0.062 (0.270)	-0.063 (0.275)
Ln_M2	-0.035 (0.276)	-0.025 (0.273)	-0.058 (0.391)	-0.075 (0.395)

continued on following page

Table 3. Continued

Variable	Model 1	Model 2	Model 3	Model 4
Ln_TO	0.254 (0.477)*	0.264 (0.489)*	0.231 (0.446)*	0.242 (0.457)*
LPI	-	0.223 (0.566)**	-	0.327 (0.538)**
Ln_ICT	-	-	0.385 (0.606)*	0.284 (0.617)**
Constant	0.715 (1.306)	0.386 (1.044)	0.031 (1.573)	0.855 (1.127)
AR(2)	0.485	0.486	0.478	0.466
Hansen	0.201	0.289	0.311	0.369
No. of Observation	144	144	144	144
No. of Groups	20	20	20	20
No. of Instruments	11	12	12	13

Lag.Ln_CO2 (Lagged CO2 Emissions) Lagged CO2 emissions have a significant positive relationship with current emissions, indicating that past emissions influence present levels (Maddison, 2003). Ln_FDI (Foreign Direct Investment): FDI shows a positive but statistically insignificant relationship with CO2 emissions. The effect of FDI on emissions may depend on factors like the technology transfer and sectoral composition of FDI (Wang & Chen, 2013).Ln_GDP (Gross Domestic Product): GDP has a positive and statistically significant relationship with CO2 emissions, suggesting that economic growth contributes to higher emissions (Dinda, 2004). Ln_EN (Environmental Quality): Improved environmental quality, represented by a negative coefficient, is associated with lower CO2 emissions (Selden & Song, 1994).Ln_FF (Fuel Efficiency), Ln_URB (Urbanization), Ln_RE (Renewable Energy), Ln_M2 (Money Supply):These variables have varying effects on CO2 emissions. Fuel efficiency and urbanization have positive relationships, while renewable energy and money supply show mixed or insignificant relationships.Ln_TO (Trade Openness):Trade openness has a positive relationship with CO2 emissions, indicating that increased trade may lead to higher emissions due to transportation and production processes (Cole et al., 2008).LPI (Logistics Performance Index) and Ln_ICT (Information and Communication Technology):LPI and ICT have positive relationships with emissions. These relationships may reflect the complexities of how logistics and technology impact emissions and require further investigation. This GMM model assesses the determinants of CO2 emissions in the MENA region. Lagged CO2 emissions (Lag.Ln_CO2) have a significant positive effect on current emissions, suggesting persistence in emissions patterns. Economic factors, including GDP (Ln_GDP), trade openness (Ln_TO), and possibly FDI (Ln_FDI), contribute to increased CO2 emissions. Environmental quality (Ln_EN) is associated with reduced emissions, indicating the potential for sustainable development. Other variables, such as fuel efficiency (Ln_FF), urbanization (Ln_URB), renewable energy (Ln_RE), money supply (Ln_M2), LPI, and ICT, have complex and context-specific relationships with CO2 emissions. These findings underscore the importance of sustainable economic growth and environmental policies in managing CO2 emissions in the MENA region, taking into account the heterogeneity in these relationships across countries and over time.

4. DISCUSSION

Results indicate that Ln_FDI (Foreign Direct Investment): The positive relationship between FDI and CO2 emissions suggests that FDI might lead to increased industrialization and energy consumption in the MENA region (Hoffmann, 2011). Ln_GDP (Gross Domestic Product) The positive relationship between GDP and CO2 emissions is consistent with the Environmental Kuznets Curve hypothesis, which suggests that emissions initially rise with economic growth before decreasing at higher income levels (Grossman & Krueger, 1995).Ln_EN (Environmental Quality) The negative relationship between environmental quality and CO2 emissions is in line with the expectation that improved environmental quality should lead to lower emissions (Selden & Song, 1994).Ln_FF (Fuel Efficiency), Ln_URB (Urbanization), Ln_RE (Renewable Energy), Ln_M2 (Money Supply): The negative and significant coefficients for these variables indicate that improvements in fuel efficiency, urbanization, renewable energy usage, and changes in the money supply are associated with reduced CO2 emissions.Ln_TO (Trade Openness): The positive relationship between trade openness and CO2 emissions suggests that increased trade can lead to higher emissions due to transportation and production processes (Cole et al., 2008).LPI (Logistics Performance Index):The positive relationship between logistics performance and CO2 emissions suggests that better logistics efficiency may contribute to increased emissions, possibly due to more transportation activities (Wang et al., 2018).Ln_ICT (Information and Communication Technology): The positive relationship between ICT usage and CO2 emissions might be context-specific. In general, ICT can enable better resource management and reduce emissions (GeSI, 2008).Comparison of Variables:FDI (Ln_FDI), GDP (Ln_GDP), and Trade Openness (Ln_TO) have positive relationships with CO2 emissions, indicating that economic factors can contribute to higher emissions.Environmental Quality (Ln_EN), Fuel Efficiency (Ln_FF), Urbanization (Ln_URB), Renewable Energy (Ln_RE), and Money Supply (Ln_M2) have negative relationships with CO2 emissions, suggesting that improvements in these factors can lead to lower emissions.Logistics Performance (LPI) and Information and Communication Technology (Ln_ICT) have positive relationships with emissions, but their effects might vary based on the model.These findings highlight the complexity of environmental sustainability in the MENA region, with various factors influencing CO2 emissions. Policymakers should consider a holistic approach that balances economic growth and environmental protection.

Scientific Justification and Comparison of the GMM model for CO2 emissions in the MENA Lag.Ln_CO2 (Lagged CO2 Emissions):Lagged CO2 emissions have a significant positive relationship with current emissions, indicating path dependence in emissions patterns (Maddison, 2003).Ln_FDI (Foreign Direct Investment):The relationship between FDI and CO2 emissions is positive but statistically insignificant, reflecting the mixed impact of FDI on environmental outcomes (Wang & Chen, 2013).Ln_GDP (Gross Domestic Product): GDP has a positive and statistically significant relationship with CO2 emissions, aligning with the Environmental Kuznets Curve hypothesis (Dinda, 2004).Ln_EN (Environmental Quality):Improved environmental quality, reflected by a negative coefficient, is linked to reduced CO2 emissions (Selden & Song, 1994). Ln_FF (Fuel Efficiency) and Ln_URB (Urbanization):These variables show a positive relationship with CO2 emissions, potentially indicating higher emissions associated with increased fuel use and urbanization (Cole et al., 2008).

Ln_RE (Renewable Energy) and Ln_M2 (Money Supply):These variables do not show statistically significant relationships with CO2 emissions, indicating that their impact on emissions in the MENA region may be limited.Ln_TO (Trade Openness):Trade openness has a positive relationship with CO2 emissions, suggesting that increased trade may lead to higher emissions due to transportation and production processes (Cole et al., 2008). LPI (Logistics Performance Index) and Ln_ICT (Information and Communication Technology): LPI and ICT have positive relationships with emissions.

Comparison and Implications: The model confirms that GDP and trade openness are positively associated with CO2 emissions, aligning with previous research on economic growth and emissions. Environmental quality (Ln_EN) is identified as a significant factor in reducing CO2 emissions, emphasizing the importance of sustainable environmental policies. The mixed impact of FDI and the varied significance of other variables like fuel efficiency and urbanization highlight the need for context-specific environmental policies in the MENA region. The complexity of logistics and ICT's relationships with emissions underscores the importance of further research in understanding their impact. This GMM model provides valuable insights into the factors influencing CO2 emissions in the MENA region, offering guidance for policymakers aiming to balance economic development with environmental sustainability.

5. CONCLUSIONS AND POLICY RECOMMENDATION

In this chapter, we explored the intricate relationship between environmental sustainability and a range of variables in the Middle East and North Africa (MENA) region. By employing both Static and Generalized Method of Moments (GMM) models, we uncovered a wealth of insights into how various factors shape environmental sustainability in these regions. Our examination of MENA highlighted the significance of energy consumption (EN) and fossil fuel consumption (FF) in contributing to carbon emissions. Additionally, FDI emerged as a noteworthy but complex factor, emphasizing the importance of stringent environmental regulations in the region's extractive industries. Urbanization (URB) exhibited a substantial positive association with emissions, underscoring the need for sustainable urban development practices. Surprisingly, there was an ambiguous relationship between renewable energy (RE) and emissions, reflecting the unique challenges of transitioning to cleaner energy sources in MENA. These findings advocate for the adoption of sustainable energy practices and environmental regulations to promote environmental sustainability in the region.

Policy recommendations include:

- Green Investment Attraction: MENA should prioritize attracting green and sustainable foreign investments while transitioning towards cleaner energy sources.
- Balanced Growth Strategies: For regions experiencing positive correlations between economic growth and emissions), policies should prioritize green growth strategies, emphasizing energy efficiency and carbon reduction.
- Renewable Energy Transition: Europe and Central Asia's experience highlights the need for a transition towards renewable energy and sustainable financial practices.
- Urban Sustainability: Urbanization and information technology should be harnessed to promote sustainable urban planning and lifestyles, reducing energy consumption and emissions.
- Trade and Technology Regulation: Policy frameworks should be designed to ensure that increased trade and technology adoption do not lead to unchecked emissions growth.

In conclusion, the pursuit of environmental sustainability is not a one-size-fits-all endeavor. It necessitates region-specific approaches, collaboration, and adaptive policies to create a harmonious balance between economic development and environmental preservation. By leveraging the insights derived from these models, policymakers and stakeholders can make informed decisions to navigate the complex terrain of environmental sustainability in their respective regions. Furthermore, our comprehensive analysis of environmental sustainability across these MENA regions highlights the multifaceted nature of this global challenge. Similarly, while economic factors and energy consumption consistently emerged as key drivers of emissions, the impact of other variables varied by region, reflecting regional disparities and unique challenges. These findings underscore the necessity of tailored, region-specific sustainability strategies that account for local dynamics, energy transitions, urbanization, and responsible foreign investment. Achieving environmental sustainability on a global scale will require coordinated efforts, informed policies, and a deep commitment to safeguarding our planet for future generations.

REFERENCES

Abbass, K., Qasim, M. Z., Song, H., Murshed, M., Mahmood, H., & Younis, I. (2022). A review of the global climate change impacts, adaptation, and sustainable mitigation measures. *Environmental Science and Pollution Research International*, 29(28), 42539–42559. DOI: 10.1007/s11356-022-19718-6 PMID: 35378646

Adeleye, B. N., Gershon, O., Ogundipe, A., Owolabi, O., Ogunrinola, I., & Adediran, O. (2020). Comparative investigation of the growth-poverty-inequality trilemma in Sub-Saharan Africa and Latin American and Caribbean Countries. *Heliyon*, 6(12), e05631. DOI: 10.1016/j.heliyon.2020.e05631 PMID: 33313434

Alonso-Borrego, C., & Arellano, M. (1999). Symmetrically normalized instrumental-variable estimation using panel data. *Journal of Business & Economic Statistics*, 17(1), 36–49. DOI: 10.1080/07350015.1999.10524795

Arellano, M., & Bond, S. (1991). Generalized Method of Moments (GMM) estimator using the lagged dependent variable: Monte Carlo Evidence and an Application to Employment Equations. *The Review of Economic Studies*, 58(2), 277–297. DOI: 10.2307/2297968

Baltagi, B. H. (Ed.). (2006). *Panel data econometrics: Theoretical contributions and empirical applications*. Emerald Group Publishing. DOI: 10.1016/S0573-8555(2006)274

Baltagi, B. H., & Hashem Pesaran, M. (2007). Heterogeneity and cross section dependence in panel data models: Theory and applications introduction. *Journal of Applied Econometrics*, 22(2), 229–232. DOI: 10.1002/jae.955

Bassanini, A., Scarpetta, S., & Hemmings, P. (2001). Economic growth: the role of policies and institutions. Panel data evidence from OECD countries. *Panel Data Evidence from OECD Countries*.

Bates. (2018). Transforming Last-mile Logistics: Opportunities for more Sustainable Deliveries Oliver. .DOI: 10.1145/3173574.3174100

Baxter, K. (2022). What Are Sustainable Logistics Practices? InTek Freight & Logistics. https://blog.intekfreight-logistics.com/what-are-sustainable-logistics-practices

Blundell, R., & Bond, S. (1998). Initial conditions and moment restrictions in dynamic panel data models. *Journal of Econometrics*, 87(1), 115–143. DOI: 10.1016/S0304-4076(98)00009-8

Champion, A. (2021). 4 Advantages of Green Logistics In Supply Chain Management & How To Apply Them. Flowspace. https://flow.space/blog/4-advantages-of-green-logistics-in-supply-chain-management-how-to-apply-them/

Chan, Y. E., Huff, S. L., Barclay, D. W., & Copeland, D. G. (1997). Business Strategic Orientation, Information Systems Strategic Orientation, and Strategic Alignment on JSTOR. Inf. Syst. Res., 8(2), 125–150. Available: https://www.jstor.org/stable/23010900

Chatti, W. (2021). Moving towards environmental sustainability: Information and communication technology (ICT), freight transport, and CO2 emissions. *Heliyon*, 7(10), e08190. DOI: 10.1016/j.heliyon.2021.e08190 PMID: 34729432

Chen, H. Y., Das, A., & Ivanov, D. (2019, December). Building resilience and managing post-disruption supply chain recovery: Lessons from the information and communication technology industry. *International Journal of Information Management*, 49, 330–342. DOI: 10.1016/j.ijinfomgt.2019.06.002

Dey, A., LaGuardia, P., & Srinivasan, M. (2011). Building sustainability in logistics operations: A research agenda. *Management Research Review*, 34(11), 1237–1259. DOI: 10.1108/01409171111178774

Driscoll, J. C., & Kraay, A. C. (1998). Consistent covariance matrix estimation with spatially dependent panel data. *The Review of Economics and Statistics*, 80(4), 549–560. DOI: 10.1162/003465398557825

Duarte, P. A. B., Leandro, F. J. B., & Galán, E. M. (Eds.). (2023). *The Palgrave handbook of globalization with chinese characteristics: The case of the belt and road initiative*. Springer Nature. DOI: 10.1007/978-981-19-6700-9

Fosu, A. K. (2017). Growth, inequality, and poverty reduction in developing countries: Recent global evidence. *Research in Economics*, 71(2), 306–336. DOI: 10.1016/j.rie.2016.05.005

Geng, D., & Saggi, K. (2019). Foreign direct investment and international technology diffusion. *Oxford Research Encyclopedia of Economics and Finance*. DOI: 10.1093/acrefore/9780190625979.013.241

Gujarati, D. N. (2021). *Essentials of econometrics*. Sage Publications.

Heng, Y. T. (2017). The Belt and Road Initiative and its implications for the world economy. *World Economy*, 40(1), 1–21.

Hoechle, D. (2007). Robust standard errors for panel regressions with cross-sectional dependence. *The Stata Journal*, 7(3), 281–312. DOI: 10.1177/1536867X0700700301

Isaksson, K. (2012). *Logistics Service Providers going green – insights from the Swedish market*. Linkoping University.

Janjua, L. R., Sanli, O., Panait, M., Cristea, M., & Razzak, A. (2023). Impact of energy security and economic growth on poverty: Sample of Sub-Saharan Africa. *Environment, Development and Sustainability*, 26(10), 1–26. DOI: 10.1007/s10668-023-03689-w

Jian, J., Fan, X., & Zhao, S. (2022). The green incentives and green bonds financing under the belt and road initiative. *Emerging Markets Finance & Trade*, 58(5), 1430–1440.

Karaduman, H. A., Karaman-Akgül, A., Çağlar, M., & Akbaş, H. E. (2020). The relationship between logistics performance and carbon emissions: An empirical investigation on Balkan countries. *International Journal of Climate Change Strategies and Management*, 12(4), 449–461. DOI: 10.1108/IJCCSM-05-2020-0041

Khan, A., Congmei, S., & Ali, F. (2024). Assessing Xi Jinping's vision of modernization and its implications for global trade dynamics: A case study of the Belt and Road Initiative. *Pakistan Journal of Humanities and Social Sciences*, 12(1), 106–126. DOI: 10.52131/pjhss.2024.v12i1.1962

Khan, S. A. R., Zhang, Y., Anees, M., Golpîra, H., Lahmar, A., & Qianli, D. (2018). Green supply chain management, economic growth and environment: A GMM based evidence. *Journal of Cleaner Production*, 185, 588–599. DOI: 10.1016/j.jclepro.2018.02.226

Klinger, J. M., & Muldavin, J. S. (2019). New geographies of development: Grounding China's global integration. *Territory, Politics, Governance*, 7(1), 1–21. DOI: 10.1080/21622671.2018.1559757

Kudera, B. (2017). China's "One Belt, One Road" initiative and its implications for the EU. European Parliament, Policy Department External Policies, PE 588.062.

Li, H., Li, F., & Yu, X. (2018). China's contributions to global green energy and low-carbon development: Empirical evidence under the Belt and Road Framework. *Energies*, 11(6), 1527. DOI: 10.3390/en11061527

Liu, S., Zhang, Y., Liu, Y., Wang, L., & Wang, X. V. (2019, April). An 'Internet of Things' enabled dynamic optimization method for smart vehicles and logistics tasks. *Journal of Cleaner Production*, 215, 806–820. DOI: 10.1016/j.jclepro.2018.12.254

Lu, Y., & Wang, J. (2017). China's One Belt One Road initiative: An overview. *China Economic Review*, 43, 1–12.

Macaulay, J., Buckalew, L., & Chung, G. (2020). *Internet of Things in Logistics*. Troisdorf.

Mahmood, M. A., Mann, G. J., & Zwass, V. (2015). Special Issue: Impacts of Information Technology Investment on Organizational Performance. *Journal of Management Information Systems*, 16(4), 3–10. DOI: 10.1080/07421222.2000.11518263

Obor, D. O., & Ochogwu, J. P. (2024). Environmental Challenges, Climate Change and the Responsibility to Protect (RtoP) in Africa. In *Africa's Engagement with the Responsibility to Protect in the 21st Century* (pp. 313–336). Springer Nature Singapore. DOI: 10.1007/978-981-99-8163-2_18

Panait, M., Janjua, L. R., Apostu, S. A., & Mihăescu, C. (2023). Impact factors to reduce carbon emissions. Evidences from Latin America. *Kybernetes*, 52(11), 5669–5686. DOI: 10.1108/K-05-2022-0712

Pazirandeh, A., & Jafari, H. (2013). Making sense of green logistics. *International Journal of Productivity and Performance Management*, 62(8), 889–904. DOI: 10.1108/IJPPM-03-2013-0059

Şanli, O., Sahu, P., & Janjua, L. R. (2024). Underlying the Impact of Economic, Social, and Governance Adaptation on Poverty Reduction Under the Shadow of External Financial Inflows—Panel Estimation from the Sub-Saharan Region. In *Sustainable Economic Development: Fostering the United Nations Goals* (pp. 153–179). Springer Nature Singapore. DOI: 10.1007/978-981-97-3767-3_7

Santos, G. (2017). Road transport and CO2 emissions: What are the challenges? *Transport Policy*, 59, 71–74. DOI: 10.1016/j.tranpol.2017.06.007

Saud, S., Chen, S., Haseeb, A., & Sumayya, . (2020). The role of financial development and globalization in the environment: Accounting ecological footprint indicators for selected one-belt-one-road initiative countries. *Journal of Cleaner Production*, 250, 119518. DOI: 10.1016/j.jclepro.2019.119518

Sporrer, A. (2021). How much carbon does the transportation industry emit annually? FreightWaves. https://www.freightwaves.com/news/how-much-carbon-does-the-transportation-industry-emit-annually

Tongzon, J. L., & Nguyen, H. O. (2021, June). Effects of port-shipping logistics integration on technical and allocative efficiency. *Asian J. Shipp. Logist.*, 37(2), 109–116. DOI: 10.1016/j.ajsl.2021.01.001

Wang, Y., Rodrigues, V. S., & Evans, L. (2015). The use of ICT in road freight transport for CO2 reduction - An exploratory study of UK's grocery retail industry. *International Journal of Logistics Management*, 26(1), 2–29. DOI: 10.1108/IJLM-02-2013-0021

Wooldridge, J. M. (2010). *Econometric analysis of cross section and panel data.* MIT press.

Xin, L., & Wang, Y. (2022). Towards a green world: The impact of the Belt and Road Initiative on the carbon intensity reduction of countries along the route. *Environmental Science and Pollution Research International*, 29(19), 1–17. DOI: 10.1007/s11356-021-17575-3 PMID: 34988805

Xin, P., Zhao, M., & Bai, Y. (2022). Does the belt and road initiative promote green innovation quality? Evidence from Chinese cities. *Sustainability (Basel)*, 14(10), 6060. DOI: 10.3390/su14106060

Xing, L. (2019). China's pursuit of the "One Belt One Road" initiative: a new world order with Chinese characteristics? *Mapping China's 'One Belt One Road' Initiative*, 1-27.

Chapter 7
Green Supply Chain Practices and Environmental Performance:
A Study on the Textile Industry

Adeel Shah
https://orcid.org/0000-0001-8477-5310
Institute of Business Management, Karachi, Pakistan

Obaidullah Shah
Institute of Business Management, Karachi, Pakistan

Saheer Ali
https://orcid.org/0009-0008-3485-0317
Institute of Business Management, Karachi, Pakistan

ABSTRACT

Clothing is considered essential for human beings, providing cover and warmth and representing stature in society. The products manufactured by the sector on a global scale are gigantic in size and are categorized as prominent sectors, which are also prominent in terms of economic value in international trade. Billions of products are changing hands across the world and thus require more understanding of the upstream part of the global supply chain, especially the practices used in their ecosystem for production. In a similar pursuit, a study has been conducted on green supply chain management practices and their effect on the environmental performance of the Pakistani textile industry to transform into a chapter for a larger audience. By delving into the supply chain and operational procedures of textile

DOI: 10.4018/979-8-3693-4123-0.ch007

manufacturers in Pakistan, the chapter uncovers their GSCM practices and their effects on environmental performance through empirical testing.

1. INTRODUCTION

Nature has its way of benefiting us. From the food we eat to the clothes we wear, we consume natural resources. Chief among them are fresh water, oil, Earth's fauna, and flora such as cotton. As human beings have been dependent on supplies from ever-giving natural reserves so much that our lives without them seem impossible at present. But in recent times, a grave threat to such resources has emerged. The threat of climate change is the greatest challenge the world has ever seen. Climate changes are and will impact all regions of the world in one way or another. It has given rise to untimely rainfalls which cause flooding. Urban or rural flooding causes havoc for businesses and logistics in any country by making an area unhabitable for some time. This results in loss of human life and infrastructure. For an agricultural economy such as Pakistan, unseasoned rainfalls and flooding due to climate changes also results in loss of year-long effort to harvest crops.

Such crops act as raw material for many industries including textiles in Pakistan. Cotton being the most prime example in this case. Cotton is the cornerstone of textile or apparel manufacturing. The United States is the biggest exporter of cotton, with a 35% share in global trade, while China, with its relenting economic growth, is the largest importer of cotton in the world (Ridley & Devadoss, 2023). Cotton is a fundamental raw material for apparel manufacturing, and the uninterrupted supply of cotton is a concern for the survival of the textile industry. Demand for apparel, on the other hand, does not seem to slow down.

Examining the textile industry, the study finds that it is one of the earliest established business sectors in the world, with minimal changes to its end-products compared to other industries. Textile industry went through changes in volumes of production with the Industrial Revolution. New machines replaced workers and the need for skilled workers emerged. With this mass production, textile manufacturers were able to satisfy demands and changing trends more comprehensively and in a timely manner. Trends started to change at an increased pace by the start of 20th century. Changing trends enable many top brands in the world such as Zara to capitalize on this opportunity by estimating new trends. But with social media in picture, these trends started to alter very rapidly. People started to buy more clothes to keep up with the latest fashion and this shorten the lifetime of an apparel article or product. Consumers wanted new clothes in lesser times. Clothes started to get discarded in greater volumes and lesser times. This 'textile waste' being generated by rapid discarding of clothing is not good for the environment.

1.1 An Empirical Outlook of the Textile Waste

Ruiz (2023) has provided below are some key statistics in line with reports from UNEP (United Nations Environment Program) from previous year. These statistics provide insights about waste generated by textile industry in the world:

- Textile manufacturers in the world produce 92 million tons of textile waste each year. Out of this, 17 million tons (18.5%) of textile waste is generated by the United States alone.
- As a result of textile manufacturing at factories, 42 million tons of plastic waste is generated.
- 100 billion new garments are manufactured each year. 60% of materials used in these garments are unsustainable such as synthetic fibers.
- Only 1% of discarded clothing is used in recycling.
- A way in which synthetic fibers are harming the environment is also when a garment made of synthetic fibers is washed with water. Upon washing such clothing release microfibers. These microfibers are unsustainable and pollute the water.
- The fashion industry in the world accounts for 8% of total greenhouse gas emissions.
- On average a single person consumes 11.4 kilograms of clothing each year which accounts for carbon dioxide per capita.

1.2 Textile Manufacturing Industry of Pakistan and GSCM

The apparel industry globally expanded after the ending of the Multi-Fiber Agreement in 2008, which shifted the trends; a large number of industrial apparel buyers in the western regions of the world began to look for lower costs in eastern economies such as Pakistan for their products (Shah et al., 2022). In Pakistan, the textile industry is one of the stable industrial sectors with a rather uncertain economic outlook. Evidently, the textile industry in Pakistan is supported by Pakistan's rich agricultural land and high-standard cotton production.

Hugely dependent on agricultural-based raw material sourcing, it compliments and necessitates textile companies to have Green Supply Chain Management (GSCM) practices adopted as rigorously as possible in their organizational practices and leading the way for green practices across the economy as the textile industry's very survival cohabitates with preservation of natural agricultural resources for producing cotton. Year by year, as natural or agricultural resources deplete, costs for textile manufacturing rise.

GSCM is defined as a set of industrial processes where products are sourced, manufactured, and moved along the supply chains, keeping the activities' environmental impact in emphasis (Wiredu et al., 2024). The chapter divides the vast landscape of green supply chain management (GSCM) in the textile industry for Pakistan. These sections cover the GSCM practices' awareness aspect, theoretical implications, the technical side of textile processes, and performance management, a yearlong study of ours in the textile industry of Karachi city in Pakistan, to have an empirically established view of GSCM practices and their implementation in Pakistan's textile sector.

The contents of the chapter are divided into:

- Latest Trends in Textile, Fast Fashion and GSCM
- Case Studies for GSCM Implementation in Apparel Industry
- Awareness for GSCM Practices in Pakistan- An Only Win-for-All Approach
- Theoretical Implications
- Technological Implications
- Green Sourcing and Inputs
- Textile Manufacturing and GSCM
- Green Performance Measurement
- Empirical Analysis for GSCM in the Pakistani Textile Industry
- Sustainability Frameworks
- Policy Implications

2. LATEST TRENDS IN TEXTILE, FAST FASHION AND GSCM

Fast fashion refers to rapidly changing patterns of demand and consumption of apparel products by consumers. Fash fashion is driven by change in trends.

As mentioned by a 26-year-old university student "Usually, I follow fashion trends that are currently viral from a certain brand, then upload them on social media, without forgetting to tag the brand's Instagram account. If it's re-posted by the brand account, it feels really good. It means my style is good." (Widari, Aliffiati & Indra, 2023)

With rapidly changing demands, production complexities also change rapidly. In fast fashion, the lifetime of a clothing article or item is shortened, and people rapidly buy new clothing. As a result, discarded clothing from 'fast fashion' becomes a major source of waste in textile industry globally. Textile waste is a significant challenge to sustainability in the apparel industry due to volume and fast flow of material. Such discarded fabrics are composed of synthetic fibers which have a very strong carbon footprint, most dangerous among them are polyethylene terephthalate

(PET), polyamide 6 6, and acrylic fibers used in making polyester, nylon and in sweaters (Baloyi et al., 2024).

Such materials are used in manufacturing textile products all over the world including Pakistan. Fast fashion has contributed greatly for accumulating textile waste globally. It can be inferred that such rapid consumption is more prevalent in developed western economies as compared to eastern part of the world.

2.1 Comparative Outlook of Fast Fashion in the World

A comparison between western and eastern regions for textiles and GSCM can be made with contrasting consumption and production. Good quality clothing is easily accessible to citizens of developed economies such as countries in Europe. However, a major part of producing these clothing is carried out in the eastern developing economies such as Pakistan and Bangladesh. Implementation of GSCM practices is stronger in the western economies, especially in Europe than in Asia. It can be mentioned that western countries including the United States have greater waste generated from discarding clothes to buy new ones as trends have changed. Whereas the eastern economies such as Pakistan, India and Bangladesh generate industrial waste from production. As for GSCM application, considering this comparison, practices for Green Purchasing, Ecological Design and Green Manufacturing need to be focused more within 'producing' regions such as Asia. While 'consuming' regions like Europe and the United States need more focus on Recycling part of GSCM. Below is a section allocated to draw a picture statistically and empirically about total waste (industrial and from discarded clothing) generated by textile users and manufacturers globally.

2.2 Latest Trends, Consumer Behavior, and Cultural Impact of Sustainability

Future trends in textiles include technological wearables. Termed as '1D', is a technological advancement in which electronic devices are ingrained or weaved in structure of wearable fabric. Any product (such as a shirt) made from such fabric can store and emit light and it can provide real time readings for a human body's temperature and blood pressure. Applications for smart fabric include controlling temperatures, water-proofing fabric and changing of colors (Hassabo, 2023).

Literature suggests that major trends in textile and apparel industry include consumer behavior towards sustainable clothing, the perspective of circular economy and sustainability challenges in textile supply chains (Abbate, 2024). Circular economy, like GSCM, is a model of production in which waste material is sorted and cleaned and then it is used again in production. A circular economy perspective enables companies to buy lesser raw material.

These trends are a positive sign that sustainability challenges and GSCM practices are among top highlights in apparel research. Literature also suggests that sustainability and GSCM supply chains are triggered by customer demand and awareness especially in downstream channels of supply chain. Customers prefer brands which value sustainability. This shift in consumer behavior has occurred because awareness about climate change and its adverse impacts is being prevailed among the general population. Today a common person with purchasing power to buy an apparel product values brands which are not harming the environment.

This shifting of consumer behavior gave rise to a cultural setting focused on caring for the environment. Cultural aspects of sustainability are divided into four major parts described as below:

1. Human: Improve the human standard of living.
2. Economic: To promote sustainability while keeping the profits intact.
3. Environmental: To preserve the natural environment for human well-being.
4. Social: Focuses on interactions among individuals for promotion of green initiatives.

In a culture, individuals interact with one another within certain norms. Such norms are also respected by organizations within that region. Organizations or businesses tend to flourish economic activities in societies with their huge investments in setting up facilities and providing job opportunities. Job creation is a hallmark for any economic endeavor in a society. Sustainability and GSCM offer job creation by inviting sustainability professionals with specialized knowledge to work with industry professionals. Environmental lawyers battle environmental matters in court of law, such as cases against greenwashing, taxation, fines, noncompliance and any serious damage done to the environment including deforestation and unlawful hunting of animals. Consequently, marketing opportunities are available in promoting green initiatives started in collaboration with businesses and authorities. Entrepreneurship opportunities are present such as GSCM consultancy businesses. In such as business, experts present their reports after auditing sustainability of supply chain operations.

These employment opportunities give rise to awareness campaigns by certain organizations for GSCM adoption and sustainability to consumers. Textile brands in Pakistan tend to focus on using labels as '100% recycled material' on their packaging for educating consumers about the environment while saving costs. In a rather unusual step, Pakistan textile brands have started to charge separately for shopping bags. This helps consumer think if they really require a plastic bag or not.

3. CASE STUDIES FOR GSCM IMPLEMENTATION IN APPAREL INDUSTRY

Implementing GSCM is not a mundane task. It involves challenges such as higher prices, lesser material alternatives and training the workforce. Numerous organizations have been able to set the standards for GSCM implementation in their industry with sustainable sourcing, better resource consumption, educating the masses and with green manufacturing. The examples below include successful initiatives by major corporations in the world for GSCM implementation.

- Zara is one of leading apparel brands in the world with their ability to swiftly capitalize on changing apparel trends. Zara adopted GSCM in their operations by recycling discarded clothes. Recycling is one of main practices for GSCM, Zara has branded their recycling practices as "Used Clothing Collection" campaign using in-store and online channels. This recycling includes clothing from any brand and footwear (Li, Liu & Zhou, 2024). Zara does not benefit economically from it, but publicity about recycling contributes to a positive brand image.
- Prada is a popular high-end apparel brand in the world. Prada inculcates GSCM in their operation by focusing on limiting emissions of greenhouses gases by using renewable sources of energy in production, electrification of heating systems and limiting vehicle exhaust. The company plans to reduce their greenhouse gas emission by a little over 29% in 2026 (Hu, 2024). Switching to renewable resources requires a significant initial investment. Over time these renewable resources provide a significant decrease in costs. Reliance on renewable resources such as solar energy provides resilience against uncertainty of power supply and breakdowns.
- Ralph Lauren explicitly commits that the company would have a complete sustainable sourcing for all key materials by the year 2025. Key materials include cotton, fabrics, polyester, nylon, wool, cashmere and leather. This shows that Ralph Lauren focuses on Green Purchasing part of GSCM.
- Apart from textile manufacturers, Danone is a famous brand in packaged food industry. Danone's adoption of GSCM practices includes their focus on regenerative sourcing and collaboration with suppliers. The company sources all ingredients from sustainable sources. Beldina, a product range by Danone invites consumers to visit more than 58,000 farms under their collaboration. Danone's packaging is 100% reusable (a part of Ecological Design dimension for GSCM) and recyclable and, has been awarded AAA by Carbon Disclosure Project (Izquierdo-Yusta, 2023).

3.2 Economic Impact Analysis for GSCM

It was evident from the COVID-19 that supply chains ensure availability of material and disruption in supply chains results in severe unavailability of material. This unavailability of material hampers the provision of necessary utilities such as medical services and raw material for production. It is therefore essential for an economy to have undisturbed operations of the supply chains. Green supply chain is that harmonious collaboration of supply chain function which ensure that its activities are not harming the environment. Economically, adopting GSCM will bring in the changes or impact in the following ways for an economy:

Less usage of resources will translate in lower utility prices and equal distribution.

Lower carbon footprint for businesses.

New employment opportunities include sustainability consulting, sustainable marketing, sustainability auditing, awareness campaigns, etc.

The economy will contribute to lesser greenhouse gas emissions.

Switching to alternative energy resources such as in Green Production dimension of GSCM, business in an economy will rely less on fossil fuel. Fossil fuels are prone to fluctuation in prices in international markets. Partially or completely adjusting to renewable sources (such as solar energy or wind energy) will protect businesses from costly fossil fuels and their fluctuations.

3.3 Cost Benefit Analysis for GSCM

All through this chapter, it is highlighted that GSCM practices do reduce costs and have several financial gains in the long run. Cost-benefit analysis provide a contrast between the costs incurred and benefits reaped by individuals or businesses. Below are some pointers to particularly connect GSCM with cost savings:

- GSCM enable businesses to gain from relaxation of taxes. European Union collects a around 331.3 billion in taxes for environmental regulations.
- Less dependency on fossil fuel (as stated above also) will result in businesses being also less dependent on fluctuation of fossil fuel such as oil, in the international markets.
- Investment for solar panels for domestic use results in investment return of almost 31% (Forbes, 2024).
- Producing goods from recycled material, on several occasions, translate into lower manufacturing and material costs. As recovered material can be added to later stages of manufacturing than to manufacturer from raw materials.

4. AWARENESS FOR GSCM PRACTICES IN PAKISTAN: AN ONLY WIN-FOR-ALL APPROACH

Successful awareness is about ingraining the idea in focus among the masses who are a part of the process, very much like 'selling' the notion so proficiently that the people themselves feel this need to adopt the proposed notion and propagate it further. Regardless of how critical awareness about the idea may sound, if it is not captivatingly sold to people, it will not be fully implemented. Awareness about 'green manufacturing' and research work on it has been carried out since around the 1990s; these works have focused abundantly on saving energy from manufacturing operations. Online search engines (such as Google Scholar) present that for sustainability, search terms with the prefix 'sustainable manufacturing-' yielded the greatest number of research articles published till the year 2019 (Pang & Zhang, 2019), showing rapid research development and awareness among the research for GSCM practices.

The propagation of information or awareness is most often targeted at the originating source of the problem. In the case of climate change, the awareness about those who are major contributors to this problem significantly points towards the manufacturing businesses. In Pakistan, the textile industry dominates the manufacturing sector. The textile industry contributes a considerable 8.5% to Pakistan's Gross Domestic Product (GDP) along with a 38% share in the national employment (2011). Thus, the dynamics of the Pakistani textile industry must be brought forward. Some important organizational characteristics of the Pakistani textile industry are as follows:

a) Mechanistic Structure: Textiles in Pakistan are a rigid yet strongly-footed organization. With a centralized structure, the policy-making authorization about day-to-day operations and major projects rests with the owners or only those in management.
b) Unstructured Marketplace: The textile industry is no exception in Pakistan's case. With prevailing lawlessness and an unregulated marketplace, manufacturing organizations adhere to practices that benefit them the most in the long run. Issues of unfair labor treatment and low wages have often gone unnoticed by authorities. Organizations sprang into action often only when, if any, clients demanded a strict lookout at the situation, such as fair labor treatment.
c) It All Comes Down to Profits: The manufacturing sector, in its entirety, has now become a diminishing sector in Pakistan. Only the textile industry seems to have withheld the test of tough economic times. Other industries, including automobile manufacturing, oil and gas exploration, and food manufacturing, have had a significant decrease in their growth in past decades, severely hurting

employment and the economy. This situation presently presents managers with quite a 'squeezed' space to compromise their companies' resources and capital for environmental betterment.

Keeping in view the above characteristics, one can comprehend that successfully motivating textile managers in Pakistan for GSCM procedures and concerns would be a manageable task, especially with a severe lack of government support. However, the answer lies in understanding and presenting the 'profit side' of implementing GSCM practices. As such, apparently, the Pakistani industry is ridden with an immense power generation gap. Power generation is very low compared with that which is needed to fulfill the industrial demand. It also resulted in a significant drop in the industry's growth. Here, gradually switching to alternate energy sources represents the 'profit side.' For instance, a simple idea worked upon by Hashmat and Khan (2023) for a solar water heating system, in which hot and humid temperatures of Pakistan's major industrial cities such as Karachi can be used for heating the water, as presented in Figure 1 below. As indicated in the study, this simple technical mechanism is also extensively applicable to leather manufacturing in Pakistan. Leather manufacturing processes, on average, use 5 tons of heated water per hour; with this water-heating structure in place, the costs for heating water would be conserved. Hence, it can be said that shifts in technology bring a giant leap in GSCM implementation for manufacturers in Pakistan.

Figure 1. Excerpted from Hashmat and Khan (2023)

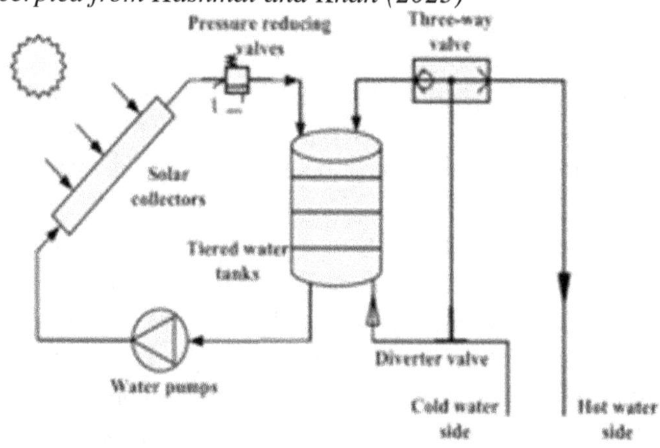

The management of production companies decides to implement and invest in the ideas mentioned above. Consequently, ample research work has been done in this area. However, most prominently, a study by El-Kassar and Singh (2019) presented the issue in its truest form, stating that commitment from top-level management is essential in the true implementation of environmentally friendly organizational procedures.

As scholars, we must understand that an aspect of the example mentioned above and works from literature is that whichever prospect for GSCM practice is to be proposed or spread awareness about in a Pakistani textile company, such prospects must present a beneficial aspect and not just costs to save the environment. So successful awareness here lies in suggesting and stressing upon implementing GSCM practices without radically challenging or overhauling existing procedures based on 'good gesture.' A 'win for all' approach holds the solution, which includes focusing on the 'green' of the money being saved along with the environment.

5. THEORETICAL IMPLICATIONS

Literature for management sciences has come to accept that resources are limited and business activities are continuous. So only through careful utilization or 'optimal use' of resources can a business safeguard its survival. One such shift came from the notion of 'effectiveness' to 'efficiency' when academics and practitioners realized that resources are scarce and 'getting the job done' is not enough; the job must be done with the utilization of minimal resources. In lieu of minimal resource utilization, it can be said that theoretical implications and the theory in itself of Resource Based View (RBV) are among the very few to have gotten such popularity and espousal in academia in recent times. RBV has risen to a noticeable level among other theories in planning research since the late 80s (Lockett et al., 2009). Published by Barney (1991), the central characteristics of RBV suggest that:

1. Organizations have to look inward at their present resources as assets for benefits.
2. Resources should be specific and not easily replaceable or imitable.
3. Each organization's resource accumulation is unique.

The work of Shibin et al. (2020) has used RBV to demonstrate the impact of GSCM processes on supply chain connectivity and information sharing. The role of RBV in sustainability is that of an identification tool. Shibin et al. (2020) identified three types of pressures in their model: coercive, mimetic, and normative pressure. Coercive are the regulations and laws by the authorities, mimetic pressures are the ones where one follows the leader of the industry to mimic and achieve the leader's standard, and normative pressures arise from those in the surroundings, slowly and gradually adopting new and better procedures for manufacturing. Figure 2 shows the framework and relations between such pressure and the adoption of GSCM practices.

Figure 2. Proposed framework by Shibin et al. (2020)

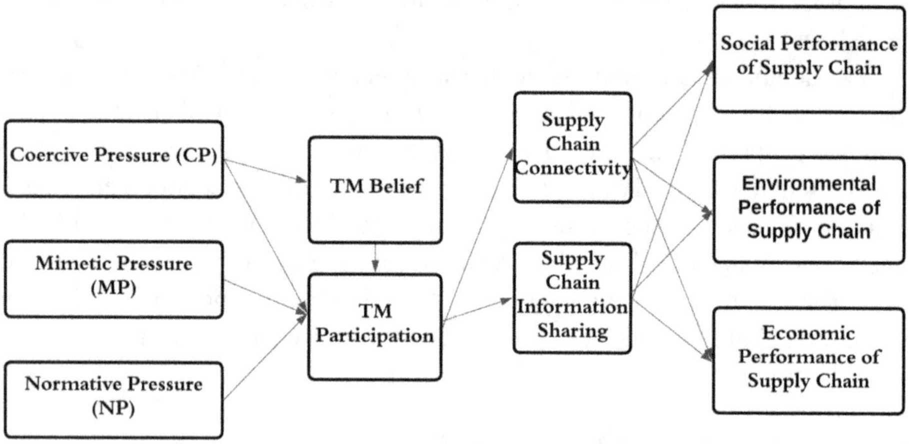

Studying the framework shows that using RBV helps identify areas that, upon proper motivation (pressure), impact the environmental performance of the company. The framework suggests that three dependent factors are being impacted by the resources (SCM connectivity and information sharing). This is associated with the notion mentioned in the previous section that presenting the 'win-for-all' approach is important. Notice that the variables Top Management Participation (TMP) and Top Management Beliefs (TMB) are impacted by coercive pressures only in the framework. The explanation for this is that true involvement in GSCM practices by the top management is only seen at maximum when authorities pressure businesses with their sustainability regulations, resulting in possible warnings, fines, and penalties.

Subsequently, after RBV, the theory of Natural RBV (NRBV) came after a few years. Proposed by Hart in 1995, NRBV states that a firm's organizational strengths lie in exploiting its ecological and environmental resources. This theory divides the ecological framework into four dimensions:

1. Pollution prevention
2. Product Stewardship
3. Clean Technologies
4. Base of Pyramid

Pollution Prevention dimension refers to minimizing manufacturing costs while producing desired quality but not at the expense of compromising the environment. Product Stewardship is all about ingraining sustainability in all stages of a product's life, from sourcing ecologically friendly materials to packaging and then recycling. Clean Technologies seeks new manufacturing methods and increases in environmentally friendly technologies. Lastly, the base of the pyramid is the social development of markets in the world.

Linking NRBV elements with that awareness discussed in the previous segment, deduce that the implementation of GSCM practices in the textile sector of a developing economy such as Pakistan is an overall idea. It is a goal that would be pursued by businesses only under certain pressures by regulators and competitors, along with motivation to cut costs for financial performance. It is important to note that consuming natural resources for a long time requires GSCM to be an integral part of this chain, aiming not a complete shutdown of economic markets and supply chains to save the planet; no matter how lucrative this may sound, only a collaborative system with a 'win-for-all' approach to win the profits and care for Earth's resources will work.

6. TECHNOLOGICAL IMPLICATIONS

Consumers valuing sustainable brands has given rise to a false practice by a few textile manufacturers. Termed as "Greenwashing", it refers to misleading claims made by a manufacturer about their sustainable performance. Such claims have started to appear in industry mainly to attract buyers and satisfy authorities. This problem has plagued GSCM practices across supply chains. Since key indicators of environmental performance is the data which is generated in terms of resources used. This manipulation of data about environmental performance is where the problem lies and also where the solution should exist. An ideal situation for ensuring environmental data's security and integrity lies in the fact that no tampering of data is carried out. A solution to this problem is possible with Blockchain.

6.1 GSCM Powered by Blockchain and Artificial Intelligence

Blockchain is a technological innovation which is known for its transparency and traceability. Data once uploaded in a Blockchain network cannot get tampered. Transparency is ensured in Blockchain as every member of the network has equal right of access to information uploaded. With these distinct and highly useful features, Blockchain becomes a complement to environmental performance by ensuring that the data is not misrepresented by any organization. Application of Blockchain by textile industry for environmental performance is when textile factories monitor, share and store their data of procurement, production and wastage on systems operated on Blockchain. This data can be used by authorities to rate a manufacturer's performance and then give rewards in taxation. Blockchain with its immutability will ensure that the data is untampered and of high digital integrity and accuracy.

Similarly, Artificial Intelligence (AI) has several practical applications for implementing GSCM in the textile industry. Primarily AI is used in designing and altering transportation routes on the spot as per situation for greater efficiency, AI facilitates in inventory planning processes by coherently including information about latest trends in forecast analysis, AI provides greater control over flow of products, Big Data Analytics (BDA) combined with AI processes necessary data needed for measuring supply chain's environmental performance, similarly AI powered Data Environment Analysis -Artificial Neural Network (DEA-ANN) is used for screening environmental performance of suppliers (Saad & Khamkham, 2022).

7. GREEN SOURCING AND INPUTS

The impact of sourcing can be understood figuratively, such as a building not being sustained if its base is frail. A product can never truly be environmentally friendly if the production materials have not been carefully sourced, keeping in view the materials' environmental impact. In Pakistan, upper management sets the company's sourcing policies for textiles. A broad division of materials can be as

- Regular Items
- Regular high-priced items
- One-time purchase

Regular items generally include maintenance, repair, and operations (MRO) supplies, often synonymously used for low-priced or 'less sensitive' items. High-priced items include dyes, chemicals for processing, and cotton. One-time purchases are expensive purchases, such as machines and plants. MROs generally have a low environmental impact; they act as support material, have the highest frequency, and make up the largest number of stored stock-keeping units (SKUs). Segregating items for production allows us to look at their sources to target GSCM practices. This segregation helps us implement GSCM practices by meeting and discussing sustainability with materials suppliers. Suppliers are often selected based on quality, price, and consistency of their delivery performance service in Pakistani textiles, and adding a new dimension will assist in nurturing a GSCM culture, beginning from these suppliers to reverse logistics. Consequently, below are prominent certifications globally that help identify a supplier or a manufacturer as sustainably responsible. They include:

- Global Organic Textile Standards (GOTS) certification testifies that at least 70% of the product's material is organic or environmentally friendly. GOTS is a collaborative certification from a body formed by associations working independently in Japan, the United Kingdom, the United States, and Germany. They focus on the sourcing of materials and audit the entire supply chain. Independent inspectors do an audit. (Global Organic Textile Standard, 2024)
- Bluesign Approved also functions the same way by auditing the entire chain of processes, but it focuses on emissions and worker safety parameters (Bluesign, 2024).
- Responsible Down Standard focuses on wildlife preservation, particularly in textiles, by checking whether any cruelty is being done to animals by sourcing their skin and hides (Textile Exchange, 2024).
- OKO TEX audits the supply chain for textiles and leather. Their certification, 'Sustainable Textile Production,' focuses on suppliers following GSCM practices by adhering to standards of chemical handling, packaging, compositions, etc. (OEKO-TEX., 2020).

Having such certifications is worthy of tax relaxations and financial benefits, but one major qualitative benefit stems from the upheaval of brand image. Brand image, a marketing notion, refers to simply what the customers think about a particular brand. Since sustainability is an issue discussed all over the world presently and will do so in decades to come, achieving such certifications will be positive for a textile manufacturer's brand image.

An argument can be made that in a country like Pakistan, consumers are not comprehensively aware of the perils of climate change, and they will prefer low prices for the same quality regardless of the items' carbon footprint. This may sound like a negative notion for textile managers, having spent so much effort and resources on 'green affiliations,' but when looked upon closely, this situation presents an opportunity. This is an opportunity to tap into a new market, an unexplored area in the Pakistani market where space is present for a 'green' or environmentally responsible textile company to lead the way while also making the general population aware of the dangers of climate change. First-mover advantage is of immense value for any brand. For Pakistan, this opportunity presently lies in first implementing GSCM sourcing practices, achieving the certifications, and then marketing as a 'green' brand. This would provide a first-mover advantage for any textile brand in this huge country of 235 million.

8. TEXTILE MANUFACTURING AND GSCM

Looking a layer beyond and understanding the source of the problem is crucial when one goes for possible improvements in processes, such as for the implementation of GSCM. The first step in this approach includes looking at the outcomes of the problem and deciding if the problem is worth investing resources in. Secondly, the chapter digs a layer below and understands the problem in its true form. GSCM practices, in a similar manner, can be understood in their truer sense in Pakistani textiles by looking at their technical processes. Textile production, in a broad view, comprises these processes below:

1. Spinning
2. Weaving and Knitting
3. Dyeing and Finishing

Spinning is the initiating process. It is the process where yarn is produced from the available fibers, such as cotton. Weaving, in its industrial meaning, refers to a process in which sets of yarn are intermingled to form a piece of woven fabric. Knitting produces a knitted fabric, in which sets of yarn are knitted via needles by machines. After these, a garment goes through a series of chemical treatments. A chemical coat is applied to have the material adhere to coloration dyes for designs and fabric quality; all such activities are included in dyeing and finishing.

Total energy consumption depends on the level of output required for each activity. Forms of energy consumed by Spinning include electricity and fossil fuel. Weaving processes include electric and thermal energy. For Dyeing and Finishing, water and chemicals are added along with electric and thermal energy consumption (Farhana et al., 2022). Figure 3 represents activities in the Spinning process and their breakdown of energy usage.

Table 1. Percentage of Energy Consumption in Spinning Activities in Textile Manufacturing. Excerpted from the work of Farhana et al. (2022)

Name of the Stages	Energy
Blow room	11
Carding	12
Drawing	5
Combing	1
Roving	7
Ring spinning	37
Open-end machines	20
Winding	7

Analyzing the above numbers and relating them with the third dimension for NRBV about 'clean technologies,' implementing GSCM practices, technological changes will bring a much greater impact than behavioral changes. With the help of the above table, realize that the resources consumed by the ring-spinning machines are the greatest. A proposal can be presented for only shifting the ring spinning machines on alternate energy; such incremental changes complement a step-by-step procedure for integrating GSCM practices in the textile sector globally.

9. GREEN KEY PERFORMANCE INDICATORS (GKPIS)

Performance metrics in management sciences have been subjective in their reliability in representing the 'true' situation or performance. Several qualitative factors need to be considered to present a true view of performance. For GSCM practices, however, issues lie on a macroeconomic level where governments must intervene, sometimes with coercive measures.

Here, the discussion is measuring GSCM practices. A framework presented almost a decade ago puts the picture in perspective for measuring sustainability for textile manufacturers. It was proposed by Acar, Kılıç, and Güner (2015), in which the ratios of environmentally hazardous elements involved per item manufactured or garment sold are calculated, as seen in Table 2.

Table 2. Ratios for Measuring Hazardous Material per Item. Excerpted from the work of Acar, Kılıç, and Güner (2015)

			Unit of Measure
Resource Consumption and Generation	I1	Overall energy consumption ratio	MJ/garment
	I2	Overall natural gas consumption ratio	MJ/garment
	I3	Overall diesel consumption ratio	MJ/garment
	I4	Electricity consumption ratio in head offices and factories	kWh/garment
	I5	Renewable energy generation and tri-generation ratio	kWh/garment
	I6	Water consumption ratio	m3/garment
Greenhouse Gas Emissions	I7	Greenhouse gas emissions ratio	g CO2eq/ garment
	I8	Greenhouse gas emissions ratio from transport	g CO2eq/garment
	I9	NOx emissions ratio	g/garment
	I10	CO emissions ratio	g/garment
	I11	SO2 emissions ratio	g/garment
General Types of Waste and Contaminators Ratio	I12	Hazardous waste ratio	g/garment
	I13	Wood wastes ratio	g/garment
	I14	Plastic wastes ratio	g/garment
	I15	Cardboard and paper waste ratio	g/garment
	I16	Textile wastes ratio	g/garment
Specific Types of Hazardous Waste Ratio	I17	Battery wastes ratio	g/garment
	I18	Electronic wastes ratio	g/garment
	I19	Floorescents waste ratio	g/garment
	I20	Oil filter waste ratio	g/garment
	I21	Contaminated metal packaging waste ratio	g/garment
	I22	Used mineral oil waste ratio	g/garment
	I23	Contaminated absorbents waste ratio	g/garment
	I24	Paint wastes ratio	g/garment
	I25	Contaminated plastic packaging wastes ratio	g/garment

Such numbers represent where the problem lies and where to begin from. Issues with GSCM practices include managers planning on implementing all measures across supply chain operations, but they need a comprehensive measurement tool, a number, to gauge their performance. Such a gap is filled by the framework described above. On examining I25, it realizes that material in this category is the stringiest, which damages the environment the most, and improvements could begin from this point and such numbers. Replacing a particular material and sourcing it from a different source with less hazardous composition are some strategies used by supply chain managers for implementing GSCM practices. Defined targets for lowering the overall negative environmental impact of materials can be set. It is also important to have the progress reporting done by independent observers.

The World Business Council for Sustainable Development (WBCSD) specified another rather interesting framework for implementation across a product's life cycle. This framework includes four modules of indicators estimating the percentage of environment-friendly material used or reused in supply chains.

Figure 3. Modules by WBCSD

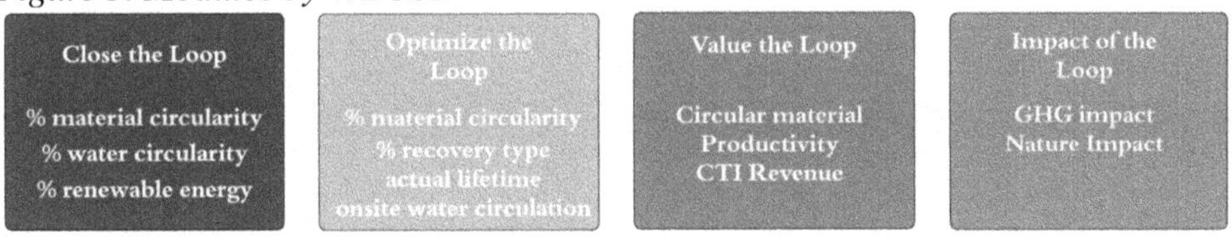

a) Close the Loop: This module measures the percentage of environmentally friendly material used in company material inflows and outflows. The inflow of materials includes measuring GSCM practices for procurement, and outflows include a percentage of material that can be recovered or recycled back into production, which is inculcated in reverse logistics for GSCM practice.
b) Optimize the Loop: It represents critical elements used in manufacturing products. Critical materials include those of high economic importance, such as rare metals, whose supply disruption could halt the entire value chain.
c) Value the Loop: This measures the extent to which a manufacturer is financially dependent on resource consumption in manufacturing and selling. In other words, the greater this ratio, the less dependent on natural resources and the greater on recycled or circular inputs.
d) Impact of the Loop: This tool helps any small or large-scale manufacturer understand the impact of their 'looped' or recycled material on the environment. It evaluates the impact of greenhouse gas (GHG). A picture of statistics is compared, such as where a textile manufacturer stands today versus where they would be with 100% reliability on recycled materials.

Independent bodies reporting on GSCM performance and implementation metrics for the textile industry in Pakistan are crucial to engender a sustained change along with the Pakistani authorities' formal intervention. Evidently, the Chinese government has not just enforced but has also evolved its environmental safeguarding policies for its giant manufacturing sector. A breakdown of their new policy for GSCM practices reveals that 52% of injunctions in the policy are targeted at lowering the negative emissions, as carbon dioxide and material supply and demand rules account for 32% and 16% of the policy measures, respectively. All these injunctions in the policy, along with setting 340 national energy saving standards and proposal of around 260 technologies to be used on an industrial level by 13 different industries across their growing economic spectrum (Zhang et al., 2022). Pakistan and China share a tremendous intensity of harmonious relations on all levels; a learning curve for

Pakistan textile owners is present by leveraging China's policies and technological tools for the implementation of GSCM practices.

9.1 The Life Cycle Assessment

Life Cycle Assessment (LCA) is a core feature of Ecological Design dimension of GSCM. LCA determines the environmental impact of any product across its lifetime. Garlet et al. (2024) divides LCA in three stages as below:

- Before Use Phase: This is the stage in which upstream channels of supply focus on GSCM practices. Such as procurement of sustainable raw materials to low energy consumed in transportation and storage of the final product.
- Use Phase: It measures hazardous impact of the product during its use.
- After Use Phase: At this phase some products can be used for a different purpose than what they were manufactured for, such as bottles of sauces. Many other products which are not reuseable are discarded resulting in pollution.

Being focused on textiles, we take the example of an apparel example and we consider LCA for a shirt. An LCA of polo shirts was analyzed manufactured in Bangladesh, a sample of 1000 units of shirts was analyzed at each stage, and it was found by Islam et al. (2024) that to produce a polo shirt following resources were consumed:

- 1.5 kWh of electricity.
- 0.015 liters of diesel fuel
- 0.072 cubic meters of natural gas
- 0.00012 hectors of land
- 0.36 kilograms of cotton
- 0.32 kilograms of yarn
- 0.32 kilograms of knitted fabric
- 0.29 kilograms of dyed fabric

All this accumulates to 1.3-kilogram CO_2-eq of the global warming potential per shirt. All these numbers above represent the 'before use' phase of LCA for a shirt.

For resource consumption during the 'Use Phase', a modern front load washing machine uses 50 liters of water per use and almost 2000 watts per use (Electrolux, 2022). Considering an average of 15 garments along with that shirt in one washing cycle then per unit water consumption would be 3.3 liters of water and 133 watts of electricity per polo shirt.

In a case where a shirt is discarded in a landfill, its environmental impact results from decomposition. When shirt's fabric decomposes in the ground, it releases methane gas and chemicals such as dyes in the soil and ground water.

10. AN EMPIRICAL ANALYSIS OF GSCM IN THE PAKISTANI TEXTILE INDUSTRY

Organizational practices such as Green Supply Chain Management (GSCM) practices have been studied under theoretical and empirical lenses, both exerting their importance and value. Theoretical approaches provide the foundation for quantitative data gathering and explanations to observe if the theory is applicable in a certain situation within set parameters. As such, many studies in management sciences and organizational behavior have focused on proving a certain theory to be applicable or being 'right' in a defined situation by gathering data from respondents, often about their perceptions and behavior. However, it can also not be denied that there exists a gap between organizational practices and the perfect implementation of theories in management sciences.

10.1 Study Foreword

This yearlong study is an attempt to understand variables of GSCM that impact green performance for textile manufacturers in Pakistan. A total of six variables were identified from the literature. Five independent variables and a dependent variable. Data was collected via survey questionnaires entailing probing questions about existing GSCM practices such as waste reduction, use of recycled material, and energy consumption in textile manufacturers of Pakistan. The textile industry in Pakistan is based mainly in the cities of Lahore and Karachi, and the study was conducted in the region of Karachi. Karachi offers a much larger number of professionals working at major textile brands' facilities. To understand the ground realities of GSCM practices in textile supply chains, the impact of Ecological Design, Internal Environmental Management, Green Purchasing, Reverse Logistics, and Green Manufacturing on Environmental Performance was made part of the project. The quantitative analysis is used on data and found that all the variables mentioned above significantly and positively impact environmental performance for textile manufacturers, with environmentally friendly procurement or Green Purchasing having the strongest impact. This study contributes to the literature by identifying factors that impact green performance and the extent to which such factors are implemented, along with what needs to be done to further strengthen such implementations of GSCM practices in the Pakistani textile industry.

Empirical studies, based on observable facts and figures, offer concrete first-hand analysis of situations. First-hand data collected from the industry experts provide insight into the practices being followed. It would not be incorrect to state that fundamental decisions by organizations are often based on empirical studies, hence supporting the perception that 'numbers speak' or, more appropriately, 'data speaks.' After data is collected and tested for authenticity, it is then upon the researcher to 'listen' to what the numbers say and produce inferences answering research questions. The inference produced is then compared to what the study was intended for and if the purpose is fulfilled. Such is the case for this study. The purpose of this year-long research is to get first-hand exposure to what is happening with Green Supply Chain Management (GSCM) practices in the Pakistani textile industry. The aim is to understand and observe the actual situation of GSCM in the Pakistani textile industry. The theoretical concept for GSCM practices is novel in many parts of the world. It would not be incorrect to state that developed countries, especially in Europe, have sternly adopted GSCM practices with their strict regulations, but in developing parts of the world, such as Pakistan, exists a significant deficiency, both in knowledge, awareness, and then subsequently in implementation of GSCM practices to save the environment. The study begins by asking the following question:

RQ1: To measure GSCM practices and their impact on environmental performance in Pakistan's textile industry.

10.2 Review of the Literature for Variables and Development of Hypotheses

Depletion of natural resources is an unfavorable natural phenomenon that will impact humans all over the world. Climate changes have begun to wreak havoc on cultivated lands with non-seasoned heavy rainfalls, rural and urban flooding, destructive forest fires, and record-high temperatures. All of this contributes to the desecration of natural reserves and lower cultivation outputs. As all sectors of the global economy are being impacted, one of the most severely negative effects would be upon the textile industry as the textile sector must have uninterrupted flow for their utterly important cultivated raw material, cotton. Therefore, it is of extreme importance or rather a question of subsistence for apparel manufacturers that the effects of climate change slow down and that textile manufacturers, who are among the most vulnerable to climate change, must lead the way by example. Environmental performance is defined as all acts by an organization for their commercial and other activities examined from two major perspectives: protecting Earth's environment from being harmed and contributing to its improvement (Li et al., 2024). In a year of working on this project, the textile sector of Karachi, Pakistan, was studied most comprehensively. The reason for selecting Environmental Performance as a dependent variable is that it inculcates a culminating impact by a manufacturer over a spectrum of their different manufacturing activities on the environment.

10.2.1 Ecological Design and Environmental Performance

Explicitly explained by the work of Wang et al. (2020) on product design. They studied the impact of changed product design on environmental performance by examining the entire cycle of a product from its manufacturing to disposal or recycling; the product under examination were LED lights, which went through a complete assessment across all their life segments from manufacturing to the end after this assessment materials incorporated in production were changed, changes included designing the LEDs with recycled material. After these specific changes, the results emerged with a significant 27 to 28 percent betterment in environmental performance. Contrastingly, electronics and textiles are two very dissimilar products; apparel has a much longer shelf life and durability, and a completely different set of resources is required for production. It can, however, be inferred that product design plays a crucial role in deciding the environmental performance of a manufacturer, and minimal changes, which are also cost-friendly, could make a significant impact on the manufacturer's carbon footprint. Hence, the variable 'Ecological Design' was incorporated, relating it to the inclusion of recycled material, and an impact this could make on Pakistani textiles' environmental performance needed to be observed. Based on the above literature review, the following is developed:

Hypothesis 1: Ecological Design has a significantly positive effect on Environmental Performance

10.2.2 Internal Environmental Management and Environmental Performance

While studying organizational practices, it can be understood that culture or values are set at the topmost level and are drilled down the lines. Organizational cultures prone to function for the betterment of the organization are dependent upon the attitude of top management towards setting such cultures (Perlman et al., 2024). Cultures are composed of organizational practices that are implemented and monitored, such as GSCM practices. GSCM practices aim to produce such a product via those industrial processes that engender the least possible negative impact on the environment. Like all organizational practices, the role of upper management is decisive in the implementation of GSCM procedures. For such, a study was conducted by Suryanto, Haseeb, and Hartani (2018), in which assistance by upper management and learning curve of companies were investigated to have an impact on implementation of GSCM practices, it was found that both the study's variables which were the learning curve such as awareness about GSCM processes and their benefits and support of the managers on top level have a significant and a contributing impact on adoption of GSCM in companies. Without addressing the top bosses' role, the strategic managers cannot move along with the implementation of GSCM practices; hence, a variable named 'Internal Environmental Management' was selected to incorporate willingness or support by the top management for implementing GSCM practices in the Pakistani textile industry also, since textile manufacturers in Pakistan work within a mechanistic structure with a strong centralized authority overlooking all decisions. With such a strongly centralized decision structure, it becomes essential that an independent variable represents the role of decision-makers in our study. Based on the inclusion of this variable, a hypothesis is developed:

Hypothesis 2: Internal Environmental Management has a significantly positive effect on environmental performance

10.2.3 Green Purchasing and Environmental Performance

As mentioned above, greener material inputs produce environmentally friendly final products. The sourcing of environmentally friendly materials ensures that the final product will be a sustainable product for the betterment of the environment, and this represents a cornerstone notion for GSCM practices. GSCM practices such as procedural wastages and optimal use of resources like water and electricity are directly aligned with higher costs or a waste of capital. Complex situations are presented to textile managers in Pakistan when a tradeoff between cost savings and expenses for sourcing greener material is to be made. Procurement, being a crucial activity as is for any supply chain, the procurement of environmentally sustainable material is highly impactful for environmental performance. Materials that have a positive impact or are least hazardous to the environment should be used, and supplier selection criteria should be designed to keep environmental concerns in sight (Jermsittiparsert et al., 2019). Having mentioned above information, a hypothesis statement is framed as:

Hypothesis 3: Green Purchasing has a significantly positive effect on Environmental Performance

10.2.4 Reverse Logistics and Environmental Performance

Logistics is the most functional part of any supply chain. It demands real-time solutions to problems, and logistics involves, among other functions, the movement and planning of goods from one place to another. Reverse logistics is where the beginning point is the customer, and the destination is usually the manufacturer with intermediaries, which may or may not be in between. The importance of reverse logistics from an environmental impact is that when an apparel or textile product's life ends after usage, it acts as a garbage material that often goes untreated and unrecycled, ultimately hurting Earth's resources in one way or another. A survey from an oil company in one of the developing economies linking the reverse flow of materials and environmental performance revealed that there is a substantially positive link between the two and that companies who actively take part in recycling the material by enabling movement of the used product back from customers and reusing it in any one way or other in their production processes (Alnoor et al., 2018). Being a controller of a responsible supply chain, managers must view this end of the chain as a stage where a product may no longer be of use to the customer, but the value of the item persists in it being recycled or used again as components in manufacturing. After including a variable for the backward flow of used goods for further processing and recycling, a hypothesis established is as below:

Hypothesis 4: Reverse Logistics has a significantly positive effect on Environmental Performance.

10.2.5 Green Manufacturing and Environmental Performance

Green manufacturing processes strive to produce products that have no or minimum negative impact on the environment; a concept here dwells on organizations working extensively to gain financial benefits while meeting their environmental concerns. To achieve this, a combination of minimum waste practices (Lean Practices - LP) are paired with green manufacturing (GM) processes where LP makes sure that there are no wastages during the production processes, and GM assures adherence to environmental responsibility. Incorporation of the variable for green manufacturing processes in this research is particularly important because implementing GSCM practices such as GM and LP demand not only that materials are procured with concerns for Earth's atmosphere and resources, but this variable is important also because textile and apparel manufacturing is comprised of multiple detailed segments of industrial production processes. Abundant facility space is needed for apparel production and storage; in short, a huge financial investment is required for setting up a textile factory, so for a setup of this magnitude, there is always a squeeze for eliminating waste and finding innovative ways to protect the environment from a number of processes and equipment involved. Having inculcated all the above information, which leads to framing the final hypothesis below:

Hypothesis 5: Green Manufacturing has a significantly positive effect on Environmental Performance.

Table 3. Description of variables

S.No.	Variable	Explanation	Support from Literature
1	Ecological Design	[illegible]	[illegible]
2	Internal Environmental Management	[illegible]	[illegible]
3	Reverse Logistics	[illegible]	[illegible]
4	Green Purchasing	[illegible]	[illegible]
5	Green Manufacturing	[illegible]	[illegible]
6	Environmental Performance	[illegible]	[illegible]

The hypotheses developed are listed below in the table:

Table 4. Hypotheses Statements

Hypotheses No.	Hypotheses Statement
1	Ecological Design has a significantly positive effect on Environmental Performance.
2	Internal Environmental Management has a significantly positive effect on environmental performance.
3	Green Purchasing has a significantly positive effect on Environmental Performance.
4	Reverse Logistics has a significantly positive effect on Environmental Performance.
5	Green manufacturing has a significantly positive effect on environmental performance.

10.3 Theoretical Framework

Figure 4. Theoretical framework

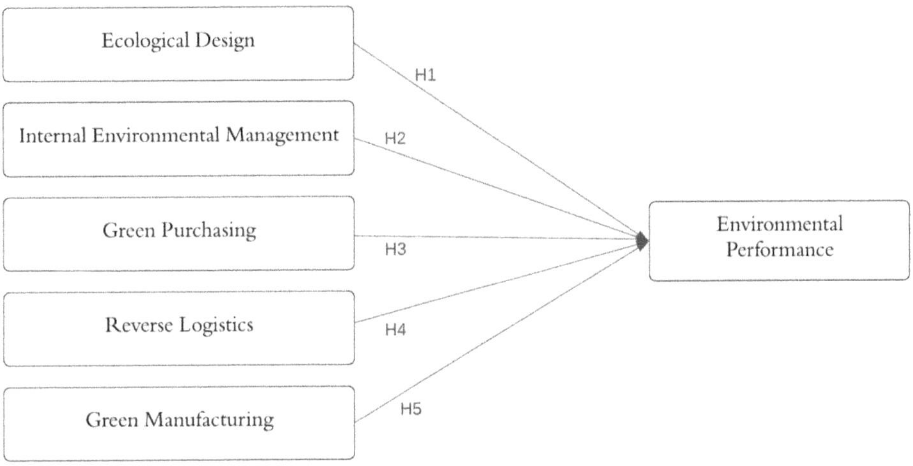

Figure 4 is the theoretical framework illustrating an overall view of environmental performance.

10.4 Methodology

Methodology is the most procedural aspect of any research work. Each notion in this section requires a skilled justification. Different methodologies can be used to study a single subject or similar variables. The choice of methodological parameters depends upon the study's requirements.

For clarity for our readers, table 5 presents the methodological sequence in the following table:

Table 5. Methodology parameters excerpted from Saunders et al. (2007)

S.No.	Parameters of Methodology	Selected Dimension	Justification for Selection
1	Purpose of Research	Explanatory	[illegible]
2	Epistemological Approach	Positivism	[illegible]
3	Ontological Approach	Pragmatism	[illegible]
4	Research Approach	Deductive	[illegible]
5	Research Strategy	Survey	[illegible]
6	Research Paradigm	Functionalist	[illegible]
7	Research Choices	Mono Method	[illegible]
8	Time Horizon	Cross-Sectional	[illegible]
9	Techniques and Procedures	Quantitative	[illegible]

10.5 Results and Discussion

Parameters of this year-long project were set as the data is collected from supply chain managers presently working in managerial positions in the Pakistani textile industry. Such professionals are prime sources for getting the data needed to have an idea of GSCM practices in their companies. Therefore, 'Purposive Sampling,' which dictates targeting only relevant people contributing to research, was applied. The frequency table shows that male managers dominate the Pakistani textile sector; however, 21% of participation by females is higher than is seen in previous textile sector studies in Pakistan. Below is the frequency distribution of the respondents from Pakistani textile companies in Karachi city who took part as respondents in the study.

Table 6. Gender-Based Frequency table for respondents who took part in the study.

		Frequency	Percent
Valid	Male	154	79
	Female	41	21
	Total	195	100

The table below represents the age groups of people who gave us the data for this study. Since data was gathered from concerned professionals, only those who were involved in working with GSCM practices in any capacity to a decision-making level in their supply operations. The data shows that GSCM decision-making in the supply chain is majorly associated with managers between 31 and 40 years of age. Then, in the second position, there are respondents or managers in their fifties and sixties. This is because, as mentioned above, textile companies in Pakistan have a mechanistic structure. Employees are promoted to managerial or authoritative 'decision-making' levels, usually after a minimum of 7 to 10 years spent in the field (such as supervising machines on the production floor). So, starting a career in the supply chain of a textile company in Pakistan at a certain age after obtaining a college degree, most employees get promoted to the company's 'decision-making' hierarchy when they usually reach the age group of 31 to 40 years.

Table 7. Age Group-based division of respondents.

		Frequency	Percent
Valid	22-30 years	15	8
	31-40 years	68	35
	41-50 years	55	28
	51 years and above	57	29
	Total	195	100

The education frequency table shows that the majority of respondents possess a Master's degree. It is associated with a recent industrial trend in Pakistan, where it gets included in organizational policies of all major textile brands, and any employee considered for the 'Manager' designation must possess a Master's degree. It can be said that, like textiles in many manufacturing supply chains of Pakistan, such as in pharmaceuticals and food manufacturing, frequency distribution for managers would not differ much from the table below, and a Master's degree would be a prerequisite for managers. For M. Phil and Doctorate, such individuals are rarely hired internally. Rather, most of them act and work in the capacity of a 'consultant,' impacting their life-long knowledge and experiences for higher efficiencies. Below is the table showing the frequency distribution of respondents.

Table 8. Qualification-based division of respondents.

		Frequency	Percent
Valid	Bachelor's degree	75	38.5
	Master's degree	93	47.7
	M.Phil degree	26	13.3
	Doctorate	1	0.5
	Total	195	100

Data was collected from 195 industry professionals. Data collection was performed with a survey questionnaire. This questionnaire was sent to supply chain professionals, probing about their GSCM practices, and professionals' responses were recorded. The respondents had to answer each question from being 'Strongly Agreed' (point 1) to 'Strongly Disagreed' (point 5) on a scale of 1 to 5. The impact of the above independent variables on the environmental performance (EP) of textile companies was observed through an analysis of the data gathered. EP is, in its essence, all about the incorporation of GSCM practices such as waste mitigation, reducing carbon emissions, and increased use of environmentally friendly material. EP is basically the overall extent to which a manufacturer contributes to bettering the environment (Afum et al., 2020). Analysis of data was carried out via SPSS (Statistical Package for Social Sciences), a software for analyzing quantitative data. Cronbach Alpha checked the data's reliability, and all variables scored above the accepted limit of 0.7. The regression test was applied to the data to observe if there was any relationship between each independent variable and environmental performance. Then, based on such statistics, hypotheses developed in the literature above were evaluated. Table 7 shows the numbers obtained after processing the data:

Table 9. Table for Coefficients summarizing values from the Regression analysis.

S. No.	Hypothesis	Beta	T-Value	Sig.-Value
H1	Ecological Design has a significantly positive effect on Environmental Performance.	0.33	4.028	0.00
H2	Internal Environmental Management has a significantly positive effect on environmental performance.	0.592	7.544	0.00
H3	Green Purchasing has a significantly positive effect on Environmental Performance.	0.312	4.191	0.00
H4	Reverse Logistics has a significantly positive effect on Environmental Performance.	0.277	3.571	0.00
H5	Green manufacturing has a significantly positive effect on environmental performance.	0.36	4.747	0.00

In the table above, Beta values, which show the intensity or extent of increase or decrease (if the value is negative), occur when an independent variable is changed. Beta values show all positive relations (an increase in independent variables will also increase environmental performance value). This means that all five independent variables positively impact environmental performance. Among all independent variables, green purchasing has the largest positive impact. A unit increase in metrics of Internal Environmental Management metric will bring an increase of 0.59 in metric value for Environmental Performance for a textile company in Pakistan.

Significance (Sig.) values are the decisive criteria applied to conclude if this data supports or does not support the developed hypothesis. The basic criteria for the Sig.-value is for it to be below 0.05, and the t-value represents how much the means of the sample differ from each other. Following concluding results are presented after setting the Sig. Values as standard for hypothesis decision:

Table 10. Final Hypotheses Summary.

Hypothesis	Statement	Result
H1	Ecological Design has a significantly positive effect on Environmental Performance.	Supported
H2	Internal Environmental Management has a significantly positive effect on environmental performance.	Supported
H3	Green Purchasing has a significantly positive effect on Environmental Performance.	Supported
H4	Reverse Logistics has a significantly positive effect on Environmental Performance.	Supported
H5	Green manufacturing has a significantly positive effect on environmental performance.	Supported

Data supports all hypotheses that Ecological Design, which is the use of sustainable recycled material, impacts environmental performance. Incorporating recycled material as GSCM practice for textiles could mean incorporating fiber left in used apparel items in their manufacturing processes. Implementing this GSCM procedure will save costs significantly and lead to an escalation in environmental performance for textile manufacturers in Pakistan. Internal Environmental Management is more of a behavioral variable. It can be assumed that the role of upper management is evident in most organizational behavioral studies, be it theoretical or empirical. GSCM practices require decisions and changes in procedural workings, such as including certain environmental certifications to be mandatory in supplier selection criteria; implementation of this and similar GSCM practices are not possible without approval from the 'above' in management. Literature is abundantly clear that procuring sustainable material will produce a considerable impact, showcasing a textile manufacturer's efforts to take care of the environment. The situation for Pakistani textile companies may prominently rise in procurement of dyes and chemicals, and non-certified vendors with no sustainability certification may give better prices, which overshadows GSCM's perspective in lieu of profits. For Reverse Logistics, a two-facet mechanism is required. The textile industry in Pakistan is strong enough to play its part in structuring collection points to bring in used material for further processing into production. The second half of this two-facet mechanism includes customers being aware and practicing taking their used clothing to collection points. Lastly, green manufacturing is all about adopting the lowest wastage along with green management, which is decisions concerning their impact on the environment. Low waste is ideal, and it serves the 'green' purpose, but processes, where costs are incurred to implement a responsible GSCM practice to increase environmental performance, are an area that needs attention in the textile sector of Pakistan. Chief among such concerns is the disposal of used chemicals and dyes, after production, directly into the city drainage pipeline without any treatment. Wastewater treatment plants are costly and add no value to financial profits. Such GSCM practices with high investment are possible with authorities intervening with regulations and with tax evasions to reward the industry initiators and front-runners for investing in GSCM practices implementation.

10.6 Relationship Between Variables

This study has observed, with the help of statistical data, the impact of five independent variables on the dependent variable, Environmental Performance (EP). A brief description of the relationships of each independent variable with the dependent variable is as follows:

10.6.1 Ecological Design and EP

Ecological Design and its implementation as a GSCM practice for the textile industry in Pakistan depends on using recycled material obtained through Reverse Logistics in apparel manufacturing. Certain chemicals and fiber can be extracted even from the most used-up and torn pieces of fabric. This GSCM practice would require a significant expenditure in the beginning, but as shown from the literature study by Wang et al. (2020) that changing the composition of the produced items with the inclusion of recycled material could bring betterment in EP by 27 to 28%.

10.6.2 Internal Environmental Management and EP

It can be inferred logically and supported by provisions in the literature that the role of management in implementing GSCM practices to improve EP is detrimental. All other variables and investments in their implementation are not possible without management's support. The results of the study also denote that this variable engenders the strongest impact; an increase in a unit of Internal Environmental Management brings an increase of 0.59 to EP.

10.6.3 Green Purchasing Design and EP

Purchasing environmentally sustainable materials or Green Purchasing directly relates to producing a better product with minimal environmental impact. Reverse Logistics can have an indirect relation in such a situation where textile manufacturers of Pakistan outsource the collection of used apparel for their recycling and procure the said material via contract or purchase orders. Furthermore, sustainability certifications must be taken into account while inducting a supplier. This also ensures a textile manufacturer's high standards for EP.

10.6.4 Reverse Logistics Design and EP

Reverse logistics could be done in-house or outsourced. In whichever case, a two-facet mechanism with manufacturers or the outsourced business and customers playing their parts is needed. The data, on the other hand, ranks Reverse Logistics as the least impactful variable on EP. This could be because recycling in Pakistan's textile industry has never been an area of concern. However, in the present view of GSCM and its implementation, there is a need to begin recycling materials.

10.6.5 Green Manufacturing Design and EP

Green Manufacturing is basically an optimal use of 'Green Purchased' materials. It includes all the manufacturing processes that could influence the EP. As mentioned, the functions of spinning, weaving, knitting, and dyeing are the most energy-consuming in textile manufacturing. Given the fact that after Internal Environmental Management scored the highest in impact for influencing EP, Green Manufacturing comes in second place with a Beta value of 0.36. This means that respondents who were managers of leading textile value the technical side of textile and GSCM practices of EP.

11. SUSTAINABILITY FRAMEWORKS

Environmental, Social and Governance (ESG) is a reporting mechanism. Under this framework the 'environmental' part is a business's impact on environment such as carbon footprint, the 'social' part is for communal and workforce concerns and 'governance is about the top decision making. Under this mechanism businesses are liable to present their details about the environmental impact of their activities to public and authorities. This set of policies serves organizations and governments in the ways below:

1. ESG compels manufacturers of textile industry to be aware of the environmental impact of their processes, inputs and outputs. It discovers areas which consume most resources.
2. ESG helps in assessing companies with their environmental performance.

3. ESG enables organizations to adopt sustainability in their reporting and decision making.

Several regulatory reporting frameworks were adopted by companies from the ESG framework, some of them include:

Global Reporting Initiative (GRI)

- Founded by the UN. It is one of most popular reporting practices standards
- Manufacturers have to report using three series of standards for GRI which include

  1. Universal Standards – Information about minimum requirements for applying GRI standards and about materials being used.
  2. Sector Standards – Set of standards per each sector
  3. Topic Standards - Set of information and numbers required in reporting.

Sustainability Accounting Standards Board (SASB)

- Developed in 2011. SASB spans across 77 industries.
- It focuses on rules for reporting cash flows, access to financing and cost of capital regarding sustainability including GSCM practices.
- The framework includes research, participation from decision makers and approval from the SASB board about financing and accounting activities for sustainability such as taxation.

UN Principles for Responsible Investment (PRI)

- UN PRI is a set of financial organizations working for the UN to implement its 6 principles, which are as below:

  1. To include ESG framework in investment decisions.
  2. Implement ESG framework in entities owned.
  3. Disclose information in invested entities.
  4. Promote UN PRI in investment industries.
  5. Collaboration for better UN PRI implementation.
  6. Reporting about implementation of UN PRI.

12. POLICY IMPLICATIONS AND REGULATORY FRAMEWORKS FOR SUSTAINABILITY

It would not be incorrect to state that Europe has the most comprehensive policies for environmental protection. European countries lead the way with sustainable efforts. The European Commission (EU) has policies in place to cut 55% greenhouse gas emissions by 2030 (European Commission, 2019). Some policy frameworks are described below for GSCM in Europe:

European Green Deal

- Proposed and accepted in 2020.
- It is a set of policies by EU aimed at achieving climate neutrality by 2050. Climate neutrality
- Under this policy framework economic growth will be dissociated from resource consumption.
- It will be applied to all citizens and places alike.
- As even for best Green Manufacturing practices in GSCM, there is always a certain part which depends on natural resource consumption from non-renewable resources such as some machines being operated on fossil fuel. Completely decoupling economic growth from resource consumption can be a challenge.

Raw Material Initiative of EU

- Implemented and monitored by the EU.
- It focuses on sourcing with fair access to materials for businesses
- Sourcing of material must be from sustainable sources.
- Reaching out to underdeveloped regions for strategic collaboration.
- Uncertainty and lack of regulation in undeveloped area is a challenge for Green Purchasing part of GSCM for EU under this policy framework.

SME Support System of EU

- Involves appraising supply chains for raw materials.
- Based on Regulation (EU) No 2017/821
- Supply chain appraisals will be conducted for imports of tin, tungsten, tantalum and gold from conflict-affected areas.

- This poses a challenge for small-scale importers. Challenge in a way that strict regulations result in disruption of material's supply and higher costs in many cases.

Apart from EU's polices, there are several other regions and countries which have successfully implemented GSCM policies for environmental protection. Some examples ae discussed as below:

Basic Environment Law of Japan

- Enacted in 1993.
- It includes the Central Environmental Council of 80 members to be elected by the Prime Minister.
- Policy consists of 46 articles directed towards promoting sustainability by participation of authorities, businesses and citizens.
- This law sets goals and assigns responsibilities such as reporting standards and monitoring progress to local government bodies.
- Challenge arose for Japanese government when earthquake of 2011 greatly disrupted nuclear plants which generated electricity.

13. CONCLUSION

A gloomy situation persists; our Earth's resources are being depleted, but the human consumption of textiles is increasing, and Pakistan is among the front-line countries in the world to have been impacted by climate change and environmental degradation. With the supply of cotton being interrupted, the Pakistani textile industry, which employs a major chunk of the population, could face a significant collapse. Textile owners in Pakistan must lead the way with green practices across all domains of their businesses, including the supply chain. GSCM practices help supply chain managers optimize their supply chain processes to have the least adverse impact on the environment. Awareness about GSCM practices in the textile sector of Pakistan is only possible via a 'win-for-all' approach, which saves costs and the environment. Branding as a 'green' manufacturer is a massive untapped market space in Pakistan. Theoretically, NRBV urges manufacturers to look internally for resources to bring a positive environmental influence. Textile manufacturers' internal resources, such as setting environmentally concerned supplier selection criteria and breaking down procedural activities in terms of energy consumed, are the internal processes they need to focus on for GSCM practices. Literature is abundantly clear that environmentally friendly sourcing of materials produces environmentally friendly products. For textile production processes, Spinning, Weaving or Knitting, Dyeing, and Finishing are the most energy-consuming processes for textile manufacturing. Performance measures for the implementation of GSCM practices include estimating the percentage of environmentally friendly material used in each SKU sold, or it could be measured across all supply chain operations. Pakistani textile industry could leverage immensely from their every-friendly Chinese neighbors for their technology and policies for GSCM practices.

This yearlong project on GSCM practices in the Pakistani textile industry revealed that Ecological Design, which includes a measure of recycled material, and Green Purchasing, which is the procurement of materials while keeping environmental concerns in focus, both GSCM practices positively and significantly impact Environmental Performance of textile manufacturers in Pakistan. Implementation of Green Purchasing could be through obtaining and making certifications a part of supplier section criteria. Certifications such as GOTS, Bluesign Approved, and others. Implementation for ecological design means inculcating what little value is extracted from the used fabric. Such used fabric or recycled material is to be obtained by Reverse Logistics mechanisms. Reverse Logistics mechanisms ensure the flow of recycled material from customers to manufacturers, for which a two-phased mechanism has customers and Pakistani textile manufacturers work together for a harmonious backward flow of this used apparel. Finally, the role of managers in the hierarchy or Internal Environmental Management is crucial due to decision-making power and the Pakistani textile industry's centralized structure.

REFERENCES

Abbate, S., Centobelli, P., Cerchione, R., Nadeem, S. P., & Riccio, E. (2024). Sustainability trends and gaps in the textile, apparel and fashion industries. *Environment, Development and Sustainability*, 26(2), 2837–2864. DOI: 10.1007/s10668-022-02887-2 PMID: 36788931

Acar, E., Kılıç, M., & Güner, M. (2015). Measurement of sustainability performance in the textile industry by using a multi-criteria decision-making method. *Textile and Apparel, 25*(1).

Afum, E., Agyabeng-Mensah, Y., Sun, Z., Frimpong, B., Kusi, L. Y., & Acquah, I. S. K. (2020). Exploring the link between green manufacturing, operational competitiveness, firm reputation, and sustainable performance dimensions: A mediated approach. *Journal of Manufacturing Technology Management*, 31(7), 1417–1438. DOI: 10.1108/JMTM-02-2020-0036

Alnoor, A., Eneizan, B., Makhamreh, H. Z., & Rahoma, I. A. (2018). The effect of reverse logistics on sustainable manufacturing. *International Journal of Academic Research in Accounting. Finance and Management Sciences*, 9(1), 71–79.

Baloyi, R. B., Gbadeyan, O. J., Sithole, B., & Chunilall, V. (2024). Recent advances in recycling technologies for waste textile fabrics: A review. *Textile Research Journal*, 94(3-4), 508–529. DOI: 10.1177/00405175231210239

Banihashemi, T. A., Fei, J., & Chen, P. S. L. (2019). Exploring the relationship between reverse logistics and sustainability performance: A literature review. *Modern Supply Chain Research and Applications*, 1(1), 2–27. DOI: 10.1108/MSCRA-03-2019-0009

Bluesign. (2024). *Bluesign Solutions and services for a sustainable textile industry*. Bluesign. https://www.bluesign.com/en/

Cellucci, N. (2024, April 23). *Solar Panels ROI: Calculating Your Average Returns*. Forbes Home. https://www.forbes.com/home-improvement/solar/solar-panel-roi/#:~:text=A%20good%20ROI%20for%20solar%20panels%20is%20between%206%25%20and

Chin, T. A., Malik, N. F. I. A., Tat, H. H., Sulaiman, Z., & Choon, T. L. (2020). Green purchasing practices and environmental performance. *International Journal of Supply Chain Management*, 9(1), 291–297.

Edgerton, B. (2023). *Circular Transition Indicators V4.0 Metrics for Business, by Business*. World Business Council for Sustainable Development in May of.

El-Kassar, A. N., & Singh, S. K. (2019). Green innovation and organizational performance: The influence of big data and the moderating role of management commitment and HR practices. *Technological Forecasting and Social Change*, 144, 483–498. DOI: 10.1016/j.techfore.2017.12.016

European Commission. (2019). *The European Green Deal*. European Commission. https://commission.europa.eu/strategy-and-policy/priorities-2019-2024/european-green-deal_en

Exchange, T. (2024). *Responsible Down Standard (RDS)*. Textile Exchange. https://textileexchange.org/responsible-down-standard/

Farhana, K., Kadirgama, K., Mahamude, A. S. F., & Mica, M. T. (2022). Energy consumption, environmental impact, and implementation of renewable energy resources in global textile industries: An overview towards circularity and sustainability. *Materials Circular Economy*, 4(1), 15. DOI: 10.1007/s42824-022-00059-1

Garlet, T. B., de Medeiros, J. F., Ribeiro, J. L. D., & Perin, M. G. (2024). Understanding ethical products: Definitions and attributes to consider throughout the product lifecycle. *Sustainable Production and Consumption*, 45, 228–243. DOI: 10.1016/j.spc.2024.01.010

Global Organic Textile Standard. (2019). *Global Organic Textile Standard International Working Group (IWG) - Global Standard gGmbH*. https://global-standard.org/

Hashmat, H. U., & Khan, M. A. (2023). Design and simulation of efficient solar thermal water heating system for textile industries in Pakistan. *Mehran University Research Journal Of Engineering & Technology*, 42(4), 8–18. DOI: 10.22581/muet1982.2304.2655

Hassabo, A. G., Gamal, N., Sediek, A., Saad, F., Hegazy, B. M., Elmorsy, H., & Othman, H. (2023). Smart wearable fabric using electronic textiles–a review. *Journal of Textiles. Coloration and Polymer Science*, 20(1), 29–39.

Hu, Y. (2024). Analyzing the Comprehensive Influence of Prada's Business Strategies. *Highlights in Business. Economics and Management*, 24, 1563–1567.

India, E. (2022, October 10). *How much is the electricity consumption of a washing machine?* Electrolux India. https://www.electrolux.in/blog/washing-machine-electricity-consumption/

Islam, S., Hasan, A. M., Bhuiyan, M. A. R., & Bhat, G. (2024). Evaluation of environmental impacts of cotton polo shirt production in Bangladesh using life cycle assessment. *The Science of the Total Environment*, 926, 172097. DOI: 10.1016/j.scitotenv.2024.172097 PMID: 38565355

Izquierdo-Yusta, A., Méndez-Aparicio, M. D., Jiménez-Zarco, A. I., & Martínez-Ruíz, M. P. (2023). When responsible production and consumption matter: The case of Danone. In *Responsible Consumption and Sustainability: Case Studies from Corporate Social Responsibility, Social Marketing, and Behavioral Economics* (pp. 199–211). Springer International Publishing. DOI: 10.1007/978-3-031-30742-3_12

Jassim, S., Al-Mubarak, M., & Hamdan, A. (2020). The impact of green supply chain management on firm's performance. *Journal of Information & Knowledge Management*, 19(01), 2040026. DOI: 10.1142/S0219649220400262

Jermsittiparsert, K., Siriattakul, P., & Wattanapongphasuk, S. (2019). Determining the environmental performance of Indonesian SMEs influence by green supply chain practices with moderating role of green HR practices. *International Journal of Supply Chain Management*, 8(3), 59–70.

Khan, S. A. R., Razzaq, A., Yu, Z., Shah, A., Sharif, A., & Janjua, L. (2022). Disruption in food supply chain and undernourishment challenges: An empirical study in the context of Asian countries. *Socio-Economic Planning Sciences*, 82, 101033. DOI: 10.1016/j.seps.2021.101033

Lee, V. H., Ooi, K. B., Chong, A. Y. L., & Seow, C. (2014). Creating technological innovation via green supply chain management: An empirical analysis. *Expert Systems with Applications*, 41(16), 6983–6994. DOI: 10.1016/j.eswa.2014.05.022

Li, L., Fei, C., & Fei, W. (2024). Research on investment incorporating both environmental performance and long (short) term financial performance of firms. *International Journal of Systems Science*, 55(2), 273–299. DOI: 10.1080/00207721.2023.2270402

Li, R., Liu, W., & Zhou, S. (2024). Digital Transformation of Supply Chain Management in the Fast Fashion Industry: A Case Study of Zara. In *SHS Web of Conferences* (Vol. 181, p. 04019). EDP Sciences. DOI: 10.1051/shsconf/202418104019

Lockett, A., Thompson, S., & Morgenstern, U. (2009). The development of the resource-based view of the firm: A critical appraisal. *International Journal of Management Reviews*, 11(1), 9–28. DOI: 10.1111/j.1468-2370.2008.00252.x

Mcdougall, N., Wagner, B., & MacBryde, J. (2016, June). A dynamic NRBV framework for innovative sustainable operations. *23rd innovation and product development management conference*.

OEKO-TEX. (2020, January 7). *OEKO-TEX- Tailor-made solutions for the textile and leather industry*. OEKO-TEX. https://www.oeko-tex.com/en/

Pang, R., & Zhang, X. (2019). Achieving environmental sustainability in manufacture: A 28-year bibliometric cartography of green manufacturing research. *Journal of Cleaner Production*, 233, 84–99. DOI: 10.1016/j.jclepro.2019.05.303

Perlman, B. J., Reddick, C. G., & Demir, T. (2024). Toward an Organizational Ethics Culture Framework: An Analysis of Survey Data From Local Government Managers. *Public Integrity*, 1–16. DOI: 10.1080/10999922.2023.2295643

Rejeb, A., Rejeb, K., Kayikci, Y., Appolloni, A., & Treiblmaier, H. (2023). Mapping the knowledge domain of green procurement: A review and bibliometric analysis. *Environment, Development and Sustainability*, 1–35. DOI: 10.1007/s10668-023-03948-w

Ridley, W., & Devadoss, S. (2023). Competition and trade policy in the world cotton market: Implications for US cotton exports. *American Journal of Agricultural Economics*, 105(5), 1365–1387. DOI: 10.1111/ajae.12370

Ruiz, A. (2023, April 11). *17 Most Worrying Textile Waste Statistics & Facts*. TheRoundup. https://theroundup.org/textile-waste-statistics/

Saad, S. M., & Khamkham, M. (2022). The Applications of AI in GSCM–A Systematic Literature Review. *Advances in Manufacturing Technology, 35*, 348-353.

Saunders, M., Lewis, P., & Thornhill, A. (2007). *Research methods for business students* (4th ed.). Pearson Education.

Shah, A., Mat, C. R. B. C., & Ibrahim, A. (2022). The resource and leagile strategy model for apparel export enterprises: A proposed model to mitigate COVID-19 uncertainties. *International Journal of Circular Economy and Waste Management*, 2(1), 1–14. DOI: 10.4018/IJCEWM.288502

Shibin, K. T., Dubey, R., Gunasekaran, A., Hazen, B., Roubaud, D., Gupta, S., & Foropon, C. (2020). Examining sustainable supply chain management of SMEs using resource based view and institutional theory. *Annals of Operations Research*, 290(1-2), 301–326. DOI: 10.1007/s10479-017-2706-x

State Bank of Pakistan. (2011). IFC Advisory Service in the Middle East and North Africa [Review of *IFC Advisory Service in the Middle East and North Africa*]. State Bank of Pakistan. https://www.sbp.org.pk/departments/ihfd/Sub-Segment%20Booklets/Textile%20Fabric.pdf

Suryanto, T., Haseeb, M., & Hartani, N. H. (2018). The correlates of developing green supply chain management practices: Firms level analysis in Malaysia. *International Journal of Supply Chain Management*, 7(5), 316.

Wang, S., Su, D., Wu, Y., & Chai, Z. (2020). Application of life-cycle assessment to the eco-design of LED lighting products. *Euro-Mediterranean Journal for Environmental Integration*, 5(2), 1–10. DOI: 10.1007/s41207-020-00180-0

Widari, T., Aliffiati, A., & Indra, M. (2023). Fast fashion: Consumptive behavior in fashion industry Generation Z in Yogyakarta. *IAS Journal of Localities*, 1(2), 104–113. DOI: 10.62033/iasjol.v1i2.18

Wiredu, J., Yang, Q., Sampene, A. K., Gyamfi, B. A., & Asongu, S. A. (2024). The effect of green supply chain management practices on corporate environmental performance: Does supply chain competitive advantage matter? *Business Strategy and the Environment*, 33(3), 2578–2599. DOI: 10.1002/bse.3606

Zhang, W., Zhang, C., Wei, S., Zhang, Q., Rehman, A., & Shah, A. (2022). Characteristics and evolution of China's carbon emission reduction measures: Leading towards environmental sustainability. *Frontiers in Environmental Science*, 10, 924887. DOI: 10.3389/fenvs.2022.924887

Chapter 8
Factors Impacting the Use of E-Marketing for Sustainable Business Performance

Adnan Ahmed Sheikh
https://orcid.org/0000-0002-3546-5284
University of Buraimi, Oman

Bilal Hassan
https://orcid.org/0009-0002-8955-2516
Air University, Islamabad, Pakistan

Beenish Tariq
Prince Sultan University, Saudi Arabia

ABSTRACT

This study aims to examine how numerous factors affect the sustainable business performance of major Pakistani enterprises using e-marketing as a mediating variable. Data was collected from 279 manufacturing companies in Pakistan using a cluster sampling technique. Notably, Amos revealed significant associations between e-marketing usage and sustainable business performance. The results showed partial mediation concerning e-marketing usage. The effective utilization of digital technologies assists in low-cost production and improves the flexibility and sustainability of manufacturing systems. Despite the lack of literature, digital marketing integrates to produce sustainability to overcome this problem. Therefore, this study has developed a unique framework to solve these difficulties and improve sustainable business performance.

DOI: 10.4018/979-8-3693-4123-0.ch008

INTRODUCTION

The advent of the Internet has revolutionized the company market relationship and is responsible for the augmented gap between them. Thus, it has become the most compelling challenge in the field of marketing. Digital marketing has revolutionized the business communication of firms due to access to consumers beyond geographic boundaries (Diez-Martin *et al.*, 2019). Digital marketing has been gaining popularity in resolving the marketing issues of modern businesses. Concurrently, sustainability goals have also become modern firms' high-value aspirations, particularly in marketing (Hassan *et al.*, 2023; Khan *et al.*, 2023). The researchers have initiated a continuing debate on digital marketing for sustainability. (Sheikh *et al.*, 2018). Sustainability asks for a better supply chain, linking and information to the investors, and better involvement of employees. (Diez-Martin *et al.*, 2019)

The increasing trend of using web-based activities and information technology has attracted considerable attention from scholars who are investigating their influence on commerce and business. (Stankov, Filimonau, & Slivar, 2019; Zikria, Kim, Hahm, Afzal, & Aalsalem, 2019). Digital technologies have engendered heightened competition among diverse businesses, particularly those enterprises endeavoring to secure market dominance and pursue optimal profitability through global market penetration. These companies are developing new strategies to compete with domestic and international rivals. In the current highly competitive landscape, businesses are actively venturing into intricate and saturated marketplaces, where an organization's marketing strategies and internal achievements heavily rely on the ability to establish a first-mover advantage (Sheikh, Shahzad and Ku Ishaq, 2017a). The dynamic and progressive nature of the information technology system has a profound influence on the operational effectiveness of organizations and the structure of their internal workflows (Labanauskaitė, Fiore, & Stasys, 2020). Moreover, researchers, practitioners, and academics paid close attention to industry growth and marketing performance.

The continuing performance of organizations depends on value addition to the shareholders' wealth and meeting the environment's needs (Labuschagne & Brent, 2005). Sustainability enhances the firm's efficiency and develops a culture of innovativeness and productivity (Chen, Okudan, & Riley, 2010). Such an environment for organizations would improve performance and efficient utilization of current resources for better economic and environmental results (Dunphy, 2011). These results promote economic, environmental, and social sustainability, improving the contentment of all stakeholders, including top management, traders, customers, employees, and society. The importance of sustainable development practices has been increasingly recognized, becoming a critical and evolving problem for international businesses. The triple bottom line concept has sustainability concerns regarding environmental preservation, economic progress, and social welfare (Khan *et al.*, 2023; Le *et al.*, 2022). Many disciplines like environmental conservation, management sciences, and engineering have adopted and recognized sustainability concepts. Therefore, the triple bottom line is comprehensively applicable to the textile industry wherein social considerations of firms include response to the customers and other social forces, economic considerations include cost-effective value addition, and environmental considerations include least harmful production and manufacturing of textile (Sheikh *et al.*, 2018). All the textile manufacturing countries face various problems mainly related to the triple bottom line concerns. Sustainability in manufacturing has been gaining increasing significance because the manufacturing processes produce a bulk of carbon dioxide into the environment, and mass resources are consumed with huge industrial wastes deposited into the environment (Hassan *et al.*, 2023; Khan *et al.*, 2023). Unemployment in textile manufacturing is alarming after closing dozens of companies in the last decade. The Pakistani textile manufacturers have contributed to developing triple bottom line features. Furthermore, the government of Pakistan and the top management of textile companies have also contributed significantly to developing the textile industry (Sheikh, Shahzad and Ku Ishaq, 2017a).

Besides, the e-marketing prospects for manufacturing firms, like the internet and social media promotional campaigns, assist in maintaining the sustainability of business and the environment due to its properties of effectively and efficiently reaching all stakeholders in time (Hassan *et al.*, 2023; Khan *et al.*, 2023; Sheikh *et al.*, 2018). Several studies have discussed the use of digital internet technologies (for instance, e-commerce and e-procurement), which can enhance the firm performance in terms of financial performance, firm output, market share, growth, and consumer faithfulness (Gregory, Ngo, & Karavdic, 2019; Mutlu & Sürer, 2016; Sánchez-Rodríguez et al., 2019). Besides, the industrial sector is not only the economic engine of a country; it also continuously adds to worldwide economic growth. Digitalization and consumer marketing have transformed industrial marketing (Herhausen, Miočević, Morgan, & Kleijnen, 2020). Therefore, to boost business performance, firms might consider the usage of technology in their marketing processes, which will not only bring new customers to the platform but also helps the firms in improving the effectiveness of the operational process in a sustainable manner keeping in view the triple bottom line and provide the firms with a competitive edge (Chege, Wang, & Suntu, 2020; Rusli, 2012).

Resultantly, digital communication impacts a firm's financial performance, and it assists in decreasing functioning expenses, financing, and facilitating international access. Pearce and Pearce (2019) and Ritter and Pedersen (2020) it is recognized that efficient firms adopt digital skills to develop a competitive advantage. Besides, effective stakeholder management is the most productive foundation of sustainable competitive advantage. Its significance is evident because the sustainability of organizational practices and processes has become necessary for a firm's B2B promotional and communication strategies (Sivarajah *et al.*, 2020). Notably, firms are unaware of the benefits of digital or e-marketing, and none of the studies has adequately addressed this main issue by doing an empirical investigation (Mzee et al., 2015; Adnan Ahmed Sheikh et al., 2016).

The global coronavirus epidemic and safety measures (e.g., regional lockdowns, social distancing, and quarantines) to contain it have also hampered business and economic growth (Kang, Diao, & Zanini, 2020). This unparalleled crisis has impacted many B2B organizations of different sizes operating in a varied set of industries (Mora Cortez & Johnston, 2020)., According to a report published by B2B International, manufacturing sectors (especially textile) are among the most disrupted due to the global pandemic. As of April 2020, the textile sector of Pakistan has faced a 59% decline compared to April 2019. Textile orders worth $1.3 billion have been suspended or cancelled due to a drop in global demand (Asghar, Batool, Farooq, & Rehman, 2020). Keeping the current situation in mind, managers of B2B organizations have started implementing contingency plans to deal with this pandemic and figure out ways to stay in business (Ritter & Pedersen, 2020). It has resulted in the digital transformation of sales and marketing efforts. B2B firms are shifting from traditional behaviours to digital behaviours. 96% of B2B firms have partially or fully moved to remote selling (McKinsey & Company, 2020). Thus, examining the benefits of e-marketing concerning the marketing performance of B2B firms would be interesting.

The present study has evaluated the impact of market orientation, support of higher management, and competition on the extent of e-marketing and performance in the wake of sustainability. Moreover, this study has laid its foundation on the Resource-Based View (RBV) theory and has elaborated on the mediating role of e-marketing. Moreover, the firm should extensively consider technological improvements. Implementing e-marketing and electronic means of communication are vital signs of economic development (Rahim et al., 2015). Dai and Kauffman (2015) Emphasized that the objective of B2B electronic markets is to computerize organizational work and minimize operating costs. Also, Herhausen et al.(2020) Indicated that the rising implications of digital marketing had not been studied in the existing literature on the manufacturing industry, especially the textile industry of Pakistan (Abrar *et al.*, 2018; Sheikh, Shahzad and Ishak, 2017a). The current analysis holds substantial implications for the academic research literature and industry, as outlined below. Initially, it offered a resolution to the inquiry, "To what extent does e-marketing impact the marketing performance of the manufacturing industry?" In addition, this study examines top management support, competitive pressure, and market orientation to determine if e-marketing improves marketing success.

Theoretical Development

The resource-based theory is widely accepted in performance literature. The basis of the resource-based view comes from old literature describing the significance of resources for performance (Penrose, 1959). The RBV theory became popular concerning strategic management and sustaining competitive advantage in companies (Chandler, 1990; Wernerfelt, 1984; Barney, 1991)The RBV theory assumes that the foundation of competitive advantage lies in the adequate utilization capacity of an available package of precious, material, and intangible resources that help businesses achieve sustainable performance.

Lastly, the speed of change dynamics in modern technology and the industrial world put extra pressure on today's manufacturing organizations to counteract promptly; otherwise, room for further development squeezes at an increasing rate (Stalk & Hout, 1990). The RBV theory has been used to examine the impact of IT on various firms' performance, and many research articles have been published in different journals to address the same issue. However, they could not come to a concrete conclusion about these constructs. Some studies also discovered a tenuous link between IT investment and organisational performance enhancement (Ravichandran *et al.*, 2009). The literature's findings suggest that the present research study can help address the most pressing issue of our time, particularly for manufacturing organizations where the triple bottom line has produced significant issues for corporations and societies. Furthermore, the research framework has been developed to identify the direct impact of various internal and external factors, including firm, technology, and environment, on sustainable business performance and the indirect impact of e-marketing technology.

The present study has also used the diffusion of innovation (DOI) theory to explain the adoption rate of technology in society at the individual and organizational levels. Besides, it claims creativity comes through consistent communication channels in a system or society. The theory has also stressed assisting firms and persons in choosing or rejecting the technology or the particular use of the technology mentioned above/ innovation (Rogers, 1995). The DOI theory has elucidated and examined the level of IT acceptance, like Internet or e-marketing databases, software development, and informational technology (Hoffer and Alexander, 1992; Prammanee, 2003). Based on the theoretical underpinning and identified gaps, the following research framework has been developed, as shown in Figure 1.

Figure 1. Framework

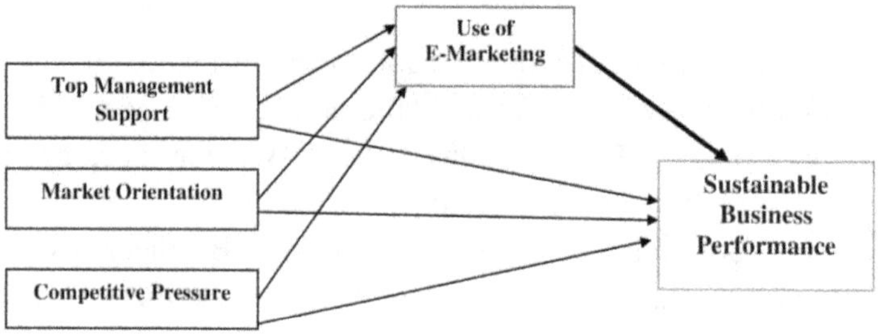

LITERATURE REVIEW

Use of E-Marketing and Sustainable Performance

Sustainable firm performance refers to producing reusable products and services that will not cause environmental pollution and enhance the organization's capacity. It can be reflected by profit, progress, and market price and represented as a combination of all three measures. In this respect, a sustainable firm creates value for its shareholders in terms of profit. It ensures environment preservation and improves living standards in society, whether it is business or manufacturing. The existing literature on sustainability has focused on critical thinking for the conservation of nature, poverty reduction, equitable distribution of resources, lesser population, and better quality of life.

Scholarly literature has established that e-marketing utilization is a noteworthy indicator of the characteristics that impact the sustainable performance of firms in business-to-business (B2B) environments. Recent literature has argued that technological adoption (e.g., e-marketing) positively influences firm performance.(Lin *et al.*, 2020). E-marketing usage improves business efficiency and significantly impacts marketing improvements (Chong *et al.*, 2018). Sheikh et al. (2018) and Sheikh, Shahzad, and Ku Ishaq (2017) Also, it concluded that e-marketing positively enhances overall firm performance. The reason behind this is the e-marketing mechanism, a technological process enabling firms to maintain 24/7 contact with customers via different mediums. E-marketing usage is important enough to study in emerging countries' business environments, such as manufacturing sectors, to learn how adoption techniques affect business performance, specifically marketing performance.

Despite the growing popularity of e-marketing, there is no evidence in the literature to support its relationship with company performance. Recently, study results on the connection between e-marketing and company success were inconsistent (Tsiotsou and Vlachopoulou, 2011). Sani et al. (2020) Indicated four different kinds of technology-based businesses and found that e-business intensity had a favourable impact on firm performance regarding company efficiency, sales performance, customer happiness, and relationship development. Further, (Babalola *et al.*, 2020) Also, e-marketing usage positively relates to marketing performance, particularly client acquisition and retention. Studies related to e-marketing are still in the infancy stage. Therefore, e-marketing adoption tactics and their impact on the manufacturing sector's market performance need more studies. According to past research, e-marketing use affects organizational performance. Hence, this study focused on B2B enterprises' marketing performance.. Thus, the proposed hypothesis is as follows;

H1: E-marketing has a positive association with sustainable business performance.

E-Marketing Applications, Sustainable Business Performance, Top Management Support

Organizational considerations relate to circumstances such as management preparedness to give assistance or an impediment (Yeh and Chen, 2018). They are used to determine whether or not a company has the technical and financial funds to put into technology (Khorram Niaki and Nonino, 2017). The degree to which senior management understands and is engaged in technology adoption is called top management support (Ooi *et al.*, 2018). Organizational barriers significantly affect adoption choices and are frequently linked to a company's strategic objectives, particularly during technology implementation (Yeh and Chen, 2018). On the other hand, senior management commitment may help spread technology, but it must stay active to accomplish the necessary outcomes (Dubey *et al.*, 2018).

The past literature has pointed out the top management's support in effectively applying innovative technology. (Sheikh et al., 2018). Tiago and Veríssimo (2014) Identify top management support as vigorous in e-marketing adoption to achieve market growth, market share, new product development, cost competence, competitive data of industry, and consumer retention for the long term. In the context of SMEs and the service industry in Western and emerging nations such as China, India, Egypt, and Taiwan, top management support has been utilized as a predictor in the literature. However, the impact of digital technology on the sustainable performance of manufacturing firms in Pakistan lacks studies. In Pakistan's manufacturing firms, the higher management has discretionary powers; thus, the decision-making is centralized to the top-level management.

The present study investigates Pakistan's manufacturing sector's sustainable performance variability to fill these gaps in the literature. E-marketing's mediating effect will be examined about top management support, market orientation, and competitive pressure (Abu Bakar and Ahmed, 2015; Mackey, 2008; Munz, 2017). This study tests the study framework to determine how e-marketing application mediates the relationship between top management support and sustainable business performance, adding to experiential, qualitative, and theoretical studies. Thus, the above discussion suggests the following hypotheses:

H2: Support from upper management has a positive effect on e-marketing implementation.

H5: Utilization of e-marketing mediates the relationship between support from upper management and sustainable business performance.

Market Orientation, Use of E-Marketing, and Sustainable Business Performance

It relates to the degree to which a company executes the marketing idea; market orientation is one of the essential terms in the marketing literature (Kohli and Jaworski, 2012). Quantitative studies have received robust evidence on market orientation and identified it as a vital strategic factor of an organization for sustainable competitive advantage (Homburg & Pflesser, 2000) Because it increases customer satisfaction, loyalty, and success in developing new products. According to the study, market orientation is the organization-wide production of market information related to present and future consumer requirements, data distribution across departments, and organization-wide response (Kohli and Jaworski, 2012). Researchers investigated different methods for understanding how market orientation affects performance by examining the impact of potential moderators and mediators, such as innovation and customer relationships (Carpenter, 2017). Market orientation is increasingly linked to innovation. Innovation may moderate the association between marketing orientation and business performance (Matear *et al.*, 2002).

According to Agarwal et al. (2003), The impact of technical and administrative innovation on the relationship between market orientation and performance is significant. E-marketing, also known as utilizing the World Wide Web and various digital tools to establish and facilitate communication between a corporation and its clients, has been widely acknowledged as a highly consequential component of marketing practice (Coviello and Brodie, 2001). Most e-marketing occurs on the Internet, which has been recognized for some time as a potent commercial resource that is being rapidly employed and incorporated into marketing strategies (Zhang *et al.*, 2024). Several factors have been examined as potential causes of widespread e-marketing adoption. Database and network marketing are examples of in-house resources and competencies (Babalola *et al.*, 2020); organizational preparedness and management support are examples of these elements Sani et al. (2020). Besides, the literature discusses inclusive, large firms that operate in different markets worldwide and focus on customer-oriented methodology, particularly in the manufacturing industry, whether it is a raw material, fabric or yarn, automobile, iron, and steel, or oil manufacturing, all are based on customer requirements and market demand. However, several studies have highlighted that most customers from various regions are shifting to India, China, and Bangladesh due to the communication edge. Most businesses have shifted their marketing activities to the Internet. Therefore, a country like Pakistan has continuously lost its global market share and has been affected drastically in the last decade (WTO, 2020). Despite several investigations, empirical investigation to identify the role of market orientation in bringing back the share of the customers for sustainable business performance.

Furthermore, the influence of various corporate factors on the firm's performance is important to understand the market orientation → innovation → performance framework better. However, it is crucial to understand the other outcomes of the firms to enhance the effectiveness of the business (Rapp, Schillewaert, and Hao, 2008). However, this study is intended to examine market orientation and innovation in the firm's performance, particularly marketing performance. As a result of previous research, the following hypotheses have been proposed:

H3: Market orientation influences e-marketing usage positively.

H6: Utilizing electronic marketing mediates the connection between market orientation and sustainable business performance.

Competitive Pressure, Use of E-Marketing, and Sustainable Business Performance

The competitive forces in the industry environment have been evaluated for sustainable performance. Introducing innovative technology like e-marketing and digital technology to gain competitive advantage inspires firms to adopt such technologies after industrial standards (Shi and Yan, 2016). The companies seek to achieve and maintain a competitive edge by introducing innovative technologies. Concurrently, competition is the environmental factor that influences industry strategy and is a key factor in characterizing the firm's level of technology adoption (Munz, 2017). The past literature on e-marketing has described that firms bring such technologies to highly competitive industries or environments; thus, it can be easily inferred that competitive pressure plays the most crucial role in the adoption of innovative technology by a firm like e-marketing. The literature on competition shows that the manufacturing sector has immense competition, which is the motivation factor of the present study for evaluating the factors of sustainable performance with the mediation of e-marketing. According to past studies, innovative technologies are adopted to create better value products at economical prices to gain a competitive advantage (Grover, 1993). Their findings were inconclusive. Thus, this study examines how top management support, market orientation, and competitive pressure through e-marketing affect sustainable business performance. Therefore, the following hypotheses have been formulated;

H4: Competitive pressure has a significant positive effect on e-marketing usage.

H7: Electronic marketing usage mediates the connection between competitive pressure and sustainable business performance.

Methodology and Measurement

There is a paucity of research on digital marketing and sustainability; consequently, the present study's methodology is related to e-marketing and sustainability research. This study employs quantitative methodologies and collects data from Pakistani manufacturing organizations. The sampling technique used to select respondents is proportionate cluster sampling because the target respondents are the top marketing managers, CEOs, directors of marketing, or marketing managers working of textile firms in Pakistan. A structured questionnaire was designed and distributed to the target respondents, i.e., the marketing managers, directors, CEOs, and top marketing managers in textile manufacturing companies scattered across Pakistan. The survey's response rate was 59%, which is adequate for the survey.

The study used the Area Cluster sampling technique for data collection. Later, the cluster was divided proportionately using a simple random sampling technique. It was made by selecting four provinces of Pakistan. Then, the study pointed out the specific cities of a textile manufacturing firm in each province of Pakistan: Punjab, Sindh, Balochistan, and KPK. During the survey, most of the industry is found in the provinces of Punjab and Sindh. In contrast, Balochistan and KPK are underdeveloped in terms of industry formation. The primary reason is that Punjab has agro-based raw material land, and Sindh has the Seaport through which most of the imports and exports have proceeded.

On the other hand, Balochistan and KPK are sand and mountainous provinces, where the availability of raw materials and transportation are the main challenges. The study has included significant cities in Pakistan based on the data provided by the Security Exchange Commission of Pakistan (SECP), the Trade Development Authority of Pakistan (TDAP), and the All Pakistan Textile Mills Association (APTMA). The respondents and the target companies are in various cities like Lahore, Faisalabad, Karachi, Multan etc. Through the sampling mentioned above technique, all the portions were chosen for the study with a proportionate multi-stage cluster sampling technique (Allen *et al.*, 2002).

Measures

As stated in the justifications, the researcher selected a seven-point Likert scale for the present study, as this is the most prevalent method of scaling in the social and behavioral sciences (Chomeya, 2010). With a 7-point Likert scale, respondents will have more room for nuanced expression of their thoughts and feelings (Hinkin, 1995). Market orientation can be evaluated with the help of a modified version of a 12-item scale Narver & Slater (1990). A four-item scale was adapted to assess top management support (Premkumar *et al.*, 1994). Besides, a six-item scale has been adapted to measure competitive pressure (Jaworski & Kohli 1993). In addition, an 8-item scale has been developed by Srinivasan et al. (2002) to assess the usage of e-marketing. Finally, a 6-item scale has been developed by (Le *et al.*, 2022)" to assess the sustainable performance of the business. The sample questions are: We achieve profitable growth over time, We achieve market share growth over time, We achieve customer database growth over time, We improve resource efficiency over time, We improve environmental performance over time, and Our contribution to improving social welfare increases over time.

DATA ANALYSIS

Confirmatory Factor Analysis (CFA)

We ran three structural equation models in AMOS 24.0 on all possible hypothetical models and finally evaluated the CR AND AVE. It allows us to examine the associations between our independent and dependent variables (Kelloway, 1998). In addition, we examined direct and indirect pathways among the manifest variables in our analysis. To assess model fit, we utilized seven fit indices: relative chi-square ($\chi 2$/DF), chi-square ($\chi 2$; Bentler & Mooijaart, 1989), CFI, Tucker-Lewis index (TLI), and RMSEA. If the model fits the data correctly, then $\chi 2$ cannot be significant as recommended by (Kline, 2004). The sensitivity of the $\chi 2$ is adjusted by dividing it by its degrees of freedom, which depends on the sample size. Further, a Relative $\chi 2$ value between 1.0 and 5.0 is measured as a good fit (Bollen, 1989).

Table 1. Fitness of Model

Model	x2	df	x2/df	SRMR	TLI	IFI	CFI	RMSEA
1-factor	1307.63	649	2.01	0.1	0.93	0.94	0.94	0.063
2-factor	1159.27	648	1.79	0.09	0.94	0.96	0.95	0.056
3-factor	624.92	369	1.69	0.07	0.95	0.96	0.96	0.052

For the first model indicated fitness as χ2= 1307.63 (χ2/df; 2.01), SRMR = .1, TLI = .93. IFI = .94, CFI =. 94, and RMSEA = .063. When we loaded all items on a single factor, All output values were determined to be within the acceptable threshold range. Next, a two-factor analysis was conducted with all dependent variables and the remaining independent variables on one factor. However, the results for the 2-factor model showed fitness as χ2= 1159.27 (χ2/df; 1.79), SRMR = .09, TLI = .94. IFI = .96, CFI = .95 and RMSEA = .056. Furthermore, all the frameworks of the current study were included in the 3rd factor, where the researcher loaded independent variables, mediating variables, and the dependent variable on the third factor separately according to the framework path analysis. The 3-factor model found fitness as χ2= 624.92 (χ2/df; 1.69), SRMR =.07, TLI =.95, IFI =.96, CFI =.96 and RMSEA =.052. Hence, the findings find the output values in the acceptable range.

Discriminant Validity and CR, AVE

Moreover, the extracted average variance (AVE) should be at least 0.50. As shown in Table 2, all variables are more dependable, and the AVE is greater than the 0.50 threshold, indicating that the measurement model is reliable (Fornell and Larcker, 1981; Sarstedt *et al.*, 2014).

Table 2. CR, AVE, Discriminant Validity

Variables Name	CR	AVE	MO	TMS	SBP	UEM	CP
Market Orientation	**0.892**	**0.533**	**0.730**				
Top Management Support	**0.813**	**0.528**	0.087	**0.727**			
Sustainable Business Performance	**0.802**	**0.534**	0.102	0.406*	**0.731**		
Use of E-Marketing	**0.888**	**0.576**	0.053	0.330*	0.395*	**0.759**	
Competitive Pressure	**0.837**	**0.519**	-0.135*	0.174**	-0.028	0.345*	**0.721**

Results

Table 3 shows the bivariate relationships between the constructs. At the zero-order level, there is a strong correlation between the dependent constructs. Our model fits the data well (χ2 = 668.65, df = 380; χ2 /df = 1.76; CFI = .96; IFI =.96; TLI = .95; SRMR =.09; RMSEA = .054. The model's empirical results with significant structural pathways and their standardized (β) regression weights were provided.

Table 3. Hypotheses Testing

Model	x2	df	x2/df	SRMR	TLI	IFI	CFI	RMSEA
Path-Analysis	668.65	380	1.76	.09	.95	.96	.96	.054

In terms of direct connections between latent variables and sustainable firm performance. Hypothesis 1, 2, 3, and 4 claim that market orientation, competitive pressure, top management support, and e-marketing usage are substantially related to firm efficiency. Moreover, top management support (β = .33) has shown a substantially favorable relation to firm efficiency, and H1 is supported. Next, market orientation (β = .104) is significant with sustainable business performance; H2 is supported. Moreover, the empirical findings revealed that competitive pressure (β = 0.15) is significantly associated with firm performance; hence, H3 is supported. Furthermore, the study discovered a significant solid positive relationship between E-marketing use (=.223) and firm performance (=.223). As a result, H4 is supported.

Next, the hypothesis proposes that support from upper management, market orientation, and competitive pressure positively affect e-marketing (UEM). In contrast, our empirical findings revealed that top management support (=.26) positively correlated with e-marketing usage. Consequently, market orientation (=.10) was significantly associated with e-marketing utilization. In addition, empirical findings revealed that competitive pressure (=0.26) is significantly associated with e-marketing usage.

Table 4. Direct Hypotheses

Direct Relationships			Beta	SE	CR	P-value	Hypothesis
SBP	**→**	**UEM**	**0.223**	**0.053**	**3.85**	**0.001**	**Accepted**
UEM	→	TMS	0.255	0.064	4.485	0.001	Accepted
UEM	→	MO	0.104	0.062	1.828	0.068	Accepted
UEM	→	CP	0.258	0.06	4.547	0.001	Accepted

Mediation Analysis

This study uses the re-sampling mediation method (bootstrapping) to examine the indirect impact of an individual construct. Similarly, most research has indicated that "bootstrapping is a non-parametric re-sampling procedure" that receives more responses because this method is considered the most promising for testing and analyzing the effect of mediation (Hayes, 2009). Besides, the AMOS bootstrapping method for mediation analysis is best for empirical studies since it is suitable for a small sample (Hair et al., 2014). During the mediation test, one should follow the mediation procedure that bootstraps the sampling distribution of indirect effects, which applies to both simple and multiple models. Consequently, the current study investigated the influence of e-marketing uses as a mediating construct by employing Amos V 20 on the bootstrapping technique and re-sampling 2000 times to determine the t-value.

Table 5. Mediation results

Indirect Relationship	Direct	Indirect	Mediation	Hypotheses
TMS → UEM → SBP	.26*	.057*	Partial	Accepted
MO → UEM → SBP	.10*	.023*	Partial	Accepted
CP → UEM → SBP	.26*	.058*	Partial	Accepted

Table 5 indicates the outcomes of the mediation effect of UEM (use of e-marketing) on the associations between latent constructs and firm performance.

DISCUSSION AND CONCLUSION

Existing research on digital marketing and sustainability was insufficient, demonstrating the need for a comprehensive study on digital marketing to bridge the gap between markets and businesses. Hypotheses have been formulated based on the research questions derived from the problem description, following the study goals. Examining these linkages has provided research prospects for enhancing the sustainable performance of the manufacturing sector, with particular emphasis on the textile manufacturing industry. This study's primary objective was to investigate the role of e-marketing as a mediator between predictor variables and the sustainable performance of manufacturing enterprises at the organizational level.

According to the fundamental hypotheses, UEM mediated the relationship between the independent variables and the performance of major firms in Pakistan. The findings affirmed that UEM positively affects business performance; consequently, it can be concluded that the greater the use of e-marketing in firms, the greater the likelihood of sustaining business performance (Sheikh, Shahzad, & Ishak, 2016). The findings supported the previous study's conclusion that e-marketing contributes to corporate success, suggesting that e-marketing adoption and use present opportunities for businesses and that e-marketing is widely acknowledged as a substantial driver of firm performance (Sheikh, Shahzad, & Ku Ishak, 2017; Sheikh et al., 2016).

The present research study has also evaluated the impact of top management support on the sustainable firm's performance (El-Gohary, 2012; Wang et al., 2010). Top management support is highly effective in improving performance sustainability for the manufacturing sector in the Pakistani textile sector. Therefore, the present study also found that top management support plays a significant role in assessing the sustainable performance of a firm. Another important aim of the study has been accomplished: the results show a link between market orientation, competitive pressure, top-level management support, and sustainable performance. The study posited that e-marketing plays a mediating role in various contexts. Subsequently, hypothesis testing concluded that e-marketing is a mediator in the link between many antecedents. The study suggests that the researcher has concluded, supported by significant evidence, that using e-marketing can yield various strategic advantages for businesses. These advantages include reducing supply chain expenses, expanding into new markets, enhancing distribution effectiveness, and establishing long-term connections with buyers through close networking. Past research studies have also established that e-marketing innovations directly influence firm performance due to increased relationships with business customers and the growth of B2B organizations in the Pakistani textile sector. The other objective of the study was to identify the antecedents of sustainable performance as a result of the direct effect of e-marketing on the firm's sustainable performance. According to the study's direct hypotheses, top management support, market orientation, and competitive pressure have a significant positive relationship with e-marketing. In addition, market orientation describes businesses that consistently consider the requirements, desires, and actions of their industry's competitors. Thus, market orientation facilitates the fulfilment of consumer needs, which is essential for the owners of the firms.

According to the findings of a subsequent hypothesis that there is a positive association between top management support and the use of e-marketing, the results were affirmative of this relationship. The finding is in line with the previous research studies on the relationship of these constructs. Thus, it has been concluded that top management support is helpful in the firm's adoption, implementation, and innovation. On the contrary, competitive pressure has shown a significant positive association with a sustainable firm's performance, implying that increased competition will increase the business's growth and market share performance, making it more sustainable. The same explanation is traced from the resource-based view theory (Kang & Park, 2012; Konings, Cayseele, & Warzynski, 2005; Rahayu & Day, 2015). The findings have vividly elaborated that competitiveness forces organizations to embrace technology to gain market share locally and internationally. Furthermore, such actions enhance consumer trust and assist the business in increasing sales to recoup its investment quickly.

Implications

The present research study has added to the literature on company performance by reviewing past research studies. The outcomes of the present research study, wherein constructs like top management support, market orientation, and competitive pressure have been evaluated for firm sustainable performance under the use of e-marketing (Hassan *et al.*, 2023; Khan *et al.*, 2023; Sheikh *et al.*, 2018). These factors affect Pakistani textile manufacturers' marketing effectiveness. RBV-Resource-based theory and DOI-Diffusion of innovation theory underpin the research to sustain all variables and their effects on marketing performance through e-marketing usage.

The study's main applied and administrative implications include understanding the group of study predictors and mediating variables to enhance the firm's performance. These predictors or antecedents include top management support, market orientation, competitive pressure, and the mediating factor of e-marketing. The policy decision-makers should create an integrated environment preservation strategy that is helpful in environmentally friendly manufacturing and sustainable performance in the long run (Zhang *et al.*, 2024). As per study findings and the corresponding research literature, these implications are possible with environmental activities and mutual collaboration from customers and raw material traders. To achieve desired outcomes and enhanced performance, the industrialists should directly involve these parties or stakeholders in achieving a triple bottom line (Sheikh *et al.*, 2018).

Furthermore, considering the evident dearth of scholarly works about e-marketing, this study aims to expand upon existing research by incorporating innovation and technology usage theories. Specifically, it seeks to explore the potential of innovation and technology in influencing the adoption of e-marketing within the manufacturing industry. The utilization of RBV theory and the DOI theory facilitated the identification of variables that could potentially influence the implementation of e-marketing practices within the manufacturing industry. This analysis was conducted in conjunction with an examination of existing literature and theories in the field. Nevertheless, there is a scarcity of scholarly investigations that have explored the integration of the DOI and RBV theories as a comprehensive theoretical framework. Furthermore, this study contributes to the existing body of literature by examining the role of e-marketing as a mediating variable in the relationship between TMS, MO, CP, and market performance. The implementation and utilization of electronic marketing play a pivotal role in enhancing operational effectiveness inside the contemporary digital era.

In addition, the strong and significant relationship between the use of e-marketing and the availability of these resources (independent variables) highlights the need for managers to prioritize these resources before implementing e-marketing strategies within their organizations. Thus, the purpose of the present study was to elucidate the essential underlying components and competencies required for transforming a traditional business model into a click-and-mortar model through the use of e-marketing strategies. This study proposed an extension of the Resource-Based View (RBV) and Diffusion of Innovation (DOI) frameworks to include characteristics more relevant to the performance of both small and large businesses in Pakistan. This study aimed to identify and analyze the factors influencing the adoption and implementation of e-marketing strategies. On the other hand, the Resource-Based View (RBV) framework concentrates on identifying and analyzing the specific tangible and intangible resources that contribute to an organization's improved performance.

This study helps researchers understand the diverse associations between TMS (Top management support), MO (Market Orientation), and CP (Competitive Pressure) in e-marketing and their direct and indirect effects on small and large businesses. This study uses e-marketing as a mediator. Thus, business owner's and marketing managers' views determine e-marketing's success. The study's unique focus on e-marketing in small and large enterprises makes it academically valuable. This study supports the research framework's theoretical links with empirical evidence. This study shows that e-marketing mediates the relationship between top management support, market orientation, and competitive pressure on sustainable business success in Pakistan (Sheikh *et al.*, 2018; Sheikh, Shahzad and Ku Ishaq, 2017b).

The present study has also evaluated the mediating role of e-marketing usage among the study variables. The study is worth researching because, as per existing literature, the antecedents of marketing performance do not affect it directly. Rather, they show the impact through the use of technology. (Laumer and Eckhardt, 2012). Pakistan's manufacturing industry's biggest performance challenge is top management's centralization chain of command decision-making. MIS professionals are hired by manufacturing senior management to administer the information system. Furthermore, because of a lack of understanding and expertise, TM hesitates to embrace such technologies, another reason Pakistan's manufacturing industry lags in global competitiveness (Pakistan Credit Rating Agency, 2011). In this research, senior management support for MIS and its implementation (particularly e-marketing acceptability and use) should be explored in detail. For contemporary leadership in the digital economy, a deeper grasp of technical innovation in the B2B environment is essential. All areas of a company's activities, including social responsibility, the environment, markets, and workers, are now subject to several internal and external demands (Khan *et al.*, 2024). Academics and corporate leaders have discussed their ability to adapt, assimilate, and regenerate. Consequently, there has been a surge in interest in a study into the different ethical types of governance associated with technological progress, such as using artificial and moral norms via questionable methods (Lin *et al.*, 2020).

Therefore, the present study has fetched many visions about the use of e-marketing and its impact on performance improvement for manufacturing companies in Pakistan, particularly in the textile industry. Thus, the present study shall assist the higher management, including directors, GM Marketing, managers, etc., in adopting and utilizing the e-marketing technology and tackling such governing independent variables from their firms to enhance sustainable performance in the long run and to access international markets through simple and efficient processes. Moreover, the present study is associated with policy decision-makers, top management, manufacturers, and stakeholders implementing e-marketing to succeed in local and international markets. Comprehensively, the present research is a worthwhile addition to the knowledge of modern marketing. The present research study has significant additions, such as the fact that the B2B and B2C markets have some similarities and their traditional differences.

Moreover, the variation of marketing practices in various constructs is studied (Coviello and Brodie, 2001). The managerial implication of this study is the use of e-marketing in Pakistan's manufacturing industry. Initially, the present study empirically assesses critical factors in the sustainable performance of manufacturing companies in Pakistan. The study findings guide the manufacturing companies' owners and marketing managers for improved comprehension of different factors of sustainable performance (Khan *et al.*, 2024). These also help in strategic planning and policy designing. Thus, ultimately, it can have a positive impact on Pakistan's overall economy.

7. LIMITATIONS AND FUTURE RECOMMENDATIONS

This research extends the existing body of knowledge and the growing literature on the crucial use of e-marketing to achieve overall marketing and firm objectives. The limited sample size of 279 respondents in this research highlights that carefulness is compulsory in understanding the outcomes since these findings are inappropriate in other states. Though the current research distillates the large firms operating only in Pakistan, there is a probability that measures of non-adoption in an emerging country and newly industrialized countries may differ from those industries operating in technologically progressive first-world countries (for instance, developed countries).

Based on this research's projected issues, future research should examine e-marketing uses and sustainable business performance in micro-businesses, medium-sized businesses, and large corporations using diverse theories and factors. E-marketing by service sector businesses can be studied using the same projected factors as present research. Finally, technological opportunism, e-business uses, e-commerce uses, and technology readiness can be utilized as independent and mediating variables to quantify firm performance in different nations or industries. Top management support moderates the relationship between technology (e-marketing, e-commerce, e-business, etc.) and firm sustainability. The TOE model can be used in future studies to demonstrate and place factors in the study framework to provide further guidance. Finally, triple bottom-line sustainable company performance characteristics can be tested separately with several antecedents for more reliable results.

ACKNOWLEDGMENT

The authors would like to thank Prince Sultan University for their support and academic guidance.

REFERENCES

Abrar, M.M., Griswold, M.G., Fullman, N., Hawley, C., Arian, N., Zimsen, S.R.M., & Tymeson, H.D. (2018). Alcohol use and burden for 195 countries and territories, 1990-2016: A systematic analysis for the Global Burden of Disease Study 2016. *The Lancet*, *392*(10152), 1015–1035. .DOI: 10.1016/S0140-6736(18)31310-2

Abu Bakar, A. R., & Ahmed, Z. U. (2015). Technology Motivation in E-Marketing Adoption Among Malaysian Manufacturers. *Journal of Transnational Management*, 20(2), 126–152. DOI: 10.1080/15475778.2015.1038949

Agarwal, S., Krishna Erramilli, M., & Dev, C. S. (2003). Market orientation and performance in service firms: Role of innovation. *Journal of Services Marketing*, 17(1), 68–82. DOI: 10.1108/08876040310461282

Al-Qirim, N. (2007). The adoption of eCommerce communications and applications technologies in small businesses in New Zealand. *Electronic Commerce Research and Applications*, 6(4), 462–473. DOI: 10.1016/j.elerap.2007.02.012

Allen, M. R., Gillett, N. P., Zwiers, F. W., Weaver, A. J., Hegerl, G. C., & Stott, P. A. (2002). Detecting anthropogenic influence with a multi-model ensemble. *Geophysical Research Letters*, 29(20), 29–32. DOI: 10.1029/2002GL015836

Asghar, N., Batool, M., Farooq, F., & Ur Rehman, H. (2020). Covid-19 Pandemic and Pakistan Economy: A Preliminary Survey. *Review of Economics and Development Studies*, 6(2), 447–459.

Babalola, H. B., Lateef, S. A., & Abu Zekeri, A. (2020). New Trends of Intelligent E-Marketing and Consumer Buying Behaviour: A Study of Selected Universities in Osun State, Nigeria. *Jurnal Aplikasi Manajemen, Ekonomi Dan Bisnis*, 5(1), 14–25. DOI: 10.51263/jameb.v5i1.109

Barney, J. (1991). Firm Resources and Sustained Competitive Advantage. *Journal of Management*, 17(1), 99–120. DOI: 10.1177/014920639101700108

Bentler, P. M., & Mooijaart, A. (1989). Choice of Structural Model via Parsimony: A Rationale Based on Precision. *Psychological Bulletin*, 106(2), 315–317. DOI: 10.1037/0033-2909.106.2.315 PMID: 2678203

Bollen, K. A. (1989). A New Incremental Fit Index for General Structural Equation Models. *Sociological Methods & Research*, 17(3), 303–316. DOI: 10.1177/0049124189017003004

Carpenter, G. S. (2017). Market orientation: Reflections on field-based, discovery-oriented research. *AMS Review*, 7(1–2), 13–19. DOI: 10.1007/s13162-017-0095-6

Chandler. (1990). Strategy and Structure: Chapters in the History of the Industrial Enterprise - Alfred Dupont Chandler - Google Books.

Chege, S. M., Wang, D., & Suntu, S. L. (2020). Impact of information technology innovation on firm performance in Kenya. *Information Technology for Development*, 26(2), 316–345. DOI: 10.1080/02681102.2019.1573717

Chomeya, D. R. (2010). Quality of Psychology Test Between Likert Scale 5 and 6 Points. *Journal of Social Sciences (New York, N. Y.)*, 6(3), 399–403. DOI: 10.3844/jssp.2010.399.403

Chong, W. K., Man, K. L., & Kim, M. (2018). The impact of e-marketing orientation on performance in Asian SMEs: A B2B perspective. *Enterprise Information Systems*, 12(1), 4–18. DOI: 10.1080/17517575.2016.1177205

Coviello, N. E., & Brodie, R. J. (2001). Contemporary marketing practices of consumer and business-to-business firms: How different are they? *Journal of Business and Industrial Marketing*, 16(5), 382–400. DOI: 10.1108/08858620110400223

Dai, Q., & Kauffman, R. J. (2002). Business models for internet-based B2B electronic markets. *International Journal of Electronic Commerce*, 6(4), 41–72. DOI: 10.1080/10864415.2002.11044247

Diez-Martin, F., Blanco-Gonzalez, A., & Prado-Roman, C. (2019). Research challenges in digital marketing: Sustainability. *Sustainability (Basel)*, 11(10), 2839. Advance online publication. DOI: 10.3390/su11102839

Djermani, F., Shahzad, A., Sheikh, A. A., Mohammed, J., & Alekam, E. (2016). Factors influencing the intention to use e-government services in algeria: An empirical study. *Studia Ubb Negotia*, LXI(3), 35–68.

Duan, X., Deng, H., & Corbitt, B. (2012). What Drives the Adoption of Electronic Markets in Australian Small-and- Medium Sized Enterprises? – An Empirical Study. *Australasian Conference on Information Systems*, 1–11.

Dubey, R., Gunasekaran, A., Childe, S. J., Papadopoulos, T., Hazen, B. T., & Roubaud, D. (2018). Examining top management commitment to TQM diffusion using institutional and upper echelon theories. *International Journal of Production Research*, 56(8), 2988–3006. DOI: 10.1080/00207543.2017.1394590

El-Gohary, H. (2012). Factors affecting E-Marketing adoption and implementation in tourism firms: An empirical investigation of Egyptian small tourism organisations. *Tourism Management*, 33(5), 1256–1269. DOI: 10.1016/j.tourman.2011.10.013

Fornell, C., & Larcker, D. F. (1981). Evaluating Structural Equation Models with Unobservable Variables and Measurement Error. *JMR, Journal of Marketing Research*, 18(1), 39–50. DOI: 10.1177/002224378101800104

Gray, B. J., & Hooley, G. J. (2002). Guest editorial. *European Journal of Marketing*, 36(9/10), 980–989. DOI: 10.1108/03090560210437280

Gregory, G. D., Ngo, L. V., & Karavdic, M. (2019). Developing e-commerce marketing capabilities and efficiencies for enhanced performance in business-to-business export ventures. *Industrial Marketing Management*, 78, 146–157. DOI: 10.1016/j.indmarman.2017.03.002

Grover, V. (1993). An empirically derived model for the adoption of customer-based interorganiza .... *Decision Sciences*, 24(3), 603–640. DOI: 10.1111/j.1540-5915.1993.tb01295.x

Hassan, N. M., Khan, S. A. R., Ashraf, M. U., & Sheikh, A. A. (2023). "Interconnection between the role of blockchain technologies, supply chain integration, and circular economy: A case of small and medium-sized enterprises in Pakistan", *Science Progress*. *Science Progress*, 106(3), 1–22. DOI: 10.1177/00368504231186527 PMID: 37437130

Hayes, A. F. (2009). Beyond Baron and Kenny: Statistical mediation analysis in the new millennium. *Communication Monographs*, 76(4), 408–420. DOI: 10.1080/03637750903310360

Herhausen, D., Miočević, D., Morgan, R. E., & Kleijnen, M. H. P. (2020). The digital marketing capabilities gap. *Industrial Marketing Management*, 90, 276–290. DOI: 10.1016/j.indmarman.2020.07.022

Hinkin, T. R. (1995). A Review of Scale Development Practices in the Study of Organizations. *Journal of Management*, 21(5), 473–478. DOI: 10.1177/014920639502100509

Hoffer, J. A., & Alexander, M. B. (1992). The diffusion of database machines. *The Data Base for Advances in Information Systems*, 23(2), 13–19. DOI: 10.1145/141342.141352

Homburg, C., & Pflesser, C. (2000). A Multiple-Layer Model of Market-Oriented Organizational Culture: Measurement Issues and Performance Outcomes. *JMR, Journal of Marketing Research*, 37(4), 449–462. DOI: 10.1509/jmkr.37.4.449.18786

Jaworski, B., & Kohli, A. (1993). Market Orientation: Antecedents and Consequences. *Journal of Marketing*, 57(3), 53–70. DOI: 10.1177/002224299305700304

Kang, J., Diao, Z., & Zanini, M. T. (2020). Business-to-business marketing responses to COVID-19 crisis: A business process perspective. *Marketing Intelligence & Planning*, (71772059). Advance online publication. DOI: 10.1108/MIP-05-2020-0217

Kang, K. N., & Park, H. (2012). Influence of government R&D support and inter-firm collaborations on innovation in Korean biotechnology SMEs. *Technovation*, 32(1), 68–78. DOI: 10.1016/j.technovation.2011.08.004

Kelloway, K. (1998). Using LISREL for Structural Equation Modeling: A Researcher's Guide - E. Kevin Kelloway - Google Books. *Sage (Atlanta, Ga.).*

Khan, S.A.R., Ahmad, Z., Sheikh, A.A. & Yu, Z. (2023). Green technology adoption paving the way toward sustainable performance in circular economy: a case of Pakistani small and medium enterprises. *International Journal of Innovation Science*. .DOI: 10.1108/IJIS-10-2022-0199

Khan, S. A. R., Sheikh, A. A., & Tahir, M. S. (2024). Corporate social responsibility-an antidote for sustainable business performance: Interconnecting role of digital technologies, employee eco-behavior, and tax avoidance. *Environmental Science and Pollution Research International*, 31(3), 4365–4383. DOI: 10.1007/s11356-023-31377-9 PMID: 38102435

Khorram Niaki, M., & Nonino, F. (2017). Additive manufacturing management: A review and future research agenda. *International Journal of Production Research*, 55(5), 1419–1439. DOI: 10.1080/00207543.2016.1229064

Kian Chong, W., Shafaghi, M., Woollaston, C., & Lui, V. (2010). B2B e-marketplace: An e-marketing framework for B2B commerce. *Marketing Intelligence & Planning*, 28(3), 310–329. DOI: 10.1108/02634501011041444

Kohli, A. K., & Jaworski, B. J. (2012). Market Orientation: The Construct, Research Propositions, and Managerial Implications. *Developing a Market Orientation*, 54(2), 7–44. DOI: 10.4135/9781452231426.n2

Konings, J., Cayseele, P., & Warzynski, F. (2005). The Effects of Privatization and Competitive Pressure on Firms' Price-Cost Margins: Micro Evidence from Emerging Economies. *The Review of Economics and Statistics*, 87(1), 124–134. DOI: 10.1162/0034653053327603

Labanauskaitė, D., Fiore, M., & Stašys, R. (2020). Use of E-marketing tools as communication management in the tourism industry. *Tourism Management Perspectives*, 34, 100652. DOI: 10.1016/j.tmp.2020.100652

Lau, Y. W., & Tong, C. Q. (2008). Are Malaysian Government-Linked Companies (GLCs) Creating Value? *International Applied Economics and Management Letters*, 1(1), 9–12.

Laumer, S., & Eckhardt, A. (2012). Integrated Series in Information Systems. Springer. DOI: 10.1007/978-1-4419-6108-2

Le, T.T., Behl, A. & Pereira, V. (2022). Establishing linkages between circular economy practices and sustainable performance: the moderating role of circular economy entrepreneurship. *Management Decision*. .DOI: 10.1108/MD-02-2022-0150

Li, Y. H. (2008). An empirical investigation on the determinants of E-procurement adoption in Chinese manufacturing enterprises. *2008 International Conference on Management Science and Engineering 15th Annual Conference Proceedings, ICMSE*, 32–37. DOI: 10.1109/ICMSE.2008.4668890

Lin, W.L., Yip, N., Ho, J.A. & Sambasivan, M. (2020). The adoption of technological innovations in a B2B context and its impact on firm performance: An ethical leadership perspective. *Industrial Marketing Management*, *89*, 61–71. .DOI: 10.1016/j.indmarman.2019.12.009

Mackey, A. (2008). The effect of CEOS on firm performance. *Strategic Management Journal*, 29(12), 1356–1367. DOI: 10.1002/smj.708

Matear, S., Osborne, P., Garrett, T., & Gray, B. J. (2002). How does market orientation contribute to service firm performance? *European Journal of Marketing*, 36(9/10), 1058–1075. DOI: 10.1108/03090560210437334

McKinsey & Company. (2020). *How B2B Sales Have Changed During COVID-19.*

Molla, A., & Licker, P. S. (2005). ECommerce adoption in developing countries: A model and instrument. *Information & Management*, 42(6), 877–899. DOI: 10.1016/j.im.2004.09.002

Munz, E. D. (2017). Psychotherapie in Der Psychiatrie. *Nervenheilkunde: Zeitschrift für Interdisziplinaere Fortbildung*. Advance online publication. DOI: 10.1007/s13398-014-0173-7.2

Mutlu, H. M., & Sürer, A. (2016). Effects of market, e-marketing, and technology orientations on innovativeness and performance in Turkish health organizations. *Health Marketing Quarterly*, 33(2), 95–111. DOI: 10.1080/07359683.2016.1166807 PMID: 27191549

Mzee, R. M., Ogweno, K. L., & Irene, N. (2015). Factors influencing Adoption of E marketing by small and Medium Enterprises (SMEs) in Kisumu Municipality. *IOSR Journal of Business and Management*, 17(5), 2319–7668. DOI: 10.9790/487X-17537883

Narver, J. C., & Slater, S. F. (1990). The Effect of a Market Orientation on Business Profitability. *Journal of Marketing*, 54(4), 20–35. DOI: 10.1177/002224299005400403

Ooi, K. B., Lee, V. H., Tan, G. W. H., Hew, T. S., & Hew, J. J. (2018). Cloud computing in manufacturing: The next industrial revolution in Malaysia? *Expert Systems with Applications*, 93, 376–394. DOI: 10.1016/j.eswa.2017.10.009

PACRA. (2011), *The Pakistan Credit Rating Agency Limited, Study of Textile Sector.*

Pearce, D. D., & Pearce, J. A. (2019). Distinguishing attributes of high-growth ventures. *Business Horizons, Elsevier Ltd*, (January). Advance online publication. DOI: 10.1016/j.bushor.2019.10.003

Prammanee, N. (2003). A critical analysis of the adoption and utilization of the internet in Thailand for education purposes. *First Monday*, 8(1). Advance online publication. DOI: 10.5210/fm.v8i1.1021

Prasad, V. K., Ramamurthy, K., & Naidu, G. M. (2001). The Influence on of Internet-Marketing Marketing Performance Competencies Integration and Export. *Journal of International Marketing*, 9(4), 82–110. DOI: 10.1509/jimk.9.4.82.19944

Premkumar, G., Ramamurthy, K., & Nilakanta, S. (1994). Implementation of electronic data interchange: An innovation diffusion perspective. *Journal of Management Information Systems*, 11(2), 157–186. DOI: 10.1080/07421222.1994.11518044

Premkumar, G., & Roberts, M. (1999). Adoption of new information technologies in rural small businesses. *Omega*, 27(4), 467–484. DOI: 10.1016/S0305-0483(98)00071-1

Rahayu, R. & Day, J. (2015). Determinant Factors of E-commerce Adoption by SMEs in Developing Country: Evidence from Indonesia. *Procedia - Social and Behavioral Sciences*, *195*, 142–150. .DOI: 10.1016/j.sbspro.2015.06.423

Rapp, A., Schillewaert, N., & Hao, A. W. (2008). The Influence of Market Orientation on E-Business Innovation and Performance: The Role of the Top Management Team. *Journal of Marketing Theory and Practice*, 16(1), 7–25. DOI: 10.2753/MTP1069-6679160101

Ravichandran, T., Liu, Y., Han, S., & Hasan, I. (2009). Diversification and Firm Performance: Exploring the Moderating Effects of Information Technology Spending. *Journal of Management Information Systems*, 25(4), 205–240. DOI: 10.2753/MIS0742-1222250407

Ritter, T., & Pedersen, C. L. (2020a). Digitization capability and the digitalization of business models in business-to-business firms: Past, present, and future. *Industrial Marketing Management*, 86(April), 180–190. Advance online publication. DOI: 10.1016/j.indmarman.2019.11.019

Ritter, T., & Pedersen, C. L. (2020b). Analyzing the impact of the coronavirus crisis on business models. *Industrial Marketing Management*, 88(May), 214–224. DOI: 10.1016/j.indmarman.2020.05.014

Rusli, E. M. (2012). Facebook buys Instagram for $1 billion. *New York Times*.

Sánchez-Rodríguez, C., Martínez-Lorente, A. R., & Hemsworth, D. (2019). E-procurement in small and medium sized enterprises; facilitators, obstacles and effect on performance. *Benchmarking*, 27(2), 839–866. DOI: 10.1108/BIJ-12-2018-0413

Sani, A., & Nawaninatyas, P. N. (2020). E-Business Adoption Models in Organizational Contexts on the TAM Extended Model: A Preliminary Assessment. *2020 8th International Conference on Cyber and IT Service Management, CITSM 2020*, 6–10. DOI: 10.1109/CITSM50537.2020.9268869

Sarstedt, M., Ringle, C. M., Henseler, J., & Hair, J. F. (2014). On the Emancipation of PLS-SEM: A Commentary on Rigdon (2012). *Long Range Planning*, 47(3), 154–160. DOI: 10.1016/j.lrp.2014.02.007

Sciences, D. (1995). The role of interorganizational and organizational factors on the .... *Decision Sciences*, 26(3), 303–336. DOI: 10.1111/j.1540-5915.1995.tb01431.x

Shah. (2012). Challenges Faced by Textile Industry of Pakistan: Suggested Solutions. *Kasbit Business*, *39*, 33–39.

Shaher, Y. A. (2012). *Strategies For Pakistan Textiles Industry To Sustain The Business*. University of Gavle.

Sheikh, A. A., Rana, N. A., Inam, A., Shahzad, A., & Awan, H. M. (2018). Is e-marketing a source of sustainable business performance? Predicting the role of top management support with various interaction factors. *Cogent Business and Management*, 5(1), 1–22. DOI: 10.1080/23311975.2018.1516487

Sheikh, A. A., & Shahzad, A., & ku Ishak, A. (2017). The Impact of Market Orientation, Top Management Support, Use of E-Marketing and Technological Opportunism on the Firm Performance: A Mediated-Moderation and Moderated-Mediation Analysis. *Abasyn University Journal of Social Sciences*, 10(2), 212–234.

Sheikh, A. A., Shahzad, A., & Ishak, A. B. K. (2016a). The mediating impact of e-marketing adoption on export performance of firms: A conceptual study. *Journal of Technology and Operations Management*, 11(1), 48–58.

Sheikh, A. A., Shahzad, A., & Ishak, A. B. K. (2017b). The Role of E-Marketing Uses among TOE Factors and Textile Sector Performance in Pakistan: An Empirical Study. *NUML International Journal of Business & Management Vol.*, 12(2), 117–135.

Sheikh, A. A., Shahzad, A., & Ishak, A. K. (2016b). The effects of e-marketing uses, market orientation, relative advantage and trading partners pressure on the performance of textile business in Pakistan: A mediated-moderation analysis. *International Journal of Economic Perspectives*, 10(4), 562–580.

Sheikh, A. A., Shahzad, A., & Ku Ishaq, A. (2017a). The Growth of E-Marketing in Business-to-Business Industry and its effect on the Performance of Businesses in Pakistan: Marketing Success. *International and Multidisciplinary Journal of Social Sciences*, 6(2), 178. DOI: 10.17583/rimcis.2017.2704

Shi, P., & Yan, B. (2016). Factors affecting RFID adoption in the agricultural product distribution industry: Empirical evidence from China. *SpringerPlus*, 5(1), 2029. DOI: 10.1186/s40064-016-3708-x PMID: 27995006

Sivarajah, U., Irani, Z., Gupta, S., & Mahroof, K. (2020). Role of big data and social media analytics for business to business sustainability: A participatory web context. *Industrial Marketing Management*, 86, 163–179. DOI: 10.1016/j.indmarman.2019.04.005

Srinivasan, R., Lilien, G. L., & Rangaswamy, A. (2002). Technological Opportunism and Radical Technology Adoption: An Application to E-Business. *Journal of Marketing*, 66(3), 47–60. Advance online publication. DOI: 10.1509/jmkg.66.3.47.18508

Stalk, G.Jr, & Hout, T. M. (1990). Competing Against Time. *Research Technology Management*, 33(2), 19–24. DOI: 10.1080/08956308.1990.11670646

Stankov, U., Filimonau, V., & Slivar, I. (2019). Calm ICT design in hotels: A critical review of applications and implications. *International Journal of Hospitality Management*, 82, 298–307. DOI: 10.1016/j.ijhm.2018.10.012

Tiago, M. T. P. M. B., & Veríssimo, J. M. C. (2014). Digital marketing and social media: Why bother? *Business Horizons*, 57(6), 703–708. DOI: 10.1016/j.bushor.2014.07.002

Tsiotsou, R. H., & Vlachopoulou, M. (2011). Understanding the effects of market orientation and e-marketing on service performance. *Marketing Intelligence & Planning*, 29(2), 141–155. DOI: 10.1108/02634501111117593

Varukolu, V. (2007). *Technology adoption of indian garment manufacturing firms* (Doctoral Dissertation). Faculty of the Louisiana State University and Agricultural and Mechanical College. doi: DOI: 10.1007/s13398-014-0173-7.2

Wang, Y. M., Wang, Y. S., & Yang, Y. F. (2010). Understanding the determinants of RFID adoption in the manufacturing industry. *Technological Forecasting and Social Change*, 77(5), 803–815. DOI: 10.1016/j.techfore.2010.03.006

Wernerfelt, B. (1984). A Resource-Based View of the Firm. *Strategic Management Journal*, 5(2), 171–180. DOI: 10.1002/smj.4250050207

Yeh, C. C., & Chen, Y. F. (2018). Critical success factors for adoption of 3D printing. *Technological Forecasting and Social Change*, 132(January), 209–216. DOI: 10.1016/j.techfore.2018.02.003

Zhang, Y., Hassan, N.M. & Sheikh, A.A. (2024). Unboxing the dilemma associated with online shopping and purchase behavior for remanufactured products: A smart strategy for waste management. *Journal of Environmental Management*, *351*, 119790. .DOI: 10.1016/j.jenvman.2023.119790

Zhao, X., Lynch, J. G.Jr, & Chen, Q. (2010). Reconsidering Baron and Kenny: Myths and truths about mediation analysis. *The Journal of Consumer Research*, 37(2), 197–206. DOI: 10.1086/651257

Zikria, Y., Kim, S.W., Hahm, O., Afzal, M.K. & Aalsalem, M.Y. (2019). Internet of things (IoT) operating systems management: Opportunities, challenges, and solution. *Sensors, 19*(8), 1793. DOI: 10.3390/s19081793

Chapter 9
Revisiting the Spectrum of the Logistics Service Providers for a Circular Logistics Service:
From 1PL to a Circular Logistics Service Provider

Muhammad Jawad Sajid
https://orcid.org/0000-0002-7220-2838
China University of Mining and Technology, China

Muhammad Tanveer
Imam Mohammad Ibn Saud Islamic University, Saudi Arabia

ABSTRACT

The logistics services providers have come a long way. From the first-party logistics service provider, whereby all of the logistics-related activities are historically managed in-house, to the advanced technologically oriented fifth- (5PL) and even sixth-party logistics service providers (6PL). However, all these spectrums of logistics service providers fail to explicitly incorporate the circular nature of modern logistics activities. That is reverse logistics alongside forward logistics is an integral part of the logistics services. Therefore, this chapter proposes the need for a circular logistics service provider service (CPL) that incorporates the key aspects of reverse supply chains like recycling, reuse, and refurbishment (alongside more advanced technology, backed by more efficient overall logistics) and is logically linked with a greener overall supply chain.

DOI: 10.4018/979-8-3693-4123-0.ch009

1. BACKGROUND

The logistics industry has undergone significant transformation, evolving from the basic First-Party Logistics (1PL), where companies manage their logistics internally, to the advanced, technology-driven Fifth-Party Logistics (5PL) and even Sixth-Party Logistics (6PL) providers. Despite these advancements, the current spectrum of logistics service providers (LSPs) remains primarily focused on forward logistics, neglecting the equally important reverse logistics that is crucial for a sustainable supply chain. The circular economy, which emphasizes the reuse, recycling, and refurbishment of materials, necessitates a new type of logistics provider that integrates these principles into both forward and reverse logistics.

This chapter proposes the concept of a Circular Logistics Service Provider (CPL), a comprehensive logistics solution that fully incorporates the principles of the circular economy. Unlike traditional LSPs, CPLs manage the entire lifecycle of products and materials, ensuring that they are reused, repaired, remanufactured, and recycled wherever possible. This approach not only optimizes logistics operations but also contributes to a greener and more sustainable supply chain, reducing the environmental impact of logistics activities.

By embracing the CPL model, companies can align their logistics practices with global sustainability goals, particularly those related to reducing waste and greenhouse gas emissions. The adoption of CPLs is essential for the future of sustainable supply chains, as they enable a closed-loop system where materials are continuously cycled back into the production process, minimizing resource consumption and environmental degradation. This chapter emphasizes the critical role that CPLs will play in driving the transition to a circular economy, highlighting the potential benefits for both businesses and the environment.

2. UNDERSTANDING THE DIFFERENT PERCEPTIVE ON THE LOGISTICS

It is vital to know that researchers disagree on a universal definition of logistics and supply chain management. As far as the researcher is concerned, there are at least four different perspectives on the differences between supply chain management and logistics (Larson et al., 2007). In this regard, the figure 1 shows the details. In particular, the traditionalist school believes that supply chain management is a sub-part of logistics. This means that logistics encompasses all the activities of supply chain management. The unionist school (perhaps the more conventional view followed in this chapter) argues that logistics is part of supply chain management. Meanwhile, the re-labeling school says that there is no considerable difference between logistics and supply chain management. In fact, the previously labeled logistics activities are the new supply chain management. In summary, there is no significant difference between the two. Finally, the intersections believe that both supply chain management and logistics simultaneously share some similarities and a few differences.

Figure 1. Different perspectives on the logistics vs supply chain management

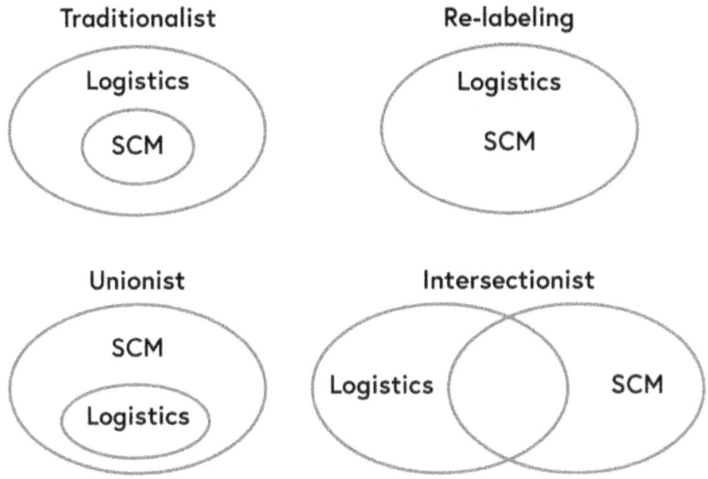

Larson, P., Poist, R. & Halldorsson, A. (2007). Perspectives on logistics vs. SCM: a survey of SCM professionals. Journal of Business Management, 28(1), 1–24.

3. DIFFERENT LEVELS OF LOGISTICS

Before, explaining the main topic. It's vital to provide the readers with a quick review of the different levels of logistics. Especially, the differences between logistics, Supply chain management, and distribution. First of all, distribution is relatively the smallest sub-part of the overall supply chain. Distribution involves all the transport and/or storage between the supplier and the manufacturer. Or, the transport and storage activities from the manufacturer to the customer/consumer. Meanwhile, conventional logistics is a much broader term. It includes all the movement and storage of products from the origin point all the way to the final consumer. Finally, the supply chain is the largest. It not only encompasses distribution, and logistics (inbound and outbound) but also includes activities like planning and improving and data analysis (WTA, 2024).

Figure 2. Different levels of logistics. Source: Authors own construct

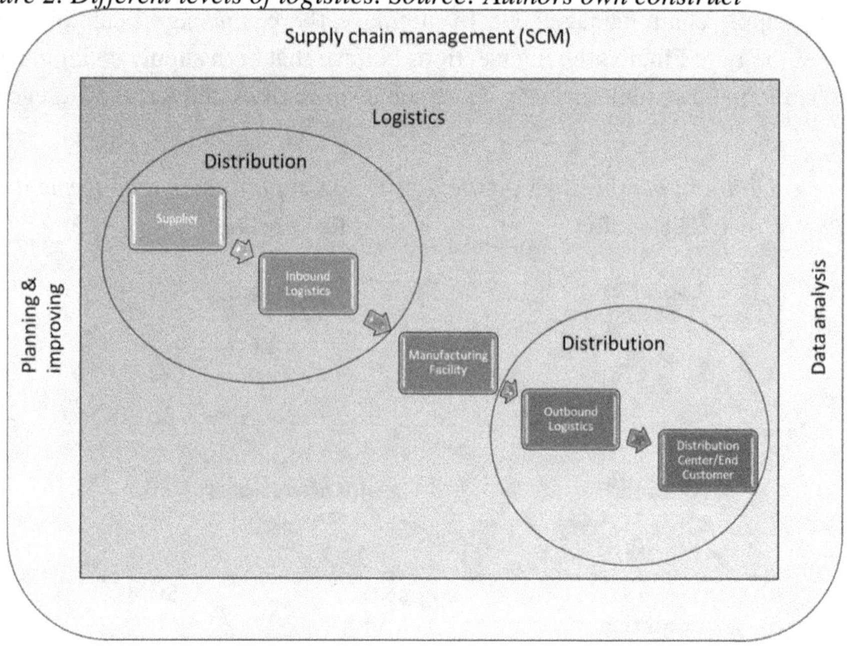

4. THE DEFINITION AND SCOPE OF 1PL TO 4PL

The definition and scope of the first to fourth party logistics is somewhat settled from the literature. In fact, a simple pyramid is often used to indicate the evolution of the IPL all the way to the 4PL in the related literature (Notteboom et al., 2021; Tripathi, 2020). Figure 3 shows a simple evolution form the 1PL all the way to the 4PL.

Figure 3. The evolution of the logistics services providers from the 1PL to the 4PL

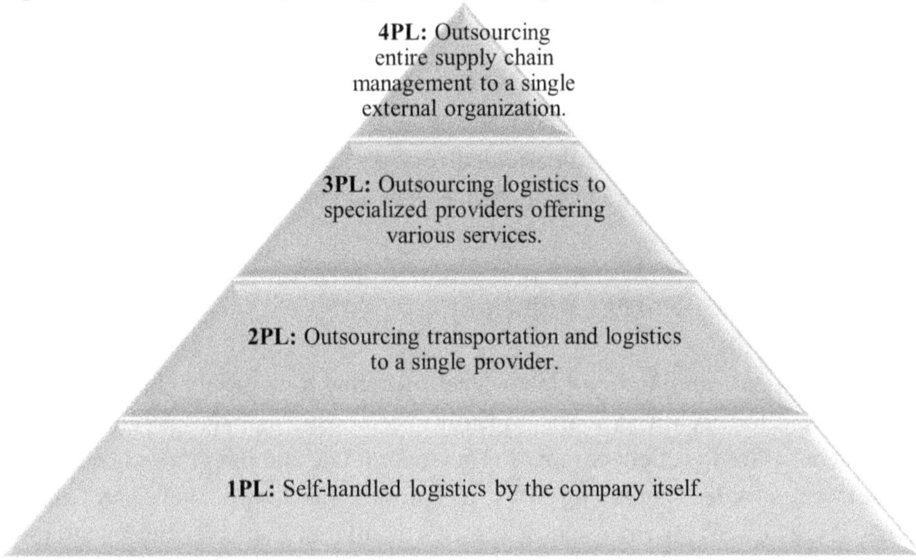

Authors own construct based on the information from Notteboom et al. (2021) and Tripathi (2020).

Broadly speaking, the first to fourth party logistics service providers are defined in the following manner.

4.1. 1PL (First-Party Logistics)

1PL refers to a company that handles its own logistics operations internally (MAERSK, 2024). In this case, the organization manages all aspects of transportation, warehousing, inventory management, and other logistics functions without outsourcing to external service providers. This means the company has direct control and responsibility over its logistics activities.

4.2. 2PL (Second-Party Logistics)

2PL represents a situation where a company outsources some specific logistics functions to a service provider (MAERSK, 2024). Unlike 1PL, where the company manages everything internally, here, certain logistics activities are delegated to a specialized logistics provider. The relationship is usually established on a contractual basis and may involve transportation, warehousing, or distribution services. Conventionally, the transportation part of logistics is outsourced to a courier company (Notteboom et al., 2021; Tripathi, 2020).

4.3. 3PL (Third-Party Logistics)

3PL involves outsourcing a significant portion of logistics operations to an external service provider (MAERSK, 2024). A 3PL provider offers a comprehensive range of logistics services, including transference, warehousing, stock management, order completion, and other value-added services. The company relying on 3PL services can focus on its core business while leveraging the expertise and resources of the logistics provider.

4.4. 4PL (Fourth-Party Logistics)

4PL takes outsourcing to a higher level by acting as a supply chain integrator (MAERSK, 2024). A 4PL provider typically oversees and manages the entire supply chain on behalf of the client company. They coordinate and integrate various logistics service providers, including 3PLs, to optimize the supply chain and enhance efficiency. The 4PL provider acts as a solitary outlet of contact, offering strategic guidance, performance monitoring, and supply chain optimization services.

5. THE DEBATE ON THE LATEST 5PL AND 6PL IS FAR FROM SETTLED

Beyond the 4PL its not much clear from the literature and logistic professionals what actually constitutes or clearly distinguishes the 5PL and 6PL. That is the researchers and the professionals are a vague about their distinction if there at all exists any actual differences. One thing is for sure both the 5PL and 6PL are heavily reliant on the latest (modern) technologies and the ongoing exponential advancements in the technologies like "internet of things (IOT), Artificial intelligence (AI), robotics, big data analytics, blockchain" and beyond. In this regard we will first try to define the 5PL followed by analysing some of the available information on the 6PL.

The 5PL is normally defined simply as the virtual logistics or in other words the virtual logistics service providers (Tripathi, 2020). 5PL is a new supply chain logistics solution that coordinates operations using e-commerce, networks, and IT, with research progress in concept, development model, role, and future. A 5PL creates, manages, and executes logistics solutions for a principal or another contractual party, mostly employing cutting-edge technology. The concept of a Fifth Party Logistics (5PL) provider, which coordinates the entire supply chain and logistics operation without physical assets, has been recognized by academia and industry (Miscevic et al., 2018).

The evolution of logistics management, driven by competitive forces and technological innovation, has led to the need for advanced logistics services (Hosie et al., 2007, 2012). This has prompted the outsourcing of 4PL services and speculation about the future form of 5PL services (Hosie et al., 2007). 5PL services are increasingly essential for businesses' competitiveness due to commercial necessities, technological revolutions, market rivalry, and managerial capacity to provide cutting-edge logistics services. Based upon this it can be said that a 5PL is a logistics service provider uses IT and other latest technologies to coordinate and optimize entire supply chains using usually without involving physical assets.

6. AN INTRODUCTORY TO THE GENERAL CONCEPT OF CIRCULAR ECONOMY

A circular economy can ensure sustainable global development (Khan et al., 2024; Rehman Khan, Ahmad, et al., 2022; Rehman Khan, Umar, et al., 2022). The circular economy has gained popularity as a solution to some of the world's most pressing sustainable development issues (United Nations General Assembly, 2018a). The circular economy is frequently associated with more sustainable patterns of production and consumption (Kostakis & Tsagarakis, 2021). A circular economy reduces material consumption, redesigns goods to need fewer resources, and reclaims “waste” as a resource for developing new materials and products (EPA: U.S. Environmental Protection Agency, 2021). In a circular economy, each and every “waste” is recycled or reused, including clothing, scrap metal, and old technology (United Nations Conference and on Trade and Development (UNCTAD), 2018). In essence, the circular economy is the most recent attempt to envision the sustainable integration of economic activity and environmental well-being (Murray et al., 2017). Consequently, by addressing the fundamental sustainability issues, the circular economy guarantees to fast-track the execution of the UN's 2030 Sustainable Development Goals [SDGs] (United Nations General Assembly, 2018b). Particularly, “SDGs 7 on affordable and clean energy, 8 on economic development, 11 on sustainable cities and communities, 12 on responsible consumption and production, 13 on climate change, 14 on life below water, and 15 on life on land” all stand to benefit from a shift to a circular economy (United Nations General Assembly, 2018b).

The circular economy is categorized into technical and biological cycles at its broadest level. The technical cycle refers to the non-biodegradable and biological cycle presents biodegradable side of a circular economy. The biological cycle restores the nutrients from biodegradable items to the earth for renaissance (Ellen MacArthur Foundation, 2019a). While the technical cycle keeps the non-biodegradable materials in circulation through “reuse, repair, remanufacture and recycling” (Ellen

MacArthur Foundation, 2019b). Specifically, the circular economy's (technical side) business models are divided into two categories: those that promote reuse and extend useful life through repair, remanufacture, renovations, and retrofits, and those that reuse materials to transform old matters into as-new resources (Stahel, 2016). Sundin and Lee (Sundin and Lee, 2012), based on a literature review of 12 articles (estimating miscellaneous environmental impacts) and their estimations, find that compared to others (reuse, remanufacture and refurbish), the recycling has the highest environmental impact. Therefore, it's evident that the circular economy's pivotal recycling sector is amongst the most significant environmental impact intensive (and hence greenhouse gas (GHG) intensive) aspects of a circular economy. And that improvements in the GHG intensity of the recycling sector can help with the climate change-friendly transition from linear to the circular economy. Recent evidence shows that only 6% of materials are recycled (Geng et al., 2019; Haas et al., 2015), indicating a massive potential of growth in global recycling of materials]. Figure 4, provides the details.

Figure 4. The technical cycle of a circular economy (Authors own construct)

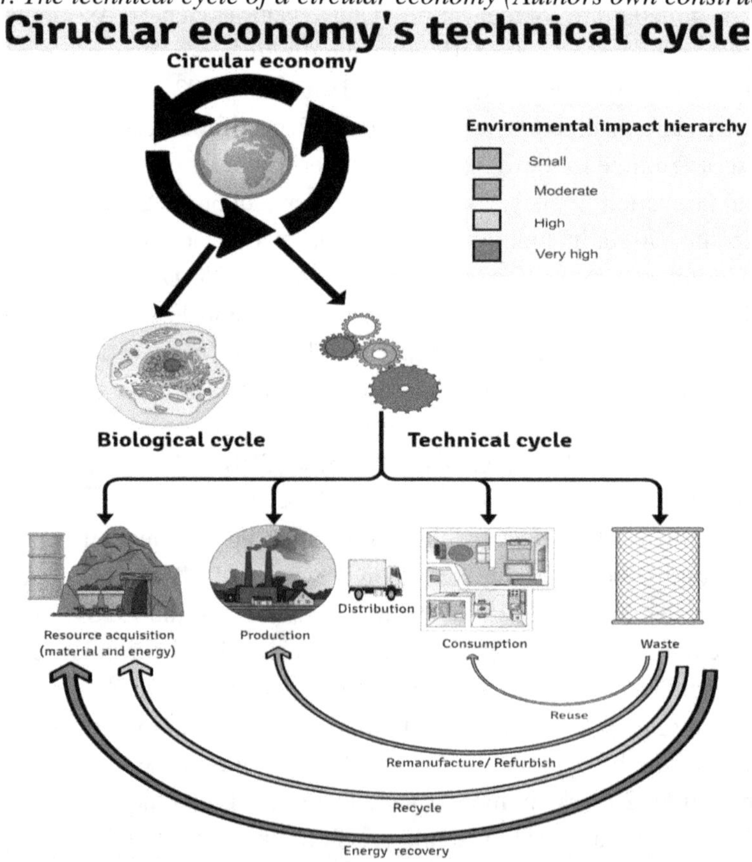

The categorization of the circular economy into biological and technical cycles is based on the Ellen MacArthur Foundation (2019), which is guided by the work of McDonough and Braungar (2002). Meanwhile, the environmental impact hierarchy is based on the literature review (12 articles) and self-investigation of Sundin and Lee (2012). This figure was developed using the "Mind the graph" premium version.

7. WHAT IS THE MAIN CONCEPT OF REVERSE LOGISTICS?

Reverse logistics is crucial for sustainability (Dabees et al., 2023; Dowlatshahi, 2000; Rogers & Tibben-Lembke, 2001). Compared to the forward logistics that involves the movement and storage of goods from point of origin to the final consumer (final destination). The process of the reverse logistics starts once the product has already been delivered to the final consumer or customer. In other words, the reverse logistics is the process of managing the flow of products, materials, and information from the point of consumption back to the point of origin (Olariu, 2013; Rogers & Lembke, 2021). It involves activities such as reuse, repair, remanufacture, and recycle, aimed at recapturing value or ensuring proper disposal (Olariu, 2013). Reverse logistics starts at consumer and ends at the producer or retailer (Thompson, 2023).

But unlike the forward logistics whose demand is somewhat predictable or it can be forecasted. The reverse logistics demand is somewhat unpredictable. A product may be in the reverse logistics because it may need repairs, remanufacturing, refurbishment, recycling and even the for the purpose of propel disposal. So, it can be safely inferred that the reverse logistics is no simply the backward movement of the conventional forward logistics. Instead, it is usually more complex. A product may in reverse for different reasons like for repairs, refurbishment, resale and even salvage. Moreover, compared to forward logistics the reverse movement of products is irregular. Figure 5 provides a simple explanation.

Figure 5. A simplified process of reverse logistics

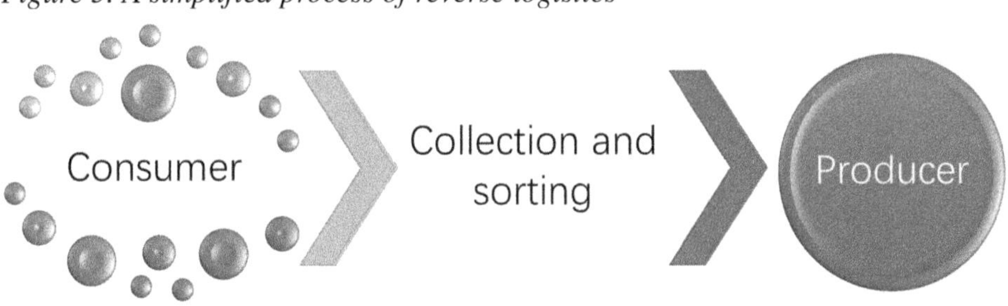

Authors own construct. Note: reverse logistics starts at consumer and ends at the producer or retailer (Thompson, 2023).

8. A CIRCULAR LOGISTICS SERVICE PROVIDER SERVICE (CPL) NECESSARY FOR AN OVERALL GREENER SUPPLY CHAIN

As the reverse logistics continues to evolve, it presents opportunities for both practitioners and researchers to develop novel solutions and explore new areas of study (Sheriff et al., 2012). One such novel endeavor is combing both the forward and reverse logistics simultnsously considering the principles of circular economy. The proposed circular logistics services provider (CPL) has to efficiently provide both the forward and the reverse logistics facilities under a single banner. In doing so, the CPL not only ensures a comprehensive logistics service to its clients. But also a greener overall supply chain. That is at the end of a product's usual life cycle, by incorporating the principles of circular economy the product can be reused, repaired, remanufactured, recycled, and for energy recovery. Similarly, the packaging must be reused, recycled or disposed of by employing the most environmentally friendly alternatives. In that manner, a CPL company ensures the incorporation of the principles of circular economy in their logistics operations. Thus, ensuring a greener logistics and supply chain. Which is inevitably linked with sustainable economy and environment. Figure 6 presents a simple overview of a CPL company's overall logistics operation.

Figure 6. An overview of a CPL company's overall logistics operation. Authors own work

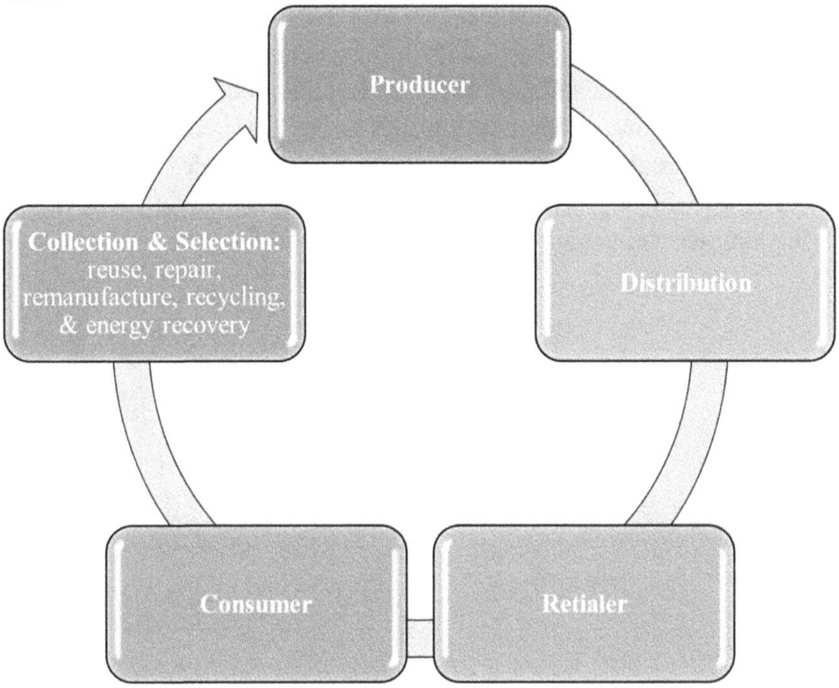

9. CONCLUSION

The evolution of logistics service providers (LSPs) has significantly transformed the logistics landscape, progressing from the basic in-house management of 1PL to the advanced, technology-driven solutions of 5PL and 6PL. However, these advancements have largely focused on optimizing forward logistics without fully integrating the principles of the circular economy, particularly the critical role of reverse logistics.

This chapter highlights the necessity for a new type of logistics service provider—the Circular Logistics Service Provider (CPL). The CPL concept integrates both forward and reverse logistics under the framework of the circular economy, ensuring that materials and products are efficiently reused, repaired, remanufactured, and recycled. By doing so, CPLs not only provide comprehensive logistics solutions but also contribute to a greener and more sustainable supply chain.

The adoption of CPLs is essential for achieving a truly sustainable economy. As industries and economies increasingly prioritize sustainability, the role of logistics service providers must evolve to meet these demands. The CPL model offers a path forward, aligning logistics practices with the principles of the circular economy and supporting the global transition to more sustainable production and consumption patterns. This shift towards circular logistics is not just an option but a necessity for the future of sustainable supply chains. As logistics service providers embrace this model, they will play a crucial role in driving environmental sustainability and achieving long-term economic resilience.

REFERENCES

Dabees, A., Barakat, M., Elbarky, S. S., & Lisec, A. (2023). A Framework for Adopting a Sustainable Reverse Logistics Service Quality for Reverse Logistics Service Providers: A Systematic Literature Review. *Sustainability (Basel)*, 15(3), 1755. DOI: 10.3390/su15031755

Dowlatshahi, S. (2000). Developing a Theory of Reverse Logistics. *Interfaces*, 30(3), 143–155. DOI: 10.1287/inte.30.3.143.11670

Ellen MacArthur Foundation. (2019). *The butterfly diagram: Visualising the circular economy.*

Geng, Y., Sarkis, J., & Bleischwitz, R. (2019). How to globalize the circular economy. *Nature*, 565(7738), 153–155. DOI: 10.1038/d41586-019-00017-z

Haas, W., Krausmann, F., Wiedenhofer, D., & Wiedenhofer, D. (2015). How Circular is the Global Economy? An Assessment of Material Flows, Waste Production, and Recycling in the European Union and the World in 2005. *Journal of Industrial Ecology*, 19(5), 765–777. DOI: 10.1111/jiec.12244

Hosie, P., Egan, V., & Li, Y. (2007). *Drivers of Fifth Party Logistics (5PL) Service Providers for Supply Chain Management.*

Hosie, P., Sundarakani, B., Tan, A. W. K., & Koźlak, A. (2012). Determinants of fifth party logistics (5PL): Service providers for supply chain management. *International Journal of Logistics Systems and Management*, 13(3), 287. DOI: 10.1504/IJLSM.2012.049700

Khan, S. A. R., Sharif, A., Panait, M., & Mardani, A. (2024). Technological innovation and circular economy approaches: Leading toward SDG-12. *Environmental Technology & Innovation*, 103827, 103827. Advance online publication. DOI: 10.1016/j.eti.2024.103827

Kostakis, I., & Tsagarakis, K. P. (2021). Social and economic determinants of materials recycling and circularity in Europe: An empirical investigation. *The Annals of Regional Science*, 68(2), 263–281. DOI: 10.1007/s00168-021-01074-x

Larson, P. D., Poist, R. F., & Halldórsson, Á. (2007). Perspectives on logistics vs. SCM: A survey of SCM professionals. *Journal of Business Logistics*, 28(1), 1–24. DOI: 10.1002/j.2158-1592.2007.tb00230.x

MAERSK. (2024). *What are 1PL, 2PL, 3PL, and 4PL logistics in supply chain management?*https://www.maersk.com/logistics-explained/supply-chain-management/2024/04/24/navigate-the-world-of-party-logistics-with-our-guide-to-1pl-2pl-3pl-4pl-models

Miscevic, G., Tijan, E., Zgaljic, D., & Jardas, M. (2018). Emerging trends in e-logistics. *2018 41st International Convention on Information and Communication Technology, Electronics and Microelectronics (MIPRO)*, 1353–1358. DOI: 10.23919/MIPRO.2018.8400244

Murray, A., Skene, K., & Haynes, K. (2017). The Circular Economy: An Interdisciplinary Exploration of the Concept and Application in a Global Context. *Journal of Business Ethics*, 140(3), 369–380. DOI: 10.1007/s10551-015-2693-2

Notteboom, T., Pallis, A., & Rodrigue, J.-P. (2021). *Port Economics, Management and Policy*. Routledge., DOI: 10.4324/9780429318184

Olariu, I. (2013). Conceptual issues regarding reverse logistics. *Studies And Scientific Researches.Economics Edition*, 18(18). Advance online publication. DOI: 10.29358/sceco.v0i18.218

Rehman Khan, S. A., Ahmad, Z., Sheikh, A. A., & Yu, Z. (2022). Digital transformation, smart technologies, and eco-innovation are paving the way toward sustainable supply chain performance. *Science Progress*, 105(4). Advance online publication. DOI: 10.1177/00368504221145648 PMID: 36573795

Rehman Khan, S. A., Umar, M., Zia-ul-haq, H. M., & Yu, Z. (2022). *Technological Advancement and Circular Economy Practices in Food Supply Chain* (pp. 65–75). DOI: 10.1108/S1877-636120220000027005

Rogers, D. S., & Lembke, R. S. (2021). Reverse Logistics. In *International Encyclopedia of Transportation* (pp. 208–218). Elsevier. DOI: 10.1016/B978-0-08-102671-7.10245-3

Rogers, D. S., & Tibben-Lembke, R. (2001). An examination of reverse logistics practices. *Journal of Business Logistics*, 22(2), 129–148. DOI: 10.1002/j.2158-1592.2001.tb00007.x

Sheriff, K. M. M., Gunasekaran, A., & Nachiappan, S. (2012). Reverse logistics network design: A review on strategic perspective. *International Journal of Logistics Systems and Management*, 12(2), 171. DOI: 10.1504/IJLSM.2012.047220

Stahel, W. (2016). The circular economy. *Nature*, 531(7595), 435–438. DOI: 10.1038/531435a PMID: 27008952

Sundin, E., & Lee, H. M. (2012). In what way is remanufacturing good for the environment? In Matsumoto, M., Umeda, Y., Masui, K., & Fukushige, S. (Eds.), *Design for Innovative Value Towards a Sustainable Society* (pp. 552–557). Springer. DOI: 10.1007/978-94-007-3010-6_106

Thompson, A. (2023). *What is Reverse Logistics?*https://www.dhl.com/discover/en-lk/logistics-advice/essential-guides/what-is-reverse-logistics

Tripathi, S. P. (2020). Perspectives On Logistics Outsourcing. *Journal of Critical Reviews*, 7(15), 2785–3795.

UNCTAD. (2018). *Circular Economy: The New Normal?*https://unctad.org/system/files/official-document/presspb2017d10_en.pdf

United Nations General Assembly. (2018). Circular Economy for the SDGs: From Concept to Practice.

WTA. (2024). *The difference between Logistics and Supply Chain Management (SCM).* https://www.wtagroup.com/resources-and-insights/blogs/the-difference-between-logistics-and-supply-chain-management-scm

Appendix

Table 1. A brief categorization of different levels of logistics service providers

Number	Service provider	Service
1	1PL	inhouse logistics
	2PL	a small portion of logistics outsourced
2	3PL	a significant or complete logistics outsourced
3	4PL	supply chain management outsourced
4	5PL	virtual logistics (for example, electronic commerce)

Compilation of References

Aamir, A., Jan, S. U., Qadus, A., Nassani, A. A., & Haffar, M. (2021). Impact of knowledge sharing on sustainable performance: Mediating role of employee's ambidexterity. *Sustainability (Basel)*, 13(22), 12788. DOI: 10.3390/su132212788

Abate, G., & Mavris, D. N. (2017). CFD Analysis of Leading Edge Tubercle Effects on Wind Turbine Performance. *15th International Energy Conversion Engineering Conference*, 1–2. DOI: 10.2514/6.2017-4626

Abbas, J., & Dogan, E. (2022). The impacts of organizational green culture and corporate social responsibility on employees' responsible behaviour towards the society.

Abbas, J., & Sağsan, M. (2019). Impact of knowledge management practices on green innovation and corporate sustainable development: A structural analysis. *Journal of Cleaner Production*, 229, 611–620. DOI: 10.1016/j.jclepro.2019.05.024

Abbass, K., Qasim, M. Z., Song, H., Murshed, M., Mahmood, H., & Younis, I. (2022). A review of the global climate change impacts, adaptation, and sustainable mitigation measures. *Environmental Science and Pollution Research International*, 29(28), 42539–42559. DOI: 10.1007/s11356-022-19718-6 PMID: 35378646

Abbas, U., Hassan, S., & Miko, N. (2022). Sustainability practices and supply chain resilience in the development of a circular economy: A study of Nigeria. *Journal of Economics and Technology Research*, 3(4), 30–46. DOI: 10.22158/jetr.v3n4p30

Abbate, S., Centobelli, P., Cerchione, R., Nadeem, S. P., & Riccio, E. (2024). Sustainability trends and gaps in the textile, apparel and fashion industries. V. *Environment, Development and Sustainability*. Advance online publication. DOI: 10.1007/s10668-022-02887-2 PMID: 36788931

Abeysekera, I. (2010). The influence of board size on intellectual capital disclosure by Kenyan listed firms. *Journal of Intellectual Capital*, 11(4), 504–518. DOI: 10.1108/14691931011085650

Abrar, M.M., Griswold, M.G., Fullman, N., Hawley, C., Arian, N., Zimsen, S.R.M., & Tymeson, H.D. (2018). Alcohol use and burden for 195 countries and territories, 1990-2016: A systematic analysis for the Global Burden of Disease Study 2016. *The Lancet, 392*(10152), 1015–1035. .DOI: 10.1016/S0140-6736(18)31310-2

Abu Bakar, A. R., & Ahmed, Z. U. (2015). Technology Motivation in E-Marketing Adoption Among Malaysian Manufacturers. *Journal of Transnational Management*, 20(2), 126–152. DOI: 10.1080/15475778.2015.1038949

Abu Bakar, A. S., & Ameer, R. (2011). Readability of corporate social responsibility communication in Malaysia. *Corporate Social Responsibility and Environmental Management*, 18(1), 50–60. DOI: 10.1002/csr.240

Abuzied, H., Senbel, H., Awad, M. & Abbas, A. (2020). A review of advances in design for disassembly with active disassembly applications. *Engineering Science and Technology, an International Journal*. DOI: 10.1016/j.jestch.2019.07.003

Acar, E., Kılıç, M., & Güner, M. (2015). Measurement of sustainability performance in the textile industry by using a multi-criteria decision-making method. *Textile and Apparel, 25*(1).

Achar, A. P. (2016). Assessment of PLS-SEM path model for coefficient of determination and predictive relevance of consumer trust on organic cosmetics. *Ushus Journal of Business Management*, 15(4), 1–19.

Adebayo, T. S., & Samour, A. (2024). Renewable energy, fiscal policy and load capacity factor in BRICS countries: Novel findings from panel nonlinear ARDL model. *Environment, Development and Sustainability*, 26(2), 4365–4389. DOI: 10.1007/s10668-022-02888-1

Adeboye, N., Fagoyinbo, I., & Olatayo, T. (2014). Estimation of the effect of multicollinearity on the standard error for regression coefficients. *Journal of Mathematics*, 10(4), 16–20.

Adeleye, B. N., Gershon, O., Ogundipe, A., Owolabi, O., Ogunrinola, I., & Adediran, O. (2020). Comparative investigation of the growth-poverty-inequality trilemma in Sub-Saharan Africa and Latin American and Caribbean Countries. *Heliyon*, 6(12), e05631. DOI: 10.1016/j.heliyon.2020.e05631 PMID: 33313434

Adenle, Y. A., Haideri, S., & Sandouka, I. (2024). Understanding the best practices of cradle to cradle in furnishings, carpet, and textile industries–A case studies analysis and conceptual model. *Cleaner and Circular Bioeconomy*, 8, 100088. DOI: 10.1016/j.clcb.2024.100088

Afum, E., Agyabeng-Mensah, Y., Sun, Z., Frimpong, B., Kusi, L. Y., & Acquah, I. S. K. (2020). Exploring the link between green manufacturing, operational competitiveness, firm reputation, and sustainable performance dimensions: A mediated approach. *Journal of Manufacturing Technology Management*, 31(7), 1417–1438. DOI: 10.1108/JMTM-02-2020-0036

Agarwal, S., Krishna Erramilli, M., & Dev, C. S. (2003). Market orientation and performance in service firms: Role of innovation. *Journal of Services Marketing*, 17(1), 68–82. DOI: 10.1108/08876040310461282

Ahmed, S., Naz, F., Abbas, Z., & Batool, K. H. (2022). Impact of green innovation on sustainable development with mediating effect of knowledge management. *Journal of Business Management Studies-JBMS*, 1(01), 1–16.

Akbar, P., & Hoffmann, S. (2018). Under which circumstances do consumers choose a product service system (PSS)? Consumer benefits and costs of sharing in PSS. *Journal of Cleaner Production*, 201, 416–427. DOI: 10.1016/j.jclepro.2018.08.010

Al Alam, M. A., Biswas, M. K., Mahiat, T., Chowdhury, R. B., Biswas, K. F., Hossain, M. M., & Sujauddin, M. (2023). Taking stock of the share of global environmental burden of knitwear production in Bangladesh: Constructing the life cycle inventory. *Journal of Cleaner Production*, 412, 137376. DOI: 10.1016/j.jclepro.2023.137376

Alan, B. (2020). *A quantified case study of the value in the circular economy for clothing and textiles*. Goong.org. https://www.linkedin.com/pulse/quantified-case-study-value-circular-economy-clothing-braithwaite

Alavi, M., Kayworth, T. R., & Leidner, D. E. (2005). An empirical examination of the influence of organizational culture on knowledge management practices. *Journal of Management Information Systems*, 22(3), 191–224. DOI: 10.2753/MIS0742-1222220307

Alavi, M., & Leidner, D. (2001). Knowledge management and knowledge management systems: Conceptual foundations and research issues. *Management Information Systems Quarterly*, 25(1), 107–136. DOI: 10.2307/3250961

Albinsson, P. A., Chaudhuri, H. R., Das, A., Ray, S. & Nayak, L. (2023). Marketing Sustainable Fashion: Trends and Future Directions. *Sustainability, 15*(7), 6202. DOI: 10.3390/su15076202

Alcácer, V., & Cruz-Machado, V. (2019). Scanning the industry 4.0: A literature review on technologies for manufacturing systems. *Engineering Science and Technology, an International Journal, 22*(3), 899-919.

Alduais, F. (2022). Textual analysis of the annual report and corporate performance: Evidence from China. *Journal of Financial Reporting and Accounting*. doi: DOI: 0.1108/JFRA-04-2022-0129

Alexander, B. (2018). *Carbios Breaks Down Plastic Textile Waste With Enzymes.* Labiotech. https://www.labiotech.eu/trends-news/carbios-plastic-textile-waste-enzymes/

Allen, M. R., Gillett, N. P., Zwiers, F. W., Weaver, A. J., Hegerl, G. C., & Stott, P. A. (2002). Detecting anthropogenic influence with a multi-model ensemble. *Geophysical Research Letters*, 29(20), 29–32. DOI: 10.1029/2002GL015836

Allwood, J. M., Soren, L. E., Cecilia, R. de M. & Nancy, B. (2006). *Well dressed? The present and future sustainability of clothing and textiles in the United Kingdom.* University of Cambridge. https://www.researchgate.net/publication/282249347_Well_Dressed_The_Present_and_Future_Sustainability_of_Clothing_and_Textiles_in_the_United_Kingdom

Alnoor, A., Eneizan, B., Makhamreh, H. Z., & Rahoma, I. A. (2018). The effect of reverse logistics on sustainable manufacturing. *International Journal of Academic Research in Accounting. Finance and Management Sciences*, 9(1), 71–79.

Alonso-Borrego, C., & Arellano, M. (1999). Symmetrically normalized instrumental-variable estimation using panel data. *Journal of Business & Economic Statistics*, 17(1), 36–49. DOI: 10.1080/07350015.1999.10524795

Al-Qirim, N. (2007). The adoption of eCommerce communications and applications technologies in small businesses in New Zealand. *Electronic Commerce Research and Applications*, 6(4), 462–473. DOI: 10.1016/j.elerap.2007.02.012

Al-Qudah, A. A., Hamdan, A., Al-Okaily, M., & Alhaddad, L. (2022). The impact of green lending on credit risk: Evidence from UAE's banks. *Environmental Science and Pollution Research International*, 30(22), 1–13. DOI: 10.1007/s11356-021-18224-5 PMID: 35067871

Alves, L., Ferreira Cruz, E., Lopes, S. I., Faria, P. M., & Rosado da Cruz, A. M. (2022). Towards circular economy in the textiles and clothing value chain through blockchain technology and IoT: A review. V. *Waste Management & Research*, 40(1), 3–23. Advance online publication. DOI: 10.1177/0734242X211052858 PMID: 34708680

Ananas-anam. (2024). *Home - Ananas Anam.* https://www.ananas-anam.com/

Andrew, M., Rob, O., Dr, H. S., Laura, B., Camille, G. & Lukas, F. (2017). *A New Textiles Economy: Redesigning Fashion's Future.*

Andrushia, A. D., Neebha, T. M., Patricia, A. T., Sagayam, K. M., & Pramanik, S. (2023). Capsule Network based Disease Classification for VitisVinifera Leaves. *Neural Computing & Applications*. Advance online publication. DOI: 10.1007/s00521-023-09058-y

Ansari, Z. N., & Kant, R. (2017). A state-of-art literature review reflecting 15 years of focus on sustainable supply chain management. *Journal of Cleaner Production*, 142, 2524–2543. DOI: 10.1016/j.jclepro.2016.11.023

Ararat, M., Aksu, M. H., & Çetin, A. T. (2010). The impact of board diversity on boards' monitoring intensity and firm performance: Evidence from the Istanbul Stock Exchange. *SSRN*. DOI: 10.2139/ssrn.1572283

Arellano, M., & Bond, S. (1991). Generalized Method of Moments (GMM) estimator using the lagged dependent variable: Monte Carlo Evidence and an Application to Employment Equations. *The Review of Economic Studies*, 58(2), 277–297. DOI: 10.2307/2297968

Arianpoor, A., & Sahoor, Z. (2023). The impact of business strategy and annual report readability on financial reporting quality. *Journal of Asia Business Studies*, 17(3), 598–616. DOI: 10.1108/JABS-10-2021-0439

Asghar, N., Batool, M., Farooq, F., & Ur Rehman, H. (2020). Covid-19 Pandemic and Pakistan Economy: A Preliminary Survey. *Review of Economics and Development Studies*, 6(2), 447–459.

Ashby, A., Callegaro, A. M., Adeyeye, K. & Granados, M. (2019). The Spiral Economy: A Socially Progressive Circular Economy Model? *Sustainable Development Goals and Sustainable Supply Chains in the Post-global Economy* (pp. 67–94). Springer Nature. https://doi.org/DOI: 10.1007/978-3-030-15066-2_5/COVER

Ashvani, G. (2021). *Management of spinning and weaving wastes. Waste Management in the Fashion and Textile Industries*. Woodhead Publishing. DOI: 10.1016/C2018-0-04057-8

Audrey, S. (2024). *What Is Fast Fashion, Anyway? The Good Trade*. https://www.thegoodtrade.com/features/what-is-fast-fashion/

Aus, R., Moora, H., Vihma, M., Unt, R., Kiisa, M., & Kapur, S. (2021). Designing for circular fashion: Integrating upcycling into conventional garment manufacturing processes. *Fashion and Textiles*, 8(1), 34. DOI: 10.1186/s40691-021-00262-9

Autry, C. W., Grawe, S. J., Daugherty, P. J., & Richey, R. G. (2010). The effects of technological turbulence and breadth on supply chain technology acceptance and adoption. *Journal of Operations Management*, 28(6), 522–536. DOI: 10.1016/j.jom.2010.03.001

Awasthi, M. K., Sarsaiya, S., Chen, H., Wang, Q., Wang, M., Awasthi, S. K., Li, J., Liu, T., Pandey, A., & Zhang, Z. (2019). *Global Status of Waste-to-Energy Technology. Current Developments in Biotechnology and Bioengineering*. Elsevier. DOI: 10.1016/B978-0-444-64083-3.00003-8

Babalola, H. B., Lateef, S. A., & Abu Zekeri, A. (2020). New Trends of Intelligent E-Marketing and Consumer Buying Behaviour: A Study of Selected Universities in Osun State, Nigeria. *Jurnal Aplikasi Manajemen, Ekonomi Dan Bisnis*, 5(1), 14–25. DOI: 10.51263/jameb.v5i1.109

Baloyi, R. B., Gbadeyan, O. J., Sithole, B., & Chunilall, V. (2024). Recent advances in recycling technologies for waste textile fabrics: A review. *Textile Research Journal*, 94(3-4), 508–529. DOI: 10.1177/00405175231210239

Baltagi, B. H. (Ed.). (2006). *Panel data econometrics: Theoretical contributions and empirical applications*. Emerald Group Publishing. DOI: 10.1016/S0573-8555(2006)274

Baltagi, B. H., & Hashem Pesaran, M. (2007). Heterogeneity and cross section dependence in panel data models: Theory and applications introduction. *Journal of Applied Econometrics*, 22(2), 229–232. DOI: 10.1002/jae.955

Banihashemi, T. A., Fei, J., & Chen, P. S. L. (2019). Exploring the relationship between reverse logistics and sustainability performance: A literature review. *Modern Supply Chain Research and Applications*, 1(1), 2–27. DOI: 10.1108/MSCRA-03-2019-0009

Barney, J. (1991). Firm resources and sustained competitive advantage. *Journal of Management*, 17(1), 99–120. DOI: 10.1177/014920639101700108

Bas, F. (2023). *The Circular Fashion Economy: A Sustainable Shift Towards a Greener Future - EcoMatcher*. EcoMatcher. https://www.ecomatcher.com/the-circular-fashion-economy-a-sustainable-shift-towards-a-greener-future/

Bassanini, A., Scarpetta, S., & Hemmings, P. (2001). Economic growth: the role of policies and institutions. Panel data evidence from OECD countries. *Panel Data Evidence from OECD Countries*.

Bates. (2018). Transforming Last-mile Logistics: Opportunities for more Sustainable Deliveries Oliver. .DOI: 10.1145/3173574.3174100

Baxter, K. (2022). What Are Sustainable Logistics Practices? InTek Freight & Logistics. https://blog.intekfreight-logistics.com/what-are-sustainable-logistics-practices

Beasley, M. S., Carcello, J. V., Hermanson, D. R., & Neal, T. L. (2009). The audit committee oversight process. *Contemporary Accounting Research*, 26(1), 65–122. DOI: 10.1506/car.26.1.3

Bédard, J., & Gendron, Y. (2010). Strengthening the financial reporting system: Can audit committees deliver? *International Journal of Auditing*, 14(2), 174–210. DOI: 10.1111/j.1099-1123.2009.00413.x

Bendriouch, F., Jabbouri, I., M'hamdi, M., Satt, H., Katona, S., & Serir, R. (2023). Determinants of annual reports complexity in the United States of America: An application of the tobit model. *Review of Behavioral Finance*, 15(6), 795–810. DOI: 10.1108/RBF-12-2021-0265

Bentaher, C., & Rajaa, M. (2022). Supply chain management 4.0: A literature review and research framework. *European Journal of Business and Management Research*, 7(1), 117–127. DOI: 10.24018/ejbmr.2022.7.1.1246

Bentler, P. M., & Mooijaart, A. (1989). Choice of Structural Model via Parsimony: A Rationale Based on Precision. *Psychological Bulletin*, 106(2), 315–317. DOI: 10.1037/0033-2909.106.2.315 PMID: 2678203

Bharadwaj, A. S. (2000). A resource-based perspective on information technology capability and firm performance: An empirical investigation. *Management Information Systems Quarterly*, 24(1), 169–196. DOI: 10.2307/3250983

BlockTexx. (2024). *Technology — BlockTexx®*. blocktexx.com. https://www.blocktexx.com/technology

Bluesign. (2024). *Bluesign Solutions and services for a sustainable textile industry*. Bluesign. https://www.bluesign.com/en/

Blundell, R., & Bond, S. (1998). Initial conditions and moment restrictions in dynamic panel data models. *Journal of Econometrics*, 87(1), 115–143. DOI: 10.1016/S0304-4076(98)00009-8

Bocken, N. M. P., Olivetti, E. A., Cullen, J. M., Potting, J., & Lifset, R. (2017). Taking the Circularity to the Next Level: A Special Issue on the Circular Economy. *Journal of Industrial Ecology*, 21(3), 476–482. DOI: 10.1111/jiec.12606

Bocken, N. M. P., Short, S. W., Rana, P., & Evans, S. (2014). A literature and practice review to develop sustainable business model archetypes. *Journal of Cleaner Production*, 65, 42–56. DOI: 10.1016/j.jclepro.2013.11.039

Bollen, K. A. (1989). A New Incremental Fit Index for General Structural Equation Models. *Sociological Methods & Research*, 17(3), 303–316. DOI: 10.1177/0049124189017003004

Bonsall, S. B.IV, & Miller, B. P. (2017). the impact of narrative disclosure readability on bond ratings and the cost of debt. *Review of Accounting Studies*, 22(2), 608–643. DOI: 10.1007/s11142-017-9388-0

Bossert, O. (2016). A two-speed architecture for the digital enterprise. *Emerging trends in the evolution of service-oriented and enterprise architectures*, 139-150.

Bradford, M., & Florin, J. (2003). Examining the role of innovation diffusion factors on the implementation success of enterprise resource planning systems. *International Journal of Accounting Information Systems*, 4(3), 205–225. DOI: 10.1016/S1467-0895(03)00026-5

Braithwaite, N. (2018). *Clothing rental could be the key to a stylishly sustainable fashion industry*. theconversation.com. https://theconversation.com/clothing-rental-could-be-the-key-to-a-stylishly-sustainable-fashion-industry-100106

Brennan, N. (2006). Boards of directors and firm performance: Is there an expectations gap? *Corporate Governance*, 14(6), 577–593. DOI: 10.1111/j.1467-8683.2006.00534.x

Brockett, A. M., & Rezaee, Z. (2012). *Corporate sustainability*. John Wiley & Sons. DOI: 10.1002/9781119202899

C&A. (2024). *Cradle-to-Cradle describes a circular economy in which products are recycled without waste. Find out how C2C works here.*https://www.c-and-a.com/eu/cz/shop/circular-economy-for-products

Cai, Y.-J., & Choi, T.-M. (2020). A United Nations' Sustainable Development Goals perspective for sustainable textile and apparel supply chain management. *Transportation Research Part E, Logistics and Transportation Review*, 141, 102010. DOI: 10.1016/j.tre.2020.102010 PMID: 32834741

Cao, H., Cobb, K., Yatvitskiy, M., Wolfe, M., & Shen, H. (2022). Textile and Product Development from End-of-Use Cotton Apparel: A Study to Reclaim Value from Waste. *Sustainability (Basel)*, 14(14), 8553. DOI: 10.3390/su14148553

Carpenter, G. S. (2017). Market orientation: Reflections on field-based, discovery-oriented research. *AMS Review*, 7(1–2), 13–19. DOI: 10.1007/s13162-017-0095-6

Celep, G., Tetik, G. D., Yilmaz, F., Celep, G., Tetik, G. D., & Yilmaz, F. (2022). *Limitations of Textile Recycling: The Reason behind the Development of Alternative Sustainable Fibers*. Next-Generation Textiles. DOI: 10.5772/intechopen.105118

Cellucci, N. (2024, April 23). *Solar Panels ROI: Calculating Your Average Returns*. Forbes Home. https://www.forbes.com/home-improvement/solar/solar-panel-roi/#:~:text=A%20good%20ROI%20for%20solar%20panels%20is%20between%206%25%20and

Chaithanapat, P., Punnakitikashem, P., Oo, N. C. K. K., & Rakthin, S. (2022). Relationships among knowledge-oriented leadership, customer knowledge management, innovation quality and firm performance in SMEs. *Journal of Innovation & Knowledge*, 7(1), 100162. DOI: 10.1016/j.jik.2022.100162

Champion, A. (2021). 4 Advantages of Green Logistics In Supply Chain Management & How To Apply Them. Flowspace. https://flow.space/blog/4-advantages-of-green-logistics-in-supply-chain-management-how-to-apply-them/

Chan, Y. E., Huff, S. L., Barclay, D. W., & Copeland, D. G. (1997). Business Strategic Orientation, Information Systems Strategic Orientation, and Strategic Alignment on JSTOR. Inf. Syst. Res., 8(2), 125–150. Available: https://www.jstor.org/stable/23010900

Chandler. (1990). Strategy and Structure: Chapters in the History of the Industrial Enterprise - Alfred Dupont Chandler - Google Books.

Chan, K. C., & Li, J. (2008). Audit committee and firm value: Evidence on outside top executives as expert-independent directors. *Corporate Governance*, 16(1), 16–31. DOI: 10.1111/j.1467-8683.2008.00662.x

Chatti, W. (2021). Moving towards environmental sustainability: Information and communication technology (ICT), freight transport, and CO2 emissions. *Heliyon*, 7(10), e08190. DOI: 10.1016/j.heliyon.2021.e08190 PMID: 34729432

Chauhan, C., Kaur, P., Arrawatia, R., Ractham, P., & Dhir, A. (2022). Supply chain collaboration and sustainable development goals (SDGs). Teamwork makes achieving SDGs dream work. *Journal of Business Research*, 147, 290–307. DOI: 10.1016/j.jbusres.2022.03.044

Chauhan, N., Kumar, V., & Dixit, S. (2023). To achieve sustainability in a supply chain with Digital integration: A TISM approach. *International Journal of Experimental Research and Review*, 30, 442–451. DOI: 10.52756/ijerr.2023.v30.041

Chauhan, S., Singh, R., Gehlot, A., Akram, S. V., Twala, B., & Priyadarshi, N. (2022). Digitalization of supply chain management with industry 4.0 enabling technologies: A sustainable perspective. *Processes (Basel, Switzerland)*, 11(1), 96. DOI: 10.3390/pr11010096

Chege, S. M., Wang, D., & Suntu, S. L. (2020). Impact of information technology innovation on firm performance in Kenya. *Information Technology for Development*, 26(2), 316–345. DOI: 10.1080/02681102.2019.1573717

Chen, X., Memon, H. A., Wang, Y., Marriam, I. & Tebyetekerwa, M. (n.d.). Circular Economy and Sustainability of the Clothing and Textile Industry. *Materials Circular Economy, 1*, 3. DOI: 10.1007/s42824-021-00026-2

Chen, H. Y., Das, A., & Ivanov, D. (2019, December). Building resilience and managing post-disruption supply chain recovery: Lessons from the information and communication technology industry. *International Journal of Information Management*, 49, 330–342. DOI: 10.1016/j.ijinfomgt.2019.06.002

Chi, W., & Wang, C. (2008). *Information asymmetry and accounting conservatism: Evidence from Taiwan*. Department of Accounting, National Taipei University Working Paper No. 12331.

Chin, T. A., Malik, N. F. I. A., Tat, H. H., Sulaiman, Z., & Choon, T. L. (2020). Green purchasing practices and environmental performance. *International Journal of Supply Chain Management*, 9(1), 291–297.

Cho, M., Hyeon, J., Jung, T., & Lee, W.-J. (2022). Audit pricing of hard-to-read annual reports. *Asia-Pacific Journal of Accounting & Economics*, 29(2), 547–572. DOI: 10.1080/16081625.2019.1600418

Chomeya, D. R. (2010). Quality of Psychology Test Between Likert Scale 5 and 6 Points. *Journal of Social Sciences (New York, N. Y.)*, 6(3), 399–403. DOI: 10.3844/jssp.2010.399.403

Chong, W. K., Man, K. L., & Kim, M. (2018). The impact of e-marketing orientation on performance in Asian SMEs: A B2B perspective. *Enterprise Information Systems*, 12(1), 4–18. DOI: 10.1080/17517575.2016.1177205

Chopra, M., Saini, N., Kumar, S., Varma, A., Mangla, S. K., & Lim, W. M. (2021). Past, present, and future of knowledge management for business sustainability. *Journal of Cleaner Production*, 328, 129592. DOI: 10.1016/j.jclepro.2021.129592

Choudhary, S., Narayan, V., Faiz, M., & Pramanik, S. (2022). Fuzzy Approach-Based Stable Energy-Efficient AODV Routing Protocol in Mobile Ad hoc Networks. In Ghonge, M. M., Pramanik, S., & Potgantwar, A. D. (Eds.), *Software Defined Networking for Ad Hoc Networks*. Springer. DOI: 10.1007/978-3-030-91149-2_6

Chowdhury, M. M. H., Rahman, S., Quaddus, M. A., & Shi, Y. (2023). Strategies to mitigate barriers to supply chain sustainability: An apparel manufacturing case study. *Journal of Business and Industrial Marketing*, 38(4), 869–885. DOI: 10.1108/JBIM-04-2021-0233

Chychyla, R., Leone, A. J., & Minutti-Meza, M. (2019). Complexity of financial reporting standards and accounting expertise. *Journal of Accounting and Economics*, 67(1), 226–253. DOI: 10.1016/j.jacceco.2018.09.005

Clerck, J. (2017). Digitization, digitalization and digital transformation: the differences. I SCOOP. Available at: www. i-scoop. eu/digitization-digitalization-digital-transformation-disruption/

Colucci, M., & Vecchi, A. (2021). Close the loop: Evidence on the implementation of the circular economy from the Italian fashion industry. *Business Strategy and the Environment*, 30(2), 856–873. DOI: 10.1002/bse.2658

Coppola, C., Vollero, A., & Siano, A. (2023). Developing dynamic capabilities for the circular economy in the textile and clothing industry in Italy: A natural-resource-based view. *Business Strategy and the Environment*, 32(7), 4798–4820. DOI: 10.1002/bse.3394

Corvellec, H., & Stål, H. I. (2017). Evidencing the waste effect of Product-Service Systems (PSSs). *Journal of Cleaner Production*, 145, 14–24. Advance online publication. DOI: 10.1016/j.jclepro.2017.01.033

Coscieme, L., Mortensen, L. F., Anderson, S., Ward, J., Donohue, I., & Sutton, P. C. (2020). Going beyond gross domestic product as an indicator to bring coherence to the sustainable development goals. *Journal of Cleaner Production*, 248, 119232. DOI: 10.1016/j.jclepro.2019.119232

Cousineau, D., & Chartier, S. (2010). Outliers detection and treatment: A review. *International Journal of Psychological Research*, 3(1), 58–67. DOI: 10.21500/20112084.844

Coviello, N. E., & Brodie, R. J. (2001). Contemporary marketing practices of consumer and business-to-business firms: How different are they? *Journal of Business and Industrial Marketing*, 16(5), 382–400. DOI: 10.1108/08858620110400223

Dabees, A., Barakat, M., Elbarky, S. S., & Lisec, A. (2023). A Framework for Adopting a Sustainable Reverse Logistics Service Quality for Reverse Logistics Service Providers: A Systematic Literature Review. *Sustainability (Basel)*, 15(3), 1755. DOI: 10.3390/su15031755

Dadashi, Z., Mahmoudi, A., & Rashidi, S. (2022). Capacity and strategies of energy production from renewable sources in Arab countries until 2030: A review from renewable energy potentials to environmental issues. *Environmental Science and Pollution Research International*, 29(32), 47837–47866. DOI: 10.1007/s11356-022-20544-z PMID: 35522406

Daidj, N., Sugahara, S., & Ushio, S. (2017). *Value creation in management accounting and strategic management: An integrated approach*. John Wiley & Sons.

Dai, Q., & Kauffman, R. J. (2002). Business models for internet-based B2B electronic markets. *International Journal of Electronic Commerce*, 6(4), 41–72. DOI: 10.1080/10864415.2002.11044247

Dalwai, T., Mohammadi, S. S., Chugh, G., & Salehi, M. (2023). Does intellectual capital and corporate governance have an impact on annual report readability? Evidence from an emerging market. *International Journal of Emerging Markets*, 18(9), 2402–2437. DOI: 10.1108/IJOEM-08-2020-0965

Dan, M. C., & Østergaard, T. (2021). Circular Fashion: The New Roles of Designers in Organizations Transitioning to a Circular Economy. *The Design Journal*, 24(6), 1001–1021. Advance online publication. DOI: 10.1080/14606925.2021.1936748

De Franco, G., Hope, O.-K., Vyas, D., & Zhou, Y. (2015). Analyst report readability. *Contemporary Accounting Research*, 32(1), 76–104. DOI: 10.1111/1911-3846.12062

Demirdelen, T., Aksu, İ. Ö., Yilmaz, K., Koç, D. D., Arikan, M., & Şener, A. (2023). Investigation of the Carbon Footprint of the Textile Industry: PES- and PP-Based Products with Monte Carlo Uncertainty Analysis. *Sustainability (Basel)*, 15(19), 14237. DOI: 10.3390/su151914237

Denizel, M., & Schumm, C. Z. (2024). Closed loop supply chains in apparel: Current state and future directions. *Journal of Operations Management*, 70(2), 190–223. DOI: 10.1002/joom.1274

Desa, A. L., Hairom, N. H. H., Ng, L. Y., Ng, C. Y., Ahmad, M. K., & Mohammad, A. W. (2019). Industrial textile wastewater treatment via membrane photocatalytic reactor (MPR) in the presence of ZnO-PEG nanoparticles and tight ultrafiltration. *Journal of Water Process Engineering*, 31, 100872. Advance online publication. DOI: 10.1016/j.jwpe.2019.100872

Desing, H., Brunner, D., Takacs, F., Nahrath, S., Frankenberger, K., & Hischier, R. (2020). A circular economy within the planetary boundaries: Towards a resource-based, systemic approach. *Resources, Conservation and Recycling*, 155, 104673. Advance online publication. DOI: 10.1016/j.resconrec.2019.104673

Dey, A., LaGuardia, P., & Srinivasan, M. (2011). Building sustainability in logistics operations: A research agenda. *Management Research Review*, 34(11), 1237–1259. DOI: 10.1108/01409171111178774

Diamantopoulos, A., & Siguaw, J. A. (2006). Formative versus reflective indicators in organizational measure development: A comparison and empirical illustration. *British Journal of Management*, 17(4), 263–282. DOI: 10.1111/j.1467-8551.2006.00500.x

Diez-Martin, F., Blanco-Gonzalez, A., & Prado-Roman, C. (2019). Research challenges in digital marketing: Sustainability. *Sustainability (Basel)*, 11(10), 2839. Advance online publication. DOI: 10.3390/su11102839

Dissanayake, D. G. K. (2020). *Does Mass Customization Enable Sustainability in the Fashion Industry? V.* Fashion Industry - An Itinerary Between Feelings and Technology., DOI: 10.5772/intechopen.88281

Dissanayake, D. G. K., & Weerasinghe, D. (2020). *Does Mass Customization Enable Sustainability in the Fashion Industry? Fashion Industry - An Itinerary Between Feelings and Technology*. IntechOpen. DOI: 10.1007/s43615-021-00090-5

Djermani, F., Shahzad, A., Sheikh, A. A., Mohammed, J., & Alekam, E. (2016). Factors influencing the intention to use e-government services in algeria: An empirical study. *Studia Ubb Negotia*, LXI(3), 35–68.

Doctor, S. J., & Khatwani, P. A. (2022). Solid Textile Wastes : Different Types and their Causes of Generation. *Journal of the Textile Association, 83*(1), 422–426. https://doi.org/https://doi.org/10.17605/OSF.IO/QC6DT

Domina, T., & Koch, K. (1997). The Textile Waste Lifecycle. *Clothing & Textiles Research Journal*, 15(2), 96–102. DOI: 10.1177/0887302X9701500204

Dominick, A.-F. (2023). *The Fashion Industry Needs to Reduce Its Carbon Footprint | Industry Insights*. https://www.ana.net/miccontent/show/id/ii-2023-01-sustainable-fashion

Dong, C., Shen, B., Chow, P.-S., Yang, L., & Ng, C. T. (2016). Sustainability investment under cap-and-trade regulation. *Annals of Operations Research*, 240(2), 509–531. DOI: 10.1007/s10479-013-1514-1

Dowlatshahi, S. (2000). Developing a Theory of Reverse Logistics. *Interfaces*, 30(3), 143–155. DOI: 10.1287/inte.30.3.143.11670

Driscoll, J. C., & Kraay, A. C. (1998). Consistent covariance matrix estimation with spatially dependent panel data. *The Review of Economics and Statistics*, 80(4), 549–560. DOI: 10.1162/003465398557825

Duan, X., Deng, H., & Corbitt, B. (2012). What Drives the Adoption of Electronic Markets in Australian Small-and- Medium Sized Enterprises? – An Empirical Study. *Australasian Conference on Information Systems*, 1–11.

Duarte, P. A. B., Leandro, F. J. B., & Galán, E. M. (Eds.). (2023). *The Palgrave handbook of globalization with chinese characteristics: The case of the belt and road initiative*. Springer Nature. DOI: 10.1007/978-981-19-6700-9

Dubey, R., Gunasekaran, A., Childe, S. J., Papadopoulos, T., Hazen, B. T., & Roubaud, D. (2018). Examining top management commitment to TQM diffusion using institutional and upper echelon theories. *International Journal of Production Research*, 56(8), 2988–3006. DOI: 10.1080/00207543.2017.1394590

Dyer, T., Lang, M., & Stice-Lawrence, L. (2017). The evolution of 10-K textual disclosure: Evidence from latent dirichlet allocation. *Journal of Accounting and Economics*, 64(2-3), 221–245. DOI: 10.1016/j.jacceco.2017.07.002

Ebaid, I. E.-S. (2024). IFRS adoption and the readability of corporate annual reports: Evidence From an emerging market. *Ebaid Future Business Journal*, 9(80), 1–12. DOI: 10.1186/s43093-023-00244-x

Edgerton, B. (2023). *Circular Transition Indicators V4.0 Metrics for Business, by Business*. World Business Council for Sustainable Development in May of.

Ehrenfeld, J. R. (1995). Design for environment: A new framework for strategic decisions. *Environmental Quality Management*, 4(4), 37–51. DOI: 10.1002/tqem.3310040406

El Hilali, W., El Manouar, A., & Idrissi, M. A. J. (2020). Reaching sustainability during a digital transformation: A PLS approach. *International Journal of Innovation Science*, 12(1), 52–79. DOI: 10.1108/IJIS-08-2019-0083

El-Gohary, H. (2012). Factors affecting E-Marketing adoption and implementation in tourism firms: An empirical investigation of Egyptian small tourism organisations. *Tourism Management*, 33(5), 1256–1269. DOI: 10.1016/j.tourman.2011.10.013

El-Kassar, A. N., & Singh, S. K. (2019). Green innovation and organizational performance: The influence of big data and the moderating role of management commitment and HR practices. *Technological Forecasting and Social Change*, 144, 483–498. DOI: 10.1016/j.techfore.2017.12.016

Elkington, J. (1997). Cannibals with forks: The triple bottom line of 21st century business, Capstone. Oxford Capestone.

Ellen MacArthur Foundation. (2019). *The butterfly diagram: Visualising the circular economy.*

Ellen, F. M. (2024). *Schools of thought that inspired the circular economy.* https://www.ellenmacarthurfoundation.org/schools-of-thought-that-inspired-the-circular-economy

Ellenmacarthurfoundation.org. (2021). *Recycling and the circular economy: what's the difference?* Ellen Macarthur Foundation. https://www.ellenmacarthurfoundation.org/articles/recycling-and-the-circular-economy-whats-the-difference

Ellenmacarthurfoundation.org. (2024). *Fashion and the circular economy.* https://www.ellenmacarthurfoundation.org/fashion-and-the-circular-economy-deep-dive

Engin, B. (2017). *DyStar and Circular Fashion Time with C&A - Textilegence.* https://www.textilegence.com/en/circular-fashion-time-with-ca-and-dystar/

Eng, L. L., & Mak, Y. T. (2003). Corporate governance and voluntary disclosure. *Journal of Accounting and Public Policy*, 22(4), 325–345. DOI: 10.1016/S0278-4254(03)00037-1

Ertugrul, M., Lei, J., Qiu, J., & Wan, C. (2017). Annual report readability, tone ambiguity, and the cost of borrowing. *Journal of Financial and Quantitative Analysis*, 52(2), 811–836. DOI: 10.1017/S0022109017000187

ETP Fibres Textile Clothing -European Technology Platform. (n.d.). *Towards a 4th Industrial Revolution of Textiles and Clothing A Strategic Innovation and Research Agenda for the European Textile and Clothing Industry.*

European Commission. (2019). *The European Green Deal.* European Commission. https://commission.europa.eu/strategy-and-policy/priorities-2019-2024/european-green-deal_en

European Environment Agency. (2019). *Textile waste — European Environment Agency.* https://www.eea.europa.eu/media/infographics/textile-waste/view

Exchange, T. (2022). *Preferred Fiber and Materials Market Report 2022 - Textile Exchange*. https://textileexchange.org/knowledge-center/reports/materials-market-report-2022/

Exchange, T. (2024). *Responsible Down Standard (RDS)*. Textile Exchange. https://textileexchange.org/responsible-down-standard/

Fan, C. L., & Fan, T. (2020). The emergence and development of the concept of national innovation system-ideological evolution and policy application. *Science of Science and Management of Science and Technology*, 5, 27.

Farhana, K., Kadirgama, K., Mahamude, A. S. F., & Mica, M. T. (2022). Energy consumption, environmental impact, and implementation of renewable energy resources in global textile industries: An overview towards circularity and sustainability. *Materials Circular Economy*, 4(1), 15. DOI: 10.1007/s42824-022-00059-1

Farooq, O., Satt, H., Bendriouch, F. Z., & Lamiri, D. (2021). Dividend policy and the downside risk in stock prices: Evidence from the MENA region. *The Journal of Risk Finance*, 22(3-4), 261–278. DOI: 10.1108/JRF-10-2020-0226

Favi, C., Marconi, M., Germani, M., & Mandolini, M. (2019). A design for disassembly tool oriented to mechatronic product de-manufacturing and recycling. *Advanced Engineering Informatics*, 39, 62–79. Advance online publication. DOI: 10.1016/j.aei.2018.11.008

Fawcett, S. E., Osterhaus, P., Magnan, G. M., Brau, J. C., & McCarter, M. W. (2007). Information sharing and supply chain performance: The role of connectivity and willingness. *Supply Chain Management*, 12(5), 358–368. DOI: 10.1108/13598540710776935

Fernandes, A. J. C., Rodrigues, R. G., & Ferreira, J. J. (2022). National innovation systems and sustainability: What is the role of the environmental dimension? *Journal of Cleaner Production*, 347, 131164. DOI: 10.1016/j.jclepro.2022.131164

Fornell, C., & Larcker, D. F. (1981). Evaluating structural equation models with unobservable variables and measurement error. *JMR, Journal of Marketing Research*, 18(1), 39–50. DOI: 10.1177/002224378101800104

Fortuna, L. M., & Diyamandoglu, V. (2017). Disposal and acquisition trends in second-hand products. *Journal of Cleaner Production*, 142, 2454–2462. DOI: 10.1016/j.jclepro.2016.11.030

Fosu, A. K. (2017). Growth, inequality, and poverty reduction in developing countries: Recent global evidence. *Research in Economics*, 71(2), 306–336. DOI: 10.1016/j.rie.2016.05.005

Frei, R., Jack, L., & Krzyzaniak, S. (2020). Sustainable reverse supply chains and circular economy in multichannel retail returns. *Business Strategy and the Environment*, 29(5), 1925–1940. DOI: 10.1002/bse.2479

Furferi, R., Volpe, Y., & Mantellassi, F. (2022). Circular Economy Guidelines for the Textile Industry. *Sustainability (Basel)*, 14(17), 11111. DOI: 10.3390/su141711111

Gabe. (2023). *Cut, Make, Trim Clothing Manufacturing Explained – Gabe Clothing*. gabeclothing.ca. https://gabeclothing.ca/blogs/building-a-clothing-brand/cmt-clothing-manufacturing-explained

Gao, J., Zhang, B., Guo, X., Baker, T., Li, M., & Liu, Z. (2022). Secure partial aggregation: Making federated learning more robust for industry 4.0 applications. *IEEE Transactions on Industrial Informatics*, 18(9), 6340–6348. DOI: 10.1109/TII.2022.3145837

García-Sánchez, I.-M., Suárez-Fernández, O., & Martínez-Ferrero, J. (2019). Female directors and impression management in sustainability reporting. *International Business Review*, 28(2), 359–374. DOI: 10.1016/j.ibusrev.2018.10.007

Garlet, T. B., de Medeiros, J. F., Ribeiro, J. L. D., & Perin, M. G. (2024). Understanding ethical products: Definitions and attributes to consider throughout the product lifecycle. *Sustainable Production and Consumption*, 45, 228–243. DOI: 10.1016/j.spc.2024.01.010

Geng, D., & Saggi, K. (2019). Foreign direct investment and international technology diffusion. *Oxford Research Encyclopedia of Economics and Finance*. DOI: 10.1093/acrefore/9780190625979.013.241

Geng, D., Hung, L. K., & Zhu, Q. (2021). Eco-innovation and its role for performance improvement among Chinese small and medium-sized manufacturing enterprises. *International Journal of Production Economics, 231*, 107869. .DOI: 10.1016/j.ijpe.2020.107869

Geng, Y., Sarkis, J., & Bleischwitz, R. (2019). How to globalize the circular economy. *Nature*, 565(7738), 153–155. DOI: 10.1038/d41586-019-00017-z

Georgette, K. C. O. C. (2024). *Carbon Footprint of Polyester vs Cotton vs Wool vs Leather vs Nylon (Calculator)*. https://8billiontrees.com/carbon-offsets-credits/carbon-footprint-of-polyester/

Ghisellini, P., Cialani, C., & Ulgiati, S. (2016). A review on circular economy: The expected transition to a balanced interplay of environmental and economic systems. *Journal of Cleaner Production*, 114, 11–32. Advance online publication. DOI: 10.1016/j.jclepro.2015.09.007

Global Organic Textile Standard. (2019). *Global Organic Textile Standard International Working Group (IWG) - Global Standard gGmbH*. https://global-standard.org/

Good, F. F. (2020). Fashion for Good Resource Library. https://reports.fashionforgood.com/report/state-of-the-circular-innovations-in-the-indian-fashion-and-textile-industry/

Gray, B. J., & Hooley, G. J. (2002). Guest editorial. *European Journal of Marketing*, 36(9/10), 980–989. DOI: 10.1108/03090560210437280

Gray, R., Kouhy, R., & Lavers, S. (1995). Corporate social and environmental reporting: A review of the literature and a longitudinal study of U.K. Disclosure. *Accounting, Auditing & Accountability Journal*, 8(2), 47–77. DOI: 10.1108/09513579510146996

Greenhalgh, T., Wherton, J., Papoutsi, C., Lynch, J., Hughes, G., A'Court, C., Hinder, S., Procter, R., & Shaw, S. (2018). Analysing the role of complexity in explaining the fortunes of technology programmes: Empirical application of the NASSS framework. *BMC Medicine*, 16(1), 1–15. DOI: 10.1186/s12916-018-1050-6 PMID: 29754584

Gregory, G. D., Ngo, L. V., & Karavdic, M. (2019). Developing e-commerce marketing capabilities and efficiencies for enhanced performance in business-to-business export ventures. *Industrial Marketing Management*, 78, 146–157. DOI: 10.1016/j.indmarman.2017.03.002

Grover, V. (1993). An empirically derived model for the adoption of customer-based interorganiza .... *Decision Sciences*, 24(3), 603–640. DOI: 10.1111/j.1540-5915.1993.tb01295.x

Gucci. (2021). *Presenting the First Gucci Equilibrium Impact Report – Gucci Equilibrium*. https://equilibrium.gucci.com/presenting-the-first-gucci-equilibrium-impact-report/

Guide, V. D. R.Jr, & Van Wassenhove, L. N. (2009). The evolution of closed-loop supply chain research. *Operations Research*, 57(1), 10–18. Advance online publication. DOI: 10.1287/opre.1080.0628

Gujarati, D. N. (2021). *Essentials of econometrics*. Sage Publications.

Gullingsrud, A., & Perkins, L. (2015). *Designing for the Circular Economy: Cradle to Cradle® Design. V Sustainable Fashion What's Next?* Bloomsbury Publishing Inc. DOI: 10.5040/9781501312250.ch-012

Gunasekaran, A., Papadopoulos, T., Dubey, R., Wamba, S. F., Childe, S. J., Hazen, B., & Akter, S. (2017). Big data and predictive analytics for supply chain and organizational performance. *Journal of Business Research*, 70, 308–317. DOI: 10.1016/j.jbusres.2016.08.004

Gunning, R. (1952). *The technique of clear writing*. McGraw-Hill.

Guo, W. & Kim, E. (2023). Categorizing Chinese Consumers' Behavior to Identify Factors Related to Sustainable Clothing Consumption. *Sustainability, 15*(7), 6126. DOI: 10.3390/su15076126

Gupta, H., Kusi-Sarpong, S., & Rezaei, J. (2020). Barriers and overcoming strategies to supply chain sustainability innovation. *Resources, Conservation and Recycling*, 161, 104819. DOI: 10.1016/j.resconrec.2020.104819

Gwelo, A. S. (2019). Principal components to overcome multicollinearity problem. *Oradea Journal of Business and Economics*, 4(1), 79–91. DOI: 10.47535/1991ojbe062

H&M. (2024). *Sustainability - H&M Group*. https://hmgroup.com/sustainability/

Haas, W., Krausmann, F., Wiedenhofer, D., & Wiedenhofer, D. (2015). How Circular is the Global Economy? An Assessment of Material Flows, Waste Production, and Recycling in the European Union and the World in 2005. *Journal of Industrial Ecology*, 19(5), 765–777. DOI: 10.1111/jiec.12244

Habib, M. A., Bao, Y., Nabi, N., Dulal, M., Asha, A. A. & Islam, M. (2021). Impact of Strategic Orientations on the Implementation of Green Supply Chain Management Practices and Sustainable Firm Performance. *Sustainability, 13*(1), 340. DOI: 10.3390/su13010340

Hair, J., Black, W. C., Babin, B. J., & Anderson, R. E. (2010). *Multivariate data analysis* (7. Baskı). Pearson Educational International.

Hair, J. F., Hult, G. T. M., Ringle, C. M., Sarstedt, M., & Thiele, K. O. (2017). Mirror, mirror on the wall: A comparative evaluation of composite-based structural equation modeling methods. *Journal of the Academy of Marketing Science*, 45(5), 616–632. DOI: 10.1007/s11747-017-0517-x

Hair, J. F.Jr, Sarstedt, M., Hopkins, L., & Kuppelwieser, V. G. (2014). Partial least squares structural equation modeling (PLS-SEM): An emerging tool in business research. *European Business Review*, 26(2), 106–121. DOI: 10.1108/EBR-10-2013-0128

Hair, J. F., Ringle, C. M., & Sarstedt, M. (2011). PLS-SEM: Indeed a silver bullet. *Journal of Marketing Theory and Practice*, 19(2), 139–152. DOI: 10.2753/MTP1069-6679190202

Hair, J., & Alamer, A. (2022). Partial Least Squares Structural Equation Modeling (PLS-SEM) in second language and education research: Guidelines using an applied example. *Research Methods in Applied Linguistics*, 1(3), 100027. DOI: 10.1016/j.rmal.2022.100027

Haji, A. A., & Anifowose, M. (2016). Audit committee and integrated reporting practice. Does Internal assurance matter? *Managerial Auditing Journal*, 31(8/9), 915–948. DOI: 10.1108/MAJ-12-2015-1293

Ha, L. T. (2024). A wavelet analysis of dynamic connectedness between geopolitical risk and renewable energy volatility during the COVID-19 pandemic and Ukraine-Russia conflicts. *Environmental Science and Pollution Research International*, 31(12), 17994–18009. DOI: 10.1007/s11356-023-26033-1 PMID: 36914932

Haq, M., Moazzam, M., Khan, A. S., & Ahmed, W. (2023). The impact of reverse logistics process coordination on third party relationship quality: A moderated mediation model for multichannel retailers in the fashion industry. *Journal of Retailing and Consumer Services*, 73, 103362. DOI: 10.1016/j.jretconser.2023.103362

Haq, U. N., & Alam, S. M. R. (2023). Implementing circular economy principles in the apparel production process: Reusing pre-consumer waste for sustainability of environment and economy. *Cleaner Waste Systems*, 6, 100108. DOI: 10.1016/j.clwas.2023.100108

Harrison-Atlas, D., Glaws, A., King, R. N., & Lantz, E. (2024). Artificial intelligence-aided wind plant optimization for nationwide evaluation of land use and economic benefits of wake steering. *Nature Energy*, 9(6), 735–749. Advance online publication. DOI: 10.1038/s41560-024-01516-8

Hashmat, H. U., & Khan, M. A. (2023). Design and simulation of efficient solar thermal water heating system for textile industries in Pakistan. *Mehran University Research Journal Of Engineering & Technology*, 42(4), 8–18. DOI: 10.22581/muet1982.2304.2655

Hassabo, A. G., Gamal, N., Sediek, A., Saad, F., Hegazy, B. M., Elmorsy, H., & Othman, H. (2023). Smart wearable fabric using electronic textiles–a review. *Journal of Textiles. Coloration and Polymer Science*, 20(1), 29–39.

Hassan, N. M., Khan, S. A. R., Ashraf, M. U., & Sheikh, A. A. (2023). "Interconnection between the role of blockchain technologies, supply chain integration, and circular economy: A case of small and medium-sized enterprises in Pakistan", *Science Progress. Science Progress*, 106(3), 1–22. DOI: 10.1177/00368504231186527 PMID: 37437130

Hayes, A. F. (2009). Beyond Baron and Kenny: Statistical mediation analysis in the new millennium. *Communication Monographs*, 76(4), 408–420. DOI: 10.1080/03637750903310360

Heng, Y. T. (2017). The Belt and Road Initiative and its implications for the world economy. *World Economy*, 40(1), 1–21.

Henninger, C. E., Cano, M. B., Boardman, R., Jones, C., McCormick, H., & Sahab, S. (2020). *Cradle-to-Cradle Versus Consumer Preferences in the Fashion Industry. Encyclopedia of Renewable and Sustainable Materials*. Elsevier. DOI: 10.1016/B978-0-12-803581-8.10893-8

Henseler, J., Dijkstra, T. K., Sarstedt, M., Ringle, C. M., Diamantopoulos, A., Straub, D. W., Ketchen, D. J.Jr, Hair, J. F., Hult, G. T. M., & Calantone, R. J. (2014). Common beliefs and reality about PLS: Comments on Rönkkö and Evermann (2013). *Organizational Research Methods*, 17(2), 182–209. DOI: 10.1177/1094428114526928

Herhausen, D., Miočević, D., Morgan, R. E., & Kleijnen, M. H. P. (2020). The digital marketing capabilities gap. *Industrial Marketing Management*, 90, 276–290. DOI: 10.1016/j.indmarman.2020.07.022

Hinkin, T. R. (1995). A Review of Scale Development Practices in the Study of Organizations. *Journal of Management*, 21(5), 473–478. DOI: 10.1177/014920639502100509

Hmfoundation. (2017). *GCA winners – H&M Foundation*. https://hmfoundation.com/gca/winners/

Hoechle, D. (2007). Robust standard errors for panel regressions with cross-sectional dependence. *The Stata Journal*, 7(3), 281–312. DOI: 10.1177/1536867X0700700301

Hoffer, J. A., & Alexander, M. B. (1992). The diffusion of database machines. *The Data Base for Advances in Information Systems*, 23(2), 13–19. DOI: 10.1145/141342.141352

Homburg, C., & Pflesser, C. (2000). A Multiple-Layer Model of Market-Oriented Organizational Culture: Measurement Issues and Performance Outcomes. *JMR, Journal of Marketing Research*, 37(4), 449–462. DOI: 10.1509/jmkr.37.4.449.18786

Hosie, P., Egan, V., & Li, Y. (2007). *Drivers of Fifth Party Logistics (5PL) Service Providers for Supply Chain Management.*

Hosie, P., Sundarakani, B., Tan, A. W. K., & Koźlak, A. (2012). Determinants of fifth party logistics (5PL): Service providers for supply chain management. *International Journal of Logistics Systems and Management*, 13(3), 287. DOI: 10.1504/IJLSM.2012.049700

Hoxha, V., & Sadiku, S. (2019). Study of factors influencing the decision to adopt the blockchain technology in real estate transactions in Kosovo. *Property Management*, 37(5), 684–700. DOI: 10.1108/PM-01-2019-0002

Hubert, S. O. (1996). Tacit knowledge: The key to the strategic alignment of intellectual capital. *Strategy and Leadership*, 24(2), 10–16.

Hung, S. W., Chen, P. C., & Chung, C. F. (2014). Gaining or losing? The social capital perspective on supply chain members' knowledge sharing of green practices. *Technology Analysis and Strategic Management*, 26(2), 189–206. DOI: 10.1080/09537325.2013.850475

Hu, Y. (2024). Analyzing the Comprehensive Influence of Prada's Business Strategies. *Highlights in Business. Economics and Management*, 24, 1563–1567.

India, E. (2022, October 10). *How much is the electricity consumption of a washing machine?* Electrolux India. https://www.electrolux.in/blog/washing-machine-electricity-consumption/

Isaksson, K. (2012). *Logistics Service Providers going green – insights from the Swedish market.* Linkoping University.

Islam, S., Hasan, A. M., Bhuiyan, M. A. R., & Bhat, G. (2024). Evaluation of environmental impacts of cotton polo shirt production in Bangladesh using life cycle assessment. *The Science of the Total Environment*, 926, 172097. DOI: 10.1016/j.scitotenv.2024.172097 PMID: 38565355

Ivanov, D., & Dolgui, A. (2021). A digital supply chain twin for managing the disruption risks and resilience in the era of Industry 4.0. *Production Planning and Control*, 32(9), 775–788. DOI: 10.1080/09537287.2020.1768450

Izquierdo-Yusta, A., Méndez-Aparicio, M. D., Jiménez-Zarco, A. I., & Martínez-Ruíz, M. P. (2023). When responsible production and consumption matter: The case of Danone. In *Responsible Consumption and Sustainability: Case Studies from Corporate Social Responsibility, Social Marketing, and Behavioral Economics* (pp. 199–211). Springer International Publishing. DOI: 10.1007/978-3-031-30742-3_12

Jackson, T. (2020). *The Myth of Decoupling. Prosperity without Growth*. Routledge. DOI: 10.4324/9781849774338-10/MYTH-DECOUPLING-TIM-JACKSON

Jahandideh, A., Ashkani, M., & Moini, N. (2021). *Biopolymers in textile industries. Biopolymers and their Industrial Applications*. Elsevier. DOI: 10.1016/B978-0-12-819240-5.00008-0

Jain, A., Sharma, A., Jately, V., & Azzopardi, B. (2024). *Sustainable energy solutions with artificial intelligence, blockchain technology, and internet of things*. CRC Press. https://www.routledge.com/Sustainable-Energy-Solutions-with-Artificial-Intelligence-Blockchain-Technology-and-Internet-of-Things/Jain-Sharma-Jately-Azzopardi/p/book/9781032392752

Jana, P. (2022). *Challenges in the Traditional Fashion and Textile Supply Chain. Lean Supply Chain Management in Fashion and Textile Industry*. Springer. DOI: 10.1007/978-981-19-2108-7_2

Janjua, L. R., Sanli, O., Panait, M., Cristea, M., & Razzak, A. (2023). Impact of energy security and economic growth on poverty: Sample of Sub-Saharan Africa. *Environment, Development and Sustainability*, 26(10), 1–26. DOI: 10.1007/s10668-023-03689-w

Jassim, S., Al-Mubarak, M., & Hamdan, A. (2020). The impact of green supply chain management on firm's performance. *Journal of Information & Knowledge Management*, 19(01), 2040026. DOI: 10.1142/S0219649220400262

Jaworski, B., & Kohli, A. (1993). Market Orientation: Antecedents and Consequences. *Journal of Marketing*, 57(3), 53–70. DOI: 10.1177/002224299305700304

Jayasingh, R., Kumar, R. J. S., Telagathoti, D. B., Sagayam, K. M., & Pramanik, S. (2022). Speckle noise removal by SORAMA segmentation in Digital Image Processing to facilitate precise robotic surgery. *International Journal of Reliable and Quality E-Healthcare*, 11(1), 1–19. Advance online publication. DOI: 10.4018/IJRQEH.295083

Jermsittiparsert, K., Siriattakul, P., & Wattanapongphasuk, S. (2019). Determining the environmental performance of Indonesian SMEs influence by green supply chain practices with moderating role of green HR practices. *International Journal of Supply Chain Management*, 8(3), 59–70.

Jeyaraj, A., Rottman, J. W., & Lacity, M. C. (2006). A review of the predictors, linkages, and biases in IT innovation adoption research. *Journal of Information Technology*, 21(1), 1–23. DOI: 10.1057/palgrave.jit.2000056

Jia, F., Yin, S., Chen, L., & Chen, X. (2020a). The circular economy in the textile and apparel industry: A systematic literature review. *Journal of Cleaner Production*, 259, 120728. Advance online publication. DOI: 10.1016/j.jclepro.2020.120728

Jian, J., Fan, X., & Zhao, S. (2022). The green incentives and green bonds financing under the belt and road initiative. *Emerging Markets Finance & Trade*, 58(5), 1430–1440.

Jin, C., Shahzad, M., Zafar, A. U., & Suki, N. M. (2022). Socio-economic and environmental drivers of green innovation: Evidence from nonlinear ARDL. *Ekonomska Istrazivanja*, 1–21. DOI: 10.1080/1331677X.2022.2026241

Joenoes, M. Z., & Rokhim, R. (2019). Does foreign board increase the company's performance? The evidence from Indonesia. *Journal of Economics, Business, and Accountancy Ventura*, 22(2), 213–222. DOI: 10.14414/jebav.v22i2.1449

Jun, W., Ali, W., Bhutto, M. Y., Hussain, H., & Khan, N. A. (2019). Examining the determinants of green innovation adoption in SMEs: A PLS-SEM approach. *European Journal of Innovation Management*, 24(1), 67–87. DOI: 10.1108/EJIM-05-2019-0113

Kabir, S. M. F., Chakraborty, S., Hoque, S. M. A., & Mathur, K. (2019). Sustainability Assessment of Cotton-Based Textile Wet Processing. *Cleanroom Technology*, 1(1), 232–246. DOI: 10.3390/cleantechnol1010016

Kaine, G., & Wright, V. (2022). Relative advantage and complexity: Predicting the rate of adoption of agricultural innovations. *Frontiers in Agronomy*, 4, 967605. DOI: 10.3389/fagro.2022.967605

Kang, J., Diao, Z., & Zanini, M. T. (2020). Business-to-business marketing responses to COVID-19 crisis: A business process perspective. *Marketing Intelligence & Planning*, (71772059). Advance online publication. DOI: 10.1108/MIP-05-2020-0217

Kang, K. N., & Park, H. (2012). Influence of government R&D support and inter-firm collaborations on innovation in Korean biotechnology SMEs. *Technovation*, 32(1), 68–78. DOI: 10.1016/j.technovation.2011.08.004

Kang, M., Yang, M. G., Park, Y., & Huo, B. (2018). Supply chain integration and its impact on sustainability. *Industrial Management & Data Systems*, 118(9), 1749–1765. DOI: 10.1108/IMDS-01-2018-0004

Karaduman, H. A., Karaman-Akgül, A., Çağlar, M., & Akbaş, H. E. (2020). The relationship between logistics performance and carbon emissions: An empirical investigation on Balkan countries. *International Journal of Climate Change Strategies and Management*, 12(4), 449–461. DOI: 10.1108/IJCCSM-05-2020-0041

Kelloway, K. (1998). Using LISREL for Structural Equation Modeling: A Researcher's Guide - E. Kevin Kelloway - Google Books. *Sage (Atlanta, Ga.).*

Kemp, R. (2010). Eco-innovation: Definition, measurement and open research issues. *Economics and Politics*, 27(3), 397–420.

KFilippa. (2020). *Filippa-K-sustainability-report 2020.*

Khairul Akter, M. M., Haq, U. N., Islam, M. M., & Uddin, M. A. (2022). Textile-apparel manufacturing and material waste management in the circular economy: A conceptual model to achieve sustainable development goal (SDG) 12 for Bangladesh. *Cleaner Environmental Systems*, 4, 100070. DOI: 10.1016/j.cesys.2022.100070

Khan, S.A.R., Ahmad, Z., Sheikh, A.A. & Yu, Z. (2023). Green technology adoption paving the way toward sustainable performance in circular economy: a case of Pakistani small and medium enterprises. *International Journal of Innovation Science*. .DOI: 10.1108/IJIS-10-2022-0199

Khan, A., Congmei, S., & Ali, F. (2024). Assessing Xi Jinping's vision of modernization and its implications for global trade dynamics: A case study of the Belt and Road Initiative. *Pakistan Journal of Humanities and Social Sciences*, 12(1), 106–126. DOI: 10.52131/pjhss.2024.v12i1.1962

Khanh, P. T., Ng c, T. H., & Pramanik, S. (2023). Future of Smart Agriculture Techniques and Applications. In Khang, A., & Global, I. G. I. (Eds.), *Advanced Technologies and AI-Equipped IoT Applications in High Tech Agriculture*. DOI: 10.4018/978-1-6684-9231-4.ch021

Khan, M. M. R., & Islam, M. M. (2015). *Materials and manufacturing environmental sustainability evaluation of apparel product: knitted T-shirt case study*. Textiles and Clothing Sustainability. DOI: 10.1186/s40689-015-0008-8

Khan, S. A. R., Razzaq, A., Yu, Z., Shah, A., Sharif, A., & Janjua, L. (2022). Disruption in food supply chain and undernourishment challenges: An empirical study in the context of Asian countries. *Socio-Economic Planning Sciences*, 82, 101033. DOI: 10.1016/j.seps.2021.101033

Khan, S. A. R., Sharif, A., Panait, M., & Mardani, A. (2024). Technological innovation and circular economy approaches: Leading toward SDG-12. *Environmental Technology & Innovation*, 103827, 103827. Advance online publication. DOI: 10.1016/j.eti.2024.103827

Khan, S. A. R., Sheikh, A. A., & Tahir, M. S. (2024). Corporate social responsibility-an antidote for sustainable business performance: Interconnecting role of digital technologies, employee eco-behavior, and tax avoidance. *Environmental Science and Pollution Research International*, 31(3), 4365–4383. DOI: 10.1007/s11356-023-31377-9 PMID: 38102435

Khan, S. A. R., Yu, Z., Golpira, H., Sharif, A., & Mardani, A. (2021). A state-of-the-art review and meta-analysis on sustainable supply chain management: Future research directions. *Journal of Cleaner Production*, 278, 123357. DOI: 10.1016/j.jclepro.2020.123357

Khan, S. A. R., Zhang, Y., Anees, M., Golpîra, H., Lahmar, A., & Qianli, D. (2018). Green supply chain management, economic growth and environment: A GMM based evidence. *Journal of Cleaner Production*, 185, 588–599. DOI: 10.1016/j.jclepro.2018.02.226

Khorram Niaki, M., & Nonino, F. (2017). Additive manufacturing management: A review and future research agenda. *International Journal of Production Research*, 55(5), 1419–1439. DOI: 10.1080/00207543.2016.1229064

Kian Chong, W., Shafaghi, M., Woollaston, C., & Lui, V. (2010). B2B e-marketplace: An e-marketing framework for B2B commerce. *Marketing Intelligence & Planning*, 28(3), 310–329. DOI: 10.1108/02634501011041444

Kirchherr, J., Reike, D., & Hekkert, M. (2017). Conceptualizing the circular economy: An analysis of 114 definitions. V. *Resources, Conservation and Recycling*, 127, 221–232. Advance online publication. DOI: 10.1016/j.resconrec.2017.09.005

Kjaer, L. L., Pigosso, D. C. A., Niero, M., Bech, N. M., & McAloone, T. C. (2019). Product/Service-Systems for a Circular Economy: The Route to Decoupling Economic Growth from Resource Consumption? *Journal of Industrial Ecology*, 23(1), 22–35. Advance online publication. DOI: 10.1111/jiec.12747

Klewitz, J., & Hansen, E. (2014). Sustainability-oriented innovation of SMEs: A systematic review. *Journal of Cleaner Production*, 65, 57–75. DOI: 10.1016/j.jclepro.2013.07.017

Kline, R. B. (2015). *Principles and practice of structural equation modeling*. Guilford publications.

Klinger, J. M., & Muldavin, J. S. (2019). New geographies of development: Grounding China's global integration. *Territory, Politics, Governance*, 7(1), 1–21. DOI: 10.1080/21622671.2018.1559757

Klinkhammer, K., Hohenbild, H., Hoque, M. T., Elze, L., Teshay, H., & Mahltig, B. (2024). Functionalization of Technical Textiles with Chitosan. *Textiles*, 4(1), 70–90. DOI: 10.3390/textiles4010006

Knut, A., & Daniel, R. S. A. (2017). *Supply Chain 4.0 in consumer goods | McKinsey*. McKinsey & Company. https://www.mckinsey.com/industries/consumer-packaged-goods/our-insights/supply-chain-4-0-in-consumer-goods

Kohli, A. K., & Jaworski, B. J. (2012). Market Orientation: The Construct, Research Propositions, and Managerial Implications. *Developing a Market Orientation*, 54(2), 7–44. DOI: 10.4135/9781452231426.n2

Konings, J., Cayseele, P., & Warzynski, F. (2005). The Effects of Privatization and Competitive Pressure on Firms' Price-Cost Margins: Micro Evidence from Emerging Economies. *The Review of Economics and Statistics*, 87(1), 124–134. DOI: 10.1162/0034653053327603

Korhonen, J., Honkasalo, A., & Seppälä, J. (2018). Circular Economy: The Concept and its Limitations. *Ecological Economics*, 143, 37–46. Advance online publication. DOI: 10.1016/j.ecolecon.2017.06.041

Kostakis, I., & Tsagarakis, K. P. (2021). Social and economic determinants of materials recycling and circularity in Europe: An empirical investigation. *The Annals of Regional Science*, 68(2), 263–281. DOI: 10.1007/s00168-021-01074-x

Kudera, B. (2017). China's "One Belt, One Road" initiative and its implications for the EU. European Parliament, Policy Department External Policies, PE 588.062.

Kumar Singh, M. (2021). *Textiles Functionalization - A Review of Materials, Processes, and Assessment. Textiles for Functional Applications*. IntechOpen. DOI: 10.5772/intechopen.96936

Kumar, R., Chakraborty, P., Chakraborty, S., Basak, B., & Jeon, B.-H. (2023). *Synergy of textile dyeing wastewater treatment along with water reclamation using membrane-enabled approach. Current Developments in Bioengineering and Biotechnology*. Elsevier. DOI: 10.1016/B978-0-323-91235-8.00015-2

Kumar, S., & Barua, M. K. (2022). A modeling framework of green practices to explore their interrelations as a conduit to policy. *Journal of Cleaner Production*, 335, 130301. DOI: 10.1016/j.jclepro.2021.130301

Labanauskaitė, D., Fiore, M., & Stašys, R. (2020). Use of E-marketing tools as communication management in the tourism industry. *Tourism Management Perspectives*, 34, 100652. DOI: 10.1016/j.tmp.2020.100652

Lai, Y., Sun, H., & Ren, J. (2018). Understanding the determinants of big data analytics (BDA) adoption in logistics and supply chain management: An empirical investigation. *International Journal of Logistics Management*, 29(2), 676–703. DOI: 10.1108/IJLM-06-2017-0153

Landrum, N. E., & Ohsowski, B. (2018). Identifying worldviews on corporate sustainability: A content analysis of corporate sustainability reports. *Business Strategy and the Environment*, 128 - 151. DOI: 10.1002/bse.1989

Larson, P. D., Poist, R. F., & Halldórsson, Á. (2007). Perspectives on logistics vs. SCM: A survey of SCM professionals. *Journal of Business Logistics*, 28(1), 1–24. DOI: 10.1002/j.2158-1592.2007.tb00230.x

Larsson, E. (2018). *Filippa K's Fashion Manifest: Long Lasting Simplicity. Sustainable Fashion: Let. Part F625*. Springer Nature. DOI: 10.1007/978-3-319-74367-7_8

Laumer, S., & Eckhardt, A. (2012). Integrated Series in Information Systems. Springer. DOI: 10.1007/978-1-4419-6108-2

Lau, Y. W., & Tong, C. Q. (2008). Are Malaysian Government-Linked Companies (GLCs) Creating Value? *International Applied Economics and Management Letters*, 1(1), 9–12.

Lazarevic, D., & Valve, H. (2017). Narrating expectations for the circular economy: Towards a common and contested European transition. *Energy Research & Social Science*, 31, 60–69. DOI: 10.1016/j.erss.2017.05.006

Lazar, S., Klimecka-Tatar, D., & Obrecht, M. (2021). Sustainability orientation and focus in logistics and supply chains. *Sustainability (Basel)*, 13(6), 3280. DOI: 10.3390/su13063280

Le, T.T., Behl, A. & Pereira, V. (2022). Establishing linkages between circular economy practices and sustainable performance: the moderating role of circular economy entrepreneurship. *Management Decision.* .DOI: 10.1108/MD-02-2022-0150

Lee, I. (2024). SaaS –Software – As – A – Service https://www.wallarm.com/what/what-is-saas

Lee, C. S., & Wong, K. Y. (2015). Development and validation of knowledge management performance measurement constructs for small and medium enterprises. *Journal of Knowledge Management*, 19(4), 711–734. DOI: 10.1108/JKM-10-2014-0398

Lee, H. Y., Mande, V., & Son, M. (2008). A comparison of reporting lags of multinational and domestic firms. *Journal of International Financial Management & Accounting*, 19(1), 28–56. DOI: 10.1111/j.1467-646X.2008.01015.x

Lee, V. H., Ooi, K. B., Chong, A. Y. L., & Seow, C. (2014). Creating technological innovation via green supply chain management: An empirical analysis. *Expert Systems with Applications*, 41(16), 6983–6994. DOI: 10.1016/j.eswa.2014.05.022

Lenzing. (2024). *Circular economy*. https://www.lenzing.com/sustainability/sustainability-management/circular-economy

Leonas, K. K. (2017). The Use of Recycled Fibers in Fashion and Home Products. *Textile Science and Clothing Technology* (pp. 55–77). DOI: 10.1007/978-981-10-2146-6_2

Li, R., Liu, W., & Zhou, S. (2024). Digital Transformation of Supply Chain Management in the Fast Fashion Industry: A Case Study of Zara. In *SHS Web of Conferences* (Vol. 181, p. 04019). EDP Sciences. DOI: 10.1051/shsconf/202418104019

Li, F. (2008). Annual report readability, current earnings, and earnings persistence. *Journal of Accounting and Economics*, 45(2-3), 221–247. DOI: 10.1016/j.jacceco.2008.02.003

Li, H., Li, F., & Yu, X. (2018). China's contributions to global green energy and low-carbon development: Empirical evidence under the Belt and Road Framework. *Energies*, 11(6), 1527. DOI: 10.3390/en11061527

Li, L., Fei, C., & Fei, W. (2024). Research on investment incorporating both environmental performance and long (short) term financial performance of firms. *International Journal of Systems Science*, 55(2), 273–299. DOI: 10.1080/00207721.2023.2270402

Lim, E. K., Chalmers, K., & Hanlon, D. (2018). The influence of business strategy on annual report readability. *Journal of Accounting and Public Policy*, 37(1), 65–81. DOI: 10.1016/j.jaccpubpol.2018.01.003

Lin, W.L., Yip, N., Ho, J.A. & Sambasivan, M. (2020). The adoption of technological innovations in a B2B context and its impact on firm performance: An ethical leadership perspective. *Industrial Marketing Management, 89*, 61–71. .DOI: 10.1016/j.indmarman.2019.12.009

Liu, S., Zhang, Y., Liu, Y., Wang, L., & Wang, X. V. (2019, April). An 'Internet of Things' enabled dynamic optimization method for smart vehicles and logistics tasks. *Journal of Cleaner Production*, 215, 806–820. DOI: 10.1016/j.jclepro.2018.12.254

Li, Y. H. (2008). An empirical investigation on the determinants of E-procurement adoption in Chinese manufacturing enterprises. *2008 International Conference on Management Science and Engineering 15th Annual Conference Proceedings, ICMSE*, 32–37. DOI: 10.1109/ICMSE.2008.4668890

Li, Y., Janik, P., & Schwarz, H. (2024). Aggregated wind power characteristic curves and AI for the regional wind power infeed estimation. *Electrical Engineering*, 106, 655–671. DOI: 10.1007/s00202-023-02005-z

Lockett, A., Thompson, S., & Morgenstern, U. (2009). The development of the resource-based view of the firm: A critical appraisal. *International Journal of Management Reviews*, 11(1), 9–28. DOI: 10.1111/j.1468-2370.2008.00252.x

Long, X. & Gui, L. (2023). Waste Not Want Not? The Environmental Implications of Quick Response and Upcycling. https://doi.org/DOI: 10.1287/msom.2022.0040

Loop, C. (2024). *ReBlend - Case - Close The Loop*. https://www.close-the-loop.be/en/case/299/reblend

Loop, C. T. (2024). *End of life - Phase - Close The Loop*. https://www.close-the-loop.be/en/phase/3/end-of-life

Lorek, S., & Spangenberg, J. H. (2014). Sustainable consumption within a sustainable economy - Beyond green growth and green economies. *Journal of Cleaner Production*, 63, 33–44. Advance online publication. DOI: 10.1016/j.jclepro.2013.08.045

Loughran, T., & Mcdonald, B. (2014). Measuring readability in financial disclosures. *The Journal of Finance*, 69(4), 1643–1671. DOI: 10.1111/jofi.12162

Lu, M. T., Tsai, J. F., Shen, S. P., Lin, M.-H., & Hu, Y.-C. (2020). Estimating sustainable development performance in the electrical wire and cable industry: Applying the integrated fuzzy MADM approach. *Journal of Cleaner Production*, 277, 122440. DOI: 10.1016/j.jclepro.2020.122440

Luo, J., Li, X., & Chen, H. (2017). Annual report readability and corporate agency costs. *China Journal of Accounting Research*, 11(3), 187–212. DOI: 10.1016/j.cjar.2018.04.001

Lu, Y., & Wang, J. (2017). China's One Belt One Road initiative: An overview. *China Economic Review*, 43, 1–12.

Macaulay, J., Buckalew, L., & Chung, G. (2020). *Internet of Things in Logistics*. Troisdorf.

Mackey, A. (2008). The effect of CEOS on firm performance. *Strategic Management Journal*, 29(12), 1356–1367. DOI: 10.1002/smj.708

MAERSK. (2024). *What are 1PL, 2PL, 3PL, and 4PL logistics in supply chain management?*https://www.maersk.com/logistics-explained/supply-chain-management/2024/04/24/navigate-the-world-of-party-logistics-with-our-guide-to-1pl-2pl-3pl-4pl-models

Mahmood, M. A., Mann, G. J., & Zwass, V. (2015). Special Issue: Impacts of Information Technology Investment on Organizational Performance. *Journal of Management Information Systems*, 16(4), 3–10. DOI: 10.1080/07421222.2000.11518263

Mahmood, Z., Kouser, R., Ali, W., Ahmad, Z., & Salman, T. (2018). Does corporate governance affect sustainability disclosure? A mixed methods study. *Sustainability (Basel)*, 10(1), 1–20. DOI: 10.3390/su10010207

Mahmud, H., & Roy, J. (2024). Energy sector sustainability for a fast-growing economy like Bangladesh: An empirical assessment. *Sustainability Science*, 19(1), 51–73. DOI: 10.1007/s11625-023-01385-2

Malley, K., & Singh, R. T. D. (2020). *2nd Law of Thermodynamics - Chemistry LibreTexts*. https://chem.libretexts.org/Bookshelves/Physical_and_Theoretical_Chemistry_Textbook_Maps/Supplemental_Modules_(Physical_and_Theoretical_Chemistry)/Thermodynamics/The_Four_Laws_of_Thermodynamics/Second_Law_of_Thermodynamics

Maria, E., & Hanna, L. (2016). *Critical aspects in design - Mistra Future Fashion*. http://mistrafuturefashion.com/2016-1-critical-aspects/

Marques, A. D., Marques, A., & Ferreira, F. (2020). Homo Sustentabilis: Circular economy and new business models in fashion industry. *SN Applied Sciences*, 2(2), 306. Advance online publication. DOI: 10.1007/s42452-020-2094-8

Martina, I. (2023). *10 Concerning Fast Fashion Waste Statistics*. https://earth.org/statistics-about-fast-fashion-waste/

Martins, R., Oliveira, T., Thomas, M., & Tomás, S. (2019). Firms' continuance intention on SaaS use–an empirical study. *Information Technology & People*, 32(1), 189–216. DOI: 10.1108/ITP-01-2018-0027

Masuda, H., Kawakubo, S., Okitasari, M., & Morita, K. (2022). Exploring the role of local governments as intermediaries to facilitate partnerships for the Sustainable Development Goals. *Sustainable Cities and Society*, 82, 103883. DOI: 10.1016/j.scs.2022.103883

Masuda, H., Okitasari, M., Morita, K., Katramiz, T., Shimizu, H., Kawakubo, S., & Kataoka, Y. (2021). SDGs mainstreaming at the local level: Case studies from Japan. *Sustainability Science*, 16(5), 1539–1562. DOI: 10.1007/s11625-021-00977-0

Matear, S., Osborne, P., Garrett, T., & Gray, B. J. (2002). How does market orientation contribute to service firm performance? *European Journal of Marketing*, 36(9/10), 1058–1075. DOI: 10.1108/03090560210437334

Matuszewska-Pierzynka, A. (2021). Relationship between corporate sustainability performance and corporate financial performance: Evidence from US companies. *Equilibrium. Quarterly Journal of Economics and Economic Policy*, 16(4), 885–906. DOI: 10.24136/eq.2021.033

Mcdougall, N., Wagner, B., & MacBryde, J. (2016, June). A dynamic NRBV framework for innovative sustainable operations. *23rd innovation and product development management conference.*

McKinsey & Company. (2020). *How B2B Sales Have Changed During COVID-19.*

McQuillan, H. (2019). Waste, so What? A reflection on waste and the role of designers in a circular economy. *Nordes 2019: Who Cares?*, 1–9. DOI: 10.21606/nordes.2019.017

Md, R. M., & Md, H. M. (2016). Investigation of fabric wastages in Knit T-Shirt manufacturing industry in Bangladesh. *International Journal of Research in Engineering and Technology*, 05(10), 212–215. DOI: 10.15623/ijret.2016.0510035

Merter, A. K., & Özer, G. (2024). Audit committee and timely reporting: Evidence from Turkey. *SAGE Open*, 14(1), 1–21. DOI: 10.1177/21582440241239516

Millward-Hopkins, J., Purnell, P., & Baurley, S. (2023). Scenarios for reducing the environmental impacts of the UK clothing economy. *Journal of Cleaner Production*, 420, 138352. DOI: 10.1016/j.jclepro.2023.138352

Miscevic, G., Tijan, E., Zgaljic, D., & Jardas, M. (2018). Emerging trends in e-logistics. *2018 41st International Convention on Information and Communication Technology, Electronics and Microelectronics (MIPRO)*, 1353–1358. DOI: 10.23919/MIPRO.2018.8400244

Mishra, A., Dutta, P., Jayasankar, S., Jain, P., & Mathiyazhagan, K. (2023). A review of reverse logistics and closed-loop supply chains in the perspective of circular economy. *Benchmarking*, 30(3), 975–1020. DOI: 10.1108/BIJ-11-2021-0669

Mishra, S., & Das, A. P. (2023). *Microbial Remediation of Synthetic Microfiber Contaminated Wastewater. Microbial Technologies in Industrial Wastewater Treatment.* Springer Nature Singapore. DOI: 10.1007/978-981-99-2435-6_17

Moazzem, S., Crossin, E., Daver, F., & Wang, L. (2022). Environmental impact of apparel supply chain and textile products. *Environment, Development and Sustainability*, 24(8), 9757–9775. DOI: 10.1007/s10668-021-01873-4

Moazzem, S., Wang, L., Daver, F., & Crossin, E. (2021). Environmental impact of discarded apparel landfilling and recycling. *Resources, Conservation and Recycling*, 166, 105338. DOI: 10.1016/j.resconrec.2020.105338

Mohan, J., Rathi, R., Kaswan, M. S., & Nain, S. S. (2022). Green lean six sigma journey: Conceptualization and realization. *Materials Today: Proceedings*, 50, 1991–1998. DOI: 10.1016/j.matpr.2021.09.338

Molla, A., & Licker, P. S. (2005). ECommerce adoption in developing countries: A model and instrument. *Information & Management*, 42(6), 877–899. DOI: 10.1016/j.im.2004.09.002

Mölsä, K. M., Horn, S., Dahlbo, H., & Rissanen, M. (2022). Linear, reuse or recycling? An environmental comparison of different life cycle options for cotton roller towels. *Journal of Cleaner Production*, 374, 133976. DOI: 10.1016/j.jclepro.2022.133976

Montag, L., Klünder, T., & Steven, M. (2021). Paving the Way for Circular Supply Chains: Conceptualization of a Circular Supply Chain Maturity Framework. *Frontiers in Sustainability*, 2(11), 9111. DOI: 10.3389/frsus.2021.781978

Montenegro, R., Ribeiro, L. C., & Britto, G. (2020). The effects of environmental technologies: Evidences of different national innovation systems. *Journal of Cleaner Production*, 284, 124742. DOI: 10.1016/j.jclepro.2020.124742

Moorhouse, D. & Moorhouse, D. (2017). Sustainable Design: Circular Economy in Fashion and Textiles. *The Design Journal, 20*(sup1), S1948–S1959. DOI: 10.1080/14606925.2017.1352713

Moreau, V., Sahakian, M., van Griethuysen, P., & Vuille, F. (2017). Coming Full Circle: Why Social and Institutional Dimensions Matter for the Circular Economy. *Journal of Industrial Ecology*, 21(3), 497–506. DOI: 10.1111/jiec.12598

Morshed, M. N., Behary, N., Bouazizi, N., Guan, J., & Nierstrasz, V. A. (2021). An overview on biocatalysts immobilization on textiles: Preparation, progress and application in wastewater treatment. V. *Chemosphere*, 279, 130481. Advance online publication. DOI: 10.1016/j.chemosphere.2021.130481 PMID: 33894516

Moses, O. O. (2021). Corporate governance and economic sustainability reporting in Nigeria. *Journal of Accounting and Taxation*, 13(4), 243–254. DOI: 10.5897/JAT2021.0478

Munz, E. D. (2017). Psychotherapie in Der Psychiatrie. *Nervenheilkunde: Zeitschrift für Interdisziplinaere Fortbildung*. Advance online publication. DOI: 10.1007/s13398-014-0173-7.2

Murray, A., Skene, K., & Haynes, K. (2017). The Circular Economy: An Interdisciplinary Exploration of the Concept and Application in a Global Context. *Journal of Business Ethics*, 140(3), 369–380. DOI: 10.1007/s10551-015-2693-2

Mustafa, G., Zahid, M. T., Ullah, F., Zia, I., Younas, A., Batool, T., & Zahid, I. (2023). *Bacterial tools for the removal and degradation of synthetic dyes from the wastewater. Current Developments in Bioengineering and Biotechnology*. Elsevier. DOI: 10.1016/B978-0-323-91235-8.00022-X

Muthu, S. S. (2020). Life cycle assessment and product carbon footprint modelling of textile products. *Assessing the Environmental Impact of Textiles and the Clothing Supply Chain* (pp. 131–141). Elsevier. DOI: 10.1016/B978-0-12-819783-7.00007-7

Muthu, S. S. (2019). *Circular Economy in Textiles and Apparel. Circular Economy in Textiles and Apparel: Processing, Manufacturing, and Design*. Elsevier. DOI: 10.1016/C2017-0-03221-4

Mutlu, H. M., & Sürer, A. (2016). Effects of market, e-marketing, and technology orientations on innovativeness and performance in Turkish health organizations. *Health Marketing Quarterly*, 33(2), 95–111. DOI: 10.1080/07359683.2016.1166807 PMID: 27191549

Mzee, R. M., Ogweno, K. L., & Irene, N. (2015). Factors influencing Adoption of E marketing by small and Medium Enterprises (SMEs) in Kisumu Municipality. *IOSR Journal of Business and Management*, 17(5), 2319–7668. DOI: 10.9790/487X-17537883

Nambisan, S., Lyytinen, K., Majchrzak, A., & Song, M. (2017). Digital innovation management. *Management Information Systems Quarterly*, 41(1), 223–238. DOI: 10.25300/MISQ/2017/41:1.03

Narayanan, V. (2021). *Foundations for 3D Machine Knitting*. Carnegie Mellon University.

Narver, J. C., & Slater, S. F. (1990). The Effect of a Market Orientation on Business Profitability. *Journal of Marketing*, 54(4), 20–35. DOI: 10.1177/002224299005400403

Nasiri, M., Ukko, J., Saunila, M., & Rantala, T. (2020). Managing the digital supply chain: The role of smart technologies. *Technovation*, 96, 102121. DOI: 10.1016/j.technovation.2020.102121

Nayak, R. (2020). *Sustainable technologies in yarn and fabric manufacturing. Sustainable Technologies for Fashion and Textiles*. Elsevier. DOI: 10.1016/C2018-0-00610-6

Nayak, R., Akbari, M., & Maleki Far, S. (2019). Recent sustainable trends in Vietnam's fashion supply chain. *Journal of Cleaner Production*, 225, 291–303. Advance online publication. DOI: 10.1016/j.jclepro.2019.03.239

Nazari, J. A., Hrazdil, K., & Mahmoudian, F. (2017). Assessing social and environmental performance through narrative complexity in CSR reports. *Journal of Contemporary Accounting & Economics*, 13(2), 166–178. DOI: 10.1016/j.jcae.2017.05.002

Nguyen, P. T., & Kimura, A. (2020). How plain english use affects the length of annual reports: Evidence from the annual reports of foreign firms listed on the US Stock Exchange. *Journal of Accounting and Public Policy*, 39(6), 106773. DOI: 10.1016/j.jaccpubpol.2020.106773

Niinimäki, K. (2017). *Sustainable consumer satisfaction in the context of clothing. Product-Service System Design for Sustainability*. Routledge. DOI: 10.4324/9781351278003-7

Niinimäki, K. (2024). *Designing for (Extended) Product and Material Lifetimes. Recycling and Lifetime Management in the Textile and Fashion Sector*. CRC Press. DOI: 10.1201/9781003044413-3/DESIGNING-EXTENDED-PRODUCT-MATERIAL-LIFETIMES-KIRSI-NIINIM

Niinimäki, K., Peters, G., Dahlbo, H., Perry, P., Rissanen, T., & Gwilt, A. (2020). The environmental price of fast fashion. *Nature Reviews. Earth & Environment*, 1(4), 189–200. DOI: 10.1038/s43017-020-0039-9

Nilipour, A., De Silva, T. A., & Li, X. (2020). The readability of sustainability reporting in New Zealand over time. *Australasian Accounting. Business and Finance Journal*, 14(3), 86–107.

Nonaka, I. (1994). The dynamic theory of organizational knowledge creation. *Organization Science*, 5(1), 14–37. DOI: 10.1287/orsc.5.1.14

Notteboom, T., Pallis, A., & Rodrigue, J.-P. (2021). *Port Economics, Management and Policy*. Routledge., DOI: 10.4324/9780429318184

Novais, L., Maqueira, J. M., & Ortiz-Bas, Á. (2019). A systematic literature review of cloud computing use in supply chain integration. *Computers & Industrial Engineering*, 129, 296–314. DOI: 10.1016/j.cie.2019.01.056

Obor, D. O., & Ochogwu, J. P. (2024). Environmental Challenges, Climate Change and the Responsibility to Protect (RtoP) in Africa. In *Africa's Engagement with the Responsibility to Protect in the 21st Century* (pp. 313–336). Springer Nature Singapore. DOI: 10.1007/978-981-99-8163-2_18

OEKO-TEX. (2020, January 7). *OEKO-TEX- Tailor-made solutions for the textile and leather industry.* OEKO-TEX. https://www.oeko-tex.com/en/

Ohene-Asare, K., Tetteh, E. N., & Asuah, E. L. (2020). Total factor energy efficiency and economic development in Africa. *Energy Efficiency*, 13(6), 1177–1194. DOI: 10.1007/s12053-020-09877-1

Olariu, I. (2013). Conceptual issues regarding reverse logistics. *Studies And Scientific Researches.Economics Edition*, 18(18). Advance online publication. DOI: 10.29358/sceco.v0i18.218

Ooi, K. B., Lee, V. H., Tan, G. W. H., Hew, T. S., & Hew, J. J. (2018). Cloud computing in manufacturing: The next industrial revolution in Malaysia? *Expert Systems with Applications*, 93, 376–394. DOI: 10.1016/j.eswa.2017.10.009

Orangefiber. (2024). *Orange Fiber • Sustainable fabrics from citrus juice by-products.* https://orangefiber.it/

Osman, A. I., Redpath, D., Lichtfouse, E., & Rooney, D. W. (2024). Synergy between vertical farming and the hydrogen economy. *Environmental Chemistry Letters*, 22(1), 1–6. DOI: 10.1007/s10311-023-01648-5

Østergaard, P. A., Duic, N., Noorollahi, Y., Mikulcic, H., & Kalogirou, S. (2020). Sustainable development using renewable energy technology. *Renewable Energy*, 146, 2430–2437. DOI: 10.1016/j.renene.2019.08.094

Overdiek, A. (2018). Opportunities for slow fashion retail in temporary stores. *Journal of Fashion Marketing and Management*, 22(1), 67–81. Advance online publication. DOI: 10.1108/JFMM-05-2017-0042

Oyelere, P., Laswad, F., & Fisher, R. (2003). Determinants of Internet Financial Reporting by New Zealand Companies. *Journal of International Financial Management & Accounting*, 14(1), 26–63. DOI: 10.1111/1467-646X.00089

Özen, M., Demircan, G., Kisa, M., & Ilik, Z. (2020). *Investigation of usability of waste textile fabrics in composites. Emerging Materials Research.* Thomas Telford Ltd. DOI: 10.1680/jemmr.18.00106

Pabjańczyk-Wlazło, E. K., Puszkarz, A. K., Bednarowicz, A., Tarzyńska, N., & Sztajnowski, S. (2022). The Influence of Surface Modification with Biopolymers on the Structure of Melt-Blown and Spun-Bonded Poly(lactic acid) Nonwovens. *Materials (Basel)*, 15(20), 7097. Advance online publication. DOI: 10.3390/ma15207097 PMID: 36295163

PACRA. (2011), *The Pakistan Credit Rating Agency Limited, Study of Textile Sector.*

Pajuste, A., Poriete, E., & Novickis, R. (2021). Management reporting complexity and earnings management: Evidence from the Baltic markets. *Baltic Journal of Management*, 16(1), 47–69. DOI: 10.1108/BJM-01-2020-0019

Panait, M., Janjua, L. R., Apostu, S. A., & Mihăescu, C. (2023). Impact factors to reduce carbon emissions. Evidences from Latin America. *Kybernetes*, 52(11), 5669–5686. DOI: 10.1108/K-05-2022-0712

Pang, R., & Zhang, X. (2019). Achieving environmental sustainability in manufacture: A 28-year bibliometric cartography of green manufacturing research. *Journal of Cleaner Production*, 233, 84–99. DOI: 10.1016/j.jclepro.2019.05.303

Pathak, K., & Thapaliya, S. (2022). Some philosophical paradigms and their implications in health.

Patnaik, S., & Tshifularo, C. A. (2021). *Management of wastes in garment manufacturing. Waste Management in the Fashion and Textile Industries*. Elsevier. DOI: 10.1016/B978-0-12-818758-6.00004-1

Paul, U., & Mercedes, B. (2009). *Carbon Labelling: Public Perceptions of the Debate*. https://www.researchgate.net/publication/236146858_Carbon_Labelling_Public_Perceptions_of_the_Debate

Pazirandeh, A., & Jafari, H. (2013). Making sense of green logistics. *International Journal of Productivity and Performance Management*, 62(8), 889–904. DOI: 10.1108/IJPPM-03-2013-0059

Pearce, D. D., & Pearce, J. A. (2019). Distinguishing attributes of high-growth ventures. *Business Horizons, Elsevier Ltd*, (January). Advance online publication. DOI: 10.1016/j.bushor.2019.10.003

Pensupa, N., Leu, S. Y., Hu, Y., Du, C., Liu, H., Jing, H., Wang, H., & Lin, C. S. K. (2017). Recent Trends in Sustainable Textile Waste Recycling Methods: Current Situation and Future Prospects. V. *Topics in Current Chemistry*, 375(5), 76. Advance online publication. DOI: 10.1007/s41061-017-0165-0 PMID: 28815435

Perlman, B. J., Reddick, C. G., & Demir, T. (2024). Toward an Organizational Ethics Culture Framework: An Analysis of Survey Data From Local Government Managers. *Public Integrity*, 1–16. DOI: 10.1080/10999922.2023.2295643

Persson, O., & Hinton, J. B. (2023). Second-hand clothing markets and a just circular economy? Exploring the role of business forms and profit. *Journal of Cleaner Production*, 390, 136139. DOI: 10.1016/j.jclepro.2023.136139

Peter John, E., & Mishra, U. (2023). A sustainable three-layer circular economic model with controllable waste, emission, and wastewater from the textile and fashion industry. *Journal of Cleaner Production*, 388, 135642. DOI: 10.1016/j.jclepro.2022.135642

Pham, H. T., Pham, T., Truong Quang, H., & Dang, C. N. (2022). Impact of transformational leadership on green learning and green innovation in construction supply chains. *Engineering, Construction, and Architectural Management*.

Piller, L. W. (2023). Designing for circularity: Sustainable pathways for Australian fashion small to medium enterprises. *Journal of Fashion Marketing and Management*, 27(2), 287–310. DOI: 10.1108/JFMM-09-2021-0220

Podsakoff, P. M., MacKenzie, S. B., & Podsakoff, N. P. (2012). Sources of method bias in social science research and recommendations on how to control it. *Annual Review of Psychology*, 63(1), 539–569. DOI: 10.1146/annurev-psych-120710-100452 PMID: 21838546

Prajogo, D., & Olhager, J. (2012). The effect of supply chain information integration on logistics integration and firm performance. *International Journal of Production Economics*, 135(1), 514–522. DOI: 10.1016/j.ijpe.2011.09.001

Pramanik, S. (2022). An Effective Secured Privacy-Protecting Data Aggregation Method in IoT. In Odhiambo, M. O., Mwashita, W., & Global, I. G. I. (Eds.), *Achieving Full Realization and Mitigating the Challenges of the Internet of Things*. DOI: 10.4018/978-1-7998-9312-7.ch008

Prammanee, N. (2003). A critical analysis of the adoption and utilization of the internet in Thailand for education purposes. *First Monday*, 8(1). Advance online publication. DOI: 10.5210/fm.v8i1.1021

Prasad, V. K., Ramamurthy, K., & Naidu, G. M. (2001). The Influence on of Internet-Marketing Marketing Performance Competencies Integration and Export. *Journal of International Marketing*, 9(4), 82–110. DOI: 10.1509/jimk.9.4.82.19944

Premkumar, G., Ramamurthy, K., & Nilakanta, S. (1994). Implementation of electronic data interchange: An innovation diffusion perspective. *Journal of Management Information Systems*, 11(2), 157–186. DOI: 10.1080/07421222.1994.11518044

Premkumar, G., & Roberts, M. (1999). Adoption of new information technologies in rural small businesses. *Omega*, 27(4), 467–484. DOI: 10.1016/S0305-0483(98)00071-1

QUT. (2024). *Separation and recycling of fast fashion fibres - TextileR: Future Textile Industries*. QUT TextileR. https://research.qut.edu.au/textiler/research/demonstrating-effective-recycling-of-fast-fashion-fibres/

Rachel, C. (2021). *Fashion's sustainability agenda: Where to start | Vogue Business*. Vogue Business. https://www.voguebusiness.com/sustainability/fashions-sustainability-agenda-where-to-start

Radhakrishnan, S. (2021). *Circular Economy in Textiles and Fashion. Environmental Footprints and Eco-Design of Products and Processes*. Springer. DOI: 10.1007/978-981-16-3698-1_6

Rahayu, R. & Day, J. (2015). Determinant Factors of E-commerce Adoption by SMEs in Developing Country: Evidence from Indonesia. *Procedia - Social and Behavioral Sciences*, *195*, 142–150. .DOI: 10.1016/j.sbspro.2015.06.423

Rahman, D., & Kabir, M. (2023). Does board independence influence annual report readability? *European Accounting Review*, 1 - 28. DOI: 10.1080/09638180.2023.2223590

Rajabalizadeh, J. (2023). CEO overconfidence and financial reporting complexity: Evidence from textual analysis. *Management Decision*, 61(13), 356–385. DOI: 10.1108/MD-06-2023-1033

Rapp, A., Schillewaert, N., & Hao, A. W. (2008). The Influence of Market Orientation on E-Business Innovation and Performance: The Role of the Top Management Team. *Journal of Marketing Theory and Practice*, 16(1), 7–25. DOI: 10.2753/MTP1069-6679160101

Rath, S. R., Chu, W., Terzioğlu, N., & Wever, R. (2023). *Designing Interventions for Sustainability: A Conceptual Framework for Information Scoping in the Design Research Phase. EcoDesign for Sustainable Products, Services and Social Systems I*. Springer Nature Singapore. DOI: 10.1007/978-981-99-3818-6_29

Raut, R., Priyadarshinee, P., Gardas, B. B., Narkhede, B. E., & Nehete, R. (2018). The incident effects of supply chain and cloud computing integration on the business performance: An integrated SEM-ANN approach. *Benchmarking*, 25(8), 2688–2722. DOI: 10.1108/BIJ-07-2017-0170

Ravichandran, T., Liu, Y., Han, S., & Hasan, I. (2009). Diversification and Firm Performance: Exploring the Moderating Effects of Information Technology Spending. *Journal of Management Information Systems*, 25(4), 205–240. DOI: 10.2753/MIS0742-1222250407

Rehman Khan, S. A., Umar, M., Zia-ul-haq, H. M., & Yu, Z. (2022). *Technological Advancement and Circular Economy Practices in Food Supply Chain* (pp. 65–75). DOI: 10.1108/S1877-636120220000027005

Rehman Khan, S. A., Ahmad, Z., Sheikh, A. A., & Yu, Z. (2022). Digital transformation, smart technologies, and eco-innovation are paving the way toward sustainable supply chain performance. *Science Progress*, 105(4), 00368504221145648. DOI: 10.1177/00368504221145648 PMID: 36573795

Rehman, S. U., Kraus, S., Shah, S. A., Khanin, D., & Mahto, R. V. (2021). Analyzing the relationship between green innovation and environmental performance in large manufacturing firms. *Technological Forecasting and Social Change*, 163, 120481. DOI: 10.1016/j.techfore.2020.120481

Rejeb, A., Rejeb, K., Kayikci, Y., Appolloni, A., & Treiblmaier, H. (2023). Mapping the knowledge domain of green procurement: A review and bibliometric analysis. *Environment, Development and Sustainability*, 1–35. DOI: 10.1007/s10668-023-03948-w

Rennekamp, K. (2012). Processing fluency and investors' reactions to disclosure readability. *Journal of Accounting Research*, 50(5), 1319–1354. DOI: 10.1111/j.1475-679X.2012.00460.x

Ren, Z., Fang, F., Yan, N., & Wu, Y. (2022). State of the Art in Defect Detection Based on Machine Vision. *International Journal of Precision Engineering and Manufacturing-Green Technology*, 9(2), 661–691. DOI: 10.1007/s40684-021-00343-6

Resources, N. S. (2024). *How straw-based packaging can help optimize your supply chains and fight climate change?*https://www.nefab.com/news-insights/2022/how-straw-based-packaging-can-help-optimize-your-supply-chains-and-fight-climate-change/

Rick, L. (2020). *Textile and Clothes Recycling Facts and Figures*. https://www.liveabout.com/textile-recycling-facts-and-figures-2878122

Ridley, W., & Devadoss, S. (2023). Competition and trade policy in the world cotton market: Implications for US cotton exports. *American Journal of Agricultural Economics*, 105(5), 1365–1387. DOI: 10.1111/ajae.12370

Ripple, W. J., Wolf, C., Newsome, T. M., Galetti, M., Alamgir, M., Crist, E., & Laurance, W. F. (2017). World scientists' warning to humanity: A second notice. *Bioscience*, 67(12), 1026–1028. DOI: 10.1093/biosci/bix125

Ritter, T., & Pedersen, C. L. (2020a). Digitization capability and the digitalization of business models in business-to-business firms: Past, present, and future. *Industrial Marketing Management*, 86(April), 180–190. Advance online publication. DOI: 10.1016/j.indmarman.2019.11.019

Ritter, T., & Pedersen, C. L. (2020b). Analyzing the impact of the coronavirus crisis on business models. *Industrial Marketing Management*, 88(May), 214–224. DOI: 10.1016/j.indmarman.2020.05.014

Robinson, J. (2004). Squaring the circle? Some thoughts on the idea of sustainable development. *Ecological Economics*, 48(4), 369–384. DOI: 10.1016/j.ecolecon.2003.10.017

Rogers, E. M. (1995). Diffusion of Innovations: modifications of a model for telecommunications. *Die diffusion von innovationen in der telekommunikation*, 25-38.

Rogers, D. S., & Lembke, R. S. (2021). Reverse Logistics. In *International Encyclopedia of Transportation* (pp. 208–218). Elsevier. DOI: 10.1016/B978-0-08-102671-7.10245-3

Rogers, D. S., & Tibben-Lembke, R. (2001). An examination of reverse logistics practices. *Journal of Business Logistics*, 22(2), 129–148. DOI: 10.1002/j.2158-1592.2001.tb00007.x

Romaily, C. (2022). *10 Zero Waste Fashion Brands For A Sustainable Wardrobe.* https://pebblemag.com/zero-waste-fashion/

Rovshenov, A., & Sarsar, F. (2023). Research trends in programming education: A systematic review of the articles published between 2012-2020. *Journal of Educational Technology and Online Learning*, 6(1), 48–81. DOI: 10.31681/jetol.1201010

Roy Choudhury, A. K. (2014). Environmental Impacts of the Textile Industry and Its Assessment Through Life Cycle Assessment. *Roadmap to Sustainable Textiles and Clothing* (str. 1–39). DOI: 10.1007/978-981-287-110-7_1

Ruiz, A. (2023, April 11). *17 Most Worrying Textile Waste Statistics & Facts.* TheRoundup. https://theroundup.org/textile-waste-statistics/

Rusli, E. M. (2012). Facebook buys Instagram for $1 billion. *New York Times.*

Ryalat, M., ElMoaqet, H., & AlFaouri, M. (2023). Design of a smart factory based on cyber-physical systems and Internet of Things towards Industry 4.0. *Applied Sciences (Basel, Switzerland)*, 13(4), 2156. DOI: 10.3390/app13042156

Saad, S. M., & Khamkham, M. (2022). The Applications of AI in GSCM–A Systematic Literature Review. *Advances in Manufacturing Technology, 35*, 348-353.

Saha, K., Dey, P. K., & Papagiannaki, E. (2021). Implementing circular economy in the textile and clothing industry. *Business Strategy and the Environment*, 30(4), 1497–1530. Advance online publication. DOI: 10.1002/bse.2670

Sánchez-Rodríguez, C., Martínez-Lorente, A. R., & Hemsworth, D. (2019). E-procurement in small and medium sized enterprises; facilitators, obstacles and effect on performance. *Benchmarking*, 27(2), 839–866. DOI: 10.1108/BIJ-12-2018-0413

Sandberg, E. (2023). Orchestration capabilities in circular supply chains of post-consumer used clothes – A case study of a Swedish fashion retailer. *Journal of Cleaner Production*, 387, 135935. DOI: 10.1016/j.jclepro.2023.135935

Sandvik, I. M., & Stubbs, W. (2019). Circular fashion supply chain through textile-to-textile recycling. *Journal of Fashion Marketing and Management*, 23(3), 366–381. DOI: 10.1108/JFMM-04-2018-0058

Sani, A., & Nawaninatyas, P. N. (2020). E-Business Adoption Models in Organizational Contexts on the TAM Extended Model: A Preliminary Assessment. *2020 8th International Conference on Cyber and IT Service Management, CITSM 2020*, 6–10. DOI: 10.1109/CITSM50537.2020.9268869

Şanli, O., Sahu, P., & Janjua, L. R. (2024). Underlying the Impact of Economic, Social, and Governance Adaptation on Poverty Reduction Under the Shadow of External Financial Inflows—Panel Estimation from the Sub-Saharan Region. In *Sustainable Economic Development: Fostering the United Nations Goals* (pp. 153–179). Springer Nature Singapore. DOI: 10.1007/978-981-97-3767-3_7

Santos, G. (2017). Road transport and CO2 emissions: What are the challenges? *Transport Policy*, 59, 71–74. DOI: 10.1016/j.tranpol.2017.06.007

Sarstedt, M., Ringle, C. M., Henseler, J., & Hair, J. F. (2014). On the Emancipation of PLS-SEM: A Commentary on Rigdon (2012). *Long Range Planning*, 47(3), 154–160. DOI: 10.1016/j.lrp.2014.02.007

Saskia, M., Christis, M., & An, V. (2019). Textiles and the environment in a circular economy. *European Topic Centre on Waste and Materials in a Green Economy.*

Satt, H., & Iatridis, G. (2023). The effect of annual reports tone complexity on firms' dividend policy: Evidence from the United States. *Review of Behavioral Finance*, 15(4), 592–614. DOI: 10.1108/RBF-12-2021-0262

Saud, S., Chen, S., Haseeb, A., & Sumayya, . (2020). The role of financial development and globalization in the environment: Accounting ecological footprint indicators for selected one-belt-one-road initiative countries. *Journal of Cleaner Production*, 250, 119518. DOI: 10.1016/j.jclepro.2019.119518

Saunders, M., Lewis, P., & Thornhill, A. (2007). *Research methods for business students* (4th ed.). Pearson Education.

Schwab, K. (2016). *The Fourth Industrial Revolution*. World Economic Forum. www.weforum.org

Sciences, D. (1995). The role of interorganizational and organizational factors on the .... *Decision Sciences*, 26(3), 303–336. DOI: 10.1111/j.1540-5915.1995.tb01431.x

Seidu, R. K., Eghan, B., & Acquaye, R. (2024). A Review of Circular Fashion and Bio-based Materials in the Fashion Industry. *Circular Economy and Sustainability*, 4(1), 693–715. DOI: 10.1007/s43615-023-00303-z

Shafqat, A. R., & Saccavini, A. (2023). *Eco-design of Textiles. Textile Science and Clothing Technology*. Springer. DOI: 10.1007/978-3-031-49479-6_3

Shah, R. (2011). Examine the Role of Different Actors Across The Textile -Fashion Supply Chain To Understand the issues Regarding Growth Of Eco-Labeled Sustainable Textile Products [Thesis]. The University of Manchester, Manchester, UK.

Shah. (2012). Challenges Faced by Textile Industry of Pakistan: Suggested Solutions. *Kasbit Business*, *39*, 33–39.

Shah, A., Mat, C. R. B. C., & Ibrahim, A. (2022). The resource and leagile strategy model for apparel export enterprises: A proposed model to mitigate COVID-19 uncertainties. *International Journal of Circular Economy and Waste Management*, 2(1), 1–14. DOI: 10.4018/IJCEWM.288502

Shaher, Y. A. (2012). *Strategies For Pakistan Textiles Industry To Sustain The Business*. University of Gavle.

Shahzad, M., Qu, Y., Zafar, A. U., Rehman, S. U., & Islam, T. (2020). Exploring the influence of knowledge management process on corporate sustainable performance through green innovation. *Journal of Knowledge Management*, 24(9), 2079–2106. DOI: 10.1108/JKM-11-2019-0624

Shamsuzzaman, M., Islam, M. M., Hasan, H. M. R. U., Khan, A. M., & Sayem, A. S. M. (2023). Mapping environmental sustainability of knitted textile production facilities. *Journal of Cleaner Production*, 405, 136900. DOI: 10.1016/j.jclepro.2023.136900

Shee, H., & Kaswi, S. (2015). Behavioral causes of the bullwhip effect: Multinational vs. local supermarket retailers. *Operations and Supply Chain Management: An International Journal*, 9(1), 1–14. DOI: 10.31387/oscm0230156

Shee, H., Miah, S. J., Fairfield, L., & Pujawan, N. (2018). The impact of cloud-enabled process integration on supply chain performance and firm sustainability: The moderating role of top management. *Supply Chain Management*, 23(6), 500–517. DOI: 10.1108/SCM-09-2017-0309

Sheikh, A. A., Rana, N. A., Inam, A., Shahzad, A., & Awan, H. M. (2018). Is e-marketing a source of sustainable business performance? Predicting the role of top management support with various interaction factors. *Cogent Business and Management*, 5(1), 1–22. DOI: 10.1080/23311975.2018.1516487

Sheikh, A. A., & Shahzad, A., & ku Ishak, A. (2017). The Impact of Market Orientation, Top Management Support, Use of E-Marketing and Technological Opportunism on the Firm Performance: A Mediated-Moderation and Moderated-Mediation Analysis. *Abasyn University Journal of Social Sciences*, 10(2), 212–234.

Sheikh, A. A., Shahzad, A., & Ishak, A. B. K. (2016a). The mediating impact of e-marketing adoption on export performance of firms: A conceptual study. *Journal of Technology and Operations Management*, 11(1), 48–58.

Sheikh, A. A., Shahzad, A., & Ishak, A. B. K. (2017b). The Role of E-Marketing Uses among TOE Factors and Textile Sector Performance in Pakistan: An Empirical Study. *NUML International Journal of Business & Management Vol.*, 12(2), 117–135.

Sheikh, A. A., Shahzad, A., & Ishak, A. K. (2016b). The effects of e-marketing uses, market orientation, relative advantage and trading partners pressure on the performance of textile business in Pakistan: A mediated-moderation analysis. *International Journal of Economic Perspectives*, 10(4), 562–580.

Sheikh, A. A., Shahzad, A., & Ku Ishaq, A. (2017a). The Growth of E-Marketing in Business-to-Business Industry and its effect on the Performance of Businesses in Pakistan: Marketing Success. *International and Multidisciplinary Journal of Social Sciences*, 6(2), 178. DOI: 10.17583/rimcis.2017.2704

Sheriff, K. M. M., Gunasekaran, A., & Nachiappan, S. (2012). Reverse logistics network design: A review on strategic perspective. *International Journal of Logistics Systems and Management*, 12(2), 171. DOI: 10.1504/IJLSM.2012.047220

Shibin, K. T., Dubey, R., Gunasekaran, A., Hazen, B., Roubaud, D., Gupta, S., & Foropon, C. (2020). Examining sustainable supply chain management of SMEs using resource based view and institutional theory. *Annals of Operations Research*, 290(1-2), 301–326. DOI: 10.1007/s10479-017-2706-x

Shi, P., & Yan, B. (2016). Factors affecting RFID adoption in the agricultural product distribution industry: Empirical evidence from China. *SpringerPlus*, 5(1), 2029. DOI: 10.1186/s40064-016-3708-x PMID: 27995006

Shirvanimoghaddam, K., Motamed, B., Ramakrishna, S., & Naebe, M. (2020). Death by waste: Fashion and textile circular economy case. *The Science of the Total Environment*, 718, 137317. DOI: 10.1016/j.scitotenv.2020.137317 PMID: 32088483

Sianturi, N. M., Nofirman, N., Yulianti, E. B., Fatmawati, E., & Hendriarto, P. (2022). Relevancy technological innovation and community economic development in Indonesia. *Linguistics and Culture Review*, 6, 117–130. DOI: 10.21744/lingcure.v6nS3.2091

Sinclair, R. (2015). *Understanding Textile Fibres and Their Properties. Textiles and Fashion*. Elsevier., DOI: 10.1016/B978-1-84569-931-4.00001-5

Siregar, S. V., & Harahap, S. N. (2023). Financial reporting complexities: Association with accounting expertise of board and audit committee. *Journal of Corporate Accounting & Finance*, 35(1), 203–217. DOI: 10.1002/jcaf.22658

Sivarajah, U., Irani, Z., Gupta, S., & Mahroof, K. (2020). Role of big data and social media analytics for business to business sustainability: A participatory web context. *Industrial Marketing Management*, 86, 163–179. DOI: 10.1016/j.indmarman.2019.04.005

Sivaram, N. M., Gopal, P. M. & Barik, D. (2019). Toxic Waste From Textile Industries. *Energy from Toxic Organic Waste for Heat and Power Generation*, 43–54. DOI: 10.1016/B978-0-08-102528-4.00004-3

Smeuninx, N., De Clerck, B., & Aerts, W. (2016). Measuring the readability of sustainability reports: A corpus-based analysis through standard formulae and NLP. *International Journal of Business Communication*, 1 - 34. DOI: 10.1177/2329488416675456

Smithers, R. (2018). *Money for old socks: John Lewis to buy back clothes to cut waste | John Lewis | The Guardian*. https://www.theguardian.com/business/2018/jun/18/money-for-old-socks-john-lewis-to-buy-back-clothes-to-cut-waste

Soewarno, N., Tjahjadi, B., & Fithrianti, F. (2019). Green innovation strategy and green innovation: The roles of green organizational identity and environmental organizational legitimacy. *Management Decision*, 57(11), 3061–3078. DOI: 10.1108/MD-05-2018-0563

Song, M., Peng, L., Shang, Y., & Zhao, X. (2022). Green technology progress and total factor productivity of resource-based enterprises: A perspective of technical compensation of environmental regulation. *Technological Forecasting and Social Change*, 174, 121276. DOI: 10.1016/j.techfore.2021.121276

Song, M., Yang, M. X., Zeng, K. J., & Feng, W. (2020). Green knowledge sharing, stakeholder pressure, absorptive capacity, and green innovation: Evidence from Chinese manufacturing firms. *Business Strategy and the Environment*, 29(3), 1517–1531. DOI: 10.1002/bse.2450

Soni, J., & Bhattacharjee, K. (2024). Multi-objective dynamic economic emission dispatch integration with renewable energy sources and plug-in electrical vehicle using equilibrium optimizer. *Environment, Development and Sustainability*, 26(4), 8555–8586. DOI: 10.1007/s10668-023-03058-7

Sporrer, A. (2021). How much carbon does the transportation industry emit annually? FreightWaves. https://www.freightwaves.com/news/how-much-carbon-does-the-transportation-industry-emit-annually

Srinivasan, R., Lilien, G. L., & Rangaswamy, A. (2002). Technological Opportunism and Radical Technology Adoption: An Application to E-Business. *Journal of Marketing*, 66(3), 47–60. Advance online publication. DOI: 10.1509/jmkg.66.3.47.18508

Stahel, W. R. (2016). The circular economy. *Nature*, 531(7595), 435–438. DOI: 10.1038/531435a PMID: 27008952

Stalk, G.Jr, & Hout, T. M. (1990). Competing Against Time. *Research Technology Management*, 33(2), 19–24. DOI: 10.1080/08956308.1990.11670646

Stankov, U., Filimonau, V., & Slivar, I. (2019). Calm ICT design in hotels: A critical review of applications and implications. *International Journal of Hospitality Management*, 82, 298–307. DOI: 10.1016/j.ijhm.2018.10.012

State Bank of Pakistan. (2011). IFC Advisory Service in the Middle East and North Africa [Review of *IFC Advisory Service in the Middle East and North Africa*]. State Bank of Pakistan. https://www.sbp.org.pk/departments/ihfd/Sub-Segment%20Booklets/Textile%20Fabric.pdf

Sundin, E., & Lee, H. M. (2012). In what way is remanufacturing good for the environment? In Matsumoto, M., Umeda, Y., Masui, K., & Fukushige, S. (Eds.), *Design for Innovative Value Towards a Sustainable Society* (pp. 552–557). Springer. DOI: 10.1007/978-94-007-3010-6_106

Suryanto, T., Haseeb, M., & Hartani, N. H. (2018). The correlates of developing green supply chain management practices: Firms level analysis in Malaysia. *International Journal of Supply Chain Management*, 7(5), 316.

Systems, Z. (2024). *Defect Detection Using Artificial Intelligence In Software Testing – Learning From Other Industries*. https://www.zucisystems.com/blog/defect-detection-using-artificial-intelligence-in-software-testing-learning-from-other-industries/

Tabachnick, B. G., & Fidell, L. S. (2007). Using multivariate statistics.

Tang, C., & Tomlin, B. (2008). The power of flexibility for mitigating supply chain risks. *International Journal of Production Economics*, 116(1), 12–27. DOI: 10.1016/j.ijpe.2008.07.008

Tan, K. H., Ji, G., Lim, C. P., & Tseng, M. L. (2017). Using big data to make better decisions in the digital economy. *International Journal of Production Research*, 55(17), 4998–5000. DOI: 10.1080/00207543.2017.1331051

Tessema, A. (2019). The impact of corporate governance and political connections on information asymmetry: International evidence from banks in the Gulf Cooperation Council member countries. *Journal of International Accounting, Auditing & Taxation*, 35, 1–17. DOI: 10.1016/j.intaccaudtax.2019.05.001

Textile, E. (2023). *Standards - Textile Exchange*. https://textileexchange.org/standards/

Thompson, A. (2023). *What is Reverse Logistics?* https://www.dhl.com/discover/en-lk/logistics-advice/essential-guides/what-is-reverse-logistics

Tiago, M. T. P. M. B., & Veríssimo, J. M. C. (2014). Digital marketing and social media: Why bother? *Business Horizons*, 57(6), 703–708. DOI: 10.1016/j.bushor.2014.07.002

Tongzon, J. L., & Nguyen, H. O. (2021, June). Effects of port-shipping logistics integration on technical and allocative efficiency. *Asian J. Shipp. Logist.*, 37(2), 109–116. DOI: 10.1016/j.ajsl.2021.01.001

Tony, C. (2017). *Adidas pursues rival Nike with in-store personalisation and manufacturing*. The Drum. https://www.thedrum.com/news/2017/03/21/adidas-pursues-rival-nike-with-store-personalisation-and-manufacturing

Tripathi, S. P. (2020). Perspectives On Logistics Outsourcing. *Journal of Critical Reviews*, 7(15), 2785–3795.

Trust, C. T. (2018). *Three sustainability trends shaping the future of the fashion industry.* https://www.carbontrust.com/news-and-insights/insights/three-sustainability-trends-shaping-the-future-of-the-fashion-industry

Tsiotsou, R. H., & Vlachopoulou, M. (2011). Understanding the effects of market orientation and e-marketing on service performance. *Marketing Intelligence & Planning*, 29(2), 141–155. DOI: 10.1108/02634501111117593

Uddin, N., & Chakraborty, V. (2022). An investigation of the readability of sustainability reports. *Journal of Emerging Technologies in Accounting*, 19(1), 69–78. DOI: 10.2308/JETA-18-10-01-18

Ullah, S., Khan, F. U., & Ahmad, N. (2022). Promoting sustainability through green innovation adoption: A case of manufacturing industry. *Environmental Science and Pollution Research International*, 29(14), 1–21. DOI: 10.1007/s11356-021-17322-8 PMID: 34746984

Ullah, S., Luo, R., Adebayo, T. S., & Kartal, M. T. (2024). Paving the ways toward sustainable development: The asymmetric effect of economic complexity, renewable electricity, and foreign direct investment on the environmental sustainability in BRICS-T. *Environment, Development and Sustainability*, 26(4), 9115–9139. DOI: 10.1007/s10668-023-03085-4

UNCOP26. (2021). COP26: Together for our planet. United Nations Climate Action. https://www.un.org/en/climatechange/cop26

UNCTAD. (2018). *Circular Economy: The New Normal?* https://unctad.org/system/files/official-document/presspb2017d10_en.pdf

United Nations General Assembly. (2018). Circular Economy for the SDGs: From Concept to Practice.

Vadicherla, T., Saravanan, D., Muthu Ram, M., & Suganya, K. (2017). *Fashion Renovation via Upcycling. Textiles and Clothing Sustainability*. Springer. DOI: 10.1007/978-981-10-2146-6_1

Vehovar, V., Toepoel, V., & Steinmetz, S. (2016). *Non-probability sampling* (Vol. 1). The Sage Handbook of Survey Methods.

Vela, R. A. (2023). Circular Economy and Supply Chain Management: Circular SCM, a Sustainable Pathway for the Future. https://www.linkedin.com/pulse/circular-economy-supply-chain-management-scm-sustainable-vela/

Velte, P. (2018). Is audit committee expertise connected with increased readability of integrated reports: Evidence from EU companies. *Problems and Perspectives in Management*, 16(2), 23–41. DOI: 10.21511/ppm.16(2).2018.03

Vial, G. (2019). Understanding digital transformation: A review and a research agenda. *The Journal of Strategic Information Systems*, 28(2), 118–144. DOI: 10.1016/j.jsis.2019.01.003

Wang, C. H. (2019). How organizational green culture influences green performance and competitive advantage: The mediating role of green innovation. *Journal of Manufacturing Technology Management*, 30(4), 666–683. DOI: 10.1108/JMTM-09-2018-0314

Wang, C., Fan, A. Y., & Qian, M. H. (2021). Research on evaluation index system of sustainable development of logistics enterprises. *Business and Economic Review*, 09, 87–90.

Wang, G., Zhang, G., Guo, X., & Zhang, Y. (2021). Digital twin-driven service model and optimal allocation of manufacturing resources in shared manufacturing. *Journal of Manufacturing Systems*, 59, 165–179. DOI: 10.1016/j.jmsy.2021.02.008

Wang, J., Xue, Y., Sun, X., & Yang, J. (2020). Green learning orientation, green knowledge acquisition and ambidextrous green innovation. *Journal of Cleaner Production*, 250, 119475. DOI: 10.1016/j.jclepro.2019.119475

Wang, S., Abbas, J., Sial, M. S., Álvarez-Otero, S., & Cioca, L. I. (2022). Achieving green innovation and sustainable development goals through green knowledge management: Moderating role of organizational green culture. *Journal of Innovation & Knowledge*, 7(4), 100272. DOI: 10.1016/j.jik.2022.100272

Wang, S., Su, D., Wu, Y., & Chai, Z. (2020). Application of life-cycle assessment to the eco-design of LED lighting products. *Euro-Mediterranean Journal for Environmental Integration*, 5(2), 1–10. DOI: 10.1007/s41207-020-00180-0

Wang, S., Wan, J., Zhang, D., Li, D., & Zhang, C. (2016). Towards smart factory for industry 4.0: A self-organized multi-agent system with big data based feedback and coordination. *Computer Networks*, 101, 158–168. DOI: 10.1016/j.comnet.2015.12.017

Wang, Y. M., Wang, Y. S., & Yang, Y. F. (2010). Understanding the determinants of RFID adoption in the manufacturing industry. *Technological Forecasting and Social Change*, 77(5), 803–815. DOI: 10.1016/j.techfore.2010.03.006

Wang, Y., Rodrigues, V. S., & Evans, L. (2015). The use of ICT in road freight transport for CO2 reduction - An exploratory study of UK's grocery retail industry. *International Journal of Logistics Management*, 26(1), 2–29. DOI: 10.1108/IJLM-02-2013-0021

Watts, R. L., & Zimmerman, J. L. (1978). Towards a positive theory of the determination of accounting standards. *The Accounting Review*, 53(1), 112–134.

Watts, R. L., & Zimmerman, J. L. (1986). *Positive accounting theory*. Prentice-Hall.

Weill, P., & Woerner, S. L. (2018). Is your company ready for a digital future? *MIT Sloan Management Review*, 59(2), 21–25.

Wernerfelt, B. (1984). A Resource-Based View of the Firm. *Strategic Management Journal*, 5(2), 171–180. DOI: 10.1002/smj.4250050207

Westerman, G., Calméjane, C., Bonnet, D., Ferraris, P., & McAfee, A. (2011). Digital transformation: A roadmap for billion-dollar organizations. *MIT Center for Digital Business and Capgemini Consulting*, 1, 1–68.

Widari, T., Aliffiati, A., & Indra, M. (2023). Fast fashion: Consumptive behavior in fashion industry Generation Z in Yogyakarta. *IAS Journal of Localities*, 1(2), 104–113. DOI: 10.62033/iasjol.v1i2.18

Wiegand, T., & Wynn, M. (2023). Sustainability, the Circular Economy and Digitalisation in the German Textile and Clothing Industry. *Sustainability (Basel)*, 15(11), 9111. DOI: 10.3390/su15119111

Wiredu, J., Yang, Q., Sampene, A. K., Gyamfi, B. A., & Asongu, S. A. (2024). The effect of green supply chain management practices on corporate environmental performance: Does supply chain competitive advantage matter? *Business Strategy and the Environment*, 33(3), 2578–2599. DOI: 10.1002/bse.3606

Wojciechowska, P. (2021). *Fibres and textiles in the circular economy. Fundamentals of Natural Fibres and Textiles*. Elsevier. DOI: 10.1016/B978-0-12-821483-1.00019-X

Wojnowska-Baryła, I., Bernat, K., Zaborowska, M., & Kulikowska, D. (2024). The Growing Problem of Textile Waste Generation—The Current State of Textile Waste Management. *Energies*, 17(7), 1528. DOI: 10.3390/en17071528

Wooldridge, J. M. (2010). *Econometric analysis of cross section and panel data*. MIT press.

World, B. N. (2023). The Circular Supply Chain Is Driving Corporate Decarbonization.

WTA. (2024). *The difference between Logistics and Supply Chain Management (SCM).* https://www.wtagroup.com/resources-and-insights/blogs/the-difference-between-logistics-and-supply-chain-management-scm

Wu, K. J., Tseng, M. L., Yang, W. H., Ali, M. H., & Chen, X. (2023). Re-shaping sustainable value chain model under post pandemic disruptions: A fast fashion supply chain analysis. *International Journal of Production Economics*, 255, 108704. DOI: 10.1016/j.ijpe.2022.108704

Xing, L. (2019). China's pursuit of the "One Belt One Road" initiative: a new world order with Chinese characteristics? *Mapping China's 'One Belt One Road' Initiative*, 1-27.

Xin, L., & Wang, Y. (2022). Towards a green world: The impact of the Belt and Road Initiative on the carbon intensity reduction of countries along the route. *Environmental Science and Pollution Research International*, 29(19), 1–17. DOI: 10.1007/s11356-021-17575-3 PMID: 34988805

Xin, P., Zhao, M., & Bai, Y. (2022). Does the belt and road initiative promote green innovation quality? Evidence from Chinese cities. *Sustainability (Basel)*, 14(10), 6060. DOI: 10.3390/su14106060

Yeh, C. C., & Chen, Y. F. (2018). Critical success factors for adoption of 3D printing. *Technological Forecasting and Social Change*, 132(January), 209–216. DOI: 10.1016/j.techfore.2018.02.003

Yousaf, M. A., & Aqsa, R. (2023). Integrating Circular Economy, SBTI, Digital LCA, and ESG Benchmarks for Sustainable Textile Dyeing: A Critical Review of Industrial Textile Practices. *Global NEST Journal*, 25(7), 39–51. DOI: 10.30955/gnj.005145

Yu, S., Abbas, J., Alvarez-Otero, S., & Cherian, J. (2022). Green knowledge management: Scale development and validation. *Journal of Innovation & Knowledge*, 7(4), 100244. DOI: 10.1016/j.jik.2022.100244

Zbuchea, A., Pînzaru, F., Busu, M., Stan, S.-O., & Bârgăoanu, A. (2019). Sustainable knowledge management and its impact on the performances of biotechnology organizations. *Sustainability (Basel)*, 11(2), 359. DOI: 10.3390/su11020359

Zhang, Y., Hassan, N.M. & Sheikh, A.A. (2024). Unboxing the dilemma associated with online shopping and purchase behavior for remanufactured products: A smart strategy for waste management. *Journal of Environmental Management*, *351*, 119790. .DOI: 10.1016/j.jenvman.2023.119790

Zhang, D., Frei, R., Wills, G., Gerding, E., Bayer, S., & Senyo, P. K. (2023). Strategies and practices to reduce the ecological impact of product returns: An environmental sustainability framework for multichannel retail. *Business Strategy and the Environment*, 32(7), 4636–4661. DOI: 10.1002/bse.3385

Zhang, J., Cherian, J., Abbas Sandhu, Y., Abbas, J., Cismas, L. M., Negrut, C. V., & Negrut, L. (2022). Presumption of green electronic appliances purchase intention: The mediating role of personal moral norms. *Sustainability (Basel)*, 14(8), 4572. DOI: 10.3390/su14084572

Zhang, Q., Cheng, L., & Boutaba, R. (2010). Cloud computing: State-of-the-art and research challenges. *Journal of Internet Services and Applications*, 1(1), 7–18. DOI: 10.1007/s13174-010-0007-6

Zhang, W., Zhang, C., Wei, S., Zhang, Q., Rehman, A., & Shah, A. (2022). Characteristics and evolution of China's carbon emission reduction measures: Leading towards environmental sustainability. *Frontiers in Environmental Science*, 10, 924887. DOI: 10.3389/fenvs.2022.924887

Zhao, X., Lynch, J. G.Jr, & Chen, Q. (2010). Reconsidering Baron and Kenny: Myths and truths about mediation analysis. *The Journal of Consumer Research*, 37(2), 197–206. DOI: 10.1086/651257

Zheng, K., Zhang, Z., & Gauthier, J. (2020). Blockchain-based intelligent contract for factoring business in supply chains. *Annals of Operations Research*, 1–21.

Zhu, X., Song, B., Ni, Y., Ren, Y., & Li, R. (2016). *Business Trends in the Digital Era. Business Trends in the Digital Era: Evolution of Theories and Applications*. Springer Singapore. DOI: 10.1007/978-981-10-1079-8

Zikria, Y., Kim, S.W., Hahm, O., Afzal, M.K. & Aalsalem, M.Y. (2019). Internet of things (IoT) operating systems management: Opportunities, challenges, and solution. *Sensors, 19*(8), 1793. DOI: 10.3390/s19081793

About the Contributors

Adnan Ahmed is an Associate Professor (Ph.D.), College of Business, University of Buraimi, Oman. He is writing Books for Elsevier and Springer. He has 7 years of industry experience, specifically in the manufacturing sector, and 7 years of academic experience. He is also serving as a Book series editor of Elsevier USA on Topic: Developments and Advances in Supply chain Management.

Saheer Ali is a Senior Lecturer in the Logistics and Supply Chain Department. He is currently pursuing his Ph.D. in Management from Universiti Kebangsaan Malaysia. He completed his MBA from Staffordshire University and bachelor's in international business from Asia Pacific University. He has more than six years of experience in teaching and corporate exposure. He has served both in academia and industry in different positions for various projects and responsibilities.

Yavuz Selim Balcıoğlu is doctor at the management information systems department, Gebze Technical University. His research interests focus on text mining, machine learning, deep learning, artificial intelligence, timeliness and sentiment analysis.

Sedat Çerez is a research assistant at the school of business administration, Gebze Technical University. His research interests focus on sentiment analysis, text mining, corporate governance and timeliness.

Ankur Gupta has received the B.Tech and M.Tech in Computer Science and Engineering from Ganga Institute of Technology and Management, Kablana affiliated with Maharshi Dayanand University, Rohtak in 2015 and 2017. He is an Assistant Professor in the Department of Computer Science and Engineering at Vaish College of Engineering, Rohtak, and has been working there since January 2019. He has many publications in various reputed national/ international conferences, journals, and online book chapter contributions (Indexed by SCIE, Scopus, ESCI,

ACM, DBLP, etc). He is doing research in the field of cloud computing, data security & machine learning. His research work in M.Tech was based on biometric security in cloud computing.

Bilal Hassan is a dedicated and experienced professional currently serving as a Quality Assurance Officer at Air University Multan Campus, Islamabad. With a strong academic background, he is also pursuing his PhD in Business Administration. He has accumulated 13 years of diverse experience, with 5 years specifically devoted to teaching and research.

Abdullah Kürşat Merter is doctor at the school of business administration, Gebze Technical University. His research interests focus on audit committee, corporate governance, sentiment analysis, text mining, timeliness and financial reporting quality.

Gökhan Özer is Professor of Accounting at the school of business administration, Gebze Technical University. His research interests focus on audit committee, corporate governance, and management control systems.

Sabyasachi Pramanik is a professional IEEE member. He obtained a PhD in Computer Science and Engineering from Sri Satya Sai University of Technology and Medical Sciences, Bhopal, India. Presently, he is an Associate Professor, Department of Computer Science and Engineering, Haldia Institute of Technology, India. He has many publications in various reputed international conferences, journals, and book chapters (Indexed by SCIE, Scopus, ESCI, etc). He is doing research in the fields of Artificial Intelligence, Data Privacy, Cybersecurity, Network Security, and Machine Learning. He also serves on the editorial boards of several international journals. He is a reviewer of journal articles from IEEE, Springer, Elsevier, Inderscience, IET and IGI Global. He has reviewed many conference papers, has been a keynote speaker, session chair, and technical program committee member at many international conferences. He has authored a book on Wireless Sensor Network. He has edited 8 books from IGI Global, CRC Press, Springer and Wiley Publications.

Muhammad Jawad Sajid holds a PhD in "Management Science and Engineering" from "China University of Mining and Technology." He is currently an Assistant Professor at the School of Economics and Management of China University of Mining and Technology. He has a strong interest in environmental management and economics research. Furthermore, he is involved in the development of emerging technologies for the combined use of renewable resources such as wind, air, and water. He is also a regular contributor to conferences and workshops worldwide. He has been appointed as co-chair of MITM2020: Modern Informatics and its Teaching

Methods, held on May 20, 2020, in Andijan, Uzbekistan. He was invited to deliver a keynote speech at the 2021 International Conference on Ecological Environment and Green Technology (EEGT 2021), Nanjing, China, and the 2022 International Symposium on Electrochemistry and Energy Storage (EES 2022), Guangzhou, China. And he was an invited speaker at INDUSTRIALMEET2022, Copenhagen, Denmark. He also served as a technical committee member for several international conferences.

Adeel Shah is the Head of Logistics and Supply Chain Management at the College of Business Management. He has more than 20 years of experience in both industry and academia. He has been transforming the field of the supply chain by actively providing consultancy for best practices in the global supply chain. Dr Shah is a prolific author of multiple applied and scientific research papers on supply chains, circular economy, and sustainability. His works have been published in renowned journals, and he has also authored books with reputable publishers. His PhD research is based on the Leagile strategy and developing and publishing the RLS theoretical model. With his rich corporate experience and PhD., Dr. Shah is a supply chain leader in Pakistan. He serves as a bridge between industry and academia, providing valuable insights into current practices and transforming the industry for the future.

Syed Obaidullah Shah is a Lecturer in Supply Chain Management (SCM) department at the Institute of Business Management (IoBM), Karachi, Pakistan. He has corporate experience in procurement and sourcing in supply chains of textile and service industries. Having a Master's degree in supply chain management and a Master's in Philosophy (M.Phil.) degree, Syed Obaidullah's current area of research includes applications of Blockchain technology and sustainability in the supply chain. He is presently enrolled in a Ph.D. program specializing in supply chain management.

Index

A

B

C

D

E

F

G

I

L

M

R

S

T

U

www.ingramcontent.com/pod-product-compliance
Lightning Source LLC
LaVergne TN
LVHW061544290926
849162LV00004B/898